The

Architecture

Reference + Specification Book

Updated + Revised

Quarto Knows

Inspiring | Educating | Creating | Entertaining

Brimming with creative inspiration, how-to projects, and useful information to enrich your everyday life, Quarto Knows is a favorite destination for those pursuing their interests and passions. Visit our site and dig deeper with our books into your area of interest: Quarto Creates, Quarto Cooks, Quarto Homes, Quarto Lives, Quarto Drives, Quarto Explores, Quarto Gifts, or Quarto Kids.

This edition published in 2018
First published in 2013 by Rockport Publishers, an imprint of The Quarto Group,
100 Cummings Center, Suite 265-D, Beverly, MA 01915, USA.
T (978) 282-9590 F (978) 283-2742 QuartoKnows.com

Originally found under the following Library of Congress Cataloging-in-Publication Data

McMorrough, Julia.
Materials, structures, and standards : all the details architects need to know but can never find / Julia McMorrough.
p. cm.
ISBN 1-59253-193-8 (vinyl)
1. Architecture—Handbooks, manuals, etc. 2. Building—Handbooks, manuals, etc. I. Title.
NA2540.M43 2006
720—dc22
2005019669
CIP

ISBN: 978-1-63159-379-6

10

The original edition of this book, *Materials, Structures, and Standards*, was published by Rockport Publishers in 2006.

DISCLAIMER

The content of this book is for general information purposes only and has been obtained from many sources, professional organizations, manufacturers' literature, and codes. All illustrations in this book (except photographs) are those of the author. The author and publisher have made every reasonable effort to ensure that this work is accurate and current, but do not warrant, and assume no liability for, the accuracy or completeness of the text or illustrations, or their fitness for any particular purpose. It is the responsibility of the users of this book to apply their professional knowledge to the content, to consult sources referenced, as appropriate, and to consult a professional architect for expert advice if necessary.

Editor and Art Director: Alicia Kennedy
Design and Illustrations: Julia McMorrough

Production Design: Leslie Haimes
Cover Design: Burge Agency, www.burgeagency.com

Printed in China

The

Architecture

Reference + Specification Book

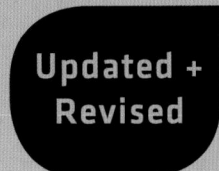

Updated + Revised

Everything Architects Need to Know Every Day

Julia McMorrough

ROCKPORT

Contents

i.

INTRODUCTION

ARCHITECTURAL DESIGN is a complex activity that involves multiple levels of knowledge, communication, and production, even on a small project. Architects often speak their own language, both in terminology and through conventions of drawings, models, and diagrams. Moreover, to make a piece of architecture requires following countless rules of which an able practitioner must remain ever knowledgeable: building codes, human dimensions, drawing standards, material properties, and relevant technologies. Familiarity with so many issues comes with schooling and long years of experience, but even the most seasoned architect must avail him- or herself of a vast and exhaustive array of resources, from code books to graphic standards, from materials libraries to manufacturers' catalogs.

The Architecture Reference + Specification Book is a unique compilation of essential information for architects, students of architecture, and anyone contemplating an architectural project. Included here are the tables, charts, diagrams, dimensions, standards, codes, and general data that many architects need on a daily basis. This book is not a replacement for other sources that architects might consult regularly, but rather a handy "first-stop" reference that is always at the ready, on a desk or in a bag.

Part 1, "Materials," provides a detailed catalog of the most common building materials—wood, masonry, concrete, metals—as well as various interior finishes. Parts 2, 3, and 4, "Systems," "Measure and Drawing," and "Codes and Guidelines," address the major aspects of undertaking an architectural project. Topics include basic measurements and geometry, architectural drawing types and conventions, parking, building codes, accessibility, structural and mechanical systems, and building components. Parts 5 and 6, "Proportion and Form" and "Context," bring together the human scale, architectural elements, a glossary, and a timeline of key moments in the history of architecture. Finally, because such a compact book cannot possibly contain everything, a directory of resources offers an extensive guide to the most helpful publications, organizations, and websites.

For every project, architects must take into account an endless number of external forces, not least of which are the codes and standards of design and construction. But these codes and standards should certainly not be viewed as limiting: Knowledge of them and their creative use can, in fact, liberate and empower.

MATERIALS 1.

A NOTE ON METRIC AND CUSTOMARY UNITS

This book acknowledges the two primary measurement systems used in the world today: the metric system, also known as the Système International d'Unités (SI), and the U.S. customary units system, referred to in the United States as English units or standard units. While the metric system has become the universally accepted system of units in science, trade, and commerce, in the United States, federal laws have yet to mandate SI as the official system.

In this book, every attempt has been made to accurately represent the relationship between customary and SI units. Except where noted, soft conversions are used throughout and, due to constraints of space, are usually written as follows: 1'-6" (457), with the numbers in parantheses representing millimeters.

See Chapter 10 (page 100) for more details on metric conversions, and Chapter 1 (page 10) for more details on wood.

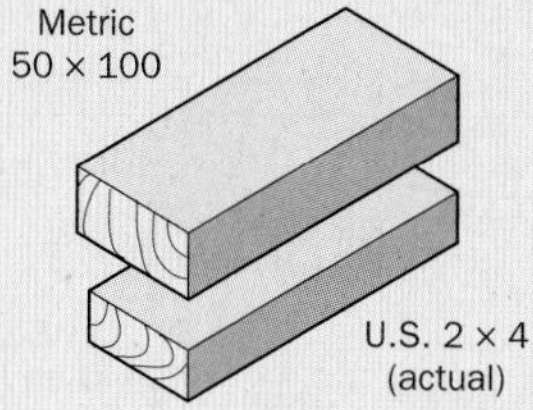
Metric
50 × 100
U.S. 2 × 4
(actual)

As an example of the factors that might influence translation from one system to the other, consider the North American 2 × 4:

Nominal dimension: 2" × 4"

Metric "soft" conversion
50.8 mm × 101.6 mm

Metric "hard" conversion
50 mm × 100 mm

Actual dimension: 1½" × 3½"

Metric "soft" conversion
38 mm × 89mm

Metric "hard" conversion
40 mm × 90 mm

Metric preferred dimension:
50 mm × 100 mm

During the design process, architects often use models as a quick way to realize and study a form or space. Frequently, the building's materials may not yet have been chosen or finalized, and there is a seductive simplicity to the foam, or wood, or cardboard model at this point: anything is still possible. Aside from the overarching impact of the project's budget, numerous factors influence the selection of materials for a building's structure, skin, and finishes. Some materials are more readily available in certain regions, or the local building trades may be more comfortable with specific construction practices. Other materials have very long lead times, and for some projects, time constraints may rule these out. Also, different climates have different material needs, and the building's program, size, and code requirements bear on the appropriateness of materials and methods of construction.

A basic sampling of common materials found in many buildings is presented here. Space limitations do not allow for discussion of other more innovative materials, but increasingly, for reasons of practicality, cost, or environmental concerns, architects are looking to less standard sources for building materials (textiles, plastics, and aerogels) or to unconventional uses for common products (concrete roof tiles, acrylic "glass blocks," and recycled cotton fabric insulation).

Chapter 1: Wood

Lightweight, strong, and durable, wood is an ideal construction material with uses that run the gamut from structure to interior finish. The two major classifications—softwood and hardwood—do not necessarily indicate relative hardness, softness, strength, or durability.

COMMON WOOD TERMS

Book-matched: Result of resawing thick lumber into thinner boards, opening the two halves like a book, and gluing the boards together along the edge to create a panel with a mirrored grain pattern.

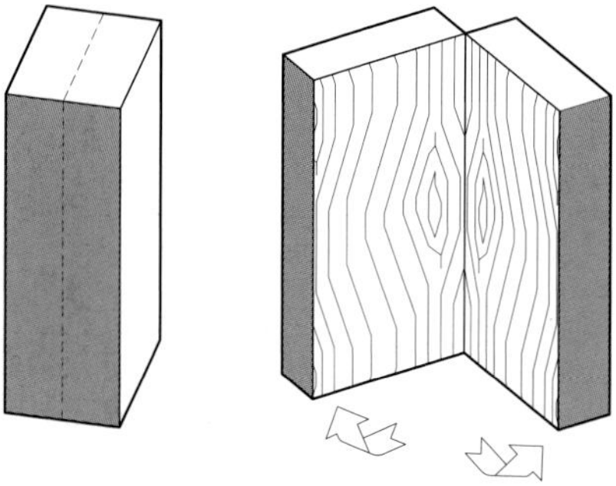

Burl: Irregular grain pattern that results from an unusual growth on the tree.

Cathedral grain: V-shaped grain pattern running the length of the board.

Check: Separation of the wood fibers running with the grain that do not go through the whole cross-section. Occurs as a result of tension and stress caused by wood movement during the drying process.

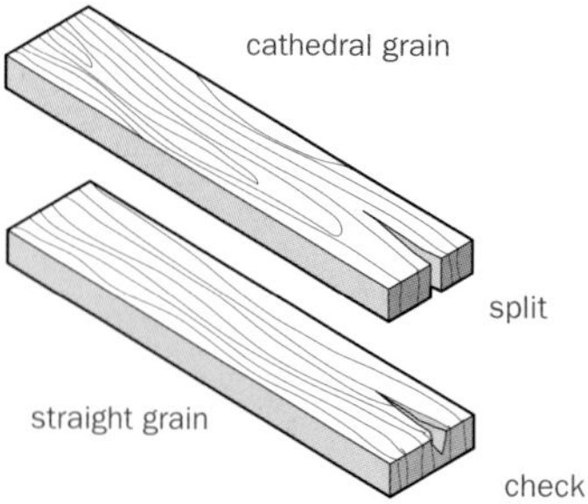
cathedral grain
split
straight grain
check

Dimensional stability: Ability of a section of wood to resist changes in volume at fluctuating moisture levels. Low dimensional stability produces expansion in humid environments and contraction in dry ones.

Early growth/late growth: In regions of little climatic change, trees tend to grow at a fairly consistent rate and have little variation in texture. In regions of seasonal climatic change, however, trees grow at different rates, depending on the season. Variations in growth contribute to the color and texture of the growth rings in the tree.

Figure: Patterns on a wood surface produced by growth rings, rays, knots, and irregular grains. Descriptors include interlocked, curly, tiger, wavy, and fiddleback, among others.

fiddleback

swirl

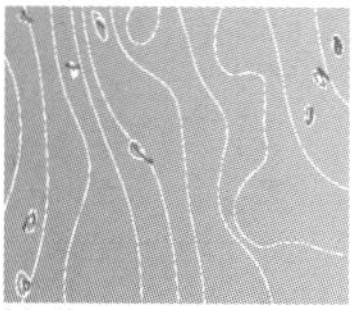

bird's-eye

crotch

Grain: Size, alignment, and appearance of wood fibers in a piece of lumber.

Gum pocket: Excessive accumulation of resin or gum in certain areas of the wood.

Hardness: Ability of wood to resist indentation. See Janka hardness test.

Hardwood: Wood from deciduous trees (which lose their leaves in the winter months). Oak and walnut constitute 50 percent of all hardwood production.

Heartwood: Harder, nonliving innermost layers of a tree. It is generally darker, denser, more durable, and less permeable than the surrounding sapwood. Good all-heartwood lumber may be difficult to obtain, and, depending on the species, it is common to find boards with both heartwood and sapwood combined.

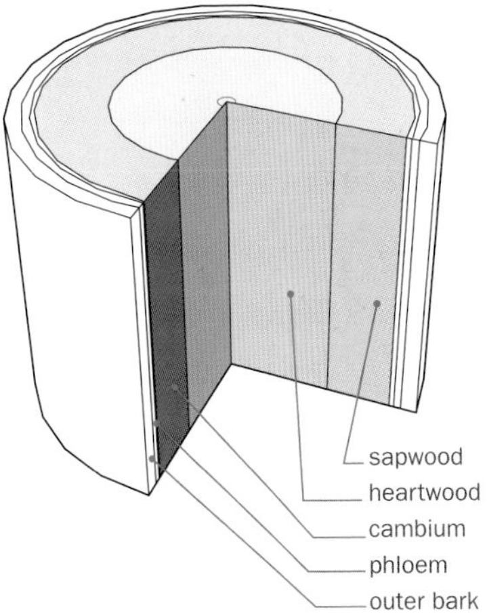
sapwood
heartwood
cambium
phloem
outer bark

Janka hardness test: Test that measures the pounds of force required to drive a 0.444" (11 mm) -diameter steel ball to half its depth into a piece of wood.

Moisture content: Percentage that represents a board's ratio of water weight to the weight of oven-dried wood.

Plainsawn: Lumber cut with less than a 30-degree angle between the face of the board and the wood's growth ring.

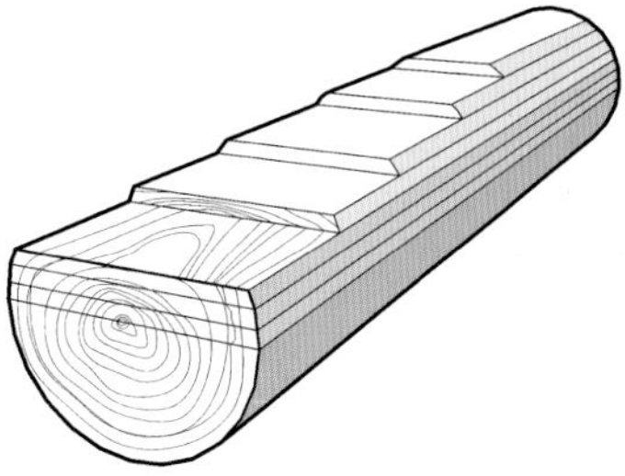

Plywood: Large sheet of wood made up of several layers of veneer that are glued together so that the grain of each layer lies perpendicular to the grain of the previous layer. There is always an odd number of layers, enabling the grain direction of both faces to run parallel to one another.

Pressure-treated lumber: Wood products that are treated with chemical preservatives to prevent decay brought on by fungi and to resist attack from insects and microorganisms. Under pressure, the preservatives are forced deep into the cellular structure of the wood.

Quartersawn: Lumber cut with a 60- to 90-degree angle between the face of the board and the wood's growth rings.

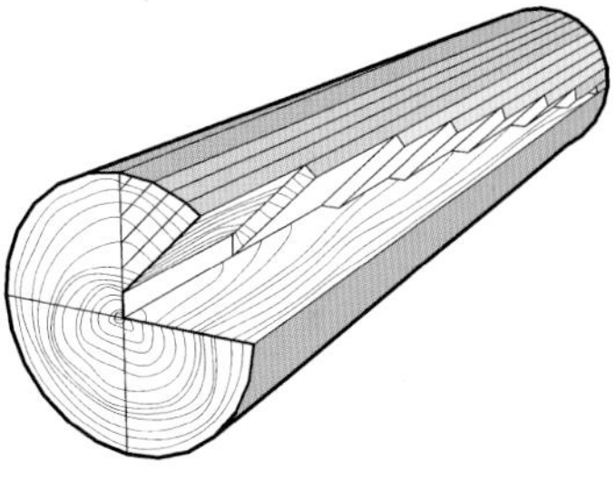

Riftsawn: Lumber cut with a 30- to 60-degree angle between the face of the board and the wood's growth rings.

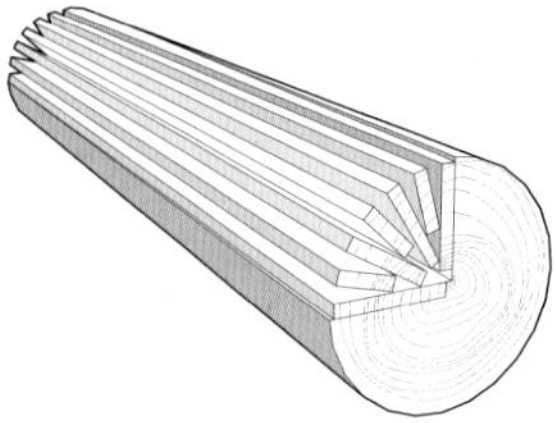

Sapwood: Living outer layers of a tree, between the outer bark and the thin formative layers of the cambium and phloem, on the one side, and the heartwood, on the other. These layers contain the sap-conducting tubes. Generally lighter in color, less durable, less dense, and more permeable than heartwood, sapwood darkens with age and becomes heartwood. Sapwood and heartwood together make up the xylem of the tree.

Softwood: Wood from coniferous (evergreen) trees.

Split: Separation of wood fibers from one face through to the next. Occurs most often at the ends of boards.

Straight grain: Wood fibers that run parallel to the axis of a piece of lumber.

Stud: 2" × 4" and 2" × 6" dimension lumber used for load-bearing and stud walls.

Warp: Bowing, cupping, and twisting distortion in lumber that occurs after it has been planed, usually during the drying process.

SOFTWOOD LUMBER

Lumber Standards*

Rough Lumber
Sawed, trimmed, and edged lumber whose faces are rough and show marks.

Surfaced (Dressed) Lumber
Rough lumber that has been smoothed by a surfacing machine.

S1S: Surfaced one side
S1E: Surfaced one edge
S2S: Surfaced two sides
S2E: Surfaced two edges
S1S1E: Surfaced one side and one edge
S1S2E: Surfaced one side and two edges
S2S1E: Surfaced two sides and one edge
S4S: Surfaced four sides

Worked Lumber
Surfaced lumber that has been matched, patterned, shiplapped, or any combination of these.

Shop and Factory Lumber
Millwork lumber for use in door jambs, moldings, and window frames.

Yard (Structural) Lumber
Lumber used for house framing, concrete forms, and sheathing.

Boards: No more than 1" (25) thick and 4"–12" (102–305) wide

Planks: Over 1" (25) thick and 6" (152) wide

Timbers: Width and thickness both greater than 5" (127)

*From U.S. Department of Commerce American Lumber Standards of Softwood Lumbers

Softwood Lumber Sizes

Nominal Size[1] inches	Actual Size, Dry[2] inches (mm)	Actual Size, Green[3] inches (mm)
1 (25)	3/4 (19)	25/32 (20)
1 1/4 (32)	1 (25)	1 1/32 (26)
1 1/2 (38)	1 1/4 (32)	1 9/32 (33)
2 (50)	1 1/2 (38)	1 9/16 (40)
2 1/2 (64)	2 (51)	2 1/16 (52)
3 (76)	2 1/2 (64)	2 9/16 (65)
3 1/2 (89)	3 (76)	3 1/16 (78)
4 (102)	3 1/2 (89)	3 9/16 (90)
4 1/2 (114)	4 (102)	4 1/16 (103)
5 (127)	4 1/2 (114)	4 5/8 (117)
6 (152)	5 1/2 (140)	5 9/16 (143)
7 (178)	6 1/2 (165)	6 5/8 (168)
8 (203)	7 1/4 (184)	7 1/2 (190)
9 (229)	8 1/4 (210)	8 1/2 (216)
10 (254)	9 1/4 (235)	9 1/2 (241)
11 (279)	10 1/4 (260)	10 1/2 (267)
12 (306)	11 1/4 (286)	11 1/2 (292)
14 (356)	13 1/4 (337)	13 1/2 (343)
16 (406)	15 1/4 (387)	15 1/2 (394)

[1]Nominal dimensions are approximate dimensions assigned to pieces of lumber and other materials as a convenience in referring to the piece.

[2]Dry lumber is defined as having a moisture content of less than 19 percent.

[3]Green (unseasoned) lumber is defined as having a moisture content of greater than 19 percent.

Softwood grading is based on the appearance, strength, and stiffness of the lumber. Numerous associations nationwide establish their own grading standards, though they must all conform to the U.S. Department of Commerce American Lumber Standards. Grading is often difficult to understand, and because it deals with both strength analysis and visual analysis, there is an allowable 5 percent variation below a given grade.

Dimensional Variations of a 2×6 Stud

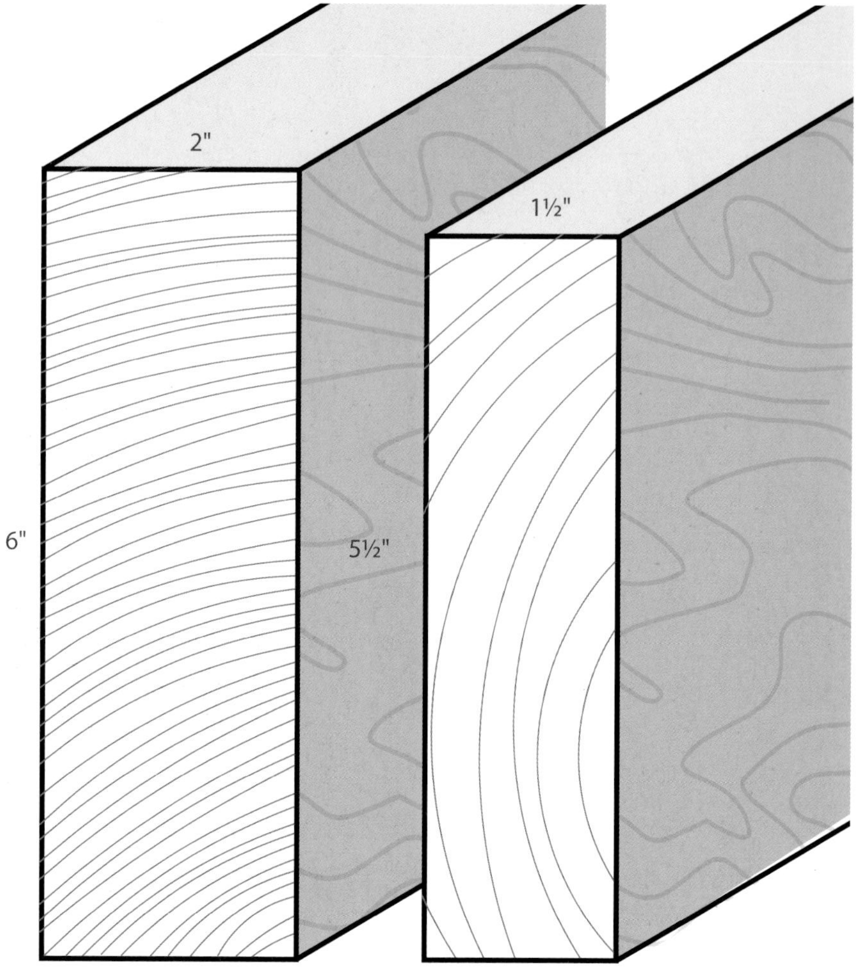
2"
1½"
6"
5½"

2×6 Old Growth
Typically, older growth wood is denser, stronger, and more dimensionally stable than younger wood. Before aggressive logging, older growth trees grew more slowly, as they competed for sunlight in more densely forested conditions, resulting in more rings per inch.

2×6 Farmed Wood
By contrast, farmed wood grows bigger faster, due to more aggressive watering, fertilizing, and exposure to sunlight. More rapid growing results in less dense wood.

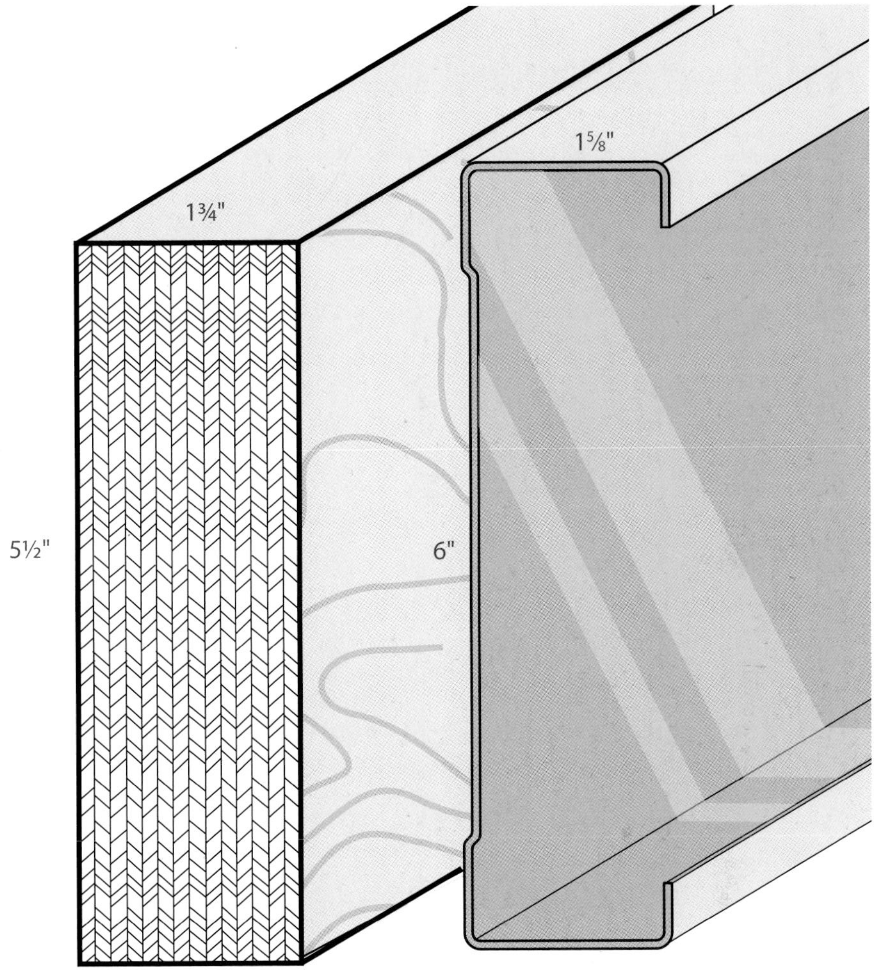
1¾"
1⅝"
5½"
6"

Laminated Veneer Lumber (LVL)—Farmed & Glued

Commonly referred to by its proprietary name of Microllam (Weyerhauser), LVL lumber is made of thin sheets of wood sandwiched and glued together, much like plywood, though resulting in heavy and dense wood members that resist warping and shrinkage, and are designed to carry significant loads.

Metal Stud

Though more expensive than wood framing members, steel studs offer more strength and dimensional stability.

Board Feet

Most lumber is measured and sold in board feet (one board foot equals 144 cubic inches), calculated as follows:

$$\frac{\text{thickness} \times \text{face width} \times \text{length}}{144}$$

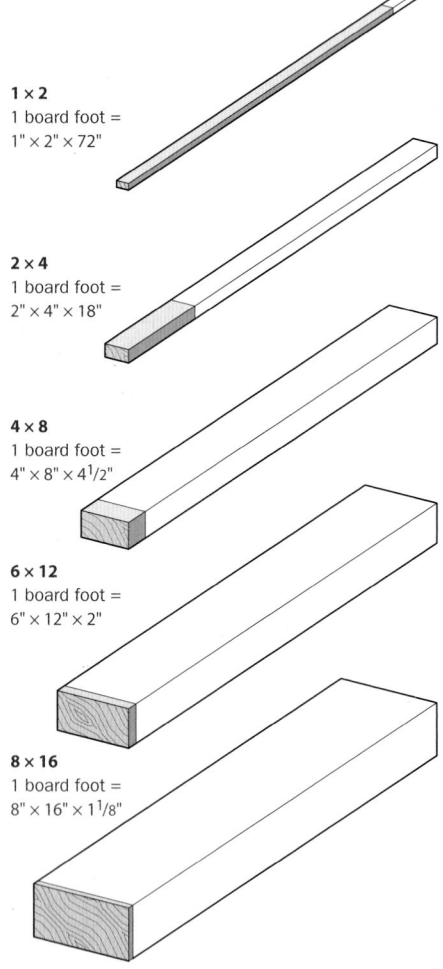

1 × 2
1 board foot =
1" × 2" × 72"

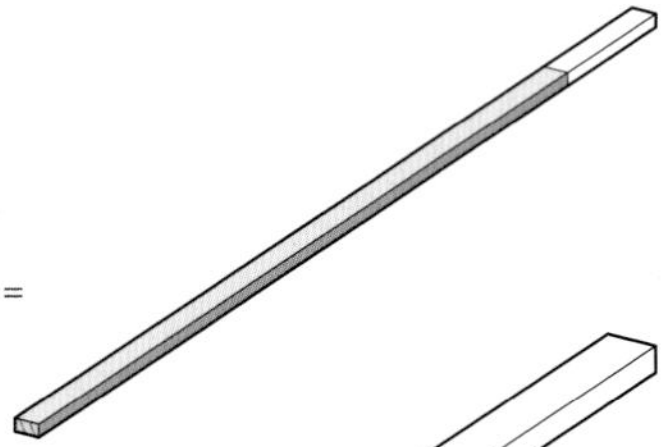

2 × 4
1 board foot =
2" × 4" × 18"

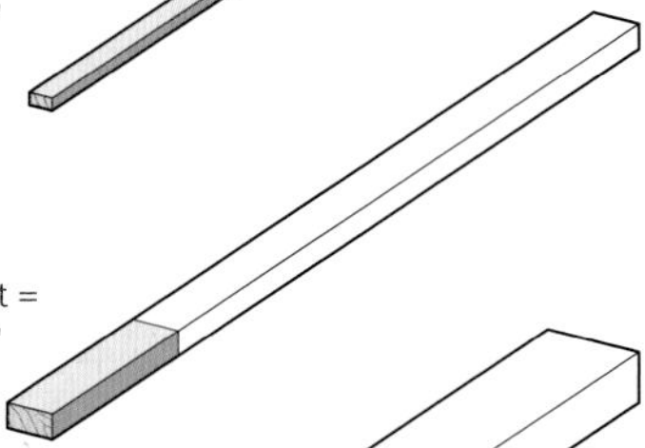

4 × 8
1 board foot =
4" × 8" × 4$^1/_2$"

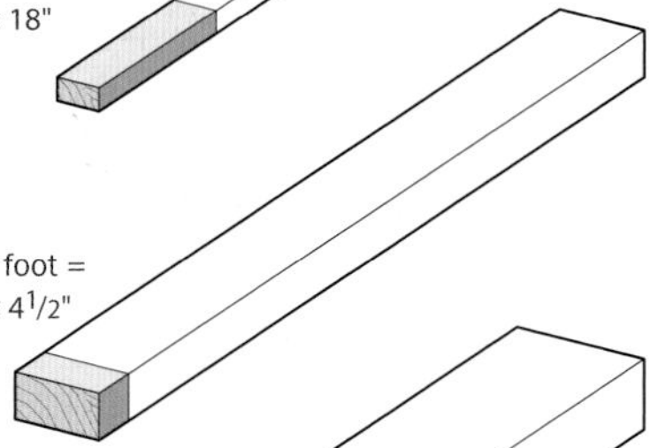

6 × 12
1 board foot =
6" × 12" × 2"

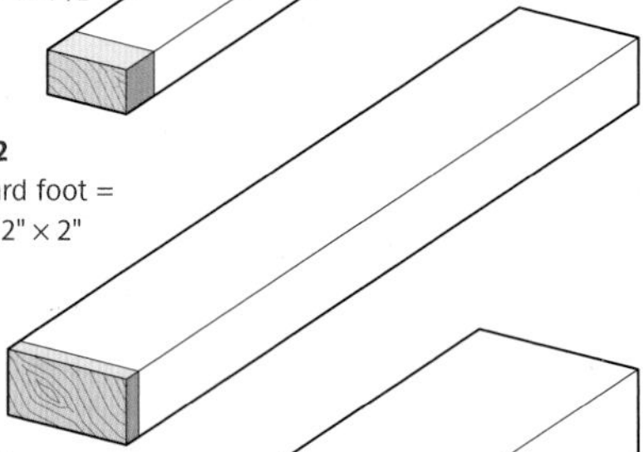

8 × 16
1 board foot =
8" × 16" × 1$^1/_8$"

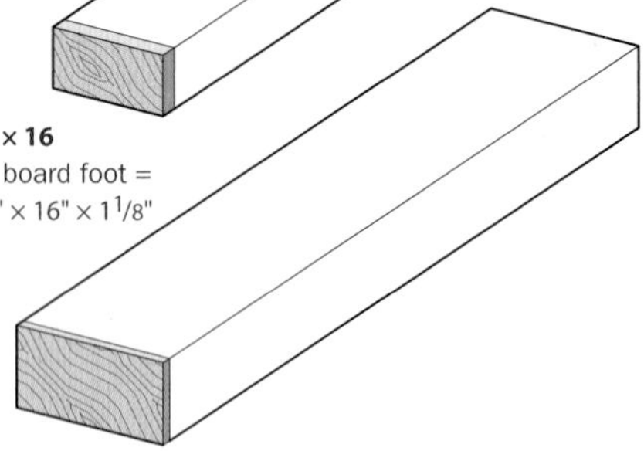

HARDWOOD

Hardwood Lumber Grades

First and Second (FAS): Best grade, normally required for a natural or stained finish. Boards must be at least 6" wide, 8'–16' long, and 83.3 percent clear on the worst face.

Select, No. 1 Common: Boards must be a minimum 3" wide, 4'–16' long, and 66.66 percent clear on the worst face.

Select, No. 2 Common

Select, No. 3 Common

Hardwood Lumber Thicknesses

Quarter*	Rough Dimension	Surfaced 1 Side (S1S)	Surfaced 2 Sides (S2S)
	3/8" (10)	1/4" (6)	3/16" (5)
	1/2" (13)	3/8" (10)	5/16" (8)
	5/8" (16)	1/2" (13)	7/16" (11)
	3/4" (19)	5/8" (16)	9/16" (14)
4/4	1" (25)	7/8" (22)	13/16" (21)
5/4	1 1/4" (32)	1 1/8" (29)	1 1/16" (27)
6/4	1 1/2" (38)	1 3/8" (35)	1 5/16" (33)
8/4	2" (51)	1 13/16" (46)	1 3/4" (44)
12/4	3" (76)	2 13/16" (71)	2 3/4" (70)
16/4	4" (102)	3 13/16" (97)	3 3/4" (95)

*Hardwood thickness is often referred to in "quarters": 4/4 equals 1" (25), 6/4 is 1 1/2" (38), and so on.

Exposure Durability

Exterior—Fully waterproof glue and minimum C-grade veneers—suitable for applications permanently exposed to the weather.

Exposure 1—Fully waterproof glue and minimum D-grade veneers suitable for applications with some exposure to weather.

Exposure 2—Glue of intermediate moisture resistance—suitable for applications of intermittent high humidity.

Interior: Protected indoor applications only.

	Veneer Grades
N	Premium grade available by special order. Select, all heartwood or all sapwood with a smooth surface and free of open defects. No more than six repairs, wood only, matched for grain and color, and parallel to the grain, allowed per 4' × 8' panel. Best for natural finish.
A	Smooth and paintable. Permits no more than eighteen neatly made repairs of boat, sled, or router type, and parallel to the grain. Used for natural finish in less demanding applications.
B	Solid surface that allows shims, circular repair plugs, and tight knots limited to 1" across grain, with minor splits permitted.
C Plugged	Improved C veneer with splits up to $\frac{1}{8}$" width and knotholes and borer holes up to $\frac{1}{4}$" x $\frac{1}{2}$". Some broken grain is permitted, and synthetic repairs are allowed.
C	Tight knots and knotholes up to $1\frac{1}{2}$" permitted if total width of knots and knotholes is within specified limits. Synthetic or wood repairs allowed. Discoloration and sanding defects that do not impair strength, limited splits, and stitching all permitted. Lowest exterior use grade.
D	Knots and knotholes up to to $2\frac{1}{2}$" across grain and $\frac{1}{2}$" larger within specified limits permitted. Limited splits and stitching also permitted. Use restricted to Interior, Exposure 1, and Exposure 2 panels.

PLYWOOD

Plywood quality is rated by the American Plywood Association (APA) and is generally graded by the quality of the veneer on both front and back sides of the panel (A-B, C-D, and so on). Veneer grades describe appearance according to natural unrepaired growth characteristics and the size and number of repairs allowed during manufacture.

Typical Plywood Construction

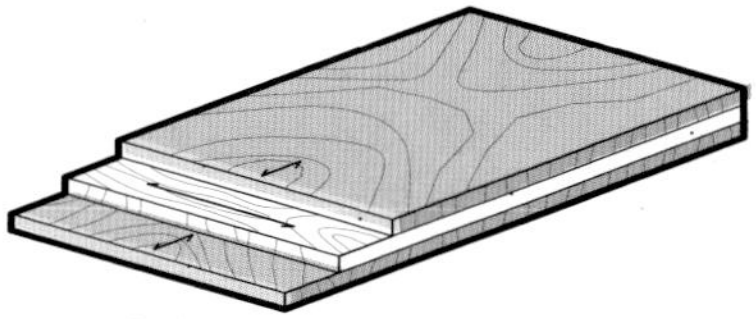

3-layer (3 ply)

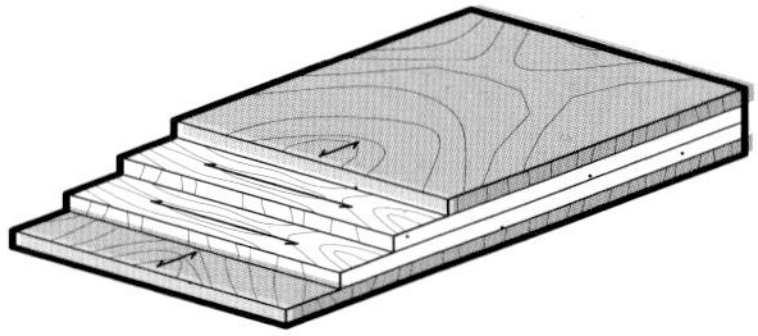

3-layer (4 ply)

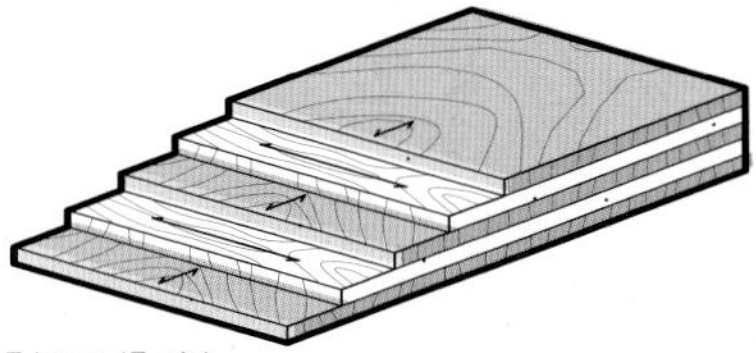

5-layer (5 ply)

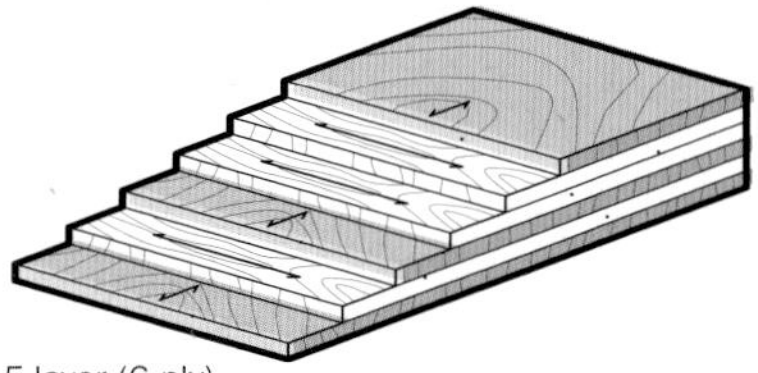

5-layer (6 ply)

WOOD TYPES AND CHARACTERISTICS

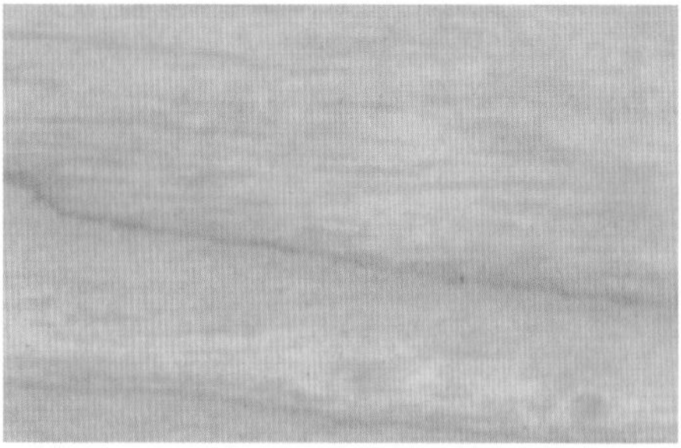

ASH white *Fraxinus americana*			
Hardness		H	
Principal Finish Uses		Trim, cabinetry	
Color		Creamy white to light brown	
Paint	n/a	Transp.	Excellent

BIRCH *Betula alleghaniensis*			
Hardness		H	
Principal Finish Uses		Trim, paneling, cabinetry	
Color		White to dark red	
Paint	Excellent	Transp.	Good

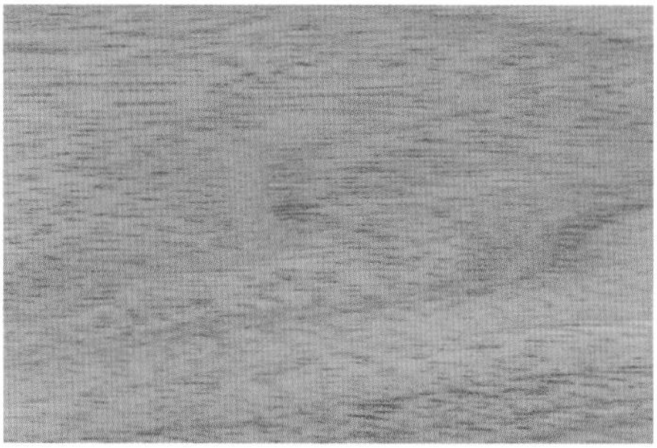

BUTTERNUT *Juglans cinerea*			
Hardness		M	
Principal Finish Uses		Trim, paneling, cabinetry	
Color		Pale brown	
Paint	n/a	Transp.	Excellent

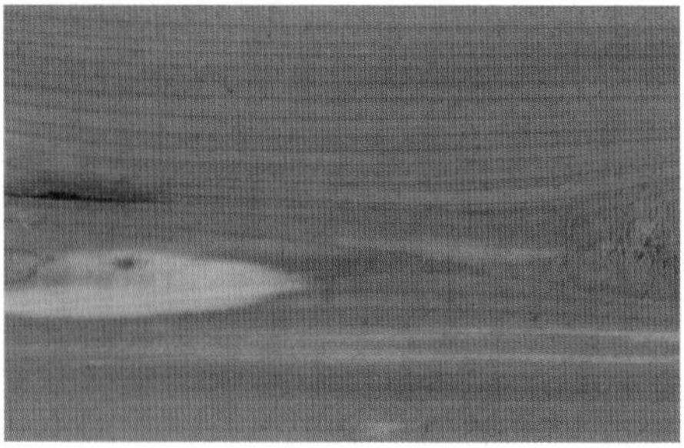

CEDAR western red *Thuja plicata*			
Hardness		S	
Principal Finish Uses		Trim, exterior & interior paneling	
Color		Reddish brown nearly white	
Paint	n/a	Transp.	Good

S=soft; M=medium; H=hard; VH=very hard; n/a=not normally used
Finishes: Painted and Transparent

CHESTNUT *Castanea dentate*			
Hardness		M	
Principal Finish Uses		Trim, paneling	
Color		Grayish brown	
Paint	n/a	Transp.	Excellent

MAHOGANY Hond. *Sweitenia macrophylla*			
Hardness		M	
Principal Finish Uses		Trim, frames, paneling, cabinetry	
Color		Rich golden brown	
Paint	n/a	Transp.	Excellent

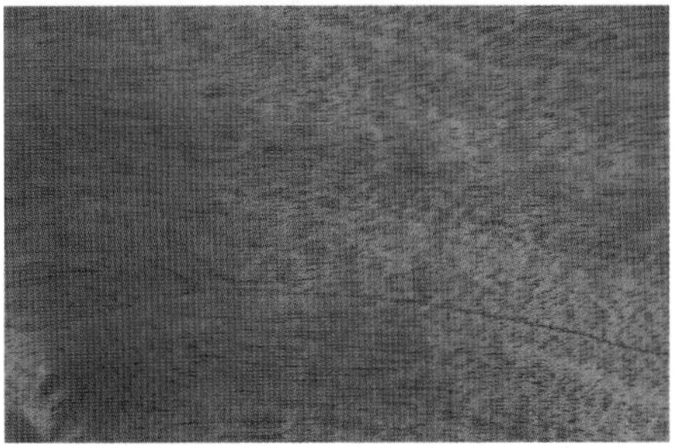

MAPLE *Acer saccharum*			
Hardness		VH	
Principal Finish Uses		Trim, paneling, cabinetry	
Color		White to reddish brown	
Paint	Excellent	Transp.	Good

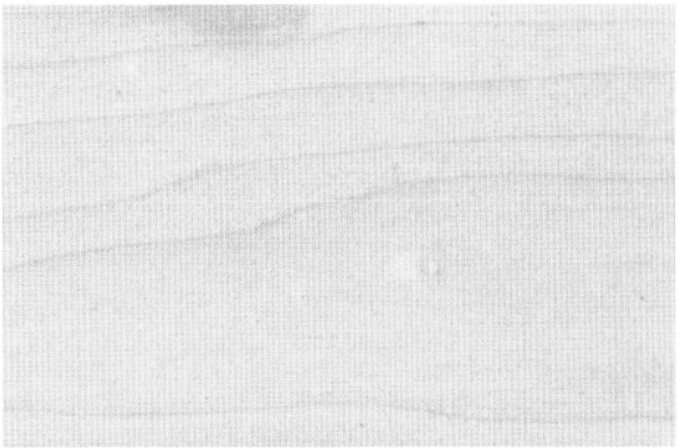

OAK English brown *Quercus robur*			
Hardness		H	
Principal Finish Uses		Veneered paneling, cabinetry	
Color		Leathery brown	
Paint	n/a	Transp.	Excellent

WOOD TYPES AND CHARACTERISTICS

OAK red *Quercus rubra*			
Hardness		H	
Principal Finish Uses		Trim, paneling, cabinetry	
Color		Reddish tan to brown	
Paint	n/a	Transp.	Excellent

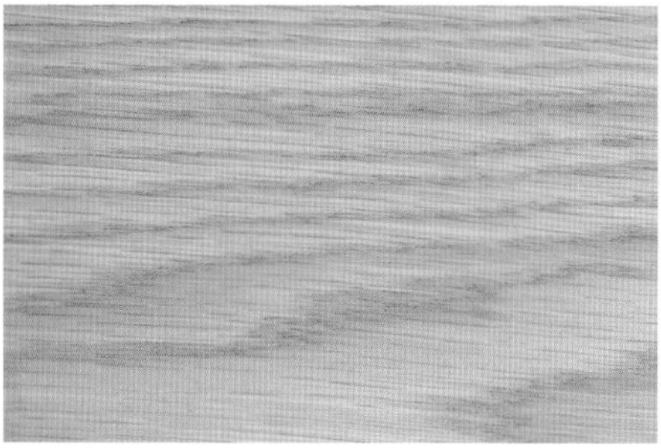

OAK white *Quercus alba*			
Hardness		H	
Principal Finish Uses		Trim, paneling, cabinetry	
Color		Grayish tan	
Paint	n/a	Transp.	Excellent

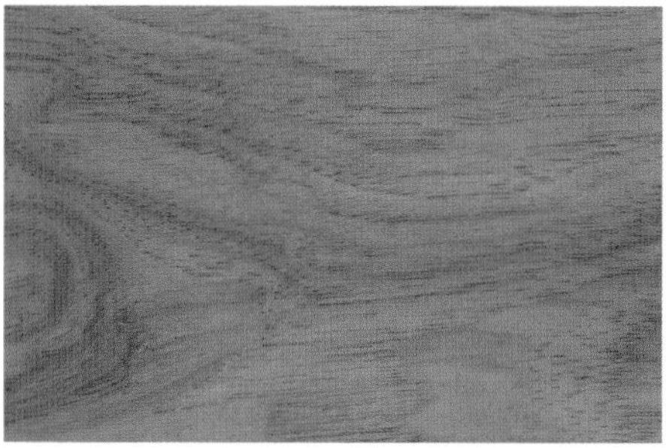

PECAN *Carya species*			
Hardness		H	
Principal Finish Uses		Trim, paneling, cabinetry	
Color		Reddish brown w/ brown stripes	
Paint	n/a	Transp.	Good

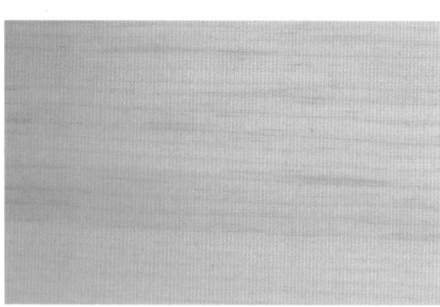

PINE east. or north. white *Pinus strobes*			
Hardness		S	
Principal Finish Uses		Trim, frames, paneling, cabinetry	
Color		Creamy white to pink	
Paint	Good	Transp.	Good

S=soft; M=medium; H=hard; VH=very hard; n/a=not normally used
Finishes: Painted and Transparent

ROSEWOOD *Dalbergia nigra*			
Hardness		VH	
Principal Finish Uses		Veneered paneling, cabinetry	
Color		Mixed red/brown/black	
Paint	n/a	Transp.	Excellent

TEAK *Tectona grandis*			
Hardness		H	
Principal Finish Uses		Trim, paneling, cabinetry	
Color		Tawny yellow to dark brown	
Paint	n/a	Transp.	Excellent

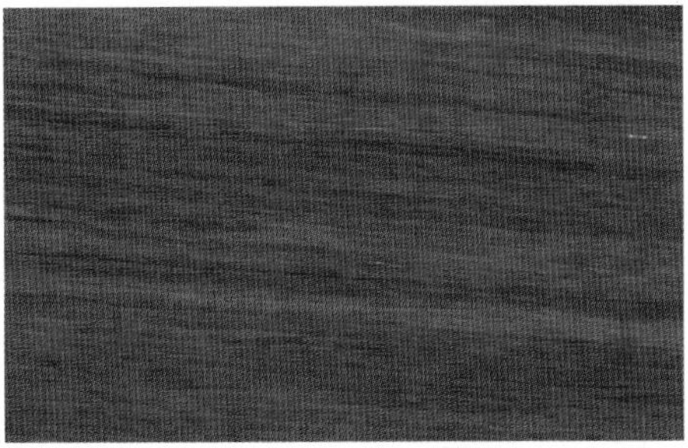

WALNUT *Juglans species*			
Hardness		H	
Principal Finish Uses		Trim, paneling, cabinetry	
Color		Chocolate brown	
Paint	n/a	Transp.	Excellent

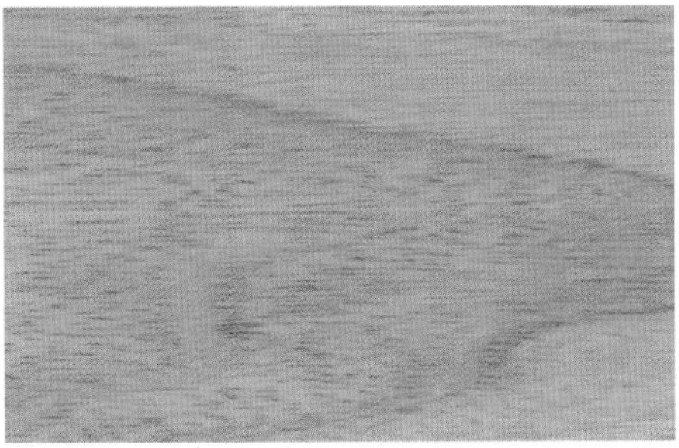

ZEBRAWOOD *Brachystegea fleuryana*			
Hardness		H	
Principal Finish Uses		Trim, paneling, cabinetry	
Color		Gold streaks on dark brown	
Paint	n/a	Transp.	Excellent

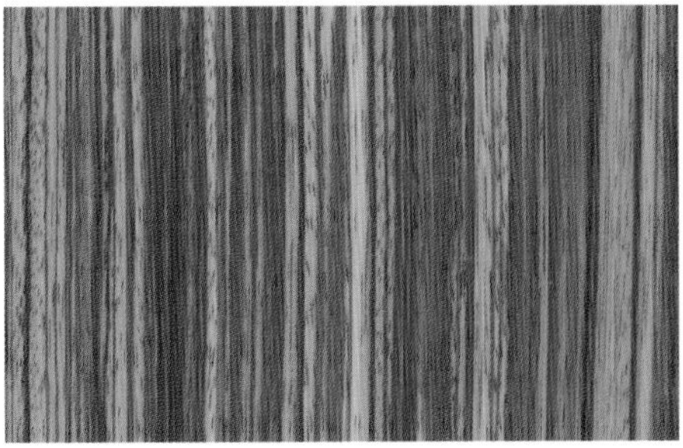

WOOD JOINERY

Edge Joints

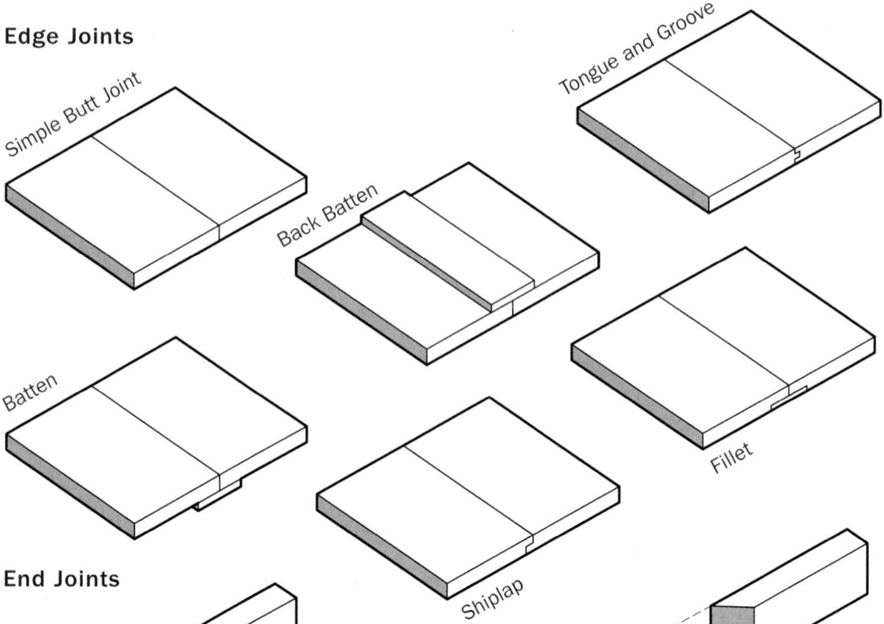
Simple Butt Joint
Tongue and Groove
Back Batten
Batten
Fillet
Shiplap

End Joints

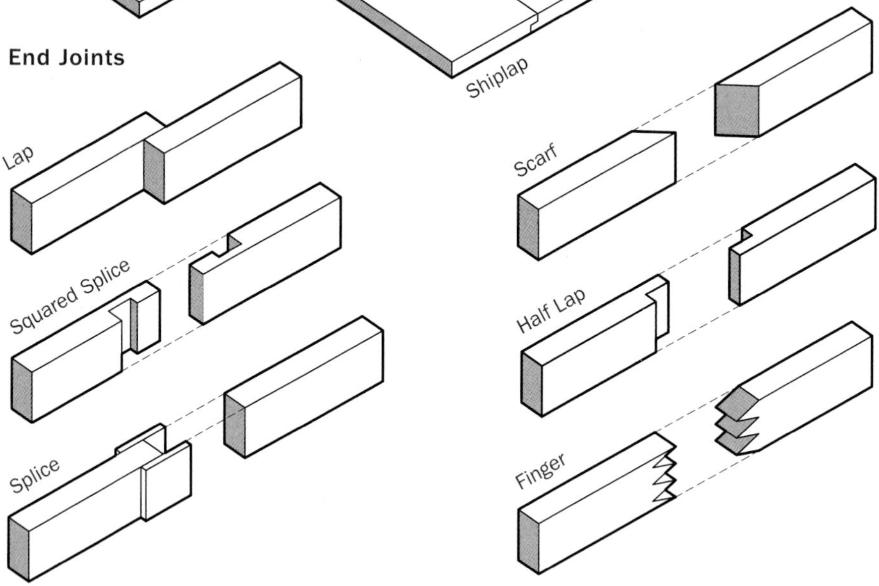
Lap
Scarf
Squared Splice
Half Lap
Splice
Finger

Right-Angle Joints (Miters)

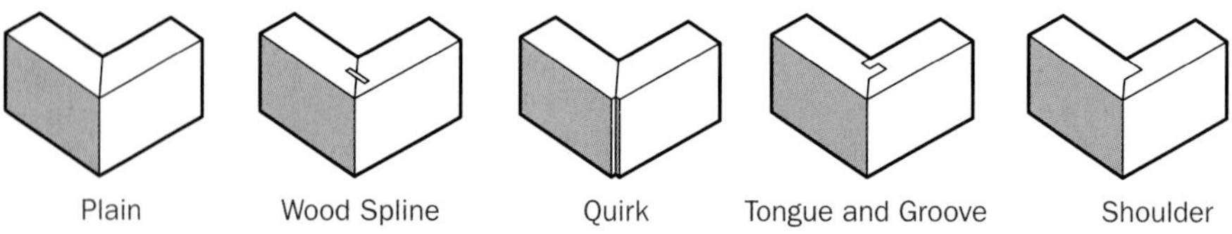
Plain
Wood Spline
Quirk
Tongue and Groove
Shoulder

Right-Angle Joints

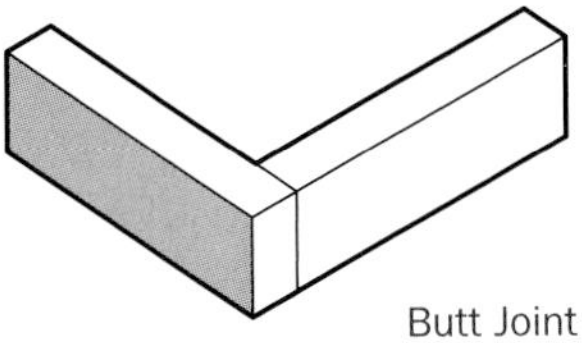

Butt Joint

Right-Angle Joints (Dovetail)

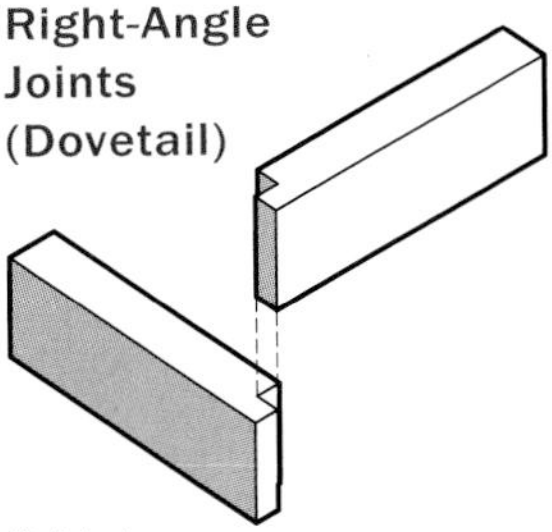

Rabbet

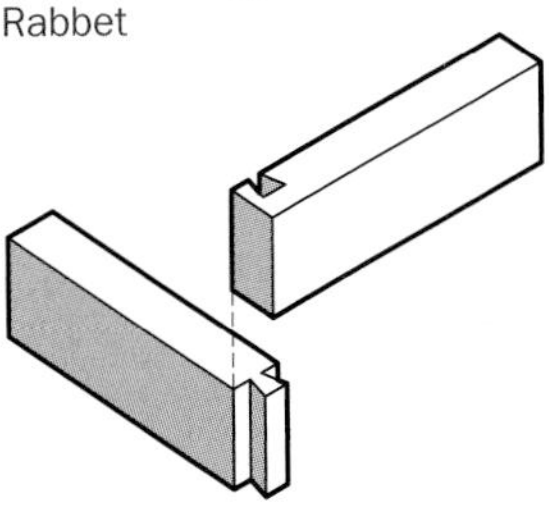

Dovetail Dado

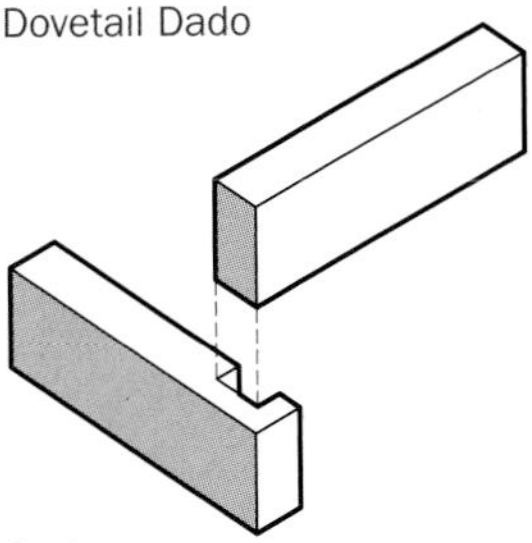

Dado

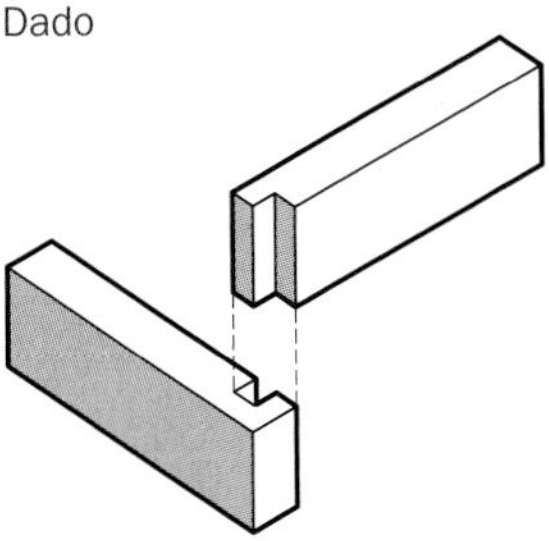

Dado and Rabbet

Right-Angle Joints (Mortise and Tenon)

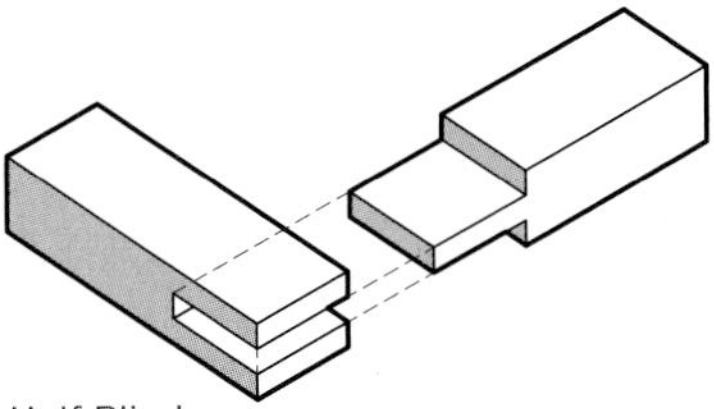

Half Blind

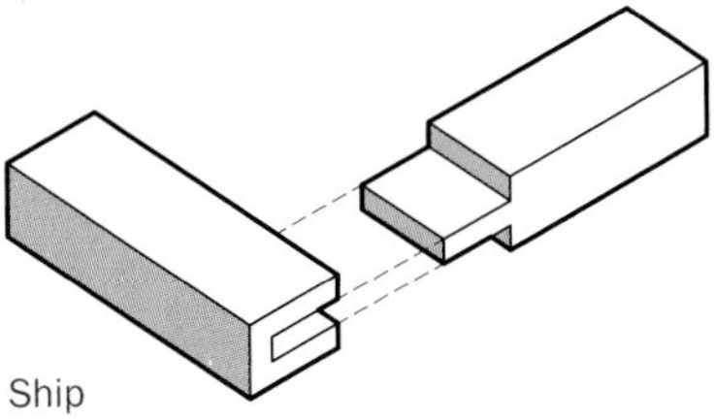

Ship

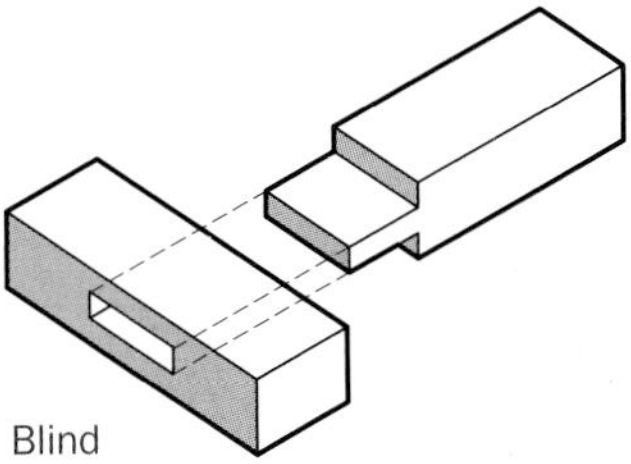

Blind

Right-Angle Joints (Lap)

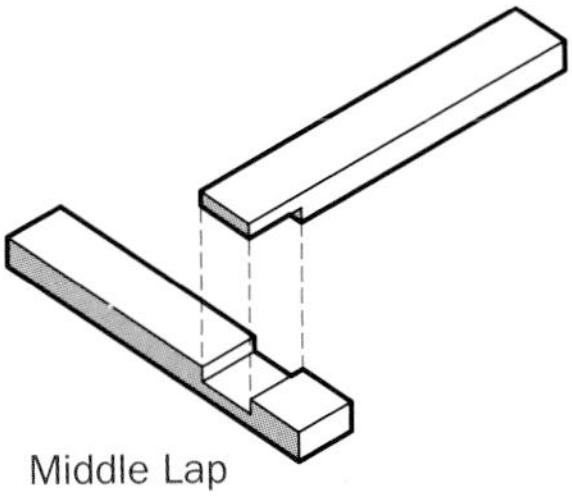

Middle Lap

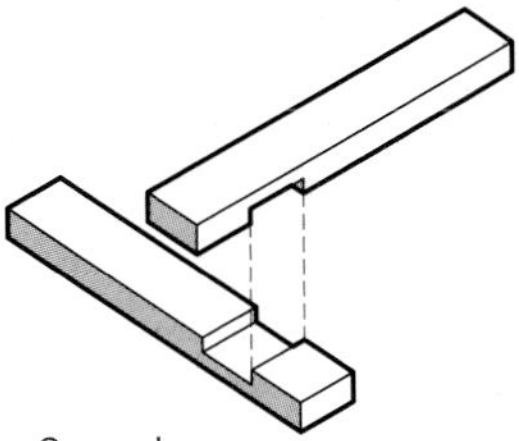

Cross Lap

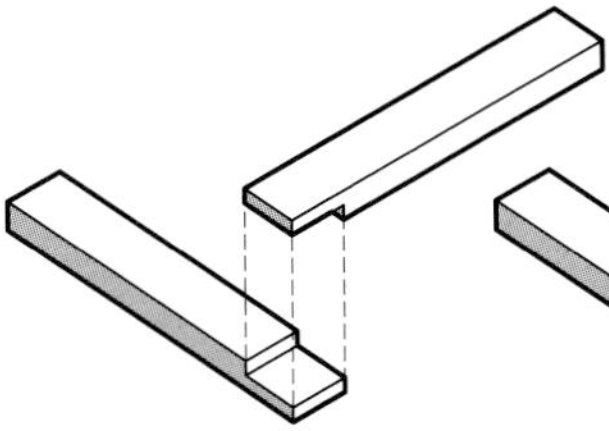

End Lap

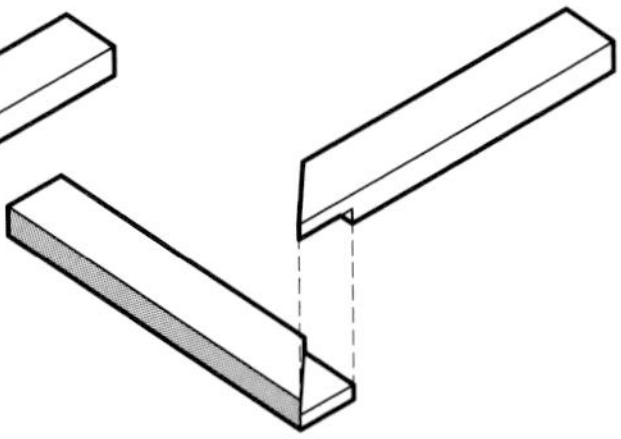

Miter Half Lap

Chapter 2: Masonry and Concrete

MASONRY

Masonry building has become quicker, stronger, and more efficient than in the past, but the basic principles of construction have changed very little since ancient times. Masonry units include bricks, stones, and concrete blocks, and because they all come from the earth, they are suitable for use as foundations, pavers, and walls embedded in the earth. The strength and durability of most masonry makes it ideal to resist fire and decay from water and air.

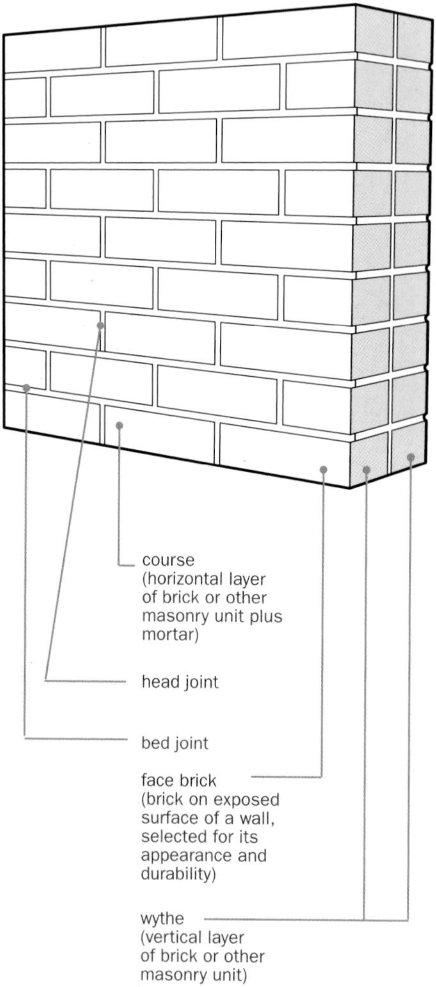
course
(horizontal layer of brick or other masonry unit plus mortar)
head joint
bed joint
face brick
(brick on exposed surface of a wall, selected for its appearance and durability)
wythe
(vertical layer of brick or other masonry unit)

Bricks

The small scale of a single brick makes it a flexible material for use in walls, floors, and even ceilings. Brick production, in which the clay is fired at very high temperatures, gives brick excellent fire-resistive qualities.

Brick Grades (Building and Facing)

SW: Severe weathering (where water may collect)

MW: Moderate weathering

NW: Negligible weathering

Brick Types (Facing)

FBS: General use in exposed exterior and interior walls; most common type and default choice if architect does not specify

FBX: Special use in exposed exterior and interior walls, where a higher degree of mechanical perfection, narrower color range, and minimal variation in size are required

FBA: Special use in exposed exterior and interior walls, where non-uniformity in size, color, and texture are desired

Brick Manufacturing

Winning (Mining) and storage: Clays are mined and enough raw material is stored for several days' use to allow continuous operation in any weather. The three principal types of clay are surface clays, shales, and fire clays.

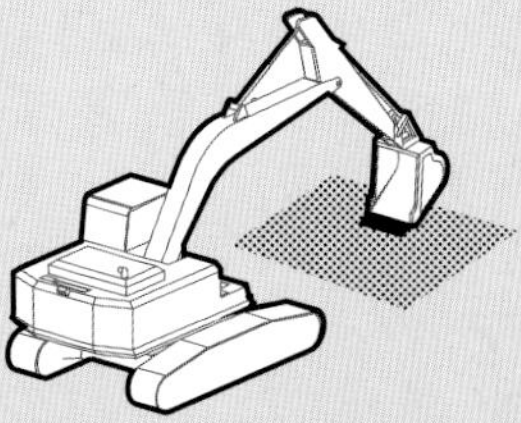

Preparation: Clay is crushed and pulverized.

Forming Processes

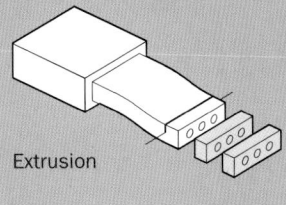

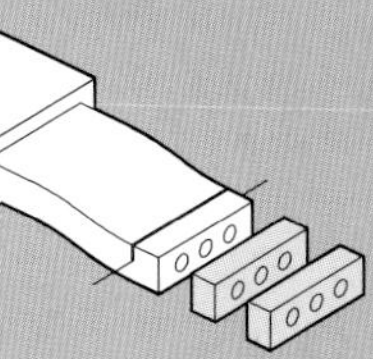

Extrusion

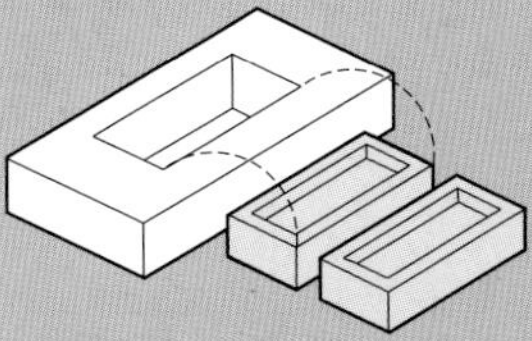

Molding

Stiff mud process (extrusion process): Clay is mixed with minimal amounts of water and then "pugged" (thoroughly mixed). Air pockets are removed from the clay as it is passed through a vacuum. Then it is extruded through a rectangular die and pushed across a cutting table where it is sliced into bricks by cutter wires.

Soft mud process (molding process): Moist clay is pressed into rectangular molds. Water or sand are used as media to prevent the clay from sticking to the molds. Water-struck bricks have a smooth surface, produced when the molds have been dipped into water before being filled; sand-struck, or sand-mold, bricks have a matte-textured surface, produced by dusting the molds with sand before forming the brick.

Dry-press process: Clay is mixed with a minimum of water and machine-pressed into steel molds.

Drying Process

Molded bricks are placed in a low-temperature kiln and dried for one to two days.

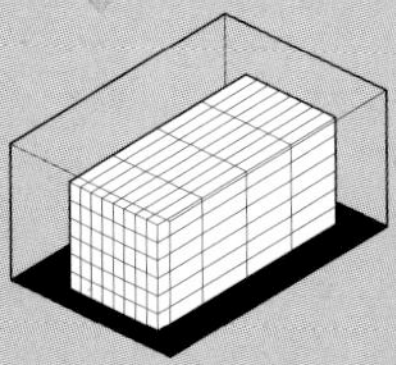

Firing Process

In periodic kilns, bricks are loaded, fired, cooled, and unloaded. In continuous tunnel kilns, bricks ride through a tunnel on railcars, where they are fired the entire time at various temperatures and emerge at the end fully burned. Firing can take from 40 to 150 hours.

Water-smoking and dehydration: Remaining water is removed from the clay.
Oxidation and vitrification: Temperatures reach up to 1,800° F (982°C) and 2,400°F (1,316°C), for these respective processes.
Flashing: Fire is regulated to produce color variations in the brick.

Bricks may also be glazed, either during the initial firing or in a special additional firing.

BRICK UNITS

Comparative Proportions

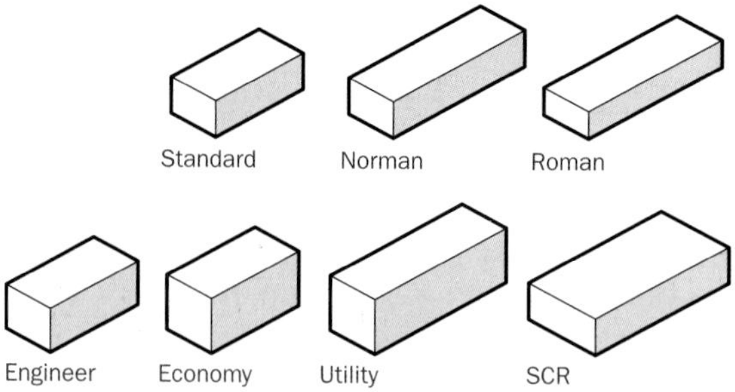
Standard
Norman
Roman
Engineer
Economy
Utility
SCR

Nominal brick dimensions are derived from combining actual brick dimensions (length, thickness, and height) with their respective mortar joints. Typical mortar joints are 3/8" (10) and 1/2" (13).

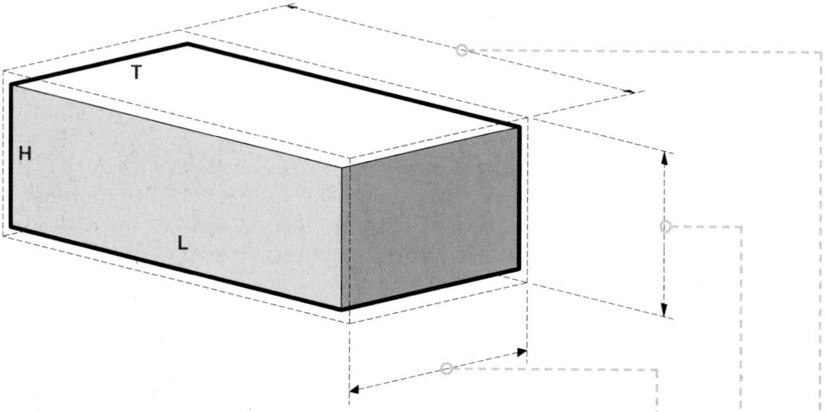
T
H
L

Standard Sizes

Unit Type	Joint Thickness in. (mm)	Brick Thickness = T in. (mm)	Brick Height = H in. (mm)	Brick Length = L in. (mm)	Vertical Coursing = (C) in. (mm)	Nominal T in. (mm)	Nominal H in. (mm)	Nominal L in. (mm)
Standard Modular	3/8 (10) 1/2 (13)	3 5/8 (92) 3 1/2 (89)	2 1/4 (57) 2 3/16 (56)	7 5/8 (194) 7 1/2 (191)	3C = 8 (203)	4 (102)	2 2/3 (68)	8 (203)
Norman	3/8 (9.5) 1/2 (12.7)	3 5/8 (92) 3 1/2 (89)	2 1/4 (57) 2 3/16 (56)	11 5/8 (295) 11 1/2 (292)	3C = 8 (203)	4 (102)	2 2/3 (68)	12 (305)
Roman	3/8 (9.5) 1/2 (12.7)	3 5/8 (92) 3 1/2 (89)	1 5/8 (41) 1 1/2 (38)	11 5/8 (295) 11 1/2 (292)	2C = 4 (102)	4 (102)	2 (51)	12 (305)
Engineer Modular	3/8 (9.5) 1/2 (12.7)	3 5/8 (92) 3 1/2 (89)	2 13/16 (71) 2 11/16 (68)	7 5/8 (194) 7 1/2 (191)	5C = 16 (406)	4 (102)	3 1/5 (81)	8 (203)
Economy	3/8 (9.5) 1/2 (12.7)	3 5/8 (92) 3 1/2 (89)	3 5/8 (92) 3 1/2 (89)	7 5/8 (194) 7 1/2 (191)	1C = 4 (102)	4 (102)	4 (102)	8 (203)
Utility	3/8 (9.5) 1/2 (12.7)	3 5/8 (92) 3 1/2 (89)	3 5/8 (92) 3 1/2 (89)	11 5/8 (295) 11 1/2 (292)	1C = 4 (102)	4 (102)	4 (102)	12 (305)
SCR	1/2 (12.7)	5 1/2 (140)	2 1/8 (54)	11 1/2 (292)	3C = 8 (203)	6 (152)	2 2/3 (68)	12 (305)

Preferred SI Dimensions for Masonry

Nominal Height (H) × Length (L)	Vertical Coursing (C)
50 × 300 mm	[2C = 100]
67 × 200 mm 67 × 300 mm	[3C = 200]
75 × 200 mm 75 × 300 mm	[4C = 300]
80 × 200 mm 80 × 300 mm	[5C = 400]
100 × 200 mm 100 × 300 mm 100 × 400 mm	[1C = 100]
133 × 200 mm 133 × 300 mm 133 × 400 mm	[3C = 400]
150 × 300 mm 150 × 400 mm	[2C = 300]
200 × 200 mm 200 × 300 mm 200 × 400 mm	[1C = 200]
300 × 300 mm	[1C = 300]

Acceptable Length Substitutions for Flexibility

200 mm	(100 mm)
300 mm	(100 mm, 150 mm, 200 mm, 250 mm)
400 mm	(100 mm, 200 mm, 300 mm)

Orientations

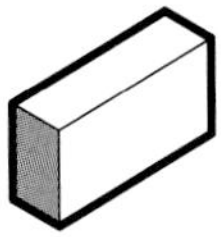
Rowlock

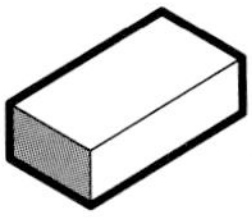
Header

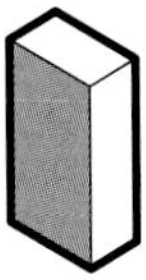
Sailor

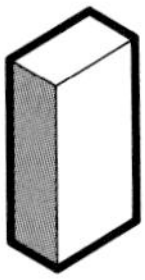
Soldier

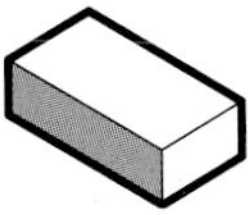
Stretcher

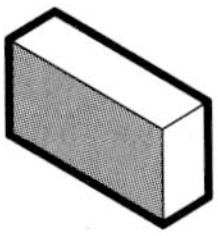
Shiner

Bond Types

Running Bond

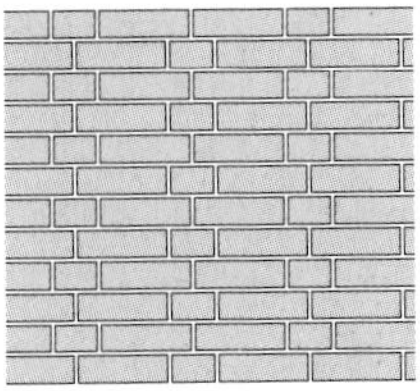
Flemish Monk Bond

1/3 Running Bond

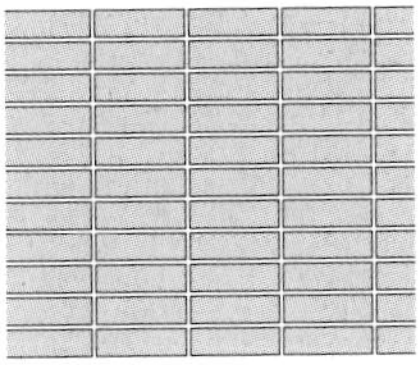
Stack Bond

Common Bond

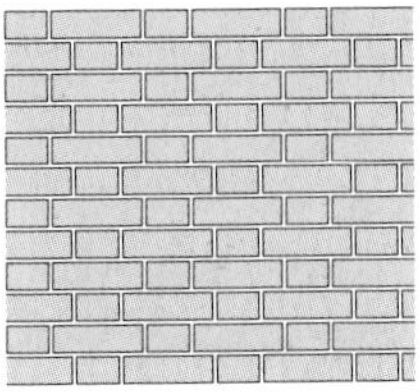
Flemish Bond

Standard Modular Brick Coursing

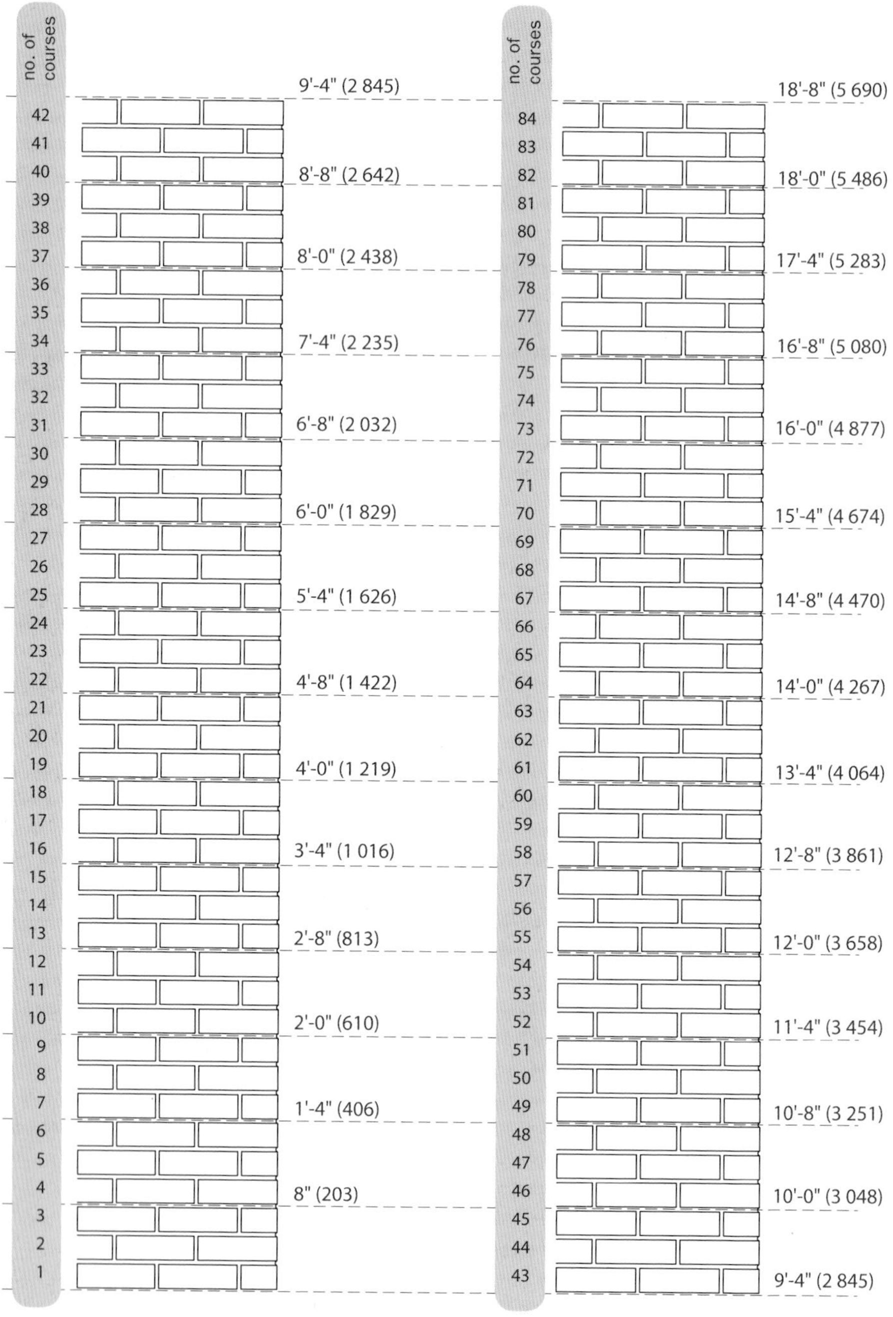
no. of courses
42
41
40
39
38
37
36
35
34
33
32
31
30
29
28
27
26
25
24
23
22
21
20
19
18
17
16
15
14
13
12
11
10
9
8
7
6
5
4
3
2
1
9'-4" (2 845)
8'-8" (2 642)
8'-0" (2 438)
7'-4" (2 235)
6'-8" (2 032)
6'-0" (1 829)
5'-4" (1 626)
4'-8" (1 422)
4'-0" (1 219)
3'-4" (1 016)
2'-8" (813)
2'-0" (610)
1'-4" (406)
8" (203)
no. of courses
84
83
82
81
80
79
78
77
76
75
74
73
72
71
70
69
68
67
66
65
64
63
62
61
60
59
58
57
56
55
54
53
52
51
50
49
48
47
46
45
44
43
18'-8" (5 690)
18'-0" (5 486)
17'-4" (5 283)
16'-8" (5 080)
16'-0" (4 877)
15'-4" (4 674)
14'-8" (4 470)
14'-0" (4 267)
13'-4" (4 064)
12'-8" (3 861)
12'-0" (3 658)
11'-4" (3 454)
10'-8" (3 251)
10'-0" (3 048)
9'-4" (2 845)

Mortar

Mortar adheres masonry units together, cushions them while mediating their surface irregularities, and provides a watertight seal. Composed of portland cement, hydrated lime, an inert aggregate (generally sand), and water, there are four basic types of mortar:

M: High strength (masonry below grade, or subjected to severe frost or to high lateral or compressive loads)

S: Medium-high strength (masonry subjected to normal compressive loads, but requiring high flexural bond strength)

N: Medium strength (masonry above grade, for general use)

O: Medium-low strength (masonry in non-load-bearing interior walls and partitions)

Mortar Joints

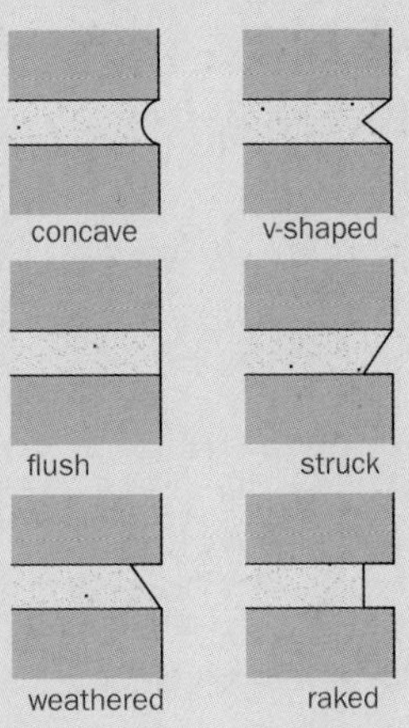
concave
v-shaped
flush
struck
weathered
raked

Colors

Bricks come in numerous textures and patterns, and both bricks and mortar are available in almost endless varieties of color (especially if either is custom produced). Coordination of brick and mortar colors can be an effective way to achieve different qualities within one brick type and color. Matching mortar to brick color, for example, produces a more monolithic look for the wall. Similarly, darker mortars can make a wall feel darker overall, and lighter mortars can make it feel lighter. Full-scale mockups are helpful for testing color combinations.

CONCRETE MASONRY UNITS

CMUs (also called concrete blocks) are available as bricks, large hollow stretcher units, and large solid units. The cores of hollow units can receive grout and reinforcing steel, making them a common element in masonry bearing-wall construction, either alone or as a backup for other cladding material. Like bricks, CMUs have nominal dimensions and accommodate mortar joints; 8" (203) nominal block heights correspond to three brick courses.

Typical Standard Sizes (W × H × L)

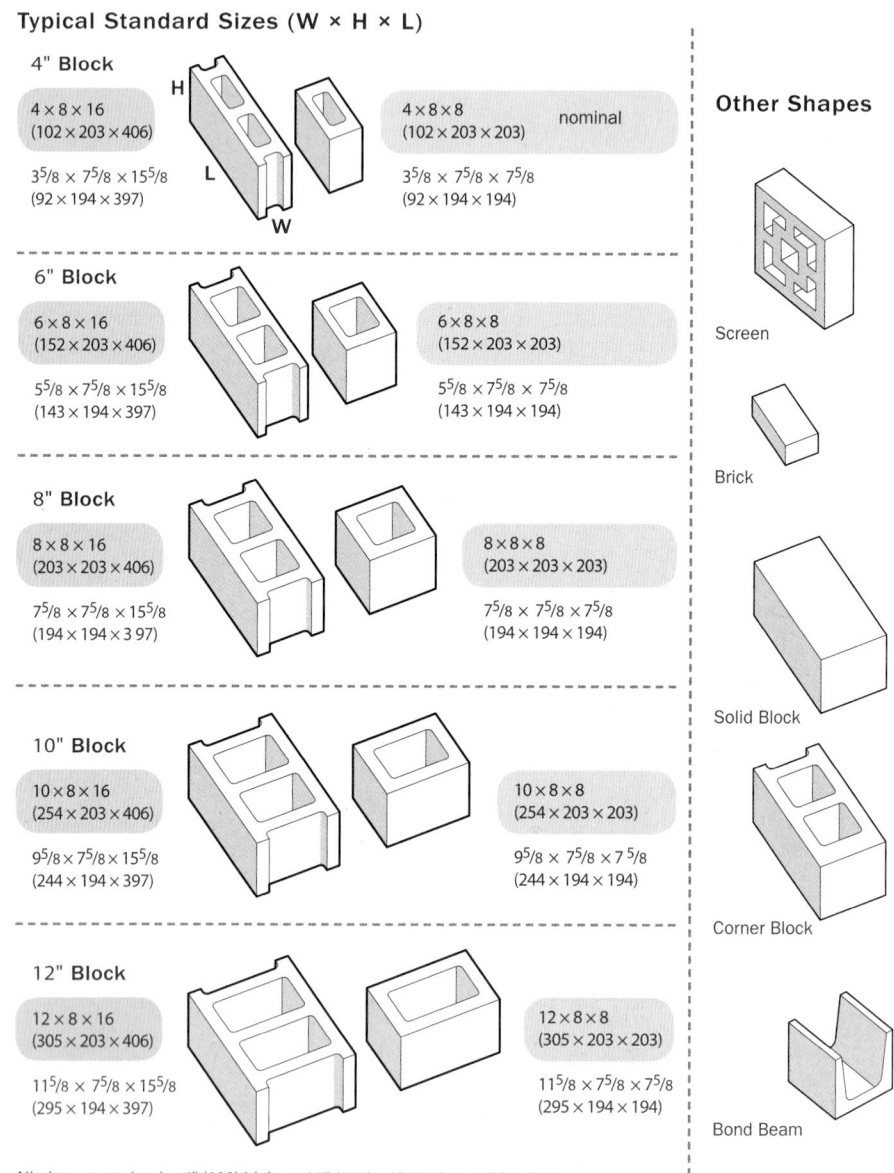

4" Block

4 × 8 × 16
(102 × 203 × 406)

3 5/8 × 7 5/8 × 15 5/8
(92 × 194 × 397)

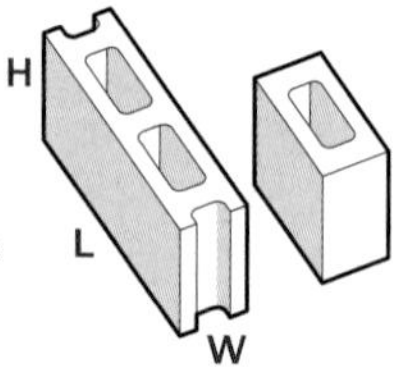
H
L
W

4 × 8 × 8
(102 × 203 × 203)

nominal

3 5/8 × 7 5/8 × 7 5/8
(92 × 194 × 194)

6" Block

6 × 8 × 16
(152 × 203 × 406)

5 5/8 × 7 5/8 × 15 5/8
(143 × 194 × 397)

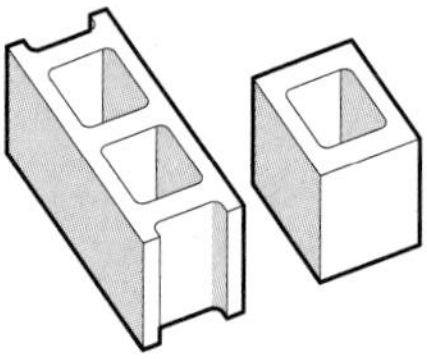

6 × 8 × 8
(152 × 203 × 203)

5 5/8 × 7 5/8 × 7 5/8
(143 × 194 × 194)

8" Block

8 × 8 × 16
(203 × 203 × 406)

7 5/8 × 7 5/8 × 15 5/8
(194 × 194 × 3 97)

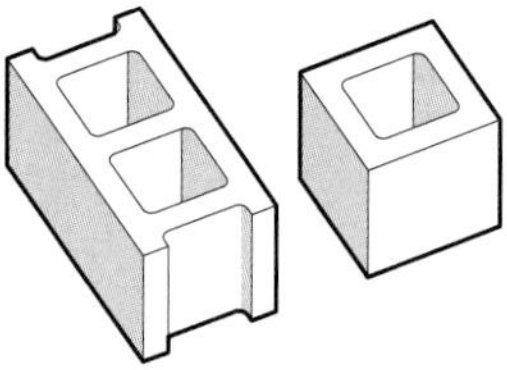

8 × 8 × 8
(203 × 203 × 203)

7 5/8 × 7 5/8 × 7 5/8
(194 × 194 × 194)

10" Block

10 × 8 × 16
(254 × 203 × 406)

9 5/8 × 7 5/8 × 15 5/8
(244 × 194 × 397)

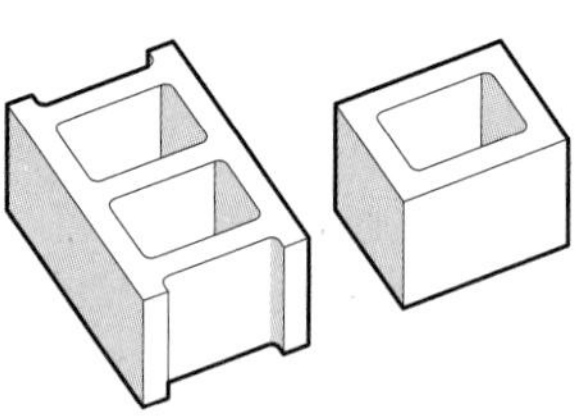

10 × 8 × 8
(254 × 203 × 203)

9 5/8 × 7 5/8 × 7 5/8
(244 × 194 × 194)

12" Block

12 × 8 × 16
(305 × 203 × 406)

11 5/8 × 7 5/8 × 15 5/8
(295 × 194 × 397)

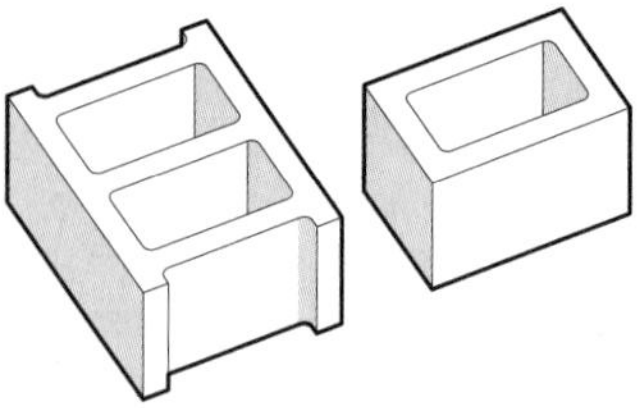

12 × 8 × 8
(305 × 203 × 203)

11 5/8 × 7 5/8 × 7 5/8
(295 × 194 × 194)

All sizes may also be 4" (102) high and 8" (203), 12" (305), or 24" (610) long.

Other Shapes

Screen

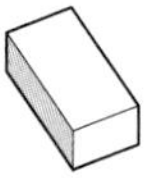

Brick

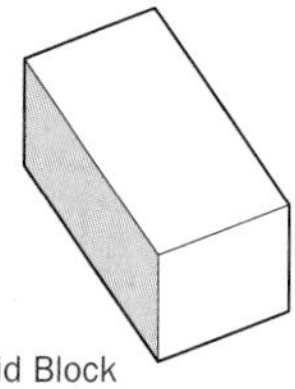

Solid Block

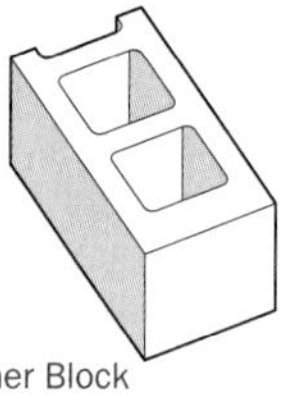

Corner Block

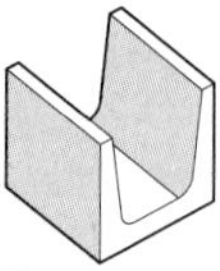

Bond Beam

CMU Production

To produce CMUs, a stiff concrete mixture is placed into molds and vibrated. The wet blocks are then removed from the molds and steam cured.

Fire-resistance ratings for CMUs vary depending on the aggregate type used in the concrete and the size of the block.

CMU Grades

N: General use above and below grade

S: Use above grade only; good where wall is not exposed to weather; if used on exterior, wall must have weather-protective coating

CMU Types

I: Moisture-controlled, for use where shrinkage of units would cause cracking

II: Not moisture-controlled

CMU Weights

Normal: Made from concrete weighing more than 125 lb. per cu. ft. (pcf) (2 000 kg/m³)

Medium: Made from concrete weighing 105–25 pcf (1 680–2 000 kg/m³)

Light: Made from concrete weighing 105 pcf (1 680 kg/m³) or less

Decorative CMUs

Concrete blocks are easily produced in many different shapes, surface textures, and colors, allowing for a variety of wall surfaces. Numerous standard decorative units exist and units may be custom designed.

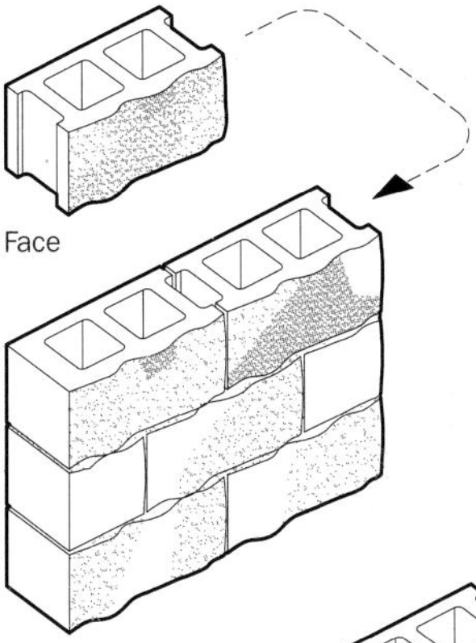

Split Face

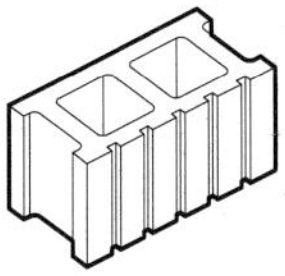

Ribbed Face

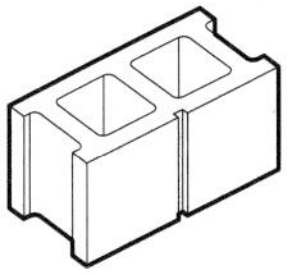

Scored Face

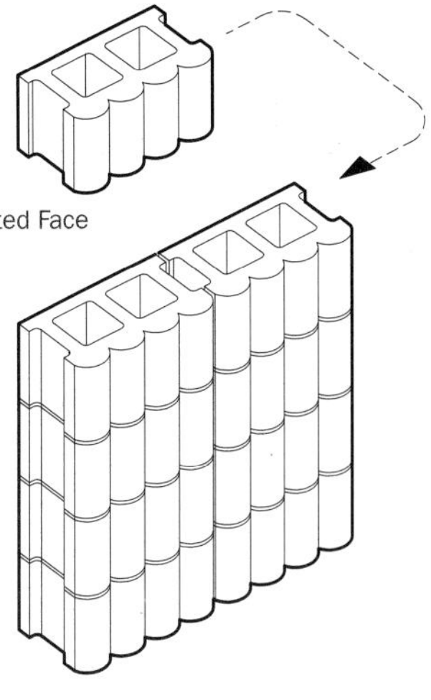

Fluted Face

CONCRETE

Concrete comprises a mixture of aggregate (sand and gravel), portland cement, and water. Because these elements are found almost everywhere, concrete is employed as a construction material throughout the world. When combined correctly with steel reinforcing, concrete becomes virtually indestructible structurally and is generally not susceptible to burning or rotting. It can be shaped into almost any form.

COMPOSITION

Aggregate: Mixture of sand and gravel. Gravel sizes can range from dust to $2\frac{1}{2}$" but should not exceed one-quarter of the thickness of the unit being poured (that is, for a 4" slab, gravel should not be greater than 1"). Rounded fragments are preferred. Larger gravel yields more cost-effective concrete and fewer problems from shrinkage.

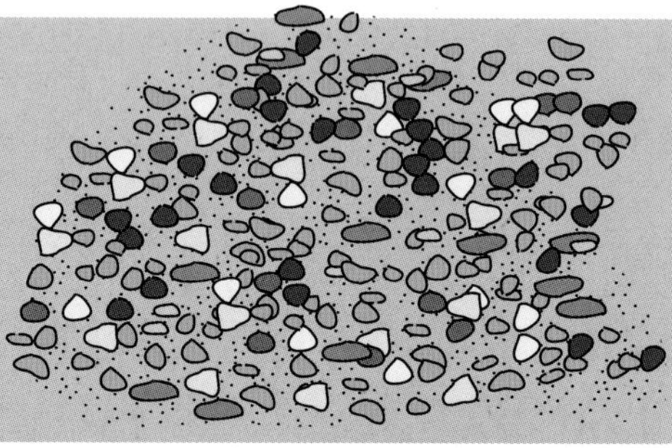

Portland cement: Chemical combination of lime, silicon, aluminum, iron, small amounts of other ingredients, and gypsum, which is added in the final grinding process. Exact ingredients vary by region, based on local availability.

There are five basic types of portland cement.

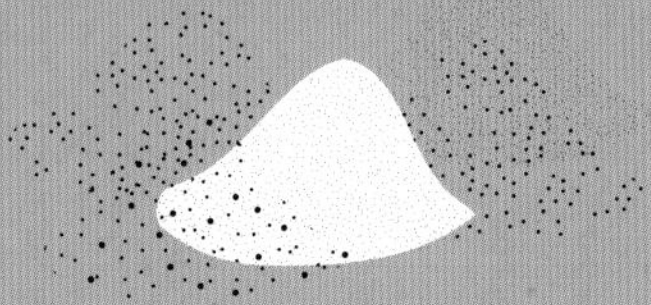

Water: Clean and impurity free.

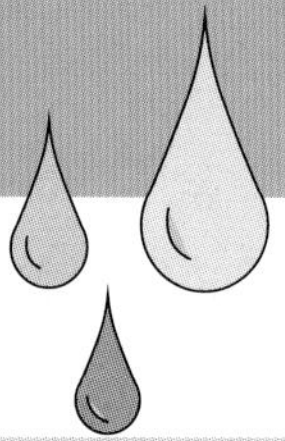

Air: Millions of tiny air bubbles in the mixture make up a fourth component of some mixes of concrete. Air makes the concrete lighter and more able to withstand the effects of freezing and thawing, and is thus useful in cold climates.

SITECAST CONCRETE FRAMING

Sitecast concrete is concrete that is cast into forms on the building site. It can be cast into any shape for which a form can be made; however, the work and time involved in building formwork, reinforcing and pouring the concrete, waiting for the concrete to cure, and dismantling the formwork makes sitecast concrete slower to erect than precast concrete or structural steel.

Concrete Casting

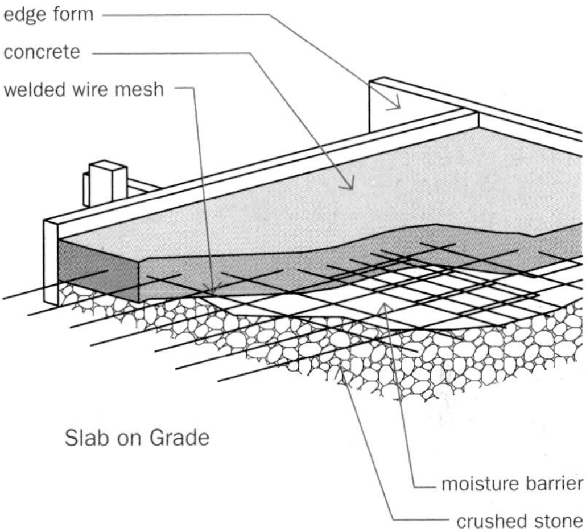
edge form
concrete
welded wire mesh
moisture barrier
crushed stone

Slab on Grade

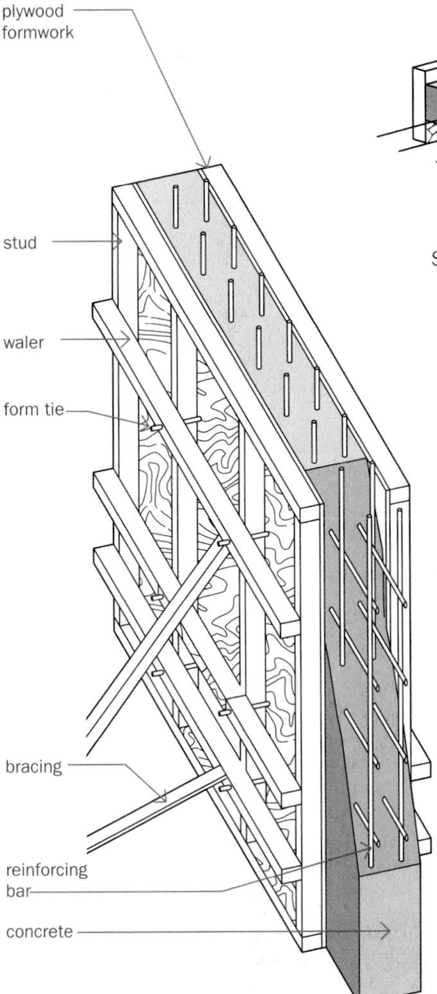
plywood formwork
stud
waler
form tie
bracing
reinforcing bar
concrete

Wall

Cast concrete uses welded wire mesh or reinforcing steel bars (rebar) to prevent cracking or uneven settling and to supply rigidity.

Casting floor slabs, slabs on grade, plates, walls, columns, beams, and girders all involve the use of formwork, which is often plywood but can also be metal or fiberboard. Standardization within a project helps to mitigate the cost of the formwork, which can be reused.

To hold formwork together during pour and curing, form ties are inserted through holes in the formwork and secured in place with fasteners; the protruding ends are snapped off after formwork comes down.

Poured concrete must have regular control joints designed into walls and slabs, either as part of the form or tooled onto the surface before the concrete has cured. A control joint is a line of discontinuity acting as a plane of weakness where movement or cracking can occur in response to forces, relieving potential cracking elsewhere.

PLACING AND CURING

As concrete is poured and placed, care must be taken to ensure that it is not subjected to excessive vibration or sudden vertical drops, which could cause segregation of the materials (course aggregate to the bottom, water and cement to the top). For this reason, vertical transportation should be done with drop chutes. If the concrete must travel excessive distances from the mixer to the formwork, it should be pumped through hoses, not transported in the formwork.

Concrete cures by hydration, as a binding chemical combination of the cement and water; it must be kept moist during this period, generally twenty-eight days, before it is adequately cured. Surfaces may be kept moist by spraying them with water or a curing compound or by covering them with moisture-resistant sheets.

Admixtures

Other ingredients may be added to concrete for various desired effects.

Accelerating admixtures: Promote faster curing (may be used in cold weather, when curing is slowed down).

Air-entraining admixtures: Increase workability of wet concrete, aid in reducing freeze-thaw damage, and may produce lightweight, thermal-insulated concrete.

Blast furnace slag: Similar to fly ash in effect.

Coloring agents: Dyes and pigments.

Corrosion inhibitors: Reduce corrosion of reinforcing steel.

Fibrous admixtures: Short glass, steel, or polypropylene fibers that act as reinforcing.

Fly ash: Improves workability of wet concrete while also increasing strength and sulfate resistance, and decreases permeability, temperature rises, and needed water.

Pozzolans: Improve workability, reduce internal temperatures while curing, and reduce reactivity caused by sulfates.

Retarding admixtures: Promote slower curing and allow more time for working with wet concrete.

Silica fume: Produces extremely high strength concrete with very low permeability.

Super-plasticizers: High-range water-reducing admixtures that turn stiff concrete into flowing liquid for placing in difficult sites.

Water-reducing admixtures: Allow for more workability with less water in the mix.

Reinforcing Steel

Without reinforcing, concrete would have few or no structural uses. Fortunately, steel and concrete are chemically compatible and have a similar rate of dimensional change due to temperature.

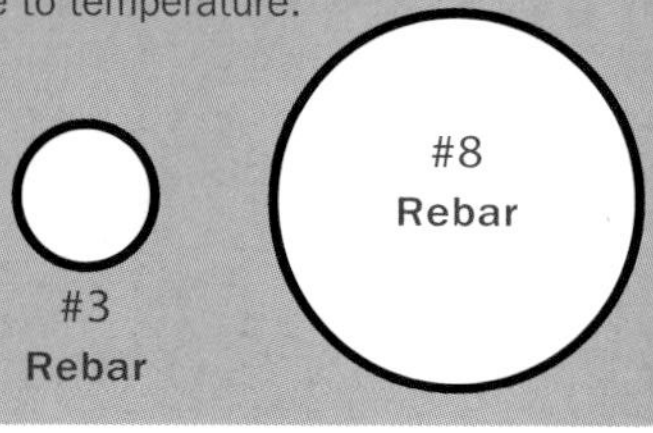
#3
Rebar
#8
Rebar

FINISHES

Concrete can be finished in a variety of ways, allowing it to be used on virtually any surface in almost any kind of space.

As cast: Concrete remains as it is after removal of forms and often bears the imprint of wood grain from the plywood.

Blasted: Various degrees of sandblasting smooth the surface while exposing successive levels of cement, sand, and aggregate.

Chemically retarded: Chemicals are applied to the surface to expose the aggregate.

Mechanically fractured: Tooling, hammering, jackhammering, and scaling produce varied aggregate-exposing effects.

Polished: Heavy-duty polishing machines polish the surface to a high gloss, with or without polishing compounds.

Sealed: Acrylic resin helps protect concrete from spalling (chipping or flaking caused by improper drainage or venting and freeze/thaw damage), dusting, efflorescence (whitening caused by water leeching soluble salts out of concrete and depositing them on the surface), stains, deicing salts, and abrasion.

Color

Colored concrete provides numerous design opportunities, It is generally achieved in one of two ways:

Integral coloring: Color is added to the wet concrete or mixed in at the jobsite—in either case, the color is distributed throughout the concrete. Because so much concrete is involved, colors are limited to earth tones and pastels. Once cured, the surface is sealed, which provides protection and a sheen that enhances the color.

Dry-shake color hardeners: Color hardeners are broadcast onto freshly placed concrete and troweled into the surface. The hardeners produce a dense and durable surface. Because the color is concentrated on top of the concrete, more vibrant and intense tones are possible. Sealers applied after curing further accentuate the richness of the color.

As in all natural materials, variations in color outcome will occur. The base color of the cement determines the ranges possible.

Reinforcing bars: Bars come in the following sizes: 3, 4, 5, 6, 7, 8, 9, 10, 11, 14, 18. Nominal diameters of #8 and lower are the bar number in eighths of an inch; that is, #3 is 3/8" (9.52). Nominal diameters of #9 and higher are slightly larger.

Welded wire fabric: Reinforcing steel is formed into a grid of wires or round bars 2"–12" (51–305) on center. Lighter styles are used in slabs on grade and some precast elements; heavier styles may be used in walls and structural slabs.

Chapter 3: Metals

Metals play an enormous role in almost every component of many projects and building types, from structural steel to sheet-metal ductwork, from drywall partition studs to oxides used as paint pigments. Metals of most varieties occur in nature as oxide ores, which can be mined and worked to extract and refine the metals, separating them from other elements and impurities. Metals fall under two broad categories: ferrous (containing iron) and nonferrous. Ferrous metals are generally stronger, more abundant, and easier to refine, but they have a tendency to rust. Nonferrous metals tend to be easier to work and most form their own thin oxide layers that protect them from corrosion.

MODIFYING METAL PROPERTIES

Most metals in their chemically pure and natural form are not very strong. To be suitable for construction and other functions, their properties must be altered, which can be done in several ways, often dependent on the proposed use of the metal.

Alloys

Metals are mixed with other elements, usually other metals, to create an alloy. For example, iron mixed with small amounts of carbon produces steel. Generally, the alloy is stronger than its primary metal ingredient. In addition to improved strength and workability, alloys provide self-protecting oxide layers.

Heat-Treated Metals

Tempering: Steel is heated at a moderate rate and slowly cooled, producing a harder and stronger metal.

Annealing: Steel and sometimes aluminum alloys are heated to very high temperatures and cooled slowly, softening the metal so that it is easier to work.

Cold-Worked Metals

At room temperature, metals are rolled thin, beaten, or drawn, making them stronger but more brittle by altering their crystalline structures. Cold-worked metals may be reversed by annealing.

Cold rolling: Metal is squeezed between rollers.

Drawing: Drawing metal through increasingly smaller orifices produces the wires and cables used to prestress concrete, which have five times the structural strength of steel.

Coated Metals

Anodizing: A thin oxide layer of controlled color and consistency is electrolytically added to aluminum to improve its surface appearance.

Electroplating: Chromium and cadmium are coated onto steel to protect it from oxidation and improve its appearance.

Galvanizing: Steel is coated with zinc to protect it against corrosion.

Other coatings: Coatings can include paints, lacquers, powders, fluoropolymers, and porcelain enamel.

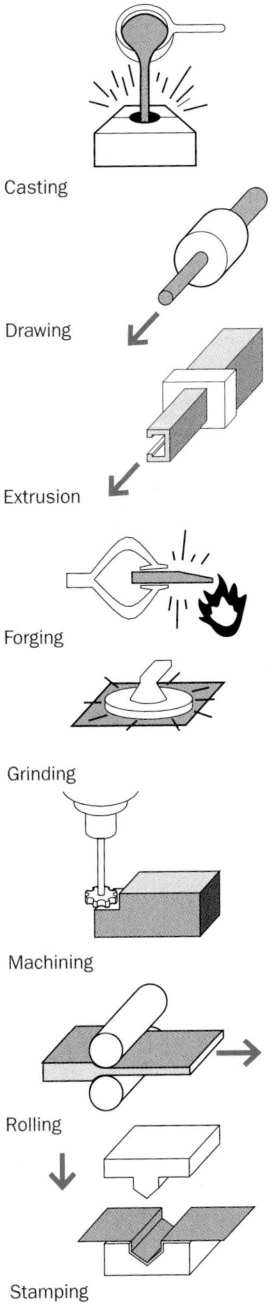
Casting
Drawing
Extrusion
Forging
Grinding
Machining
Rolling
Stamping

FABRICATION TECHNIQUES

Casting: Molten metal is poured into a shaped mold. The metal produced is weak but can be made into many shapes, such as faucets or hardware.

Drawing: Wires are produced by pulling metal through increasingly smaller holes.

Extrusion: Heated (but not molten) metal is squeezed through a die, producing a long metal piece with a shaped profile.

Forging: Metal is heated until flexible and then bent into a desired shape. This process improves structural performance by imparting a grain orientation onto the metal.

Grinding: Machines grind and polish metal to create flat, finished surfaces.

Machining: Material is cut away to achieve a desired shape. Processes include drilling, milling (with a rotating wheel), lathing (for cylindrical shapes), sawing, shearing, and punching. Sheet metal is cut with shears and folded on brakes.

Rolling: Metal is squeezed between rollers. Hot rolling, unlike cold, does not increase the strength of metal.

Stamping: Sheet metal is squeezed between matching dies to give it shape and texture.

Joining Metals

Welding: In this high-temperature fusion, a gas flame or electric arc melts two metals and allows the point of connection to flow together with additional molten metal from a welding rod. Welded connections are as strong as the metals they join and can be used for structural work.

Brazing and soldering: In these lower-temperature processes, the two metals are not themselves melted but joined with the solder of a metal with a lower melting point: brass or bronze are used in brazing, lead-tin alloy is used in soldering. Too weak for structural connections, brazing and soldering are used for plumbing pipes and roofing.

Mechanical methods: Metals can also be drilled or punched with holes, through which screws, bolts, or rivets are inserted.

Interlocking and folding: Sheet metal can be joined by such connections.

METAL TYPES

Ferrous

Cast iron: Very brittle with high compressive strength and ability to absorb vibrations; ideal for gratings and stair components but too brittle for structural work.

Malleable iron: Produced by casting, reheating, and slowly cooling to improve workability; similar to cast iron in use.

Mild steel: Ordinary structural steel with a low carbon content.

Stainless steel: Produced by alloying with other metals, primarily chromium or nickel for corrosion resistance and molybdenum when maximum resistance is required (in sea water, for example). Though harder to form and machine than mild steel, its uses are many, including flashing, coping, fasteners, anchors, hardware, and finishes that can range from matte to mirror polish.

Steel: Iron with low amounts of carbon (carbon increases strength, but decreases ductility and welding capabilities); used for structural components, studs, joists, and fasteners, and in decorative work.

Wrought iron: Soft and easily worked, with high corrosion resistance, making it ideal for use below grade. Most often cast or worked into bars, pipes, or sheets, and fashioned for ornamental purposes. Other metals like steel have virtually replaced it today.

Steel Alloys

Aluminum: Hardens surfaces

Chromium and cadmium: Resists corrosion

Copper: Resists atmospheric corrosion

Manganese: Increases hardness and helps to resist wear

Molybdenum: Often combined with other alloys, increases corrosion resistance and raises tensile strength

Nickel: Increases tensile strength and resists corrosion

Silicon: Increases strength and resists oxidation

Sulfur: Allows for free machining of mild steels

Titanium: Prevents intergranular corrosion in stainless steel

Tungsten: With vanadium and cobalt, increases hardness and resists abrasions

Aluminum Alloy Series

Wrought		Cast	
Series	**Alloying Element**	**Series**	**Alloying Element**
1000	pure aluminum	100.0	pure aluminum
2000	copper	200.0	copper
3000	manganese	300.0	silicon plus copper and/ or magnesium
4000	silicon	400.0	silicon
5000	magnesium	500.0	magnesium
6000	magnesium and silicon	600.0	unused series
7000	zinc	700.0	zinc
8000	other elements	800.0	tin
		900.0	other elements
*1*st digit is series no.; *2*nd is modification of alloy; *3*rd/*4*th are arbitrary identifiers		*1*st digit is series no.; *2*nd/*3*rd are arbitrary identifiers; no. after decimal is casting if *0*, ingot if *1* or *2*	

Nonferrous

Aluminum: When pure, it resists corrosion well, but is soft and lacks strength; with alloys, it can achieve various levels of strength and stiffness, at one-third the density of steel, and can be hot- or cold-rolled, cast, drawn, extruded, forged, or stamped. Sheets or foil, when polished to a mirror finish, have extremely high levels of light and heat reflectivity. Its uses include curtain wall components, ductwork, flashing, roofing, window and door frames, grills, siding, hardware, wiring, and coatings for other metals. Aluminum powder may be added to metallic paints and its oxide acts as an abrasive in sandpaper.

Brass: Alloy of copper, zinc, and other metals; can be polished to a high luster and is mostly used for weather stripping, ornamental work, and finish hardware.

Bronze: Alloy of copper and tin that resists corrosion; used for weather stripping, hardware, and ornamental work.

Cadmium: Similar to zinc; usually electroplated onto steel.

Chromium: Very hard and will not corrode in air; like nickel, often used as an alloy to achieve a bright polish and is excellent for plating.

Copper: Ductile and corrosion-, impact-, and fatigue-resistant; it has high thermal and electrical conductivity, and can be cast, drawn, extruded, hot-, or cold-rolled. Widely employed as an alloy with other metals, it can also be used for electrical wiring, flashing, roofing, and piping.

Lead: Extremely dense, corrosion resistant, limp, soft, and easy to work; most often combined with alloys to improve hardness and strength. Foil or sheets are ideal for waterproofing, blocking sound and vibrations, and shielding against radiation. Can also be used as roofing and flashing, or to coat copper sheets (lead-coated copper) for roofing and flashing. High toxicity of vapors and dust have made its use less common.

Magnesium: Strong and lightweight; as an alloy, serves to increase strength and corrosion resistance in aluminum. Often used in aircraft, but too expensive for most construction.

Tin: Soft and ductile; used in terneplate (80 percent lead, 20 percent tin) for plating steel.

Titanium: Low density and high strength; used in numerous alloys and its oxide has replaced lead in many paints.

Zinc: Corrosion resistant in water and air, but very brittle and low in strength. Primarily used in galvanizing steel to keep it from rusting; also electroplated onto other metals as an alloy. Other functions include flashing, roofing, hardware, and die-casting.

GALVANIC ACTION

Galvanic action is corrosion that occurs between metals under the following conditions: There exist two electrochemically dissimilar metals, an electrically conductive path between the two metals, and a conductive path for metal ions to move from the less noble metal to the more noble one. A good understanding of the material compatibilities in the galvanic series will minimize corrosion in design. The galvanic series lists metals from least noble (anodic, or most reactive to corrosion) to most noble (cathodic, or least reactive to corrosion). Generally, the farther apart two metals are on the list, the greater the corrosion of the less noble one. Therefore, combinations of metals that will be in electrical contact should be selected from groups as close together in the series as possible.

Note that the ranking of metals may differ, based on variations in alloy composition and nonuniform conditions. When specifying and detailing metals, always consult the manufacturer of the metal product.

Galvanic Series

+ Anode	Magnesium, magnesium alloys
	Zinc, zinc alloys and plates
	Zinc (hot-dipped), galvanized steel
	Aluminum (non-silicon cast alloys), cadmium
	Aluminum (wrought alloys, silicon cast)
	Iron (wrought, malleable), plain carbon and low-alloy steel
	Aluminum (wrought alloys —2000 series)
	Lead (solid, plated), lead alloys
	Tin plate, tin-lead solder
	Chromium plate
	High brasses and bronzes
	Brasses and bronzes
	Copper, low brasses and bronzes, silver solder, copper-nickel alloys
	Nickel, titanium alloys, monel
	Silver
Cathode −	Gold, platinum

The series listed here is for general information only and does not consider the anodic index of any metals. The anodic index (V) of each metal determines more precisely its compatibility thresholds with other metals.

Accurate anodic index numbers should be obtained from the specific metal manufacturer.

GAUGES AND MILS

Sheet metal thicknesses have long been expressed in terms of gauge (ga.), an antiquated term based on weight (originally for reasons of taxation) and not a reference to the precise thickness of a sheet. Thus, a sheet of mild steel and one of galvanized steel may have the same gauge but different thicknesses. As the gauge number increases, the sheet becomes thinner; sheets thicker than 1/4" (6), or about 3-gauge, are referred to as plates.

Most steel manufacturers are adapting to mils. This straightforward system allows the actual thickness of the sheet to define its mil designation.

There is no equation for a strict translation from gauge to mil thickness; however—for reference purposes only—many common mil sizes may be associated with specific gauge sizes.

Gauge Reference Chart

Mil (µm)	Gauge (ga.)	Standard Steel in.	Standard Steel (mm)	Galvanized Steel in.	Galvanized Steel (mm)	Aluminum in.	Aluminum (mm)
	3	0.2391	(6.073)			0.2294	(5.827)
	4	0.2242	(5.695)			0.2043	(5.189)
	5	0.2092	(5.314)			0.1819	(4.620)
	6	0.1943	(4.935)			0.1620	(4.115)
	7	0.1793	(4.554)			0.1443	(3.665)
	8	0.1644	(4.176)			0.1285	(3.264)
	9	0.1495	(3.797)	0.1532	(3.891)	0.1144	(2.906)
118	10	0.1345	(3.416)	0.1382	(3.510)	0.1019	(2.588)
	11	0.1196	(3.030)	0.1233	(3.132)	0.0907	(2.304)
97	12	0.1046	(2.657)	0.1084	(2.753)	0.0808	(2.052)
	13	0.0897	(2.278)	0.0934	(2.372)	0.0720	(1.829)
68	14	0.0747	(1.879)	0.0785	(1.994)	0.0641	(1.628)
	15	0.0673	(1.709)	0.0710	(1.803)	0.0571	(1.450)
54	16	0.0598	(1.519)	0.0635	(1.613)	0.0508	(1.290)
	17	0.0538	(1.367)	0.0575	(1.461)	0.0453	(1.151)
43	18	0.0478	(1.214)	0.0516	(1.311)	0.0403	(1.024)
	19	0.0418	(1.062)	0.0456	(1.158)	0.0359	(0.912)
30 | 33	20	0.0359	(0.912)	0.0396	(1.006)	0.0320	(0.813)
	21	0.0329	(0.836)	0.0366	(0.930)	0.0285	(0.724)
27	22	0.0299	(0.759)	0.0336	(0.853)	0.0253	(0.643)
	23	0.0269	(0.683)	0.0306	(0.777)	0.0226	(0.574)
	24	0.0239	(0.607)	0.0276	(0.701)	0.0201	(0.511)
18	25	0.0209	(0.531)	0.0247	(0.627)	0.0179	(0.455)
	26	0.0179	(0.455)	0.0217	(0.551)	0.0159	(0.404)
	27	0.0164	(0.417)	0.0202	(0.513)	0.0142	(0.361)
	28	0.0149	(0.378)	0.0187	(0.475)	0.0126	(0.320)
	29	0.0135	(0.343)	0.0172	(0.437)	0.0113	(0.287)
	30	0.0120	(0.305)	0.0157	(0.399)	0.0100	(0.254)
	31	0.0105	(0.267)	0.0142	(0.361)	0.0089	(0.226)
	32	0.0097	(0.246)	0.0134	(0.340)	0.0080	(0.203)
	33	0.0090	(0.229)			0.0071	(0.180)
	34	0.0082	(0.208)			0.0063	(0.160)
	35	0.0075	(0.191)			0.0056	(0.142)
	36	0.0067	(0.170)				

33 mil is considered the thinnest material allowable for structural cold-formed steel framing

20-gauge material often comes in the following two thicknesses:

30 mil for nonstructural drywall studs;

33 mil for structural studs

18 mil is considered the thinnest material allowable for nonstructural, cold-formed steel framing

LIGHT-GAUGE FRAMING

Metal studs are generally made of cold-rolled corrosion-resistant steel in standard sizes. They work in both load-bearing and non-load-bearing capacities and as floor and roof framing elements. Studs are spaced 16" (406) or 24" (610) OC inside top and bottom tracks. Metal studs with gypsum sheathing provide greatly reduced combustibility, and can be built taller than wood stud walls. Knockouts or punchouts are provided at regular intervals to allow for bridging between studs or for the passing through of electrical conduit or plumbing.

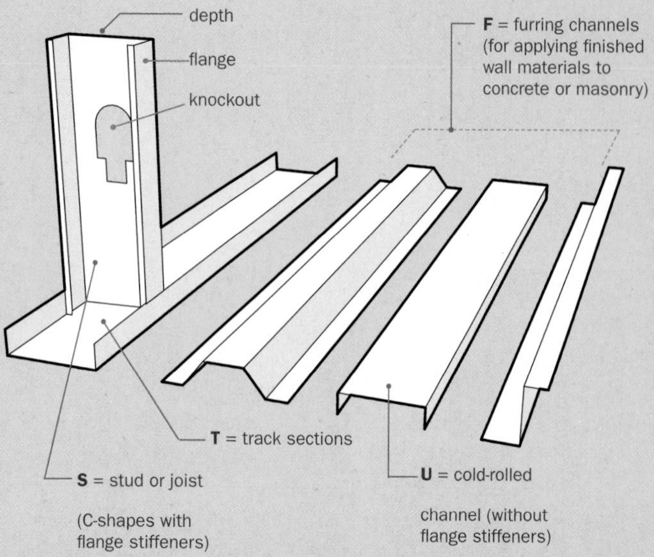
depth
flange
knockout
F = furring channels (for applying finished wall materials to concrete or masonry)
T = track sections
S = stud or joist
(C-shapes with flange stiffeners)
U = cold-rolled
channel (without flange stiffeners)

The Steel Stud Manufacturers Association (SSMA) designations for light-gauge steel framing members are written as follows: web depth (in 1/100") + S, T, U, or F designation + flange width (in 1/100") + minimum base metal thickness (in mils).

Thus, a 250S 162-33 member is a 2 1/2" (250/100") stud with a flange of 1 5/8" (162/100"), at 33 mils.

Common Metal Stud Sizes

Non-load-bearing Studs
depths: 1 5/8" (41), 2 1/2" (64), 3 5/8" (92), 4" (102), 6" (152)
gauges [mils]; 25 [18], 22 [27], 20 [30]

Non-load-bearing Curtain Wall Studs
depths: 2 1/2" (64), 3 5/8" (92), 4" (102), 6" (152)
gauges [mils]: 20 [30], 18 [43], 16 [54], 14 [68]
flange: 1 3/8" (35)

Structural C-Studs
depths: 2 1/2" (64), 3 5/8" (92), 4" (102), 6" (152), 8" (203), 10" (254), 12" (305)
gauges [mils]: 20 [33], 18 [43], 16 [54], 14 [68]
flange: 1 5/8" (41)

Structural Stud/Joist
depths: 2 1/2" (64), 3 5/8" (92), 4" (102), 6" (152), 8" (203), 10" (254), 12" (305)
gauges [mils]: 20 [33], 18 [43], 16 [54], 14 [68]
flange: 2" (51)

Sheet Thickness (actual size)

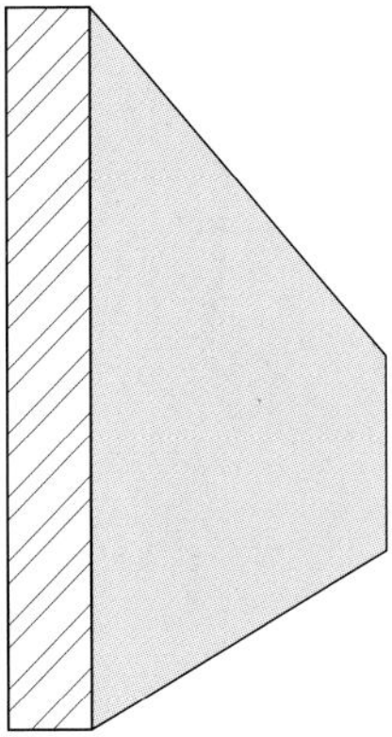

210 mils

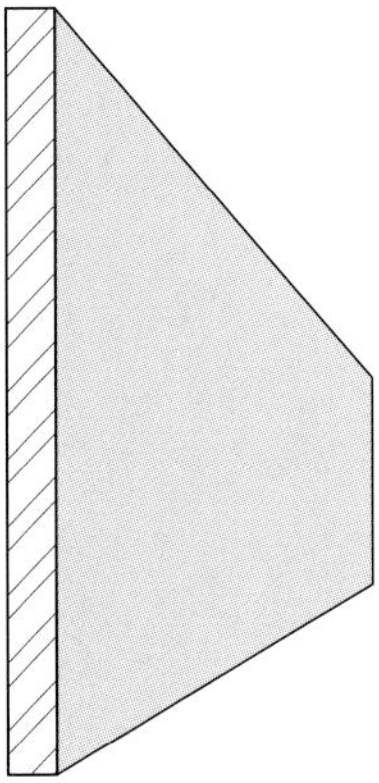

97 mils

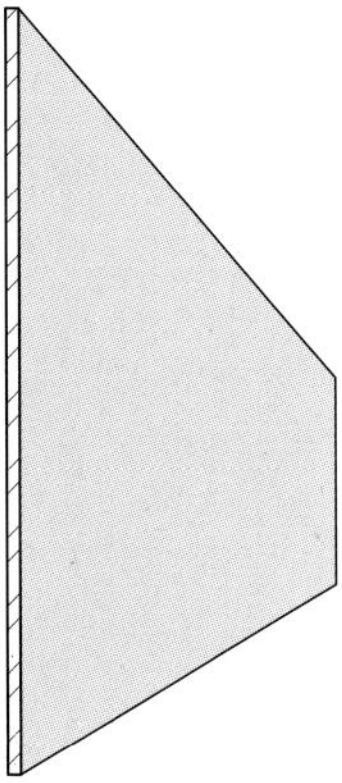

33 mils

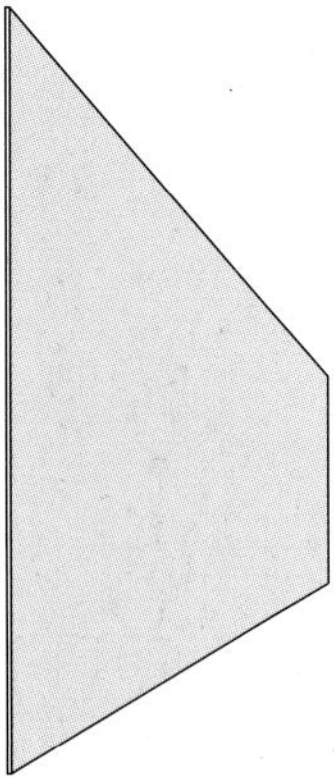

18 mils

Metal Roofing Seams

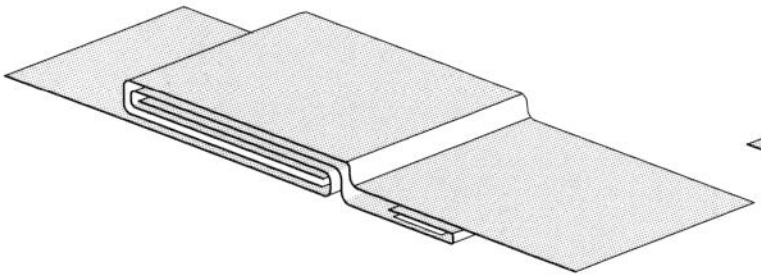

Flat Seam

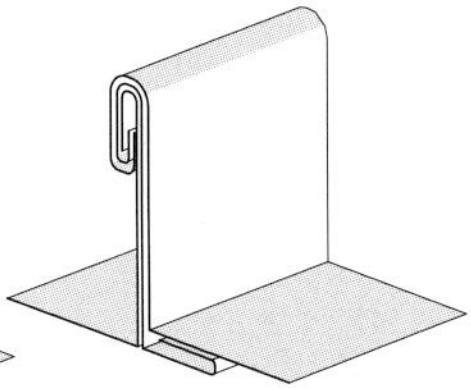

Standing Seam

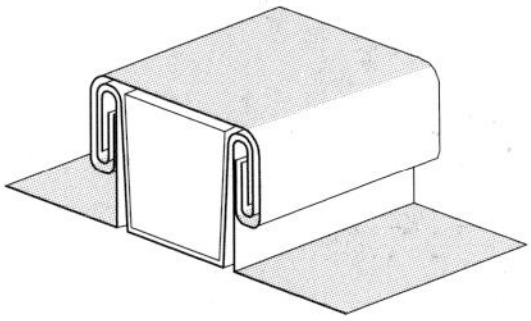

Batten Seam

Forms and Sheets

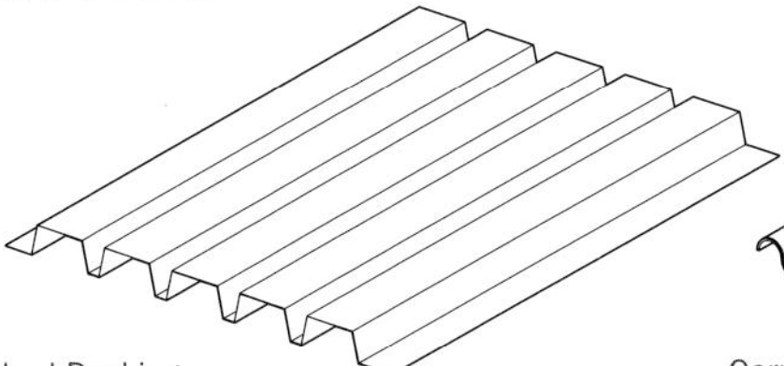

Ribbed Decking

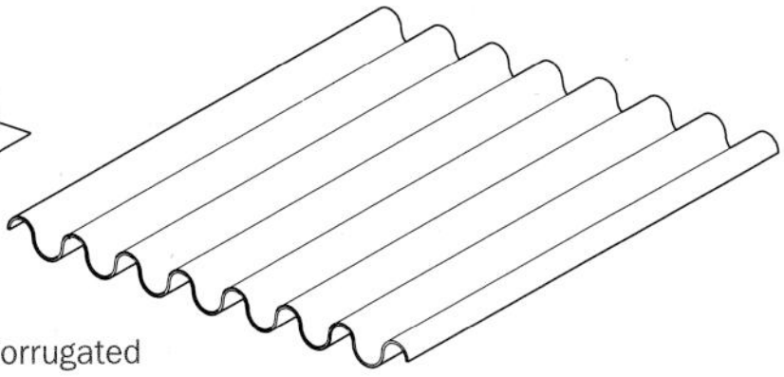

Corrugated

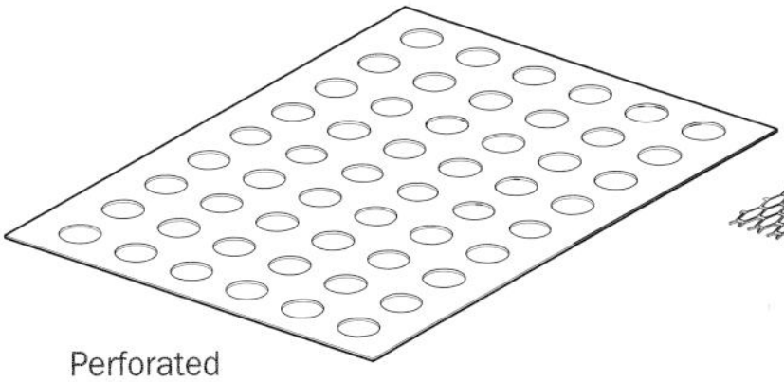

Perforated

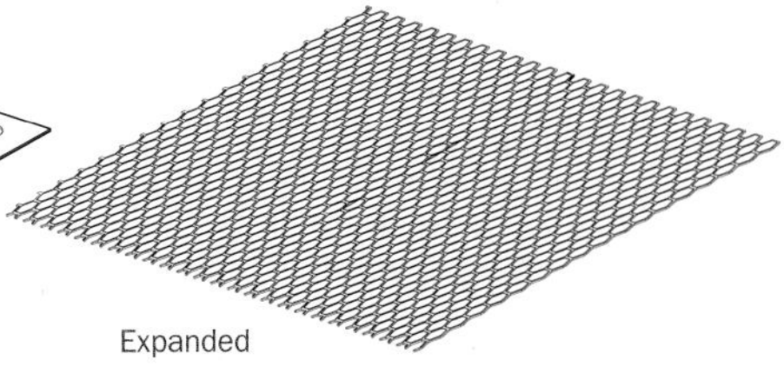

Expanded

Chapter 4: Building Enclosures

A building's enclosure systems serve many functions. Not only must they separate and protect interior from exterior, they must still allow the inside and outside to have a relationship that contributes to the most effective means of moisture, thermal, and ventilation control, all while presenting the building's public face.

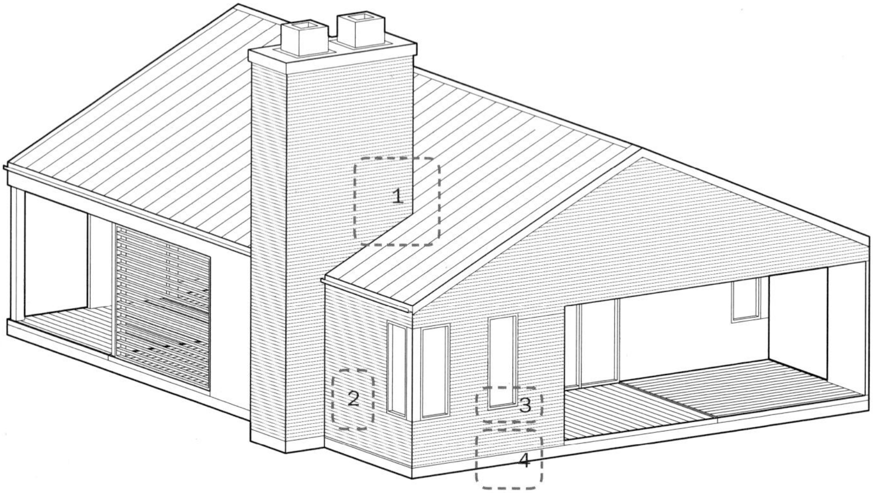
1
2
3
4

Roof Forms

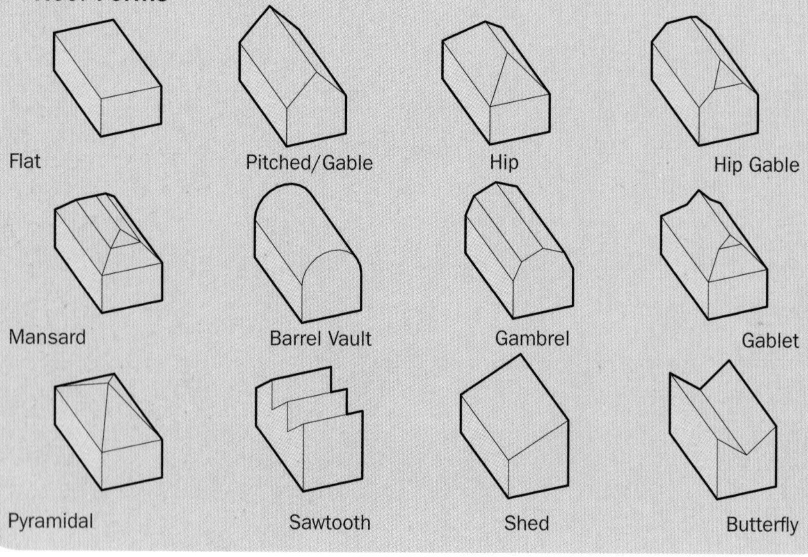
Flat
Pitched/Gable
Hip
Hip Gable
Mansard
Barrel Vault
Gambrel
Gablet
Pyramidal
Sawtooth
Shed
Butterfly

FLASHING

Flashing is used in several locations of a building's exterior to move water away and into the drainage system quickly and efficiently. Flashing is commonly thin sheet metal (copper, aluminum, stainless steel, or painted galvanized steel) or other impervious material such as rubber. Material choices often depend on whether the flashing will be exposed (metals are preferred) or concealed, and with which other materials it is likely to come into contact.

1. Roof
Flashing is wrapped around protruding objects such as chimneys and vents to keep water from settling into joints and seams.

2. Wall
Flashing may prevent water from entering a wall, or may divert water that has entered a wall cavity.

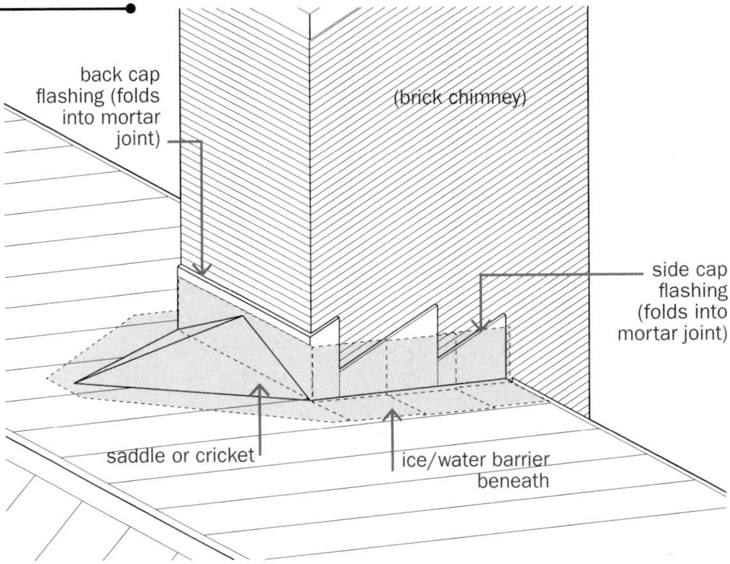
back cap flashing (folds into mortar joint)
(brick chimney)
side cap flashing (folds into mortar joint)
saddle or cricket
ice/water barrier beneath

3. Sill
Interruptions in a wall, such as doors and windows, are vulnerable to water penetration.

4. Base
Gravity helps water escape walls down the sloped surfaces of the flashing, and out through weep holes.

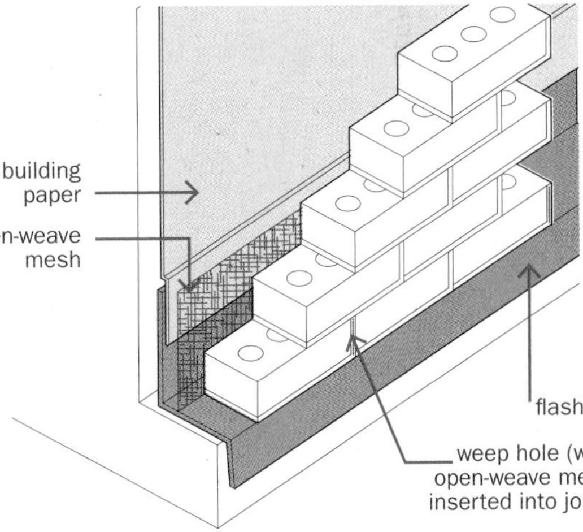
building paper
open-weave mesh
flashing
weep hole (with open-weave mesh inserted into joint)

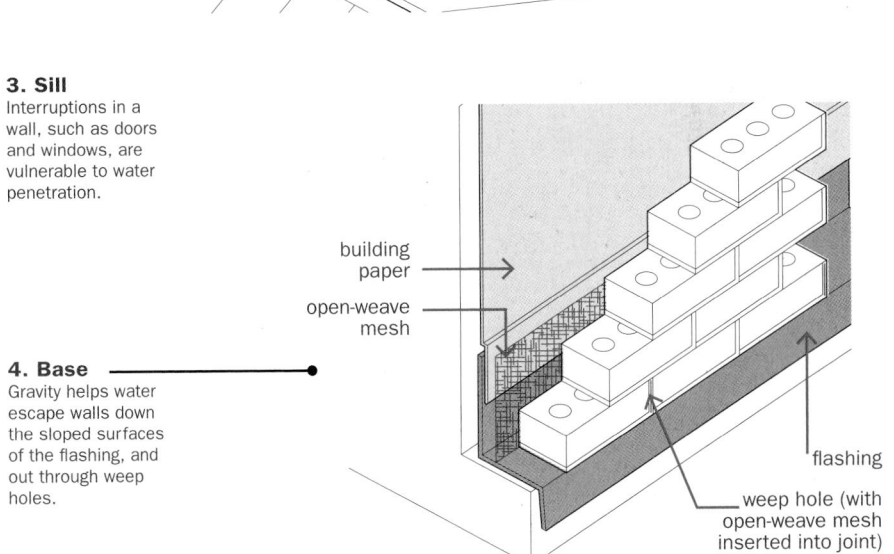

ROOF SYSTEM TYPES: STEEP SLOPES

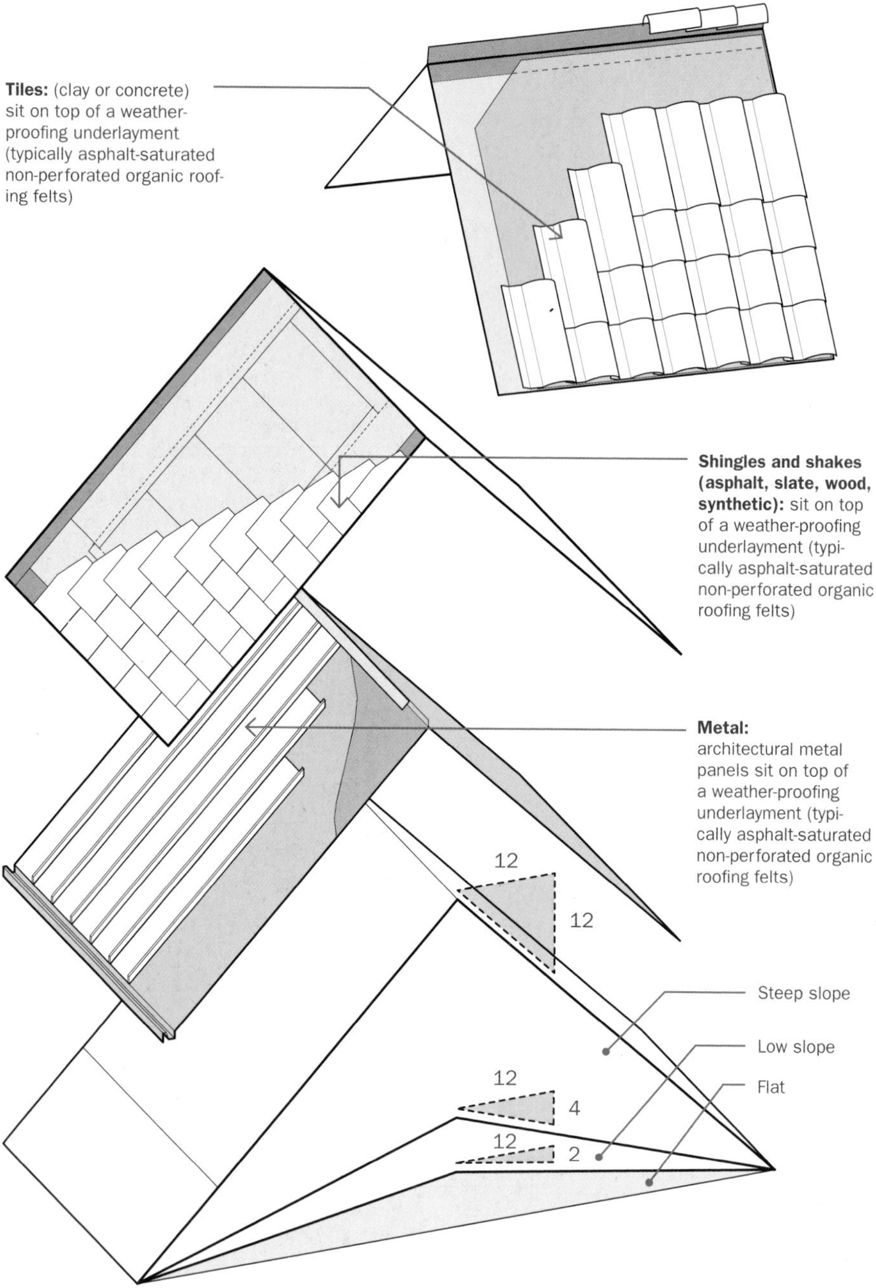
Tiles: (clay or concrete) sit on top of a weather-proofing underlayment (typically asphalt-saturated non-perforated organic roofing felts)
Shingles and shakes (asphalt, slate, wood, synthetic): sit on top of a weather-proofing underlayment (typically asphalt-saturated non-perforated organic roofing felts)
Metal: architectural metal panels sit on top of a weather-proofing underlayment (typically asphalt-saturated non-perforated organic roofing felts)
12
12
Steep slope
Low slope
Flat
12
4
12
2

ROOF SYSTEM TYPES: LOW & FLAT SLOPES

Structural metal panel: over weather-proofing under-layment

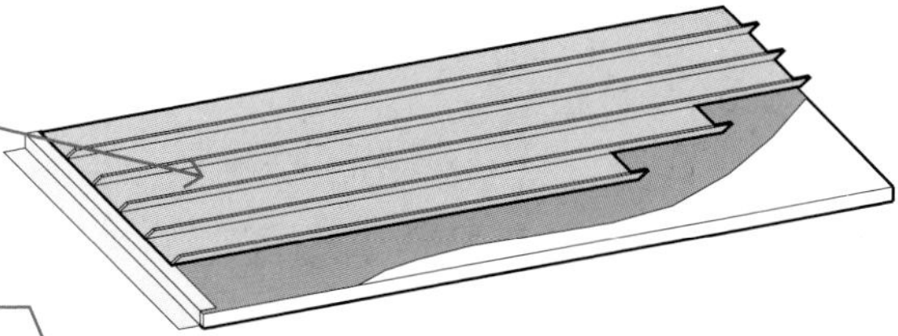

Single-ply membranes: thermoplastic or thermoset membranes are factory-made. Methods of installing include fully-adhered, mechanically-fastened, or held down with a ballast material. Shown here, the membrane is fully adhered to the insulation, which itself is mechanically fastened to the substrate.

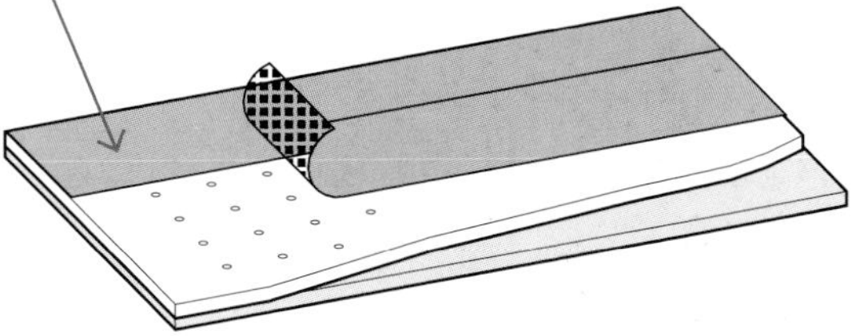

Polymer-modified bitumen sheet membranes (MB): composed of multiple layers, and most often fully-adhered as a two-ply system.

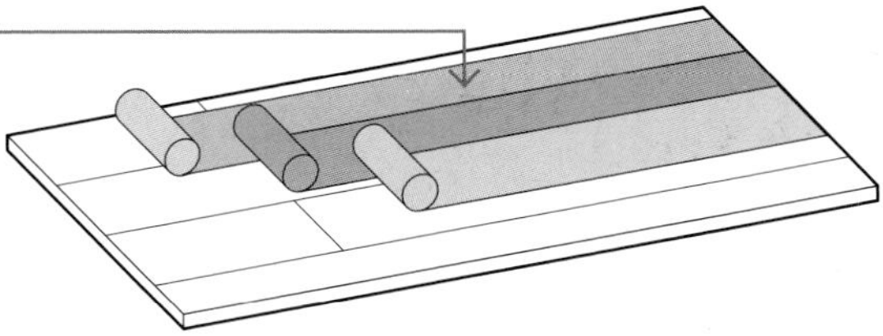

SPF (Spray polyurethane foam board): base layer is a rigid, spray foam insulation, on top of which is a spray-applied elastomeric weather-proof coating. Sand or mineral granules may be added to this layer for reasons of durability and aesthetic concerns.

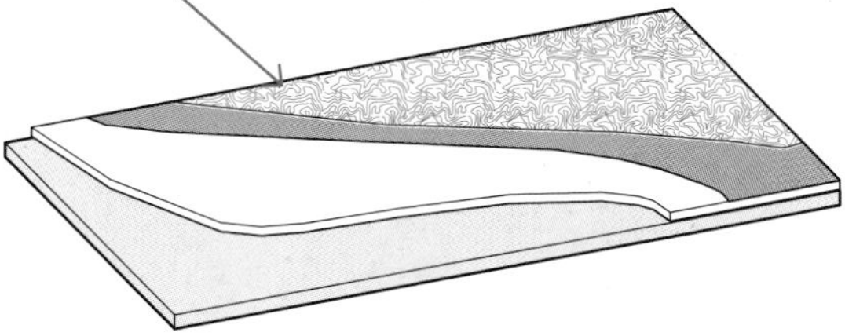

Built-up roof (BUR): bitumen (asphalt, coal tar, or cold-applied adhesive)and reinforcing fabrics (roofing felts) are applied in alternating layers to create the membrane. Sometimes referred to as 'tar and gravel' roofs. Gravel or other minerals may be added on top.

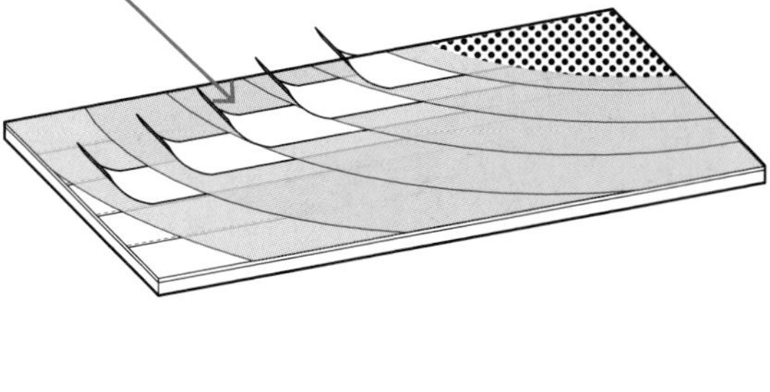

STONE

As a building material, stone may be used in two different manners: as a masonry unit laid with mortar, similar to brick or concrete blocks, or as a thin, non-load-bearing veneer facing attached to a backup wall and structural frame. Stone colors, textures, and patterns are highly varied, as are the design and detailing of unit masonry and cladding systems.

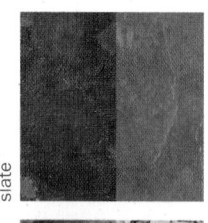

limestone

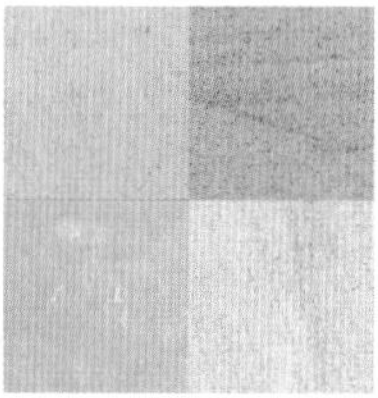

sandstone

SEDIMENTARY ROCK
(rock deposited as a result of natural action or wind)

Limestone: Colors limited mostly to white, buff, and gray. Very porous and wet when quarried, though after air seasoning, quarry sap evaporates and stone becomes harder. Suitable for wall and floor surfaces, but does not accept a polish.

Sandstone: Colors range from buff to chocolate brown to red. Suitable for most building applications, but also does not accept a high polish.

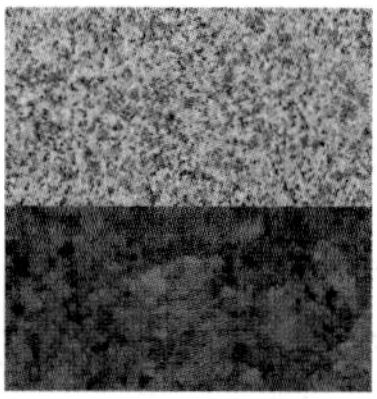

granite

IGNEOUS ROCK
(rock deposited in a molten state)

Granite: Wide range of grains and colors including gray, black, brown, red, pink, buff, and green. Nonporous and very hard. Suitable for use in the ground and with exposure to weather. Comes in many textures and may be highly polished.

slate

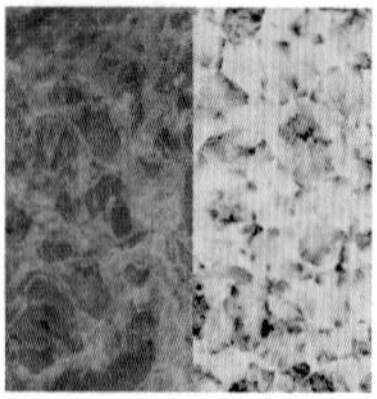

marble

METAMORPHIC ROCK
(sedimentary or igneous rock transformed into another rock type by heat or pressure)

Slate: Colors range from red and brown to grayish-green to purple and black. Sheetlike nature makes it ideal for paving, roofing, and veneer panels.

Marble: Highly varied in both color and streaking patterns. Color range includes white, black, blue, green, red, and pink, and all tones between. Suitable for use as a building stone but is most often highly polished and used as a veneer panel.

Stone masonry includes rubble stone (irregular quarried fragments), dimension stone (quarried and cut into rectangular forms called cut stone when large and ashlar when small), and flagstone (thin slabs of paving stone, irregular or cut).

Masonry Patterns

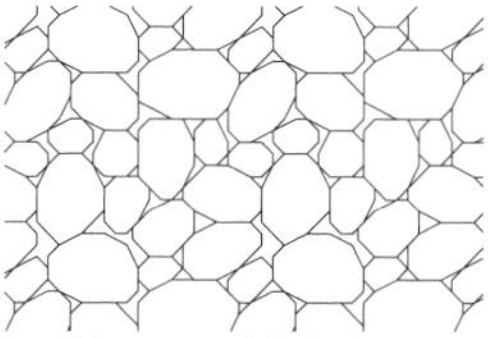

Random (Uncoursed) Rubble

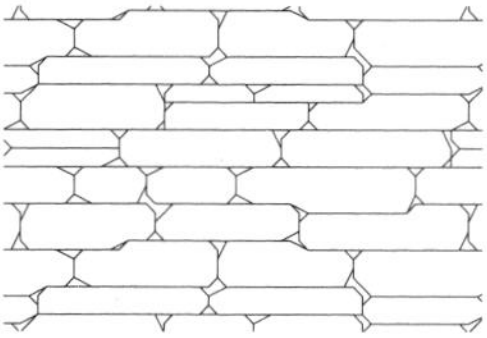

Coursed Rubble

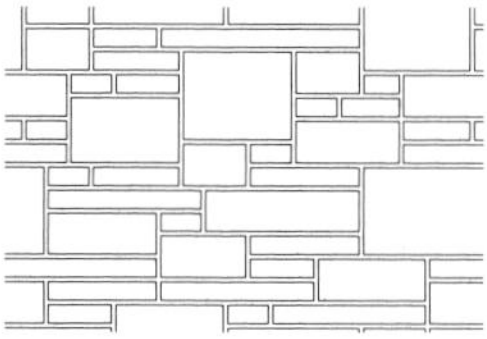

Random (Uncoursed) Ashlar

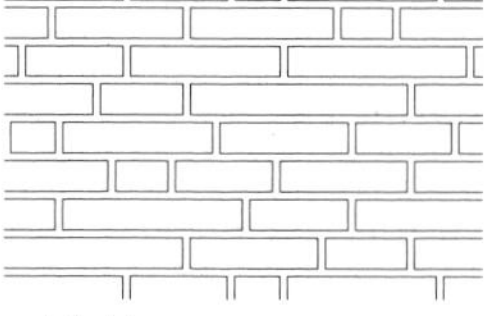

Coursed Ashlar

MASONRY BEARING WALLS

Brick, concrete block, and stone walls built as load-bearing walls will have many different characteristics, depending on whether or not they are reinforced, use more than one masonry unit type (composite wall), or are solid or cavity walls.

Reinforcing

Reinforcing masonry allows the entire wall system to be thinner and taller.

Composite Walls

Composite masonry walls employ a concrete block backup with brick or stone veneer on the exterior wythe, with the two layers bonded with steel horizontal reinforcing. Masonry ties join wythes of masonry together or to supporting wood, concrete, or steel backup structures. Anchors connect masonry units to the supporting structure.

Cavity Walls

Cavity walls have an inner and outer wythe of masonry units, separated by an air space of a minimum 2" (51). Masonry ties hold the two wythes together. If rain penetrates the outer wythe, it runs down the inner surface of the outer wythe and is collected at the base with flashing materials that divert it back to the outside through weep holes.

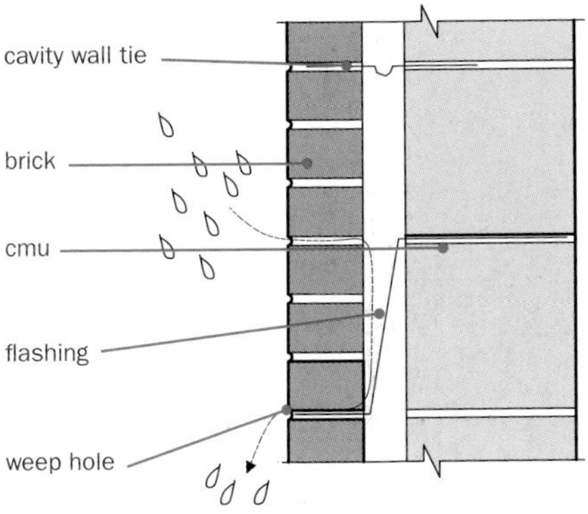
cavity wall tie
brick
cmu
flashing
weep hole

Common Wall Configurations

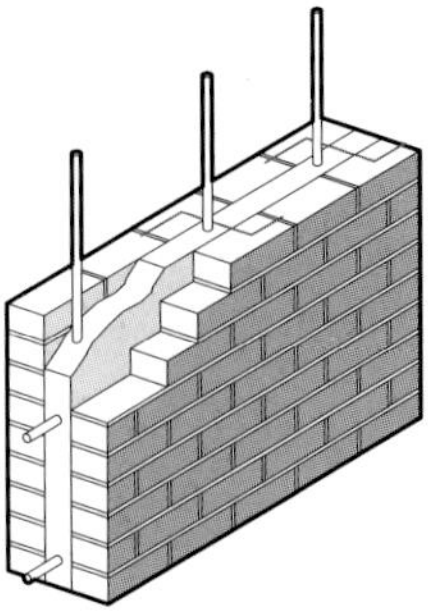

Double-wythe brick wall with concrete and steel reinforcing between

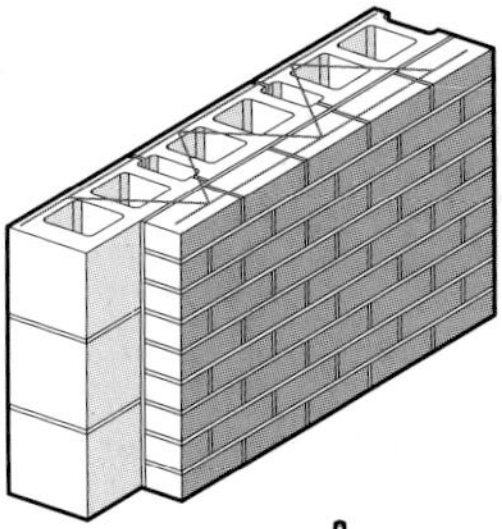

Brick wall on CMU backup (CMUs may or may not be reinforced), tied together with Z-ties

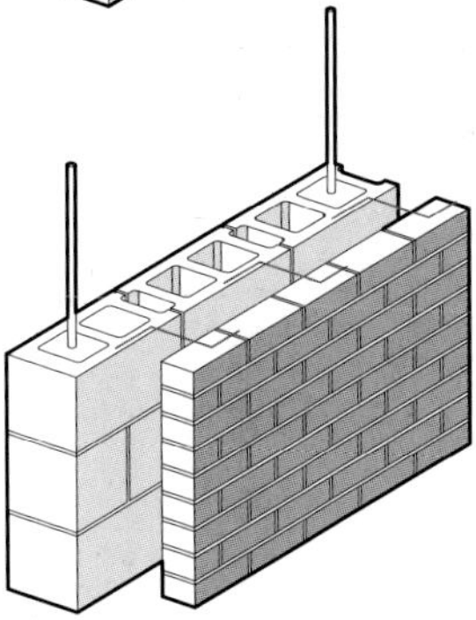

Brick and CMU cavity wall (CMU wall is reinforced)

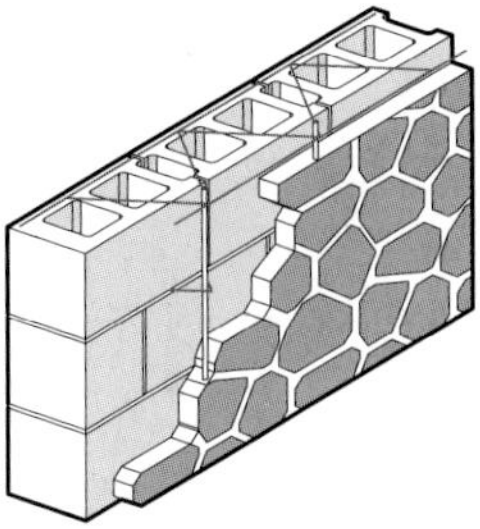

Stone veneer on CMU backup, tied together with adjustable stone ties

EXTERIOR WALLS

Common configurations are shown here, though the combinations of backup systems and exterior cladding systems are interchangeable in many cases, with changes to fastening systems dependent on the type of material being attached to specific structural elements.

Wood stud wall
Wood studs with batt insulation between; exterior sheathing with weather-resistive barrier; exterior-grade plywood panels (sealed)

SIP (Structural Insulated Panel) wall
SIP (insulated foam-core with OSB skin, either side); weather-resistive barrier; exterior siding

Metal stud wall
Metal studs with batt insulation between; exterior sheathing with weather-resistive barrier; aluminum composite material (ACM)

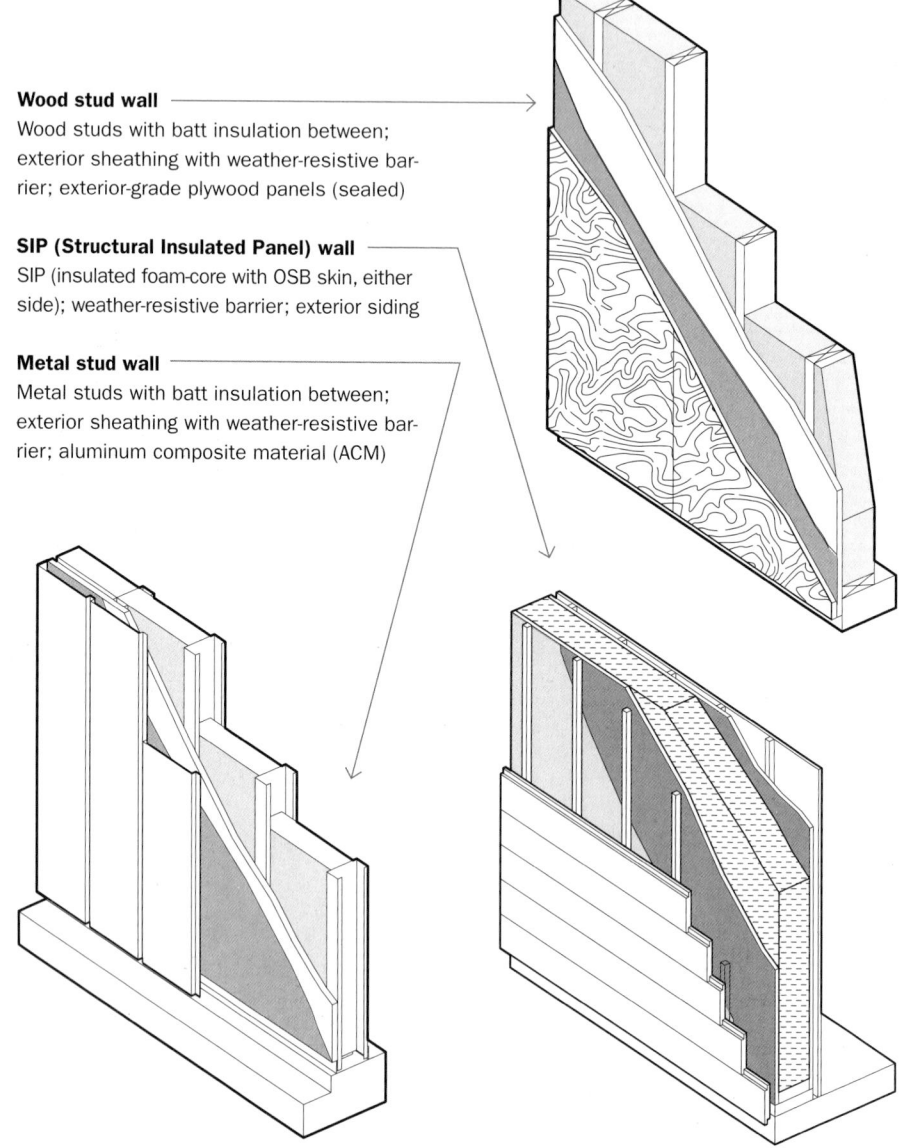

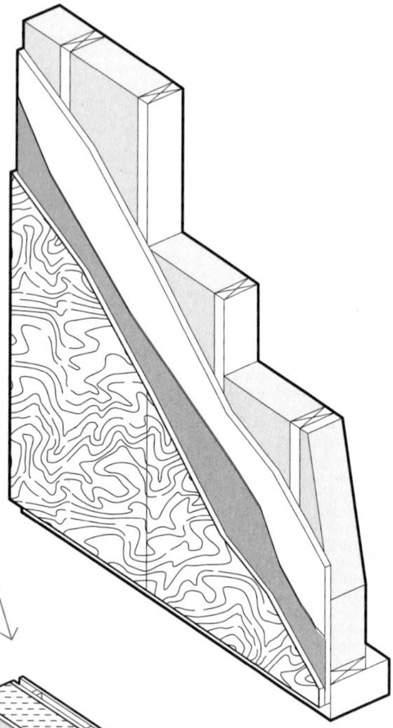

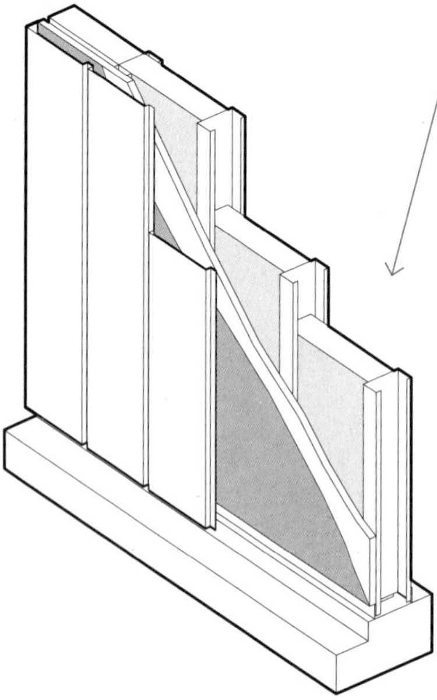

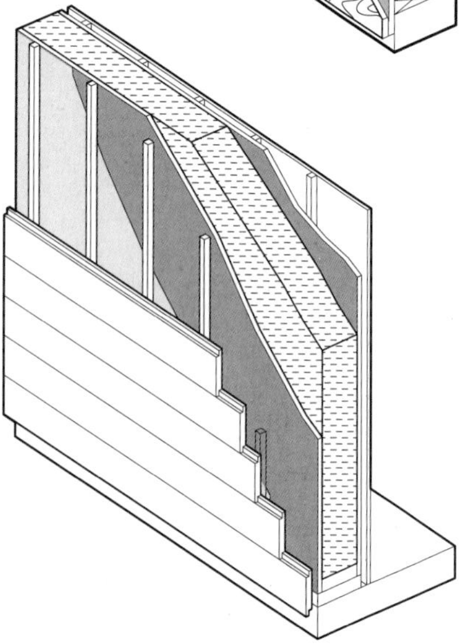

The outer skin of a building is the vertical envelope that separates interior from exterior, and must effectively keep out water and contribute effectively to maintaining the desired interior climate. Most wall constructions include structural elements, insulation, water barriers, and an exterior cladding material. Depending on many factors, including the building's size and height, backup materials such as CMUs, concrete, and stud systems may be load-bearing, or act as infill within a structural frame.

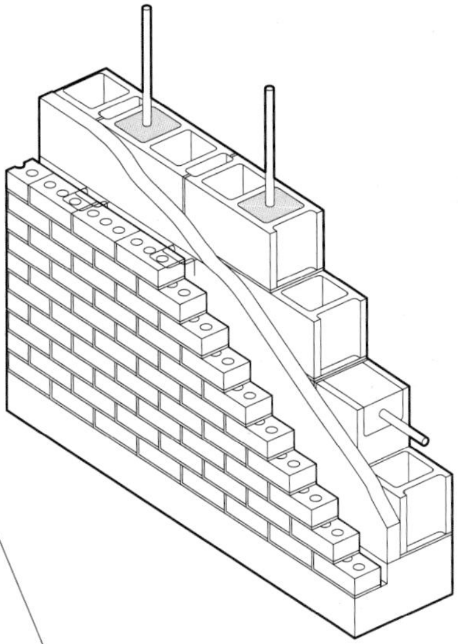

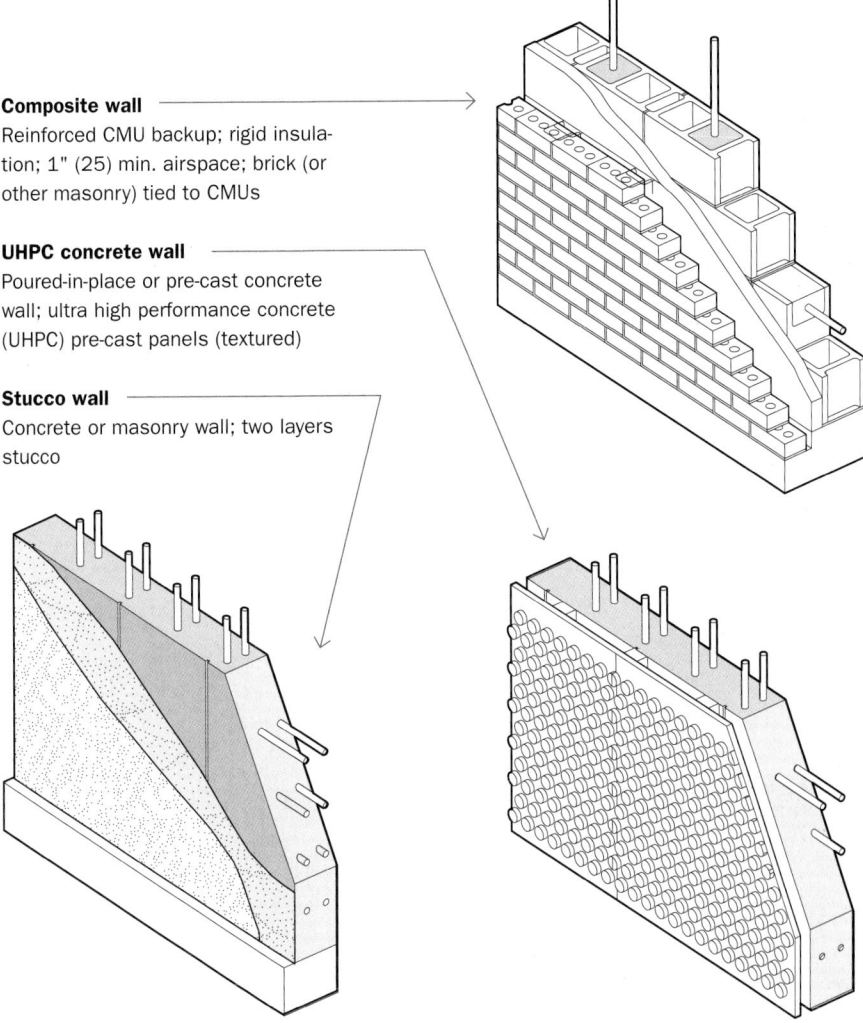

Composite wall
Reinforced CMU backup; rigid insulation; 1" (25) min. airspace; brick (or other masonry) tied to CMUs

UHPC concrete wall
Poured-in-place or pre-cast concrete wall; ultra high performance concrete (UHPC) pre-cast panels (textured)

Stucco wall
Concrete or masonry wall; two layers stucco

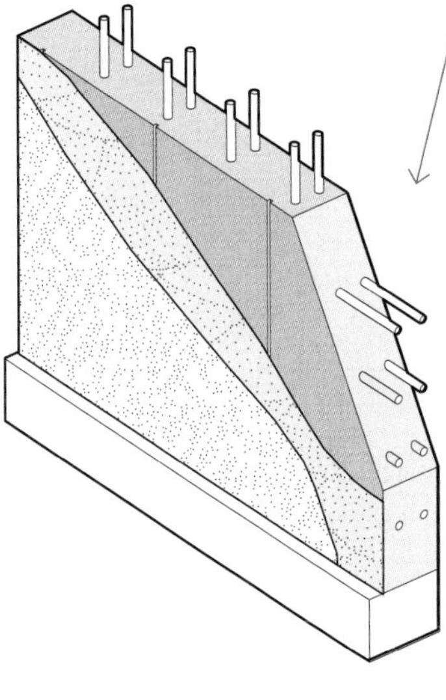

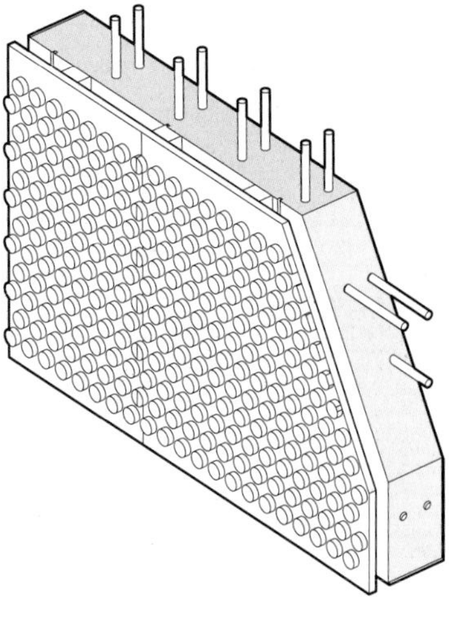

WINDOW TYPES

Fixed
Double-hung
Sliding
Single-hung
Casement
Awning
Hopper
Sliding Doors
Skylight
French Doors
Terrace Door
Roof Window

GLASS FORMS

Glass Block: Glass blocks are considered to be masonry units. Typical units are made by fusing together two hollow halves, with a vacuum inside. Solid blocks, called glass bricks, are impact resistant but can be seen through. Glass block walls are constructed in a similar fashion to other masonry walls, with mortar, metal anchors, and ties; they can be applied to interiors or exteriors.

US Customary Sizes
$4^1/2$" × $4^1/2$"
$5^3/4$" × $5^3/4$" (nominal 6" × 6")
$7^1/2$" × $7^1/2$"
$7^3/4$" × $7^3/4$" (nominal 8" × 8")
$9^1/2$" × $9^1/2$"
$11^3/4$" × $11^3/4$" (nominal 12" × 12")
$3^3/4$" × $7^3/4$" (nominal 4" × 8")
$5^3/4$" × $7^3/4$" (nominal 6" × 8")
$9^1/2$" × $4^1/2$"

thickness: 3"–4"

Preferred SI Sizes
115 × 115 mm
190 × 190 mm
240 × 240 mm
300 × 300 mm
240 × 115 mm

thickness: 80–100 mm

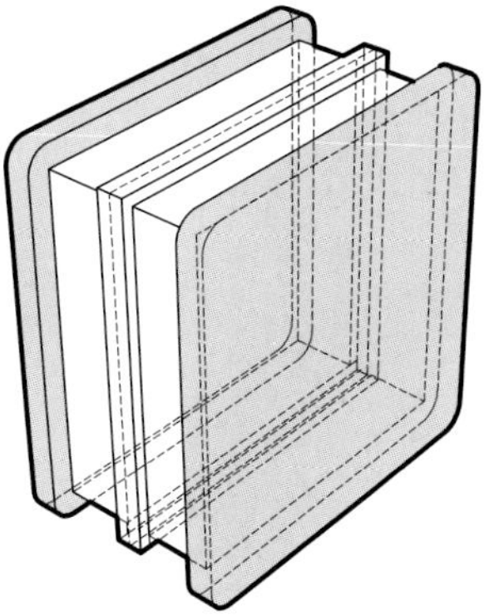

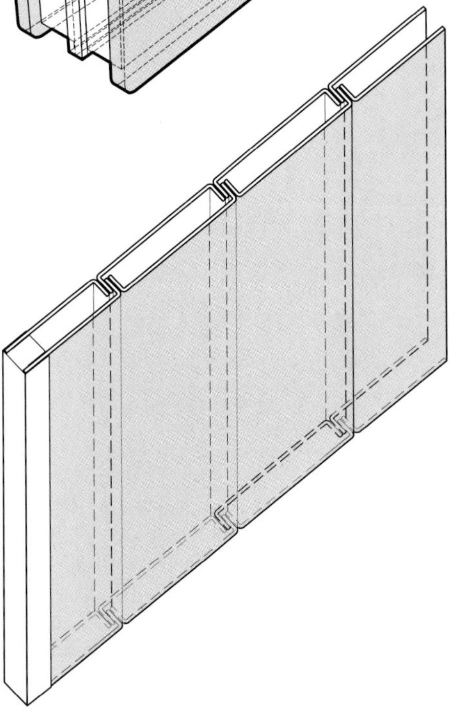

Cast or Channel Glass: U-shaped linear glass channels are self-supporting and contained within an extruded metal perimeter frame. One or two interlocking layers may be used, creating varying levels of strength, sound and thermal insulation, and translucence. Glass thicknesses are roughly $^1/4$" (6); channel widths range from 9" (230) to 19" (485), with heights varying depending on widths and wind loads. Cast glass can be employed vertically or horizontally, internally or externally, and as a curved surface. The glass itself can be made with wires, tints, and other qualities. Double layers of channels provide a natural air space that can be filled with aerogel, a latticework of glass strands with small pores, which results in an insulating substance that is 5 percent solid and 95 percent air.

WINDOW ELEMENTS

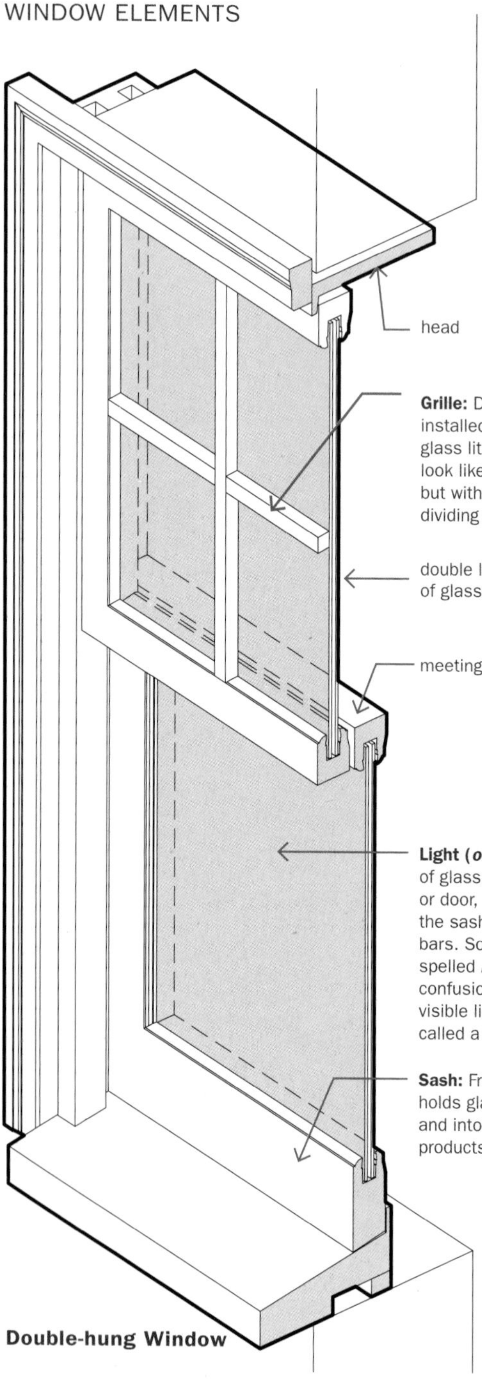
head
Grille: Decorative grid installed on or between glass lites, meant to look like a muntin bar, but without actually dividing the glass.
double layer of glass
meeting rail
Light (*or* lite): Unit of glass in a window or door, enclosed by the sash or muntin bars. Sometimes spelled *lite* to avoid confusion with visible light; also called a pane.
Sash: Frame that holds glass lites and into which glass products are glazed.

Double-hung Window

Mullion: Horizontal or vertical member holding together two adjacent lites of glass or sash.
Muntin bar: Strip that separates panes of glass in a sash.
rough opening

Window Sizing

A typical chart from a window manufacturer's catalog depicts stock sizes and types of windows (in feet and inches). Mas Opg (masonry opening) is the opening that must be provided for a brick, block, or stone wall; Rgh Opg (rough opening) is the opening required for typical stud walls; Sash Opg (sash opening) is the size of the window itself; and Glass Size is the size of the glass.

Mas Opg	2'-8½"
Rgh Opg	2'-6⅜"
Sash Opg	2'-4"
Glass Size	24"

4'-2½"
4'-1¾"
3'-10"
20"

OPENING TYPES

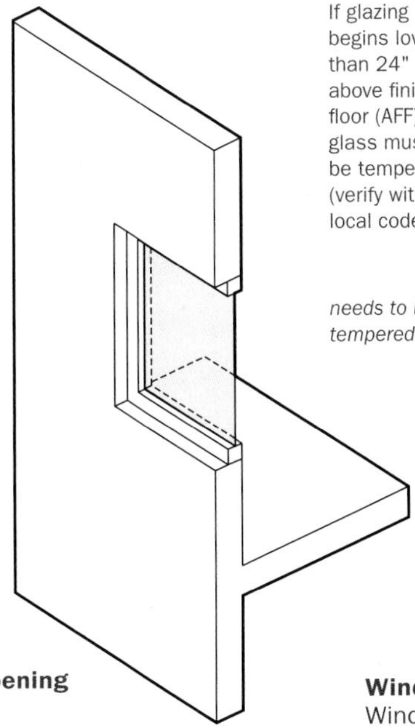

Punched opening

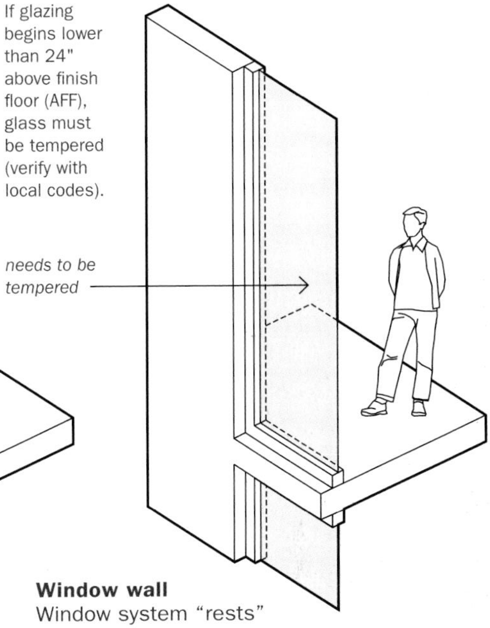
If glazing begins lower than 24" above finish floor (AFF), glass must be tempered (verify with local codes).
needs to be tempered

Window wall
Window system "rests" on floor

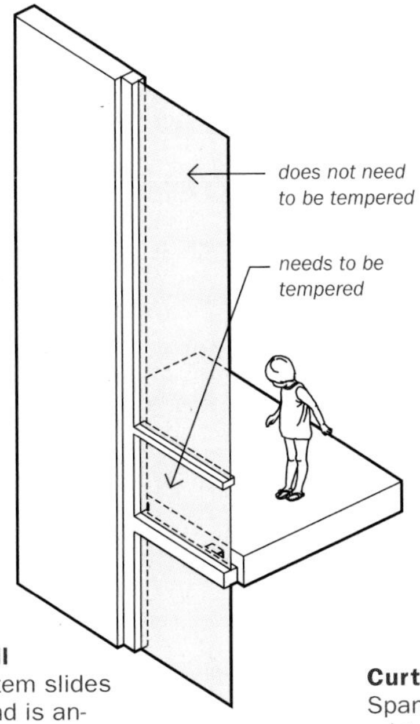
does not need to be tempered
needs to be tempered

Curtain wall
Window system slides past floor and is anchored to structure

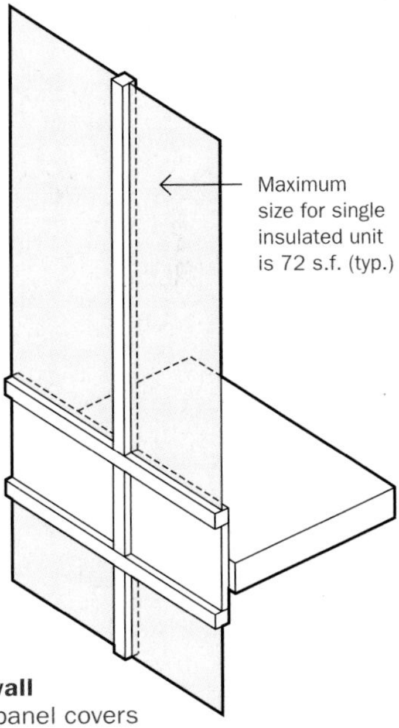
Maximum size for single insulated unit is 72 s.f. (typ.)

Curtain wall
Spandrel panel covers edge of floor

GLASS AND GLAZING

Most architectural glass comprises three major raw materials that are found naturally: silica, lime, and sodium carbonate. Secondary materials may be added to facilitate the glass-making process or to give the glass special properties, which can be broken into three basic categories:

Soda-lime Glass: Accounts for the majority of commercially produced glass. Used for bottles, glassware, and windows, its composition of silica, soda, and lime does not give it good resistance to sudden thermal changes, especially high temperatures, or to chemical corrosion.

Lead Glass: Contains about 20 percent lead oxide, and its soft surface makes it ideal for decorative cutting and engraving, though it does not withstand sudden temperature changes.

Borosilicate Glass: Refers to any silicate glass with a composition of at least 5 percent boric oxide, and has greater resistance to thermal changes and chemical corrosion.

Nominal Thickness	Actual Range
3/32" single strength	0.085"–0.101" (2.16–2.57)
laminate	0.102"–0.114" (2.59–2.90)
1/8" double strength	0.115"–0.134" (2.92–3.40)
5/32"	0.149"–0.165" (3.78–4.19)
3/16"	0.180"–0.199" (4.57–5.05)
7/32"	0.200"–0.218" (5.08–5.54)
1/4"	0.219"–0.244" (5.56–6.20)
5/16"	0.292"–0.332" (7.42–8.43)
3/8"	0.355"–0.406" (9.02–10.31)
1/2"	0.469"–0.531" (11.91–13.49)
5/8"	0.595"–0.656" (15.09–16.66)
3/4"	0.719"–0.781" (18.26–19.84)
1"	0.969"–1.031" (24.61–26.19)
1 1/4"	1.125"–1.375" (28.58–34.93)

Numbers in bubbles represent glass surface numbers, beginning with *1* on the exterior face.

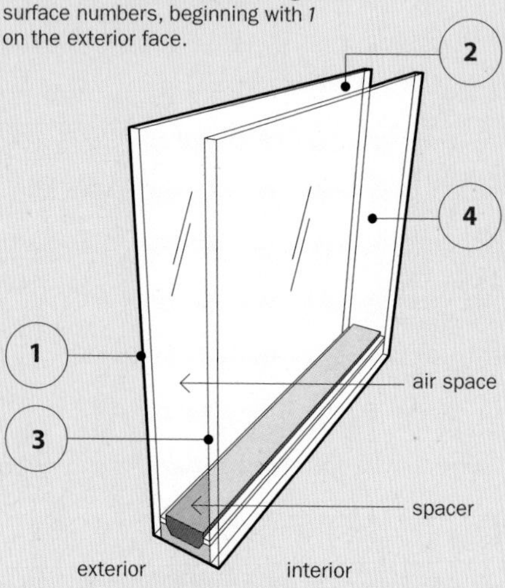
2
4
1
3
air space
spacer
exterior
interior

Insulating Glass: Two or more panes of glass enclose a hermetically sealed air space and are separated by a desiccant-filled spacer that absorbs the internal moisture of the air space. The multiple layers of glass and air space of these insulating glass units (IGUs) drastically reduce heat rates. Low-E or other coatings may be used on one or more of the glass surfaces to further improve thermal performance. Argon and sulfur hexafluoride gases may fill the space between glass sheets for even further efficiency as well as reduced sound transmission. Standard overall thickness for a double-glazed IGU is 1" (25.4), with 1/4" (6) thick glass and a 1/2" (13) air space.

Glass Production

The most common flat glass is float glass, in which properly weighed and mixed soda lime glass, silica sand, calcium, oxide, soda, and magnesium are melted in a 2 732°F (1 500°C) furnace. The highly viscous molten glass is floated across a bath of molten tin in a continuous ribbon. Because the tin is very fluid, the two materials do not mix, creating a perfectly flat surface between them. By the time the glass has left the molten tin, it has cooled enough to proceed to a lehr, where it is annealed, that is, cooled slowly under controlled conditions.

Glass may also be rolled, a process by which semimolten glass is squeezed between metal rollers to form a ribbon with predefined thicknesses and patterned surfaces. This process is used mostly for patterned and cast-glass production.

Safety Glass

Tempered Glass: Annealed glass is cut and edged before being reheated at about 1,200°F (650°C). If the glass is cooled rapidly, it is considered to be fully tempered; the glass can be up to four times as strong as annealed glass, and, when broken, it shatters into small, square-edged granules instead of into sharp shards. If cooled slowly, the glass is twice as strong as annealed glass, and the broken pieces are more linear but tend to stay in the frame.

Tempered glass is ideal for floor-to-ceiling glass, glass doors, and walls exposed to heavy winds and intense temperatures.

Chemically Strengthened Glass: Glass is dipped in a chemical solution that produces a higher mechanical resistance, giving the glass similar properties to thermal-strengthened (tempered) glass, though it breaks into sharp shards similar to annealed glass.

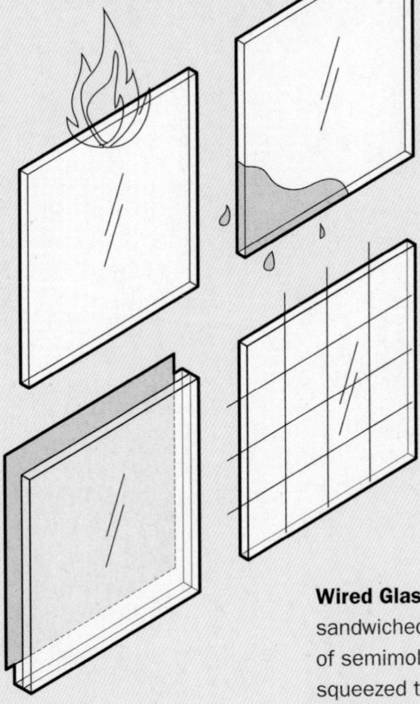

Laminated Glass: Interlayers of plastic or resin are sandwiched between two sheets of glass and the layers are bonded together under heat and pressure. When the glass breaks, the laminate interlayer holds the fragments together, making it ideal for use in overhead glazing, stair railings, and store fronts.

Security Glass: Security glass (bullet-proof) is made of multiple layers of glass and vinyl, in many thicknesses.

Wired Glass: A wire mesh is sandwiched between two ribbons of semimolten glass, which are squeezed together through a pair of metal rollers. When the glass breaks, the wire holds it in place. Wire glass is often acceptable for windows in fire doors and walls.

Chapter 5: Finishes

Interior finishes encompass all materials and surfaces that can be seen or touched. The choice of materials and the methods of construction should be based on the function of the space, the anticipated volume of traffic, acoustical effects, fire-resistance ratings, and aesthetic appearance.

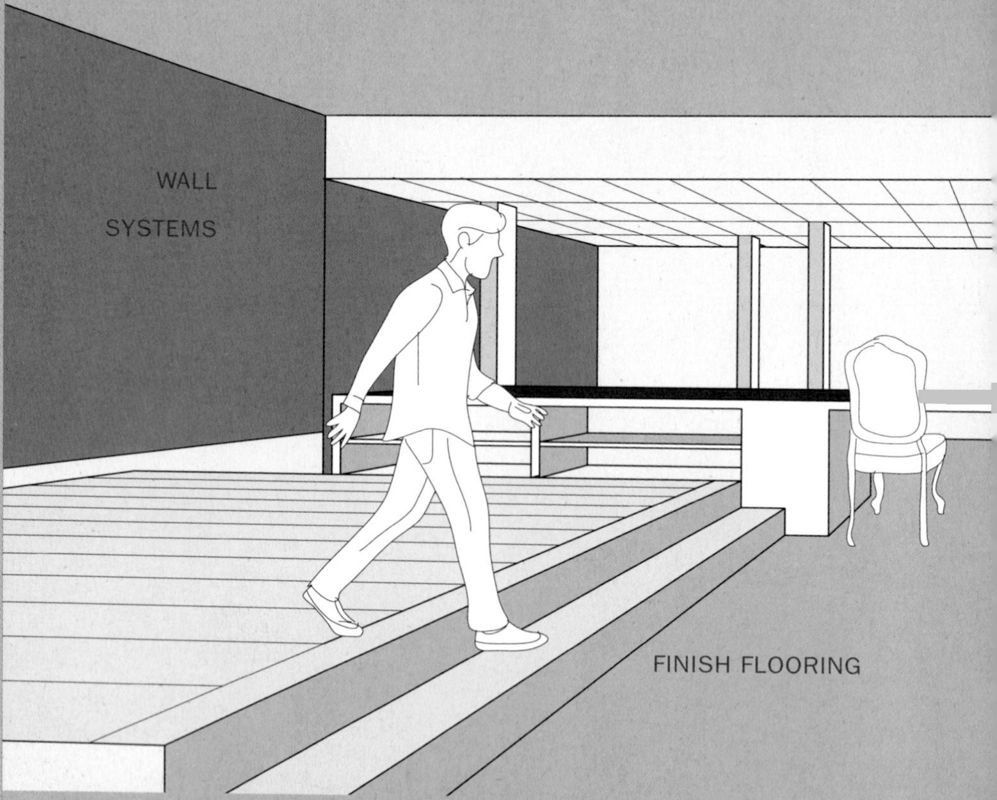
WALL
SYSTEMS
FINISH FLOORING

CEILINGS
FINISH CARPENTRY

Gypsum Board

Gypsum board goes by many names: gypsum wallboard (GWB), drywall, plasterboard, and Sheetrock (a trademarked brand name). Gypsum board is a less expensive alternative to plaster, because it requires less labor, time, and skill to install, but it still provides excellent fire-resistance and sound control.

Gypsum, a naturally occurring mineral, is formulated chemically when combined with water, starch, and other elements into a slurry and placed between paper faces to become gypsum board. When gypsum board is exposed to fire, the water is released as steam, providing a fire barrier until the water is completely eliminated (calcination). When the gypsum is completely calcined, its residue still acts as an insulating barrier to flames, preventing the structural members behind it from igniting.

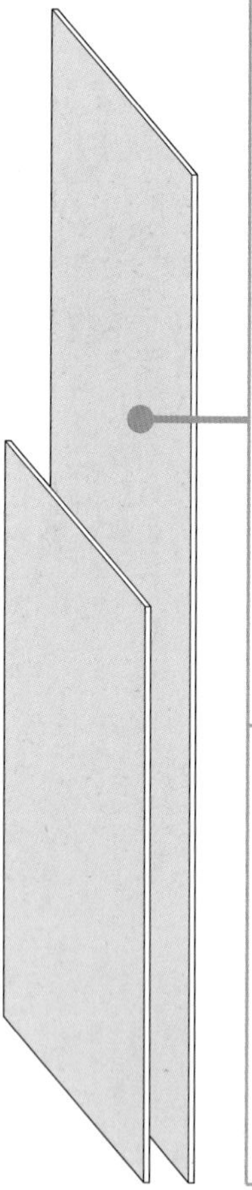

Customary Sizes

Panel sizes may vary depending on the type of board, though generally they fall in the following range: 4' (1 220) wide by 8' (2 439) to 16' (4 877) high.

Widths of 2' (610) and 2'-6" (762) and heights of 6' (1 829) may also be available for certain prefinished boards and core boards.

SI Preferred Sizes

Standard panel size is 1 200 × 2 400 mm.

Other acceptable increments are 600 mm, 800 mm, and 900 mm.

Panel Types

Backing board: Used as a base layer when multiple layers are needed, improving fire resistance and sound control.

Coreboard: Thicker boards, 1" (25.4) and 2" (50.8), used to enclose vent shafts, emergency egress stairs, elevator shafts, and other vertical chases.

Foil-backed: Can work as a vapor barrier in exterior wall assemblies and as a thermal insulator.

Prefinished: Covered in a variety of finishes such as paint, paper, or plastic film for installation without further finishing.

Regular: Used for most applications.

Type X: Short glass fibers in the core hold the calcined gypsum residue in place for increased fire resistance protection ratings.

Water-resistant (green board): Water-resistant board with a water-repellent paper facing (colored light green to distinguish it from other walls) and a moisture-resistant core (also available in type X); used as base for tiles and other nonabsorbent materials in wet locations.

Board Thicknesses

1/4" (6.4)
backing board, some acoustic work

5/16" (8)
used for manufactured housing

3/8" (9.5)
used in double-layer finishes

1/2" (12.7)
used for stud spacings up to 24" (610), most common thickness

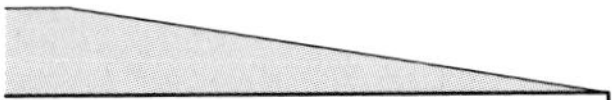

5/8" (16)
used when additional fire resistance or structural stiffness are required

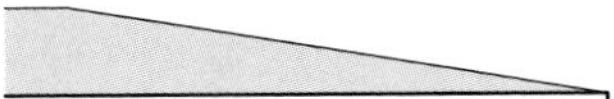

1" (25.4)
coreboard used for shaft walls

Edge Types

Square

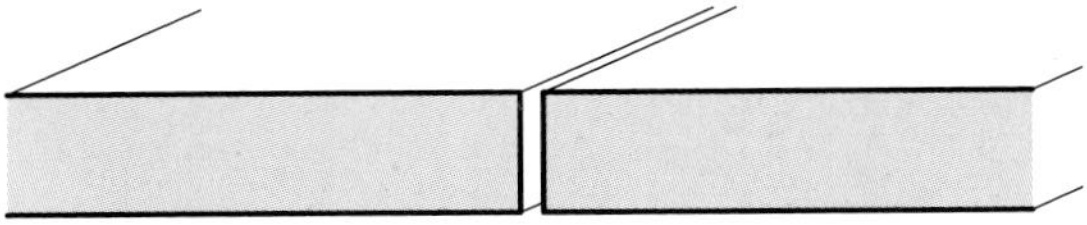

Rounded

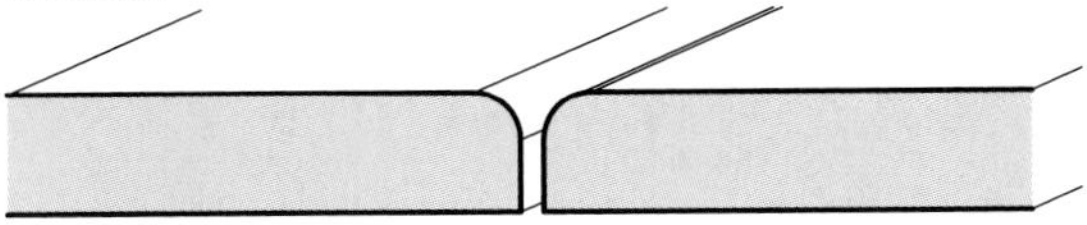

Beveled

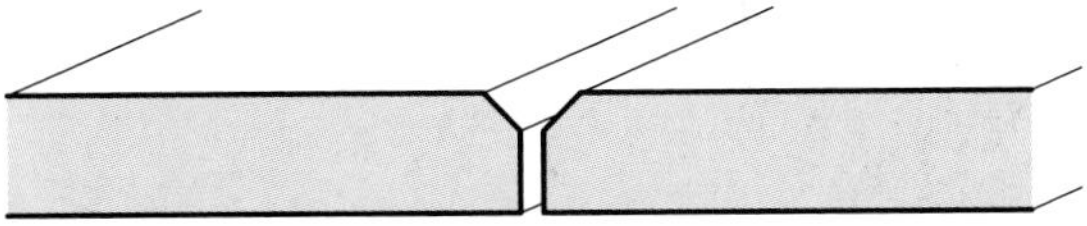

Tongue and Groove

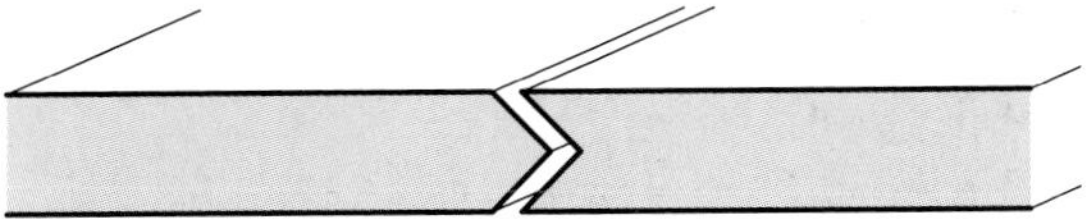

Tapered

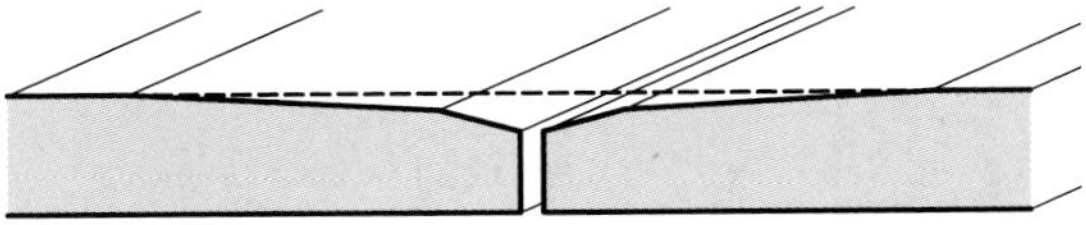

Rounded Taper

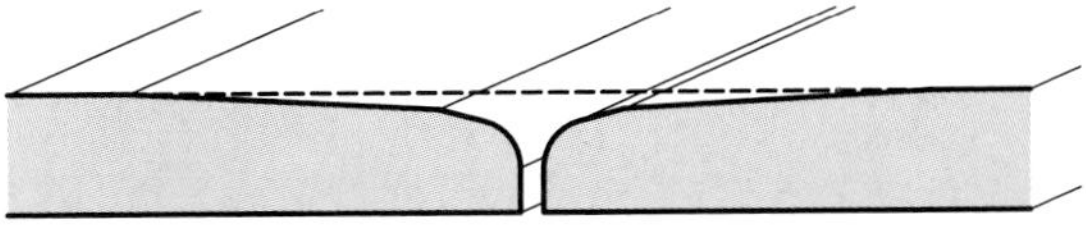

GWB Partition Wall Installation

Gypsum wallboard is placed over wood studs using nails or screws and over metal studs using screws. The orientation of the boards may differ based on the height of the wall, whether it is double-layer construction, and other factors.

Generally, it is best to minimize end joints between boards (boards have finished paper only on the face, back, and long edges, which themselves are finished in a variety of edge types), because these joints are more difficult to finish. If two or more layers of board are to be installed, joints between the layers should be staggered for added strength.

Joints are finished with joint compound and tape, usually in the following manner: A layer of joint compound is troweled into a tapered edge joint, then fiber-reinforcing mesh tape is applied; for some tapered edge joints, joint compound is forced through the tape to fill the V-shaped trough. After drying overnight, more joint compound is applied to completely smooth the joint, making it flush with the surrounding wall. Individual board manufacturers may suggest adding more layers of joint compound.

Nail or screw holes are also filled, and the whole wall receives a final light sanding before painting.

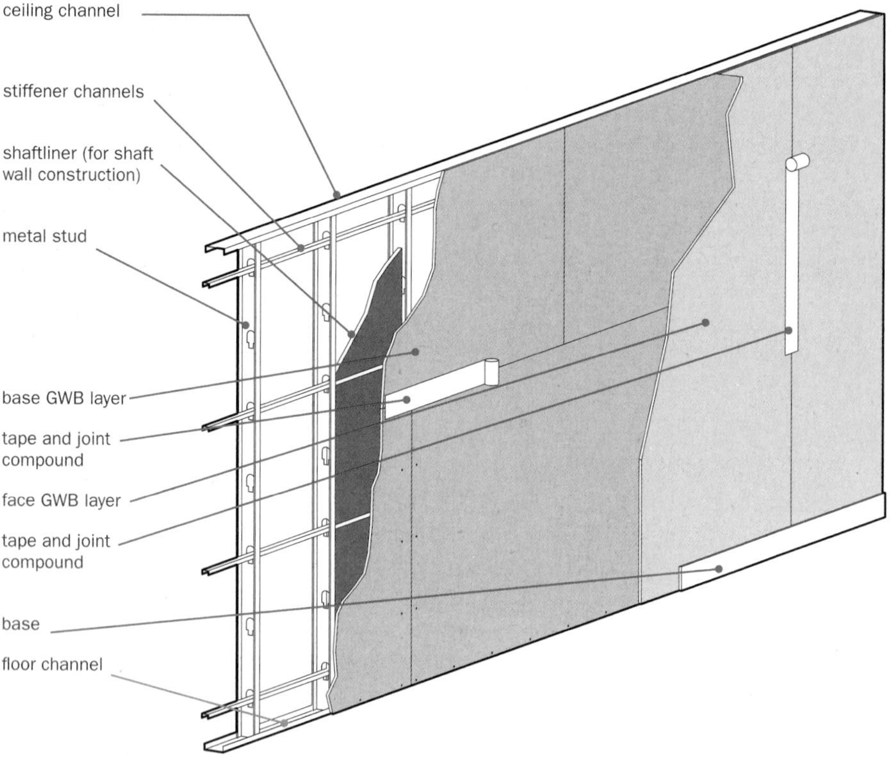
ceiling channel
stiffener channels
shaftliner (for shaft wall construction)
metal stud
base GWB layer
tape and joint compound
face GWB layer
tape and joint compound
base
floor channel

Common GWB Partition Assemblies

$3\frac{5}{8}$" STC: 40–44: (1 layer $\frac{3}{8}$" GWB on either side of $1\frac{5}{8}$" metal studs; face layers of $\frac{1}{2}$" GWB)

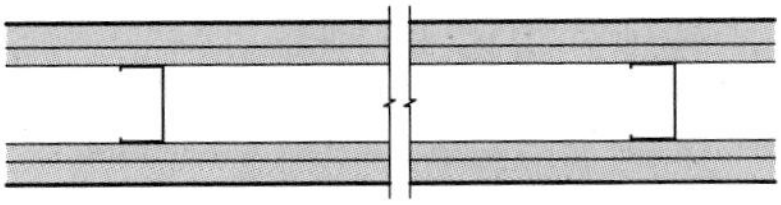

1-HR
FIRE
RATING

$4\frac{7}{8}$" STC: 40–44: (1 layer $\frac{5}{8}$" type × GWB on either side of $3\frac{5}{8}$" metal studs)

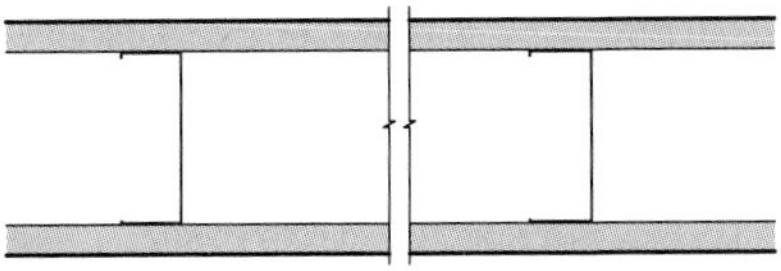

1-HR
FIRE
RATING

$5\frac{1}{2}$" STC: 45–49: (1 layer $\frac{5}{8}$" type × GWB on either side of $3\frac{5}{8}$" metal studs; one face layer $\frac{5}{8}$" GWB applied with laminating compound; $3\frac{1}{2}$" glass fiber insulation in cavity)

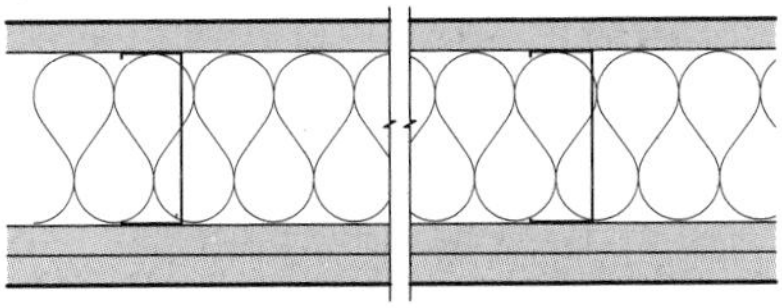

1-HR
FIRE
RATING

$6\frac{1}{4}$" STC: 55–59: (2 layers $\frac{5}{8}$" type × GWB on either side of $3\frac{5}{8}$" metal studs; one face layer $\frac{1}{4}$" GWB applied with laminating compound; $1\frac{1}{2}$" glass fiber insulation in cavity)

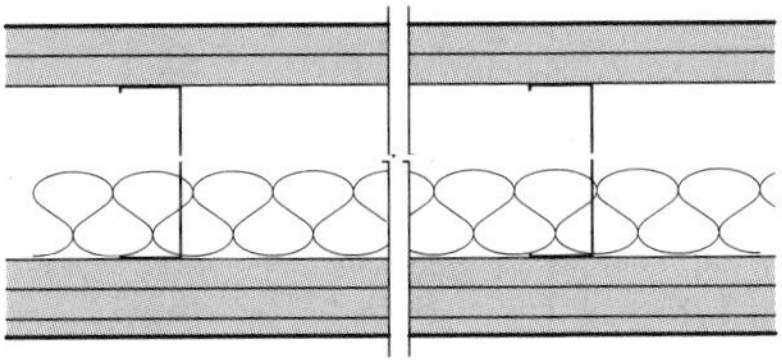

2-HR
FIRE
RATING

Fireproofing at Steel Structural Members

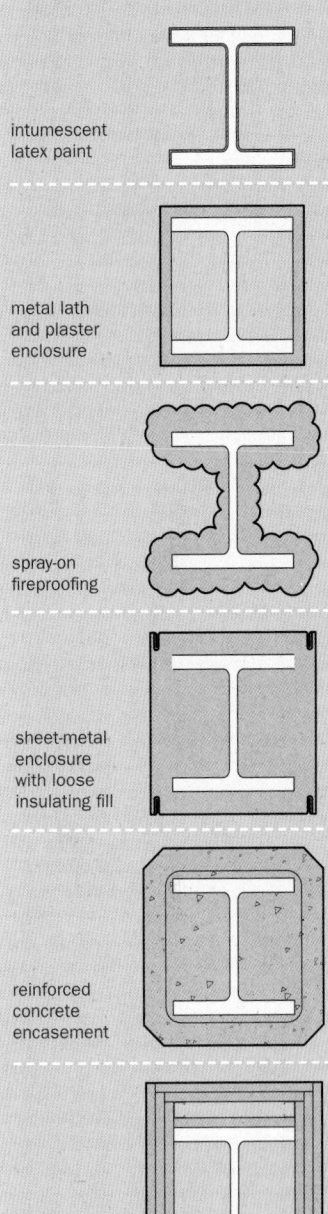

intumescent latex paint

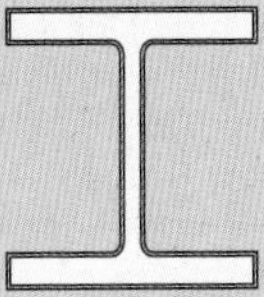

metal lath and plaster enclosure

spray-on fireproofing

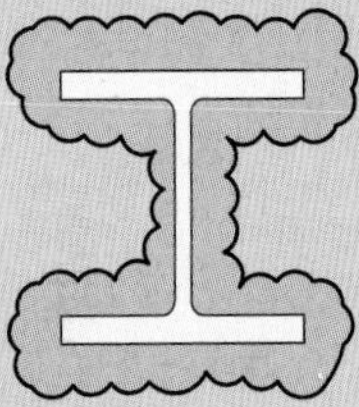

sheet-metal enclosure with loose insulating fill

reinforced concrete encasement

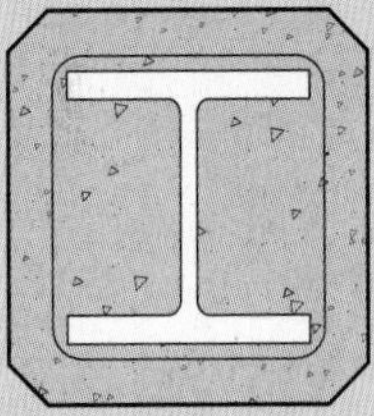

multiple layers of GWB enclosure

PLASTER

Today most plaster has a gypsum base. Gypsum is calcined and then ground into a fine powder. When mixed once again with water, it rehydrates and returns to its original state, expanding as it hardens into a plaster that possesses excellent fire-resistive qualities. This formulation can be mixed with an aggregate and applied by hand or by machine directly to masonry walls or to a lath system.

Plaster Types

Gauging plaster: Mixed with lime putty for accelerated setting and reduced cracking; may be mixed with finish lime to make a high-quality finish coat.

Gypsum plaster: Used with sand or lightweight aggregate.

High-strength basecoat: Used under high-strength finish coats.

Keenes cement: High-strength with a very strong and crack-resistant finish.

Molding plaster: Fast-setting for molding ornaments and cornices.

Stucco: Portland cement–lime plaster; used on exterior walls or where moisture is present.

With wood fiber or perlite aggregate: Lightweight with good fire resistance.

Lath Assemblies

Plaster over Metal Lath

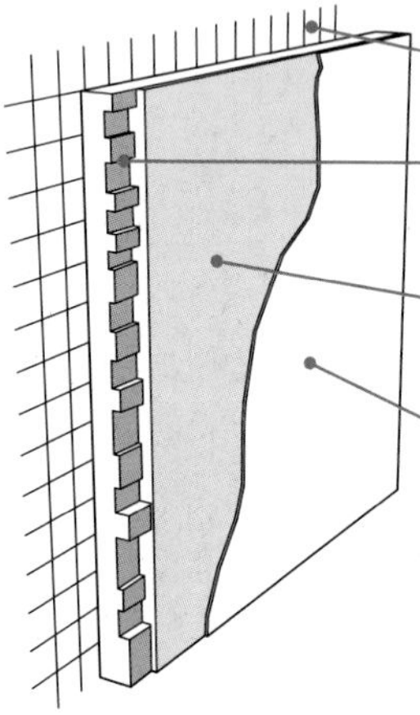

Three-Coat Plaster

metal lath: expanded metal or mesh (steel)

scratch coat: troweled on roughly and scratched to create a scored surface for the next coat

brown coat: applied over the lath and hardened scratch coat; leveled with a long straightedge

finish coat: very thin (1/16") outer layer that may be smoothed or textured.

Total thickness of all three layers is roughly 5/8" (16) and provides good fire resistance and durability.

Plaster over Gypsum Lath

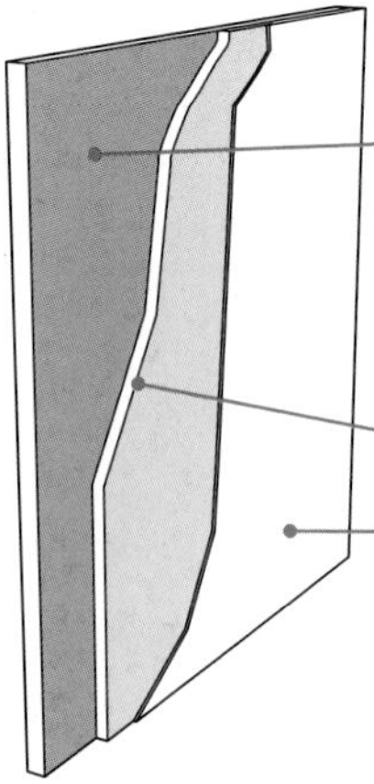

Two- or Three-Coat Plaster

gypsum lath: hardened gypsum plaster core with an outer sheet of absorbent paper to adhere to the plaster and water-resistant inner layers to protect the core; comes in 16" × 48" (406 × 1 219) boards in 3/8" (10) and 1/2" (13) thicknesses.

brown coat

finish coat

If gypsum is attached to studs, it is rigid enough to require only two coats of plaster; solid plaster walls (plaster on either side of gypsum, with no studs) require three coats. Total thickness of the plaster on one side is 1/2" (13).

Veneer Plaster

Veneer plaster is a less expensive and less labor-intensive plaster system. The special veneer base works much like a standard gypsum board wall system and is finished smooth and flat to provide the best surface for the very dense veneer plaster. The plaster is applied in two coats in quick succession; the second coat, called a skim coat, dries almost immediately. The total plaster thickness is about 1/8" (3).

Plaster over Masonry

Plaster can be applied directly to brick, concrete block, poured concrete, and stone walls. Walls should be dampened first to keep the plaster from dehydrating during application. Generally, three coats will be needed, totaling 5/8" (16) in plaster thickness, though the roughness of the masonry surface will dictate the thickness in many cases. Where the masonry or other wall is unsuitable for direct plaster application (if moisture or condensation are present or if an air space is required for insulation), plaster and lath are applied over furring channels attached to the wall.

Wall Assemblies

Plaster and lath assemblies can be applied to truss studs, steel studs, or wood studs, in addition to furring strips. Solid plaster walls of roughly 2" (51) thick are sometimes used where space is at a premium. They generally consist of plaster on either side of expanded metal mesh or gypsum lath, supported at the floor and ceiling by metal runners.

Wood lath is rarely used today in favor of cheaper and more durable lath types.

TRIM SHAPES

Ceiling Moldings

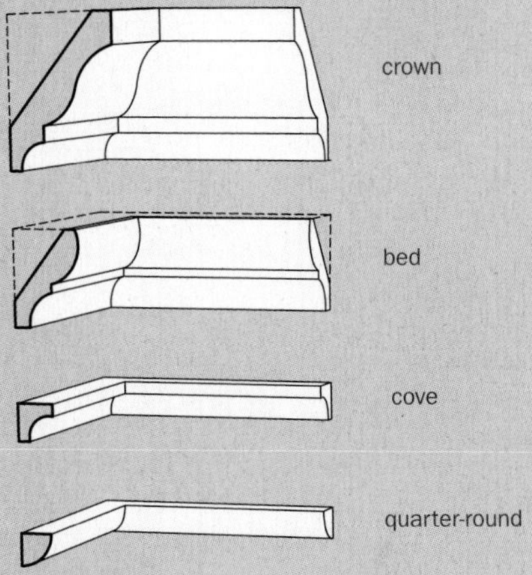
crown
bed
cove
quarter-round

General Moldings

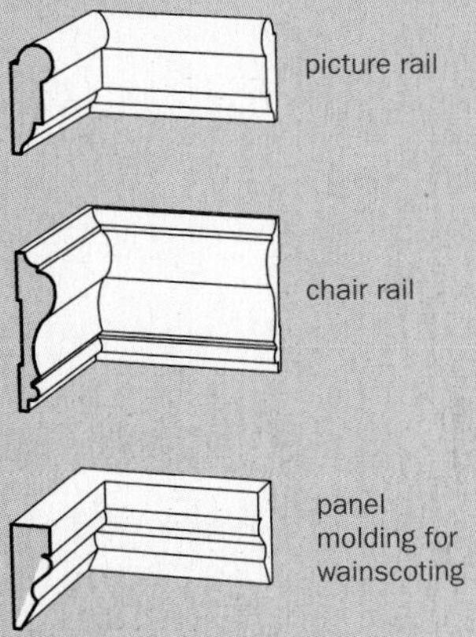
picture rail
chair rail
panel
molding for
wainscoting

Baseboards

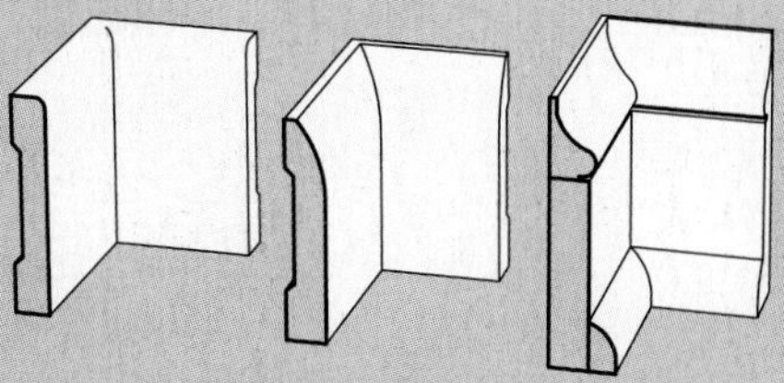

FINISH FLOORING

Floors receive regular wear and abuse, from feet, furniture, dirt, and water. Floor finish materials should be carefully chosen based on the function of the space and the amount of traffic they must endure. A wide array of finish floor types and methods of installation exist, of which the small sampling shown here represents the most common residential and commercial applications.

Carpet

Wool, nylon, polypropylene, and polyester account for most carpet fibers, with nylon the most widely used. Construction types include velvet, Axminster, Wilton, tufted, knitted, flocked, needle-punched, and fusion-bonded. Installation methods include stretch-in (using staples), direct glue down, and double glue down.

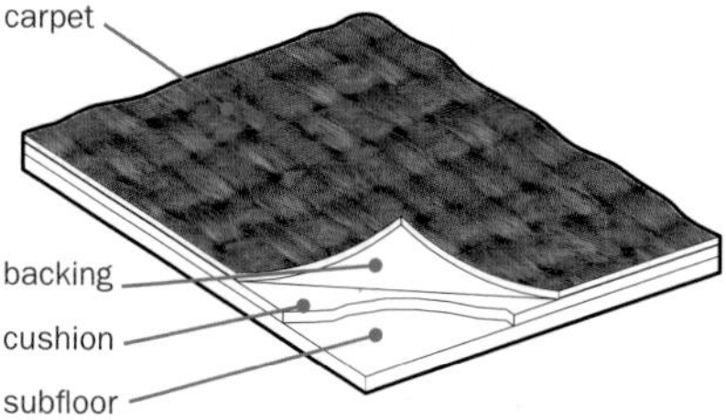
carpet
backing
cushion
subfloor

Resilient Flooring

Vinyl sheet, homogeneous vinyl tile, vinyl composition tile (VCT), cork tile, rubber tile, and linoleum are the common types. The flooring, either ±1/8" (3) thick sheets or tiles, is glued to a concrete or wood subfloor. Most types can be installed to include a seamless integral cove base.

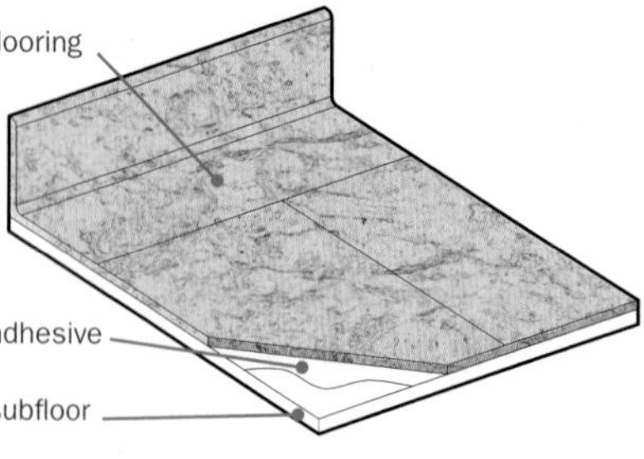
flooring
adhesive
subfloor

Wood

Wood offers a variety of widths and thicknesses, as well as methods of installation. Almost any wood can be made into strip flooring, though oak, pecan, and maple are the most common. Thicker boards should be installed in areas of heavier use.

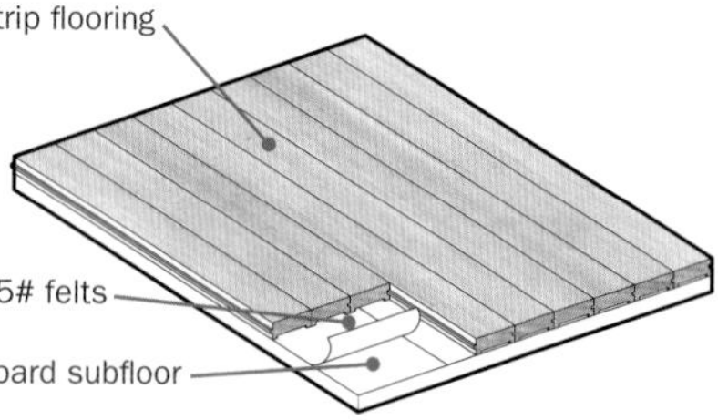
strip flooring
15# felts
board subfloor

Ceramic Tile and Quarry Tile

For thick-set installation, tiles are laid on ±1" (25) portland cement mortar. For thin-set installation, tiles are laid on ±1/8" (3) dry-set mortar, latex–portland cement mortar, organic adhesive, or modified epoxy emulsion mortar.

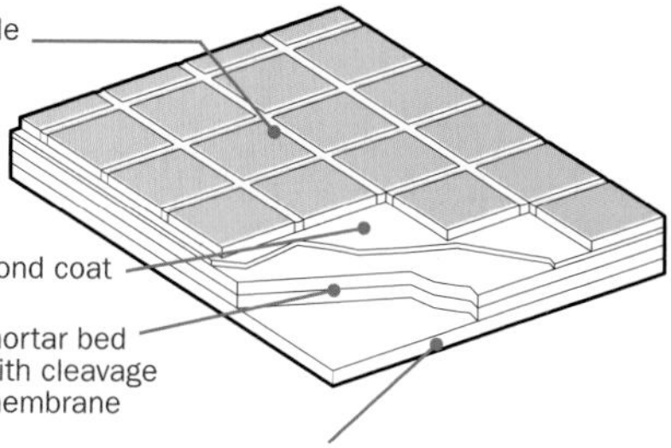
tile
bond coat
mortar bed with cleavage membrane
concrete or wood subfloor

Terrazzo

Terrazzo is a poured or precast material composed of stone chips and a cement matrix (epoxy, polyester, polyacrylate, latex, or electrically conductive).

Appearance types vary from Standard (small chip sizes) to Venetian (large chips with small chips between), Palladiana (large random marble slabs with small chips between) to Rustic (uniform texture with suppressed matrix to expose chips).

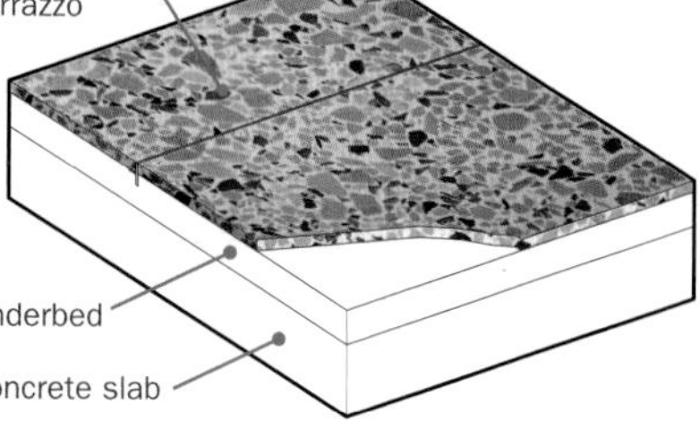
±1/2" (13) terrazzo
underbed
concrete slab

CEILINGS

Attached Ceilings

Gypsum board, plaster, metal, and other materials can be attached directly to joists, rafters, and concrete slabs. Attached ceilings are constructed in a similar manner to wall systems.

Suspended Ceilings

Suspended ceiling systems can support almost any material, although gypsum board, plaster, or fibrous board panels are most common. Regular grids of sheet metal cee channels suspended from the structure above with hanger wires support the gypsum board and plaster. The space between the structure above and the suspended ceiling, called the plenum, provides a zone for ductwork, piping, conduit, and other equipment.

Fibrous panels known as acoustic ceiling tiles (ACT) are lightweight boards made of mineral or glass fibers that are highly sound absorptive. They are easily laid into an exposed, recessed, or concealed grid of light-gauge metal tees suspended with hanger wires. Good ACT has a very high noise reduction coefficient (NRC), meaning that it absorbs the majority of the sound that reaches it. The NRC for gypsum and plaster, by contrast, is very low. Lightweight panels, however, tend to pass the sound through, which limits acoustical privacy in spaces with a shared plenum. Composite panels with acoustic material laminated to a substrate can alleviate this problem. Acoustical panels may involve other materials such as perforated metal, Mylar, and tectum.

Ceiling tiles can be easily removed, allowing access to the plenum area for maintenance of equipment and systems.

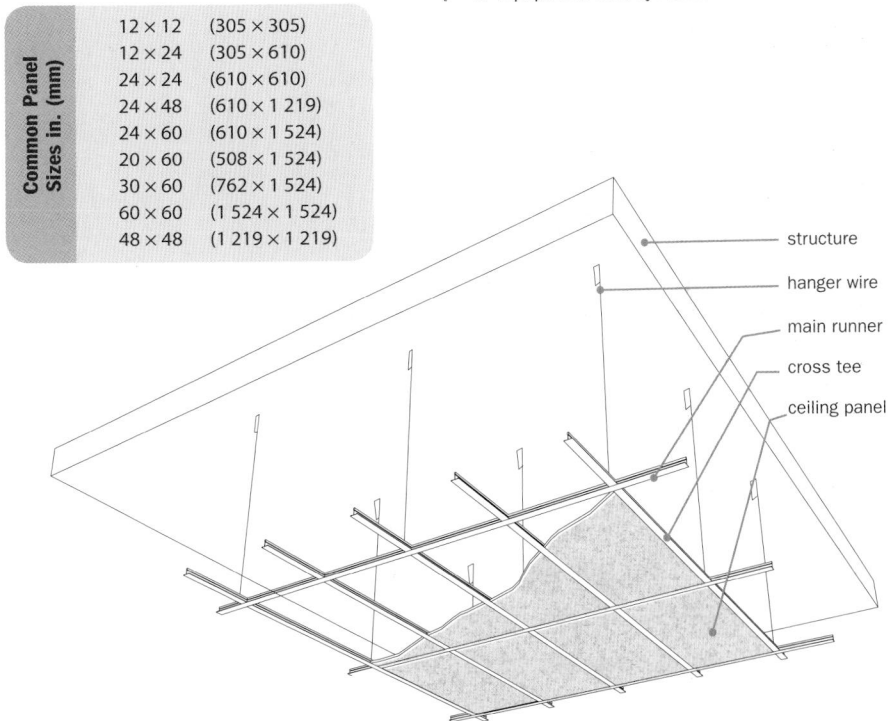

Common Panel Sizes in.	(mm)
12 × 12	(305 × 305)
12 × 24	(305 × 610)
24 × 24	(610 × 610)
24 × 48	(610 × 1 219)
24 × 60	(610 × 1 524)
20 × 60	(508 × 1 524)
30 × 60	(762 × 1 524)
60 × 60	(1 524 × 1 524)
48 × 48	(1 219 × 1 219)

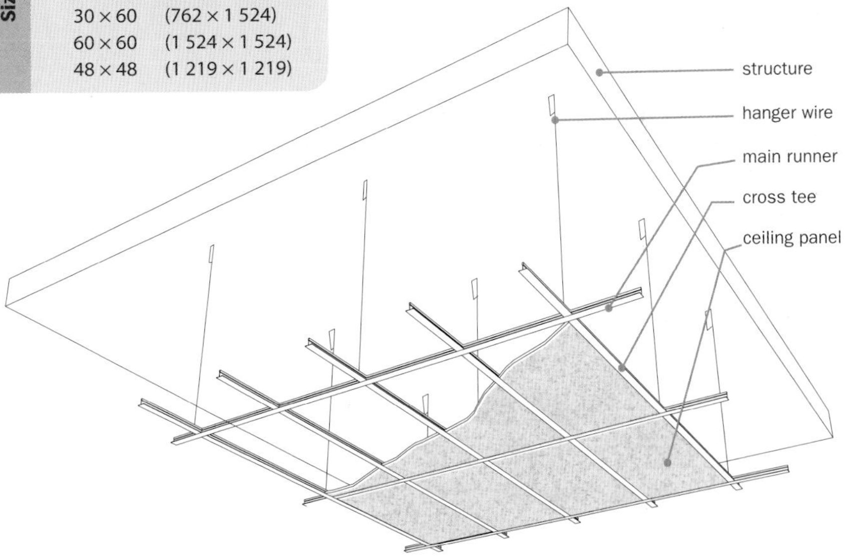
structure
hanger wire
main runner
cross tee
ceiling panel

FINISH CARPENTRY

The wood interior finish components of a building are called millwork, and their installation is known as finish carpentry. Wood used for millwork encompasses various arrangements of solid and veneer wood, but in general it is of a higher quality than that used for framing. Millwork related to cabinetry and its assembly is called casework.

Common Countertops

Plastic Laminate

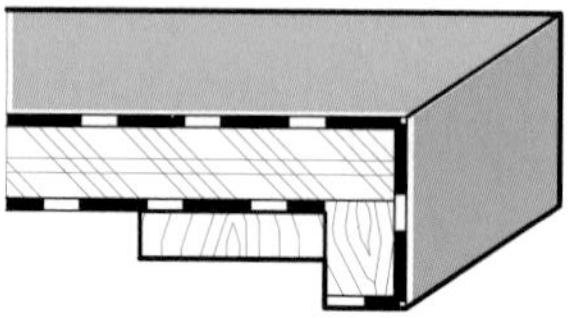

Plastic laminate counters may come postformed, with the laminate already glued to a particle board platform, complete with a backsplash and bull-nosed front edge.

It is also possible to apply p-lam as thin sheets—generally 1/16" (1.6) thick—using a contact adhesive. Decorative plastic laminates have a top sheet of paper printed with wood-grain patterns or other images.

Stone

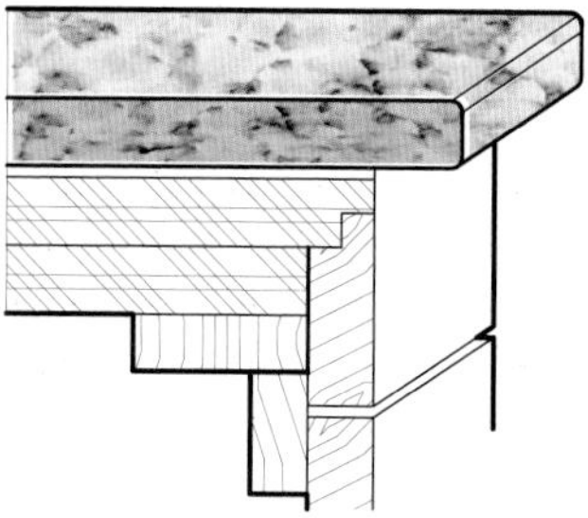

Solid stone countertops of granite, soapstone, marble, or slate (typically resting on a thin-set bed of cement) are durable and resistant to most common kitchen or bathroom wear and tear. Substrates are generally two layers of plywood or particle board. The thickness of the stone varies based on type, but is in the general range of 3/4"–1 5/16" (19–33).

Grouted stone tiles offer a lighter, less expensive alternative.

Solid Surface

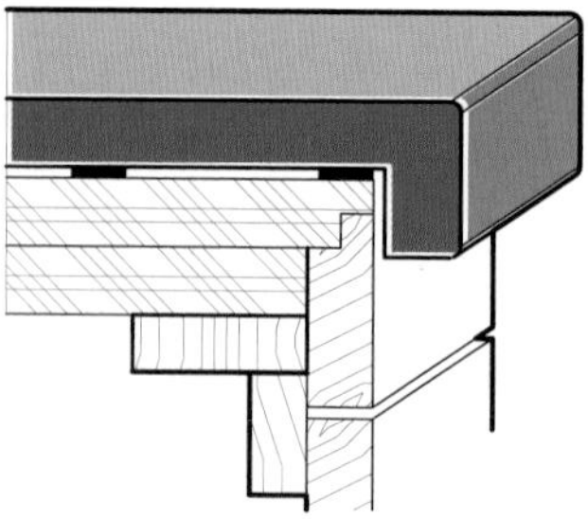

The general composition of solid surface is polymer (acrylic-based resin or unsaturated polyester resin), aluminum trihydrate filler, pigment (colorant), and a catalyst. Solid surface materials are nonporous, homogeneous (maintaining the same appearance all the way through), strong, and have UV stability and surface hardness. They resist water, impacts, chemicals, stains, and high temperatures. Moreover, solid surface can be repaired by being sanded and polished back to its original finish.

Solid surface materials are highly versatile and come in a wide variety of colors, textures, patterns, and translucencies.

Wood-based Board Types

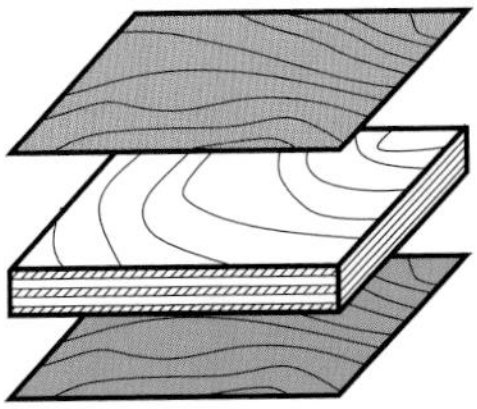
wood veneer
plywood core
wood veneer

Veneer core hardwood plywood: VC is common plywood (typically, fir) with a finished wood grain surface veneer; it is relatively lightweight and easy to handle.

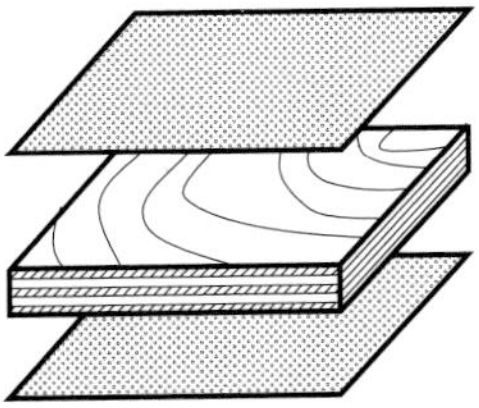
MDF veneer
plywood core
MDF veneer

Medium- and high-density overlay plywood: MDO and HDO are generally common plywood with an MDF surface, resulting in panels that weigh less than full MDF but have smoother and more stable surfaces than VC.

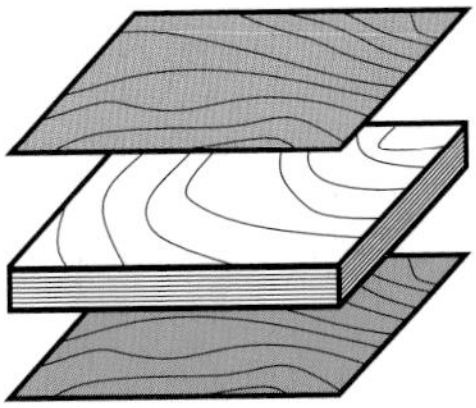
wood veneer
HDP core
wood veneer

High-density plywood: HDP has more plies and fewer voids than common plywood. Its strength and stability make it useful for cabinetry, and it typically comes in birch (Baltic) or maple (Appleby).

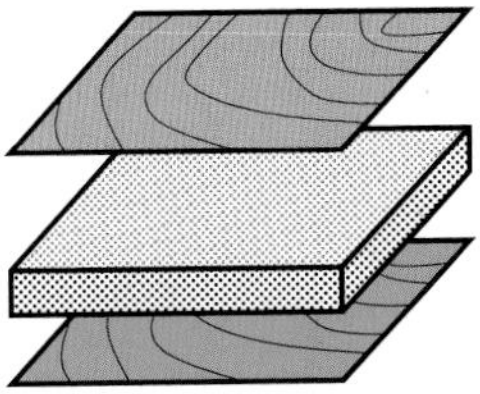
wood veneer
MDF core
wood veneer

Medium-density fiber core hardwood plywood: MDF is produced by heat-pressing a mixture of fine wood dust and a binder into panels. Paint-grade blank sheets can be used as they are or with a veneer skin, while dyed MDF has a consistent color from face to core. Though ideal for use in cabinetry and shelving, full MDF is very heavy.

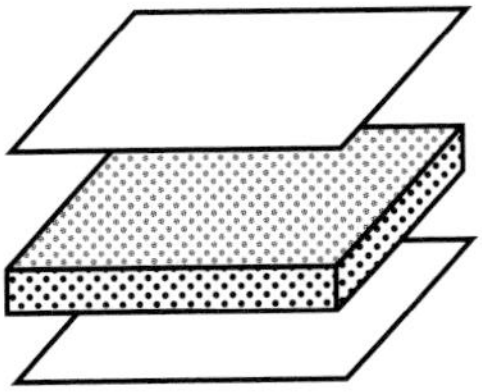
veneer, gen'l
PBC core
veneer, gen'l

Particle board core plywood: PBC produced by heat-pressing a coarse wood dust and a binder into panels, which are lower in weight than full MDF, due to the coarser dust. As the surface is rougher and less consistent, it is an ideal substrate for many other products.

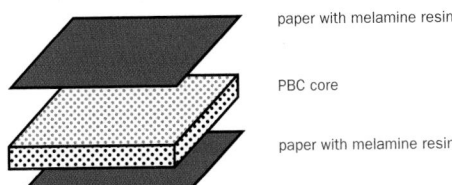

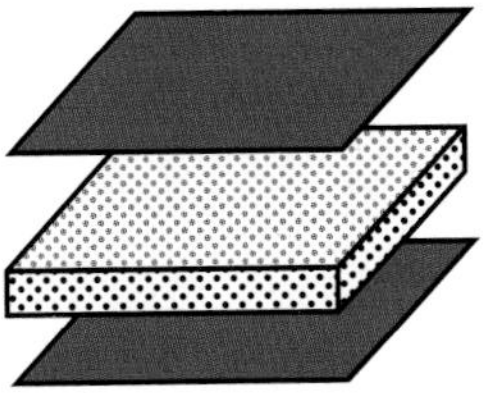
paper with melamine resin
PBC core
paper with melamine resin

Melamine: Melamine consists of a particle board core with a thermally fused, resin-saturated paper finish. Though the name refers to the resin in the paper liner, and not the paper or board, the entire product is commonly referred to as melamine. Melamine is ideal for use in cabinetry and comes in a wide variety of colors. MDF can also be used as the substrate.

SYSTEMS 2.

A single person rarely designs all aspects of a building. Numerous teams of professionals are needed to create the systems that make a building stand and function well. Coordination of these systems begins early and may continue even after the building is occupied. During design, the building is an ever-changing organism, growing and shrinking to accommodate more systems as they are shaped and sized, designed and refined, requiring continual communication between the architect and the consulting trades.

Many decisions cannot be made until specific systems are in place. For example, the materials, structure, occupancy, and layout of a building must be known before a preliminary code analysis can be attempted. This analysis may yield new information, such as the need for wider egress stairs, more exit corridors, or further provisions for sprinkler systems. The accommodation of larger stairs and more corridors will affect the arrangement of spaces—or it may generate an overall change to the size of the building, which could, in turn, require less expensive cladding materials—and more sprinklers might entail more plumbing requirements. This give-and-take process continues throughout design, resulting in a (usually) happy coexistence of systems, spaces, and materials.

Chapter 6: Structural Systems

Structural elements of a building—its walls, frame, and foundation—hold it up (or keep it down) by resisting gravity (vertical forces) and lateral (horizontal) loads such as winds and earthquakes. The primary components of a building's structural system are its foundation system and framing system. The type selected for either is contingent on many factors, including the building's use, desired height, soil conditions of the site, local building codes, and available materials. Elements of a building's structure cannot be removed without compromising its strength and stability.

Loads

All stresses acting on a building's structure, no matter how complex, can be reduced to either tension or compression. In basic terms, a building's structure must press up with the same force that the weight of the building is pressing down, which includes all fixed dead loads and varying live loads.

Tension is a pulling and stretching force.

Compression is a pressing, pushing, or squeezing force.

Dead loads: Fixed, static loads made up of the building's own structure, skin, equipment, and other fixed elements.

Live loads: Moving or transient loads such as occupants, furnishings, snow, ice, and rain.

Wind loads: Pressure from wind that affects lateral loads as well as possible uplift forces on roofs or downward pressure.

Other loads: Impact loads, shock waves, vibrations, and seismic loads.

STRUCTURAL TERMINOLOGY

Arch: Structural device that supports vertical loads by translating them into axial forces.

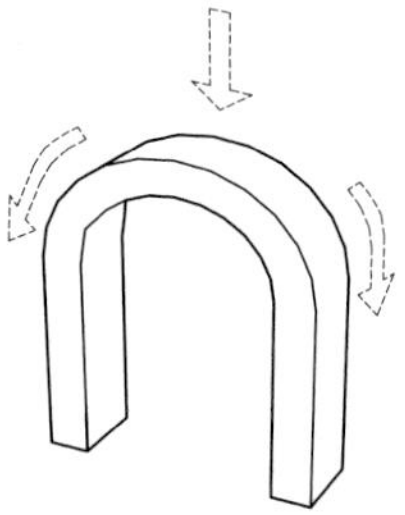

Axial force: System of internal forces whose outcome is a force acting along the longitudinal axis of a structural member or assembly.

Beam: Horizontal linear element that spans an opening and is supported at both ends by walls or columns.

Buttress: Vertical mass built against a wall to strengthen it and to resist the outward pressure of a vault.

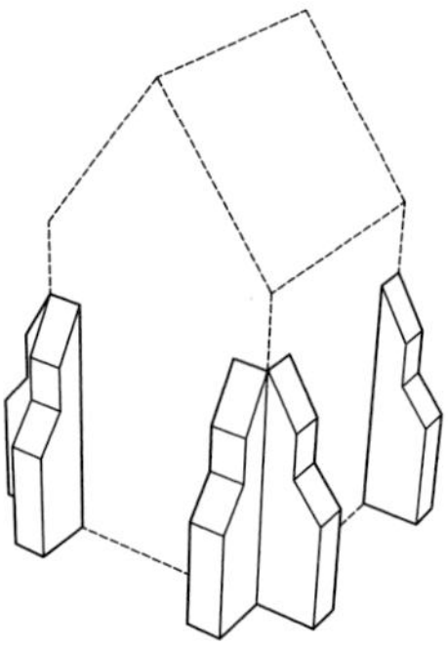

Cantilever: Horizontal beam or slab that extends beyond its last point of support.

Column: Upright structural member acting in compression.

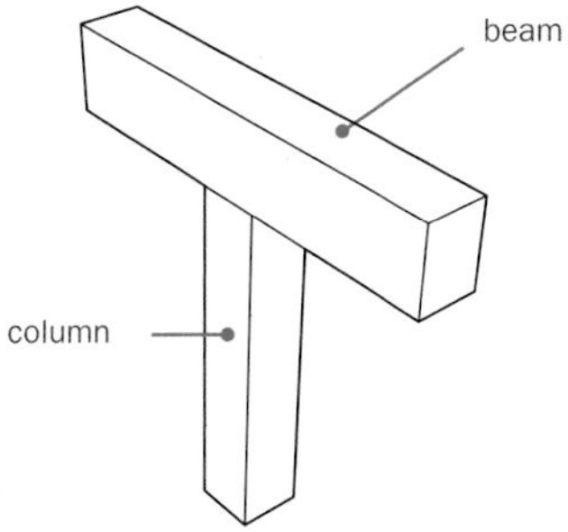
beam
column

Dome: Arch rotated in plan to produce an inverted bowl-shaped form.

Girder: Horizontal beam, which is usually very large, that supports other beams.

Lintel: Beam used to span the opening in a wall left for a window or a doorway. The lintel supports and distributes the load of the wall above the opening.

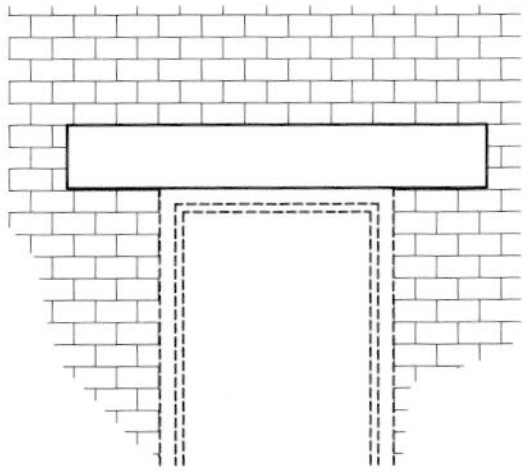

Prestressing: Applying a compressive stress to a concrete structural member, either by pre-tensioning (pouring concrete around stretched steel strands, then releasing the external tensioning force on the strands once the concrete has cured) or post-tensioning (tensioning high-strength steel tendons against a concrete structural member after the concrete has cured).

Retaining wall: Wall used to mediate abrupt changes in ground elevation and to resist lateral soil pressures.

Shear: System of internal forces whose outcome is a force acting perpendicular to the longitudinal axis of a structural member or assembly.

Shoring: Temporary vertical or sloping supports.

Slump test: Test in which wet concrete or plaster is placed in a metal cone-shaped mold of specific dimensions and allowed to slump under its own weight after the cone is removed. The index of the material's working consistency is determined by the distance between the height of the mold and the height of the slumped mixture.

Strain: Intensity of deformation at a point in an object.

Stress: Intensity of internal force acting at a point in an object.

Vault: Extruded arch.

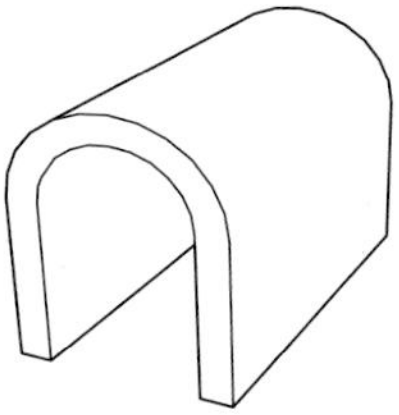
vault

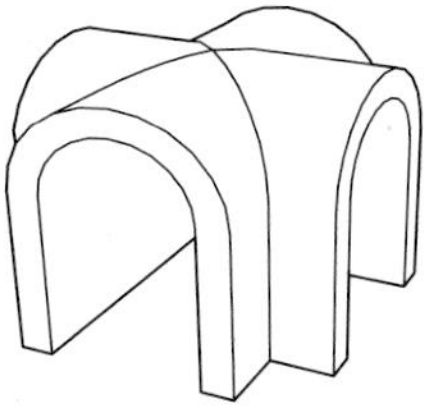
groin vault

Materials
Structural framing elements may be made of wood, heavy timbers, concrete, masonry, steel, or a combination of these.

FOUNDATION SYSTEMS

The selection of a foundation system depends on many factors, including the building size and height, the quality of the subsurface soil and groundwater conditions, construction methods, and environmental concerns.

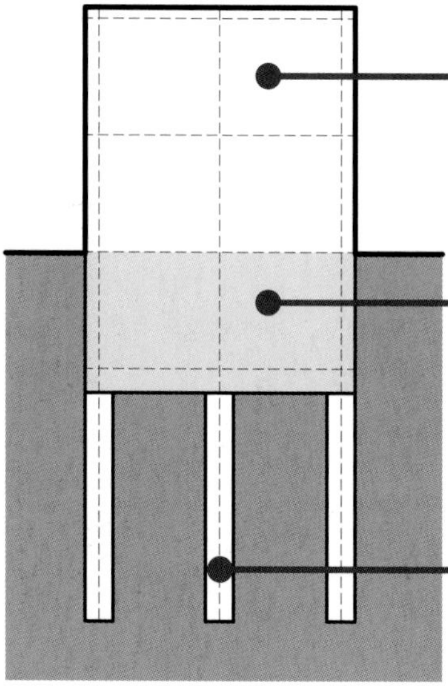

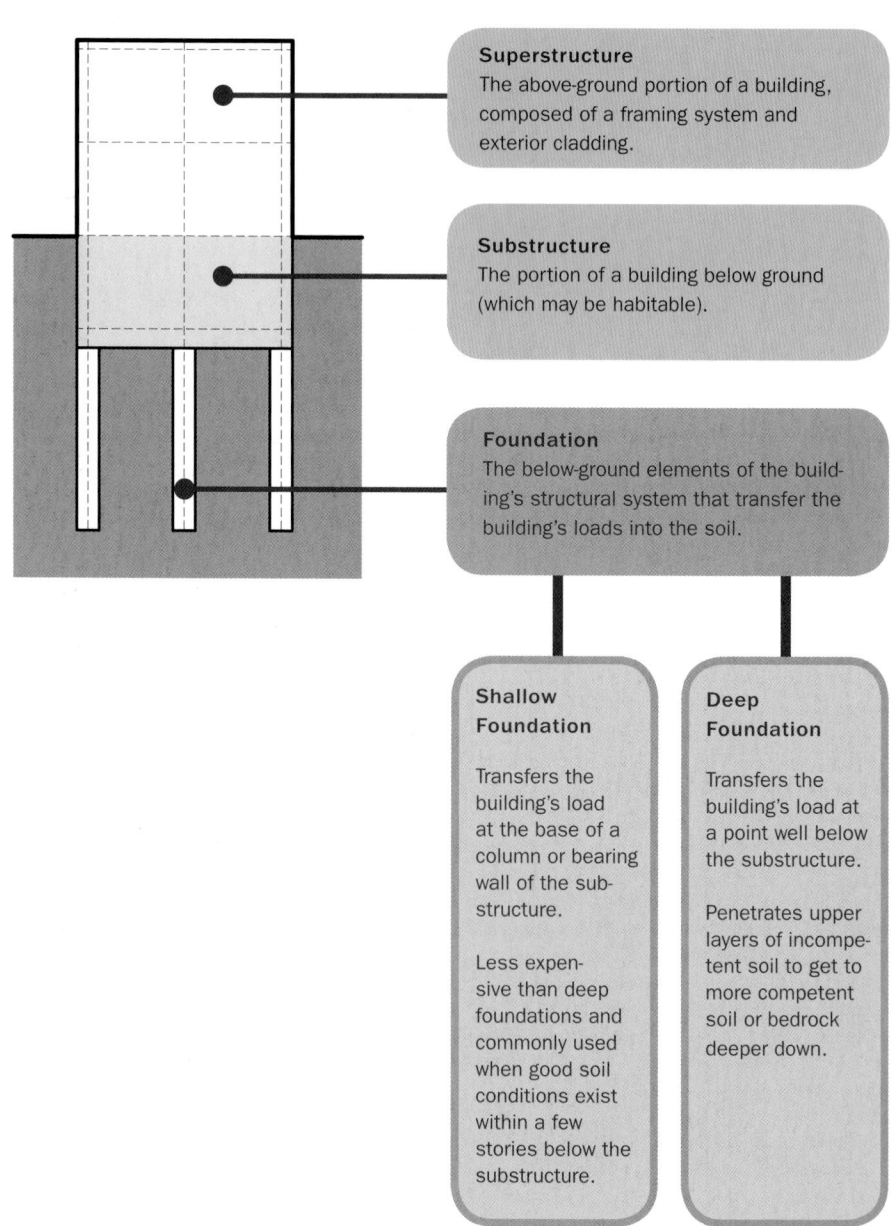

Superstructure
The above-ground portion of a building, composed of a framing system and exterior cladding.

Substructure
The portion of a building below ground (which may be habitable).

Foundation
The below-ground elements of the building's structural system that transfer the building's loads into the soil.

Shallow Foundation

Transfers the building's load at the base of a column or bearing wall of the substructure.

Less expensive than deep foundations and commonly used when good soil conditions exist within a few stories below the substructure.

Deep Foundation

Transfers the building's load at a point well below the substructure.

Penetrates upper layers of incompetent soil to get to more competent soil or bedrock deeper down.

SHALLOW SYSTEMS

Footings

Concrete footings may be in the form of a column pad, for distributing the load of a column, or a strip footing, which does the same for a bearing wall.

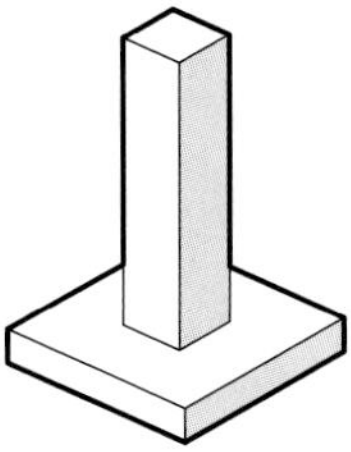

Column Footing

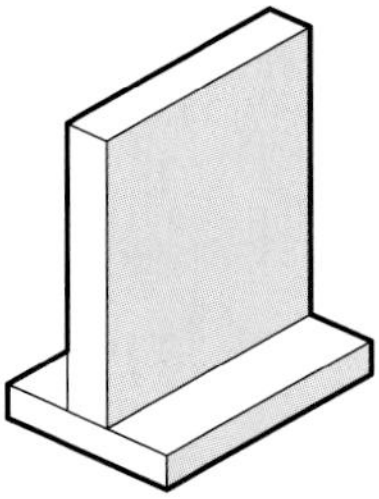

Strip Footing

Slab on Grade

Used for one- and two-story structures, this inexpensive foundation has thickened edges and rests as a continuous slab on the surface of the ground.

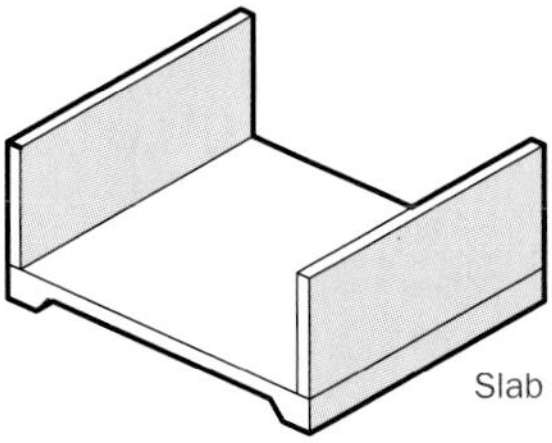

Slab on Grade

Mat Foundation

In this foundation system (also known as raft foundation), the whole building rests on a large continuous footing. It is often used to resolve special soil or design conditions. "Floating" or "compensated" mat foundations are sometimes employed in situations with weak soil. The floating foundation is placed beneath the building to a point that the amount of soil removed is equal to the total weight of the building.

DEEP SYSTEMS

Caissons

To construct a caisson (also referred to as a "drilled pier"), a hole is drilled or dug (a process known as augering) through unsatisfactory soil beneath a building's substructure, until rock, dense gravel, or firm clay is reached. If the caisson will rest on soil at the bottom, the hole is sometimes belled out to achieve a bearing area similar to a footing and the hole is then filled with concrete. Caissons may range from 18" (457) to 6' (1 829) in diameter.

Piles

Piles are similar to caissons, but are driven into place, not drilled or poured. They may be made from concrete, steel, or timber, or a combination of these materials. Piles are driven closely together in clusters and then cut off and capped in groups of two to twenty-five. The building's columns rest on top of the pile caps. Load-bearing walls, where used, rest on reinforced-concrete grade beams that span between pile caps, transmitting the walls' loads to the piles.

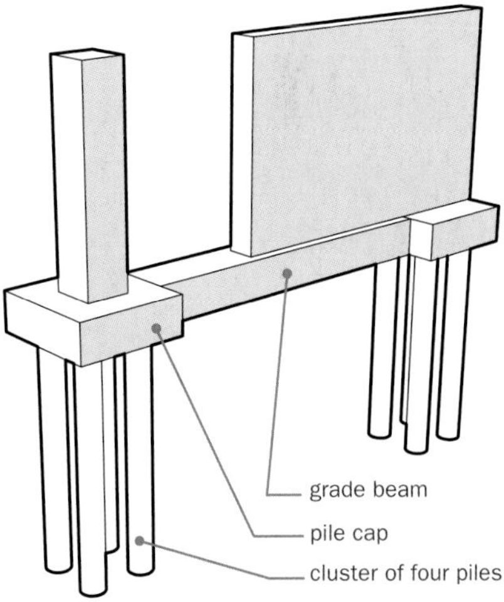
grade beam
pile cap
cluster of four piles

WOOD LIGHT-FRAMING

Wood light-frame construction uses a system of wood wall studs, floor joists, rafters, columns, and beams to create both structure and framework for applied interior and exterior finished surfaces. As a building material, wood is relatively inexpensive, versatile, and quick to erect. Typical spacing for studs and floor joists is 12" (305), 16" (406), or 24" (610) on center. These dimensions are compatible with typical wall, floor, and ceiling material unit dimensions, such as gypsum wallboard and plywood sheets. When complete SI conversion occurs in the United States, these building materials will undergo a change in unit size, and framing dimensions will shift to the metric planning grid used elsewhere in the world.

Exterior wall sheathing is typically plywood, which acts as a base for stucco, siding, or even brick and stone façades; insulation is placed between the studs. The most common framing method is platform framing, in which, in multistory buildings, the levels are built one at a time, so that each floor acts as a platform on which the walls above can rest. In balloon framing, wall studs are continuous from sill to roof; the intermediate floor joists tie into a ribbon occurring at the floor line and attached to the studs. Balloon framing is more prevalent in older houses and is seldom used today.

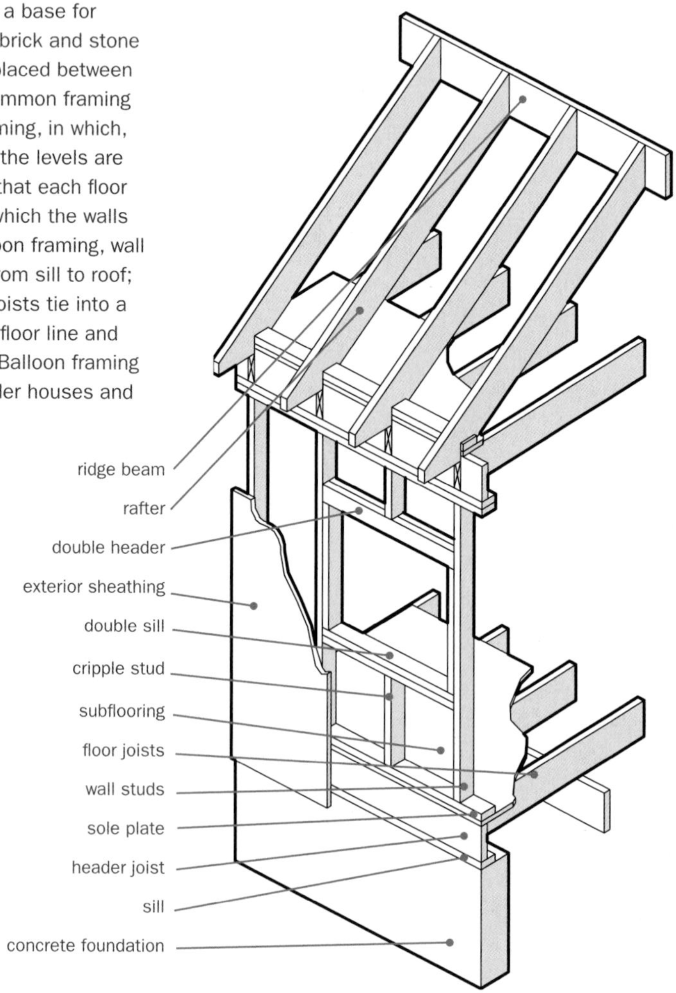
ridge beam
rafter
double header
exterior sheathing
double sill
cripple stud
subflooring
floor joists
wall studs
sole plate
header joist
sill
concrete foundation

HEAVY TIMBERS

Heavy-timber construction uses specifically engineered woods of minimum dimensions to achieve greater structural strength and fire resistance than is possible with wood light-frame construction, while also taking advantage of the aesthetic benefits of exposed wood. To achieve high levels of fire resistance, construction details, fastenings, and wood treatment are closely regulated in heavy-timber construction.

Decking

Floor deck planking spans between floor beams; finished floor material is placed above the planking, running perpendicular to it. Planks should be a minimum 3" nominal (76) thick if splined or tongue-and-grooved together, or a minimum 4" (102) nominal if set on edge and spiked together. Flooring should be 1/2"–1" (13–25) thick.

Floors

Beams and girders may be sawn or glue-laminated.

They should not be less than 6" wide × 10" deep nominal (152 × 254).

Truss members must be a minimum 8" × 8" nominal (203 × 203).

Decay

Structural members must be preservatively treated or be from the heartwood of a naturally durable wood.

Columns

Columns may be sawed or glue-laminated.

Supporting floor loads, must be a minimum 8" wide × 8" deep nominal (203 × 203).

Supporting roof and ceiling loads, must be a minimum 6" wide × 8" deep nominal (152 × 203).

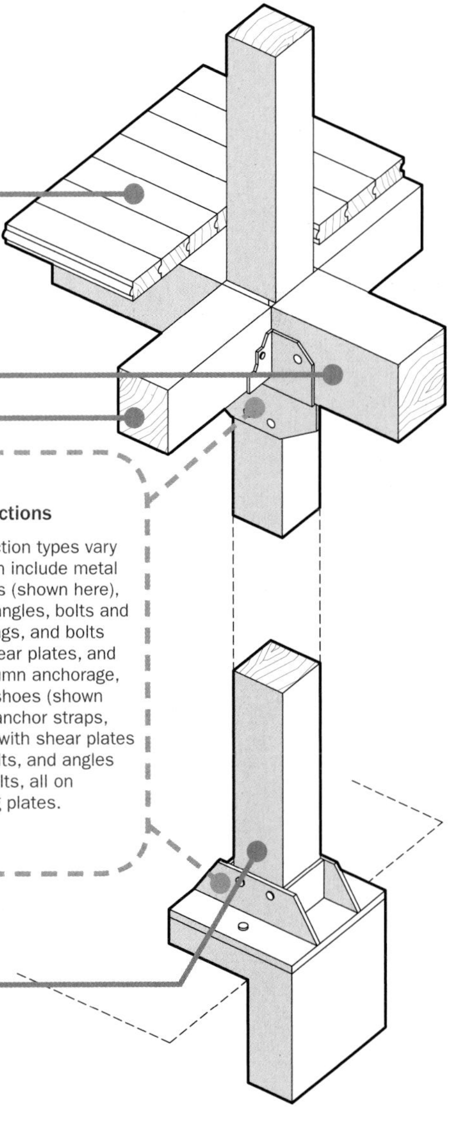
girder
beam

Connections

Connection types vary and can include metal hangers (shown here), metal angles, bolts and split rings, and bolts and shear plates, and for column anchorage, metal shoes (shown here), anchor straps, straps with shear plates and bolts, and angles with bolts, all on bearing plates.

Concrete Floor and Roof Systems

Different systems, in order of increasing load capacity, spans, and cost, are one-way solid slab (spans across parallel lines of support), two-way flat plate (uses no beams, dropped plate, or column capitals, but rather, reinforcing of various stresses), two-way flat slab (uses column capitals and/or drop panels instead of beams), one-way joist, waffle slab, one-way beam and slab, and two-way beam and slab. Two-way systems tend to be square in proportion and are supported on four sides; one-way systems have a 1:>1.5 proportion and are supported on two sides.

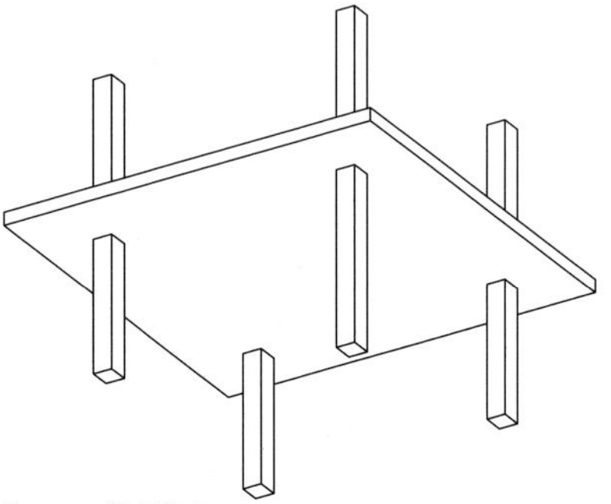
Two-way Flat Plate

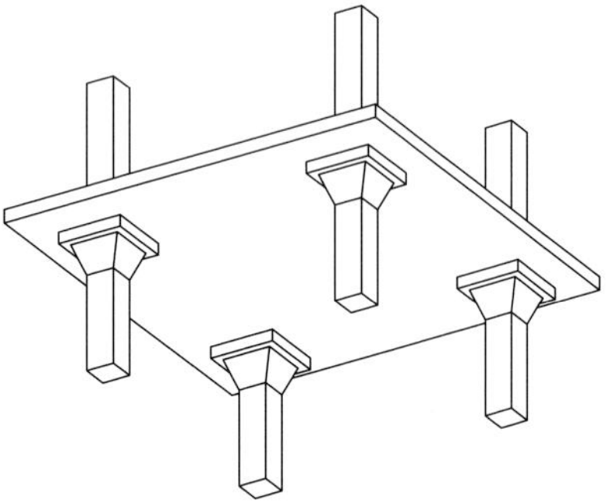
Two-way Flat Slab

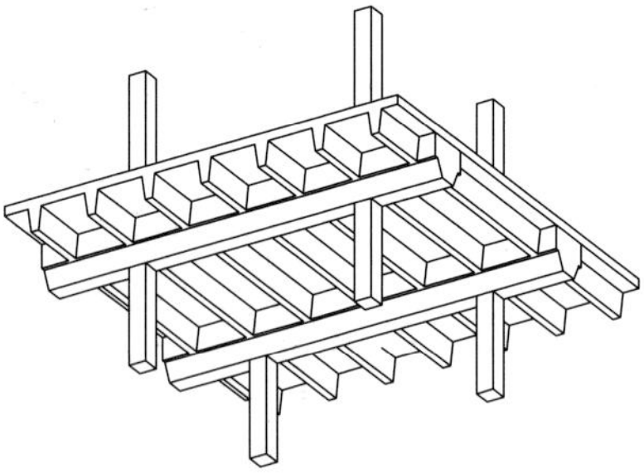
One-way Ribbed Slab (joist)

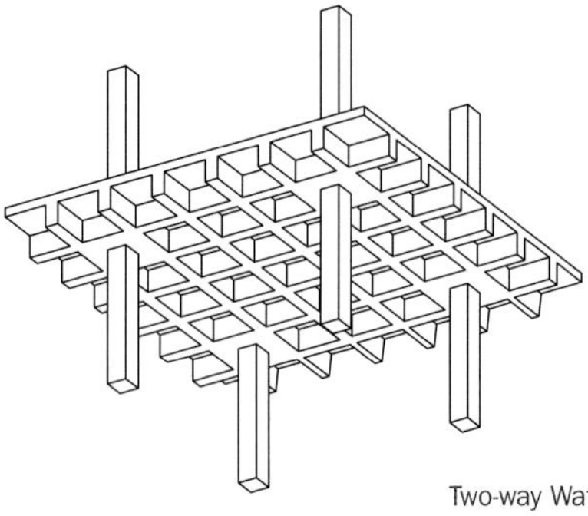
Two-way Waffle Slab

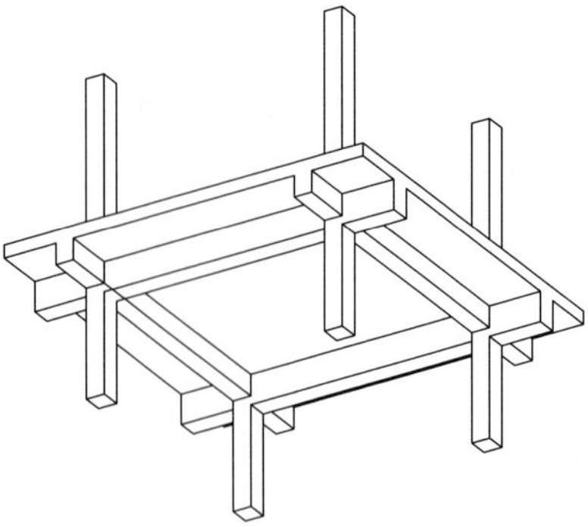
Flat Beam and Slab

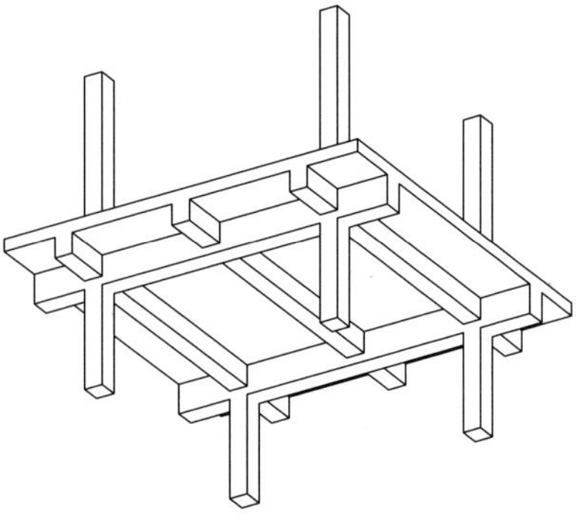
One-way Beam and Slab

Moment Frame

Rigid framework resists lateral forces

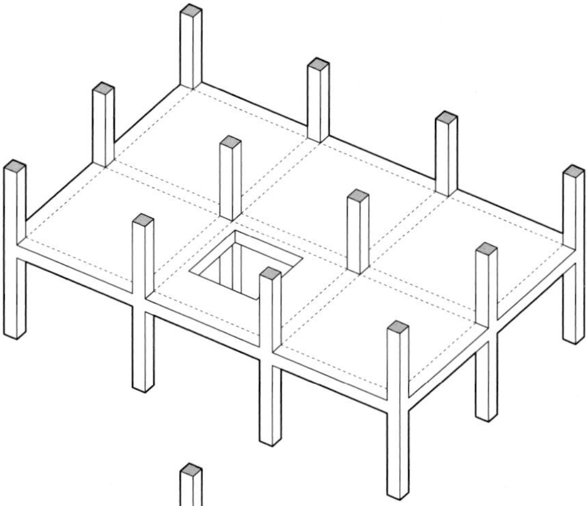

Braced Frame

Internal structure braces light frame

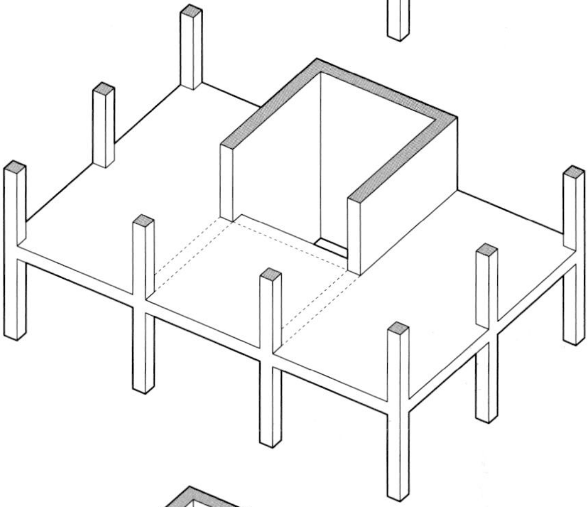

Tube

Exterior walls contribute to structural stability

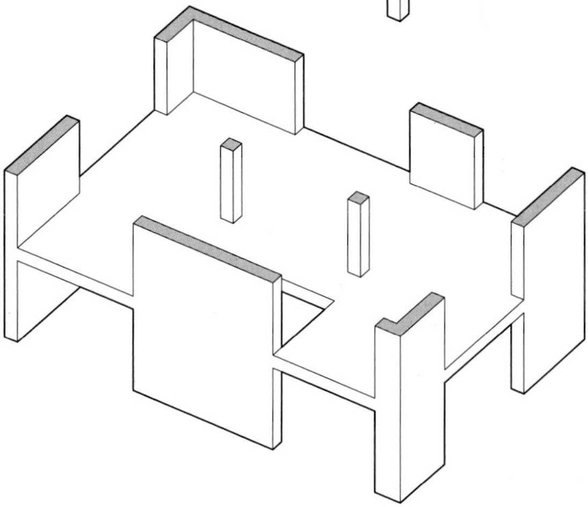

PRECAST CONCRETE FRAMING

Slab Detail

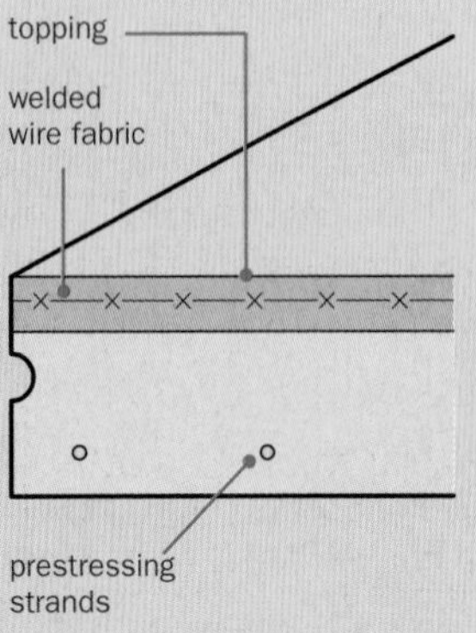
topping
welded
wire fabric
prestressing
strands

Hollow Core Slab Types

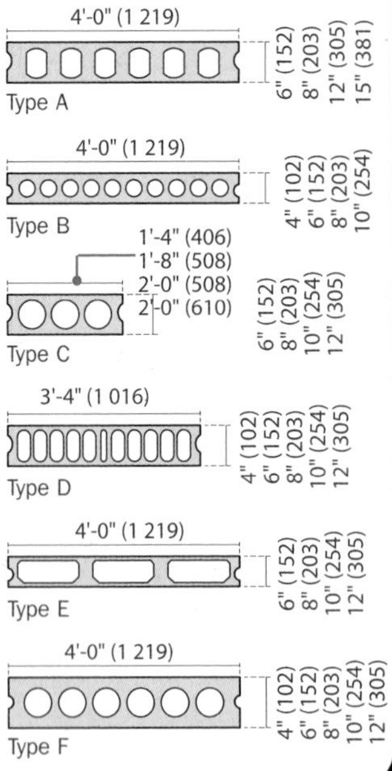
4'-0" (1 219)
6" (152)
8" (203)
12" (305)
15" (381)
Type A
4'-0" (1 219)
4" (102)
6" (152)
8" (203)
10" (254)
Type B
1'-4" (406)
1'-8" (508)
2'-0" (508)
2'-0" (610)
6" (152)
8" (203)
10" (254)
12" (305)
Type C
3'-4" (1 016)
4" (102)
6" (152)
8" (203)
10" (254)
12" (305)
Type D
4'-0" (1 219)
6" (152)
8" (203)
10" (254)
12" (305)
Type E
4'-0" (1 219)
4" (102)
6" (152)
8" (203)
10" (254)
12" (305)
Type F

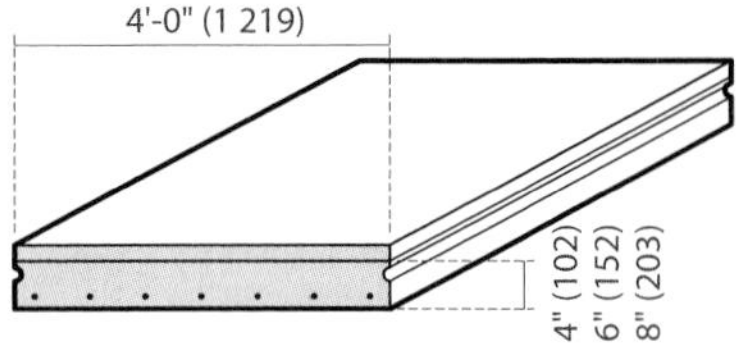
4'-0" (1 219)
4" (102)
6" (152)
8" (203)

Solid Flat Slab

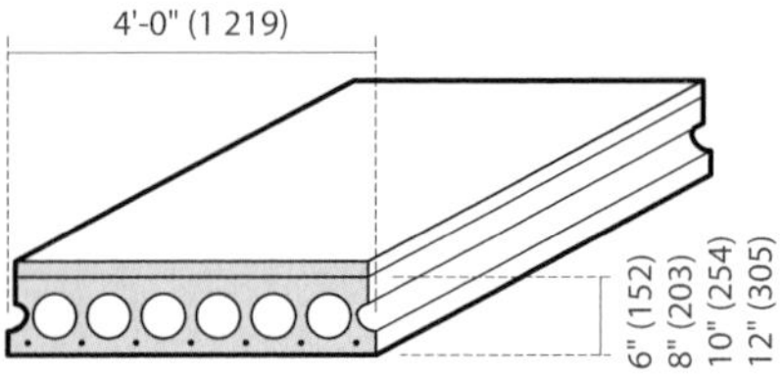
4'-0" (1 219)
6" (152)
8" (203)
10" (254)
12" (305)

Hollow Core Slab

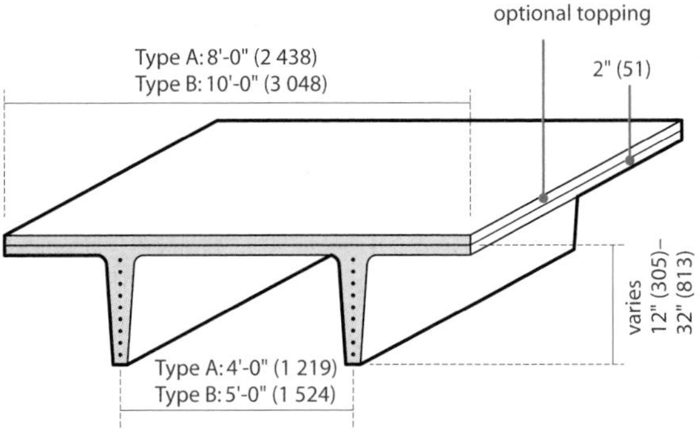
optional topping
Type A: 8'-0" (2 438)
Type B: 10'-0" (3 048)
2" (51)
varies
12" (305)–
32" (813)
Type A: 4'-0" (1 219)
Type B: 5'-0" (1 524)

Stemmed Deck, Double Tee (DT)

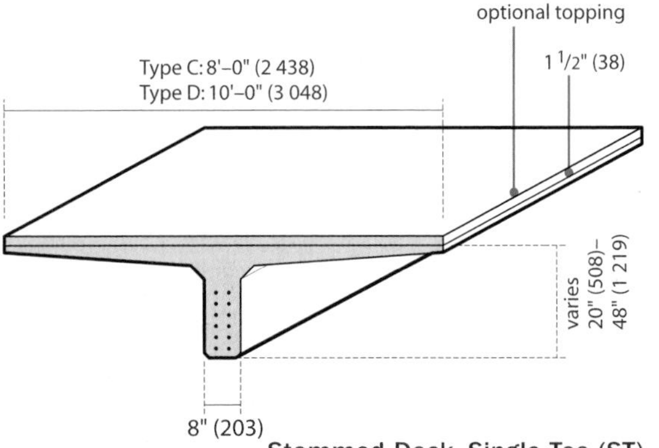
optional topping
Type C: 8'–0" (2 438)
Type D: 10'–0" (3 048)
1 1/2" (38)
varies
20" (508)–
48" (1 219)
8" (203)

Stemmed Deck, Single Tee (ST)

Hollow Slab Framing System

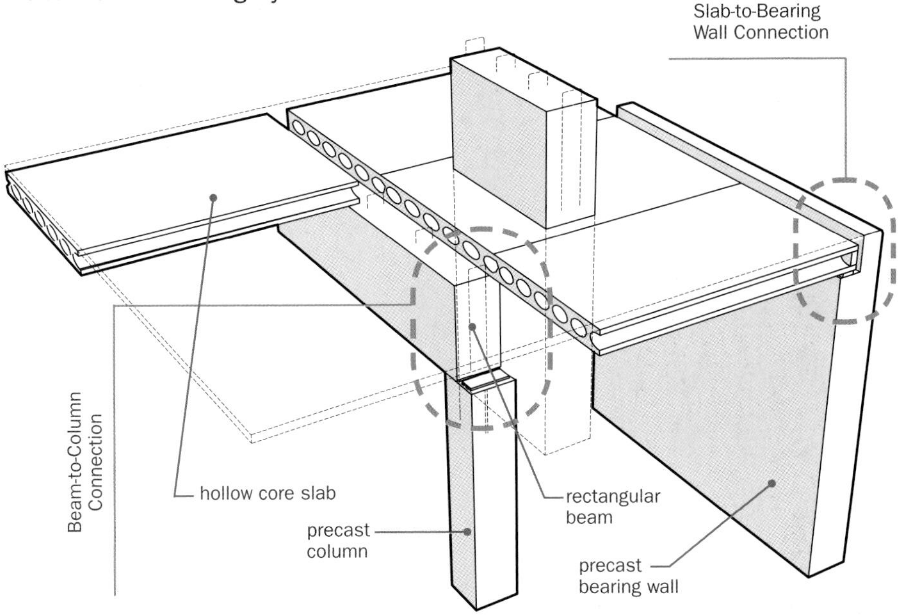
Slab-to-Bearing
Wall Connection
Beam-to-Column
Connection
hollow core slab
precast
column
rectangular
beam
precast
bearing wall

Stemmed Deck DT Framing System

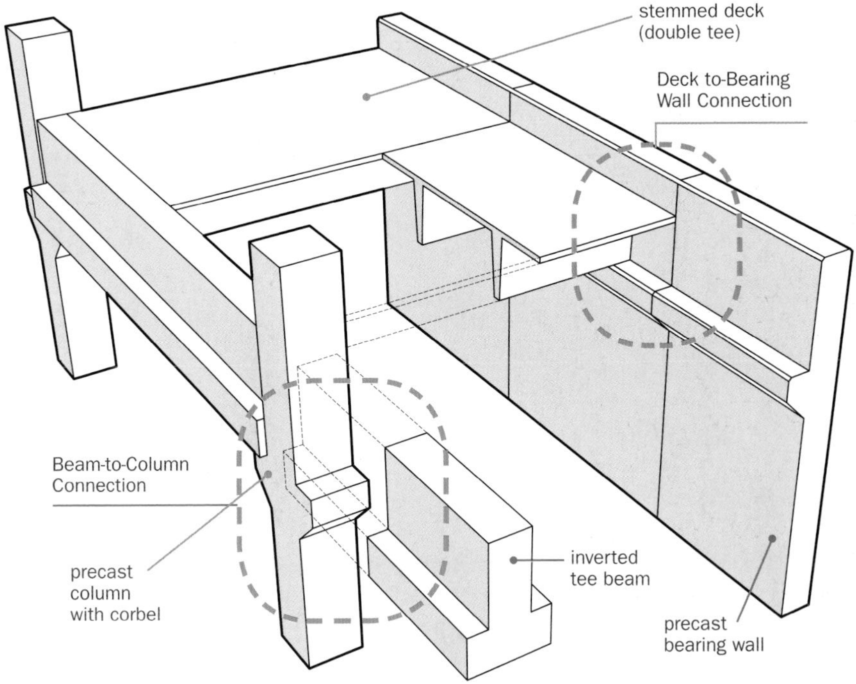
stemmed deck
(double tee)
Deck to-Bearing
Wall Connection
Beam-to-Column
Connection
precast
column
with corbel
inverted
tee beam
precast
bearing wall

Structural Steel Shape Designations

	Shape	Description
W	Wide-flange	hot-rolled, doubly symmetric wide-flange shapes used as beams and columns
HP	Wide-flange	hot-rolled, wide-flange shapes whose flanges and webs are of the same nominal thickness and whose depth and width are essentially the same; often used as bearing piles
S	American Standard beam	hot-rolled, doubly symmetric shapes produced in accordance with AASM* dimensional standards; generally being superseded by wide-flange beams, which are more structurally efficient
M	Miscellaneous	doubly symmetrical shapes that cannot be classified as W or HP shapes
L	Angle	equal leg and unequal leg angles
C	American Standard channel	hot-rolled channels produced in accordance with AASM dimensional standards
MC	Channel	hot-rolled channels from miscellaneous shape
WT	Structural tee	hot-rolled tees cut or split from W shapes
ST	Structural tee	hot-rolled tees cut or split from S shapes
MT	Structural tee	hot-rolled tees cut or split from M shapes
TU	Tube	hollow structural steel members shaped like a square or rectangle; used as beams or columns, or in bracing

*AASM: Association of American Steel Manufacturers

Steel Shape Examples

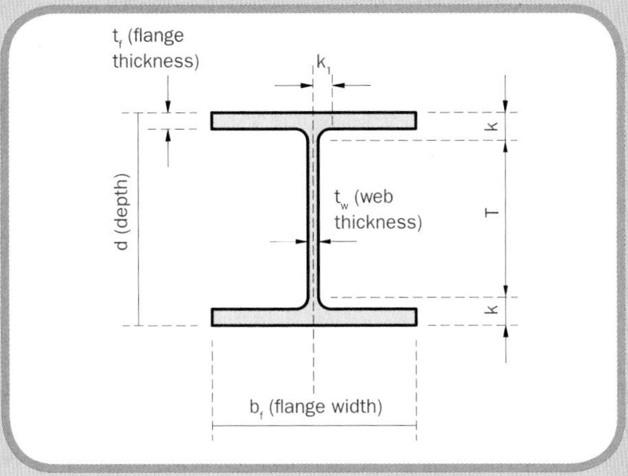

t_f (flange thickness)
k_1
k
d (depth)
t_w (web thickness)
T
k
b_f (flange width)

Wide-flange
W8×67

8 = nominal depth (in.); 67 = weight per foot of length (lb.)

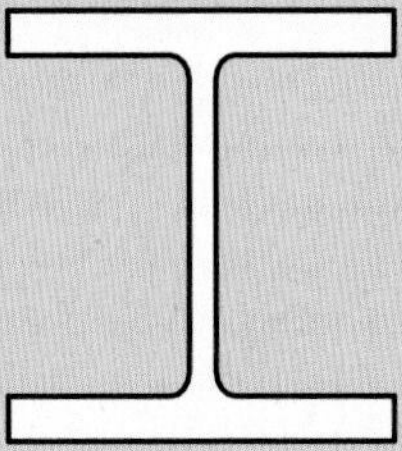

Wide-flange
HP12×84

12 = nominal depth (in.); 84 = weight per foot of length (lb.)

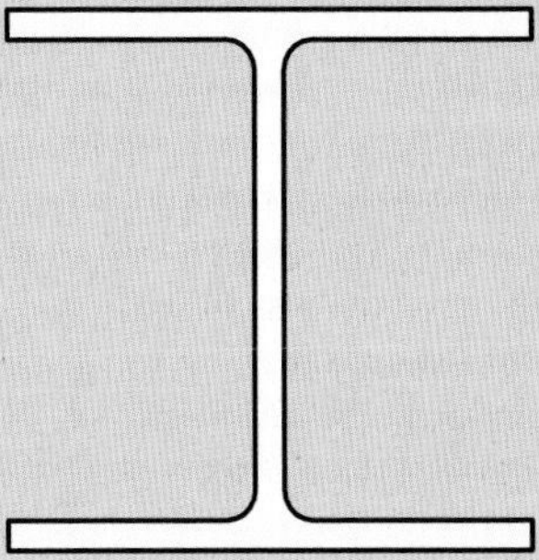

American Standard
S8×18.4

8 = nominal depth (in.); 18.4 = weight per foot of length (lb.)

Miscellaneous
M10×8

10 = nominal depth (in.); 8 = weight per foot of length (lb.)

Structural Tees
WT25×95

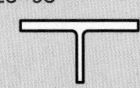

ST15×3.75

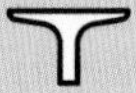

Angle
L6×4×7/8

6 and 4 = nominal depths of legs (in.); 7/8 = nominal thickness of legs (in.)

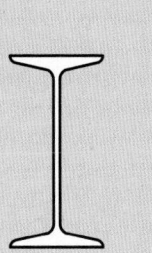

Channel
MC7×22.7

7 = nominal depth (in.); 22.7 = weight per foot of length (lb.)

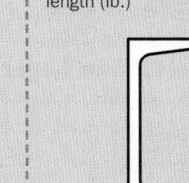

Tube
TU2×2×1/8

Steel-Frame Connections

Steel is proportionally light in weight relative to its strength and can be erected quickly but precisely. Steel-frame construction uses a combination of structural steel shapes that act as columns, beams, girders, lintels, trusses, and numerous means of connection.

The integrity and strength of steel connections are just as important as the steel shapes themselves, because a failed connection results in a failed system. Steel-frame connections include angles, plates, and tees for transitioning between members being joined.

Connections that join only the web of the beam to the column are called framed connections; they can transmit all the vertical (shear) forces from the beam to the column. If the flanges of the beam are also connected to the column, it is then capable of transmitting bending moment from beam to column.

Framed Connection: Shear connection with beam web bolted to column flange using connecting angles.

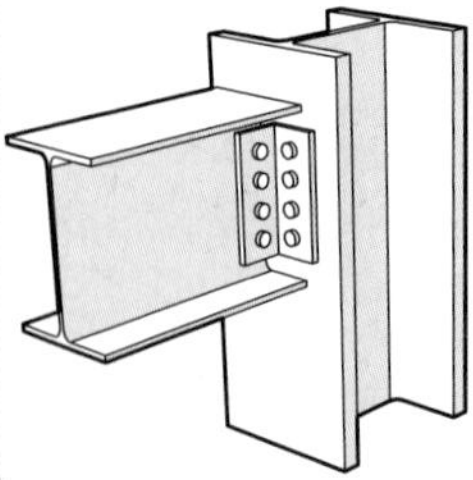

Welded Moment Connection: Moment connection between beam and column using groove welds at beam web and flange.

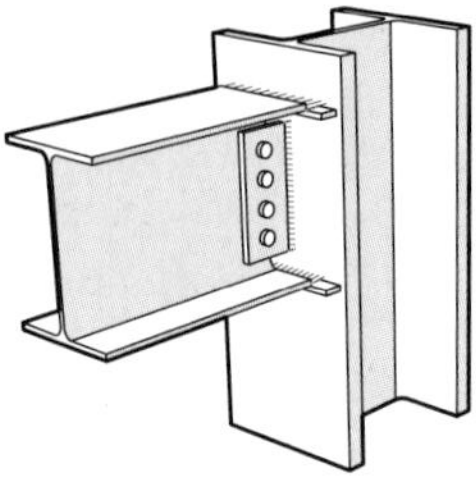

TRUSS DESIGN

Heel Conditions

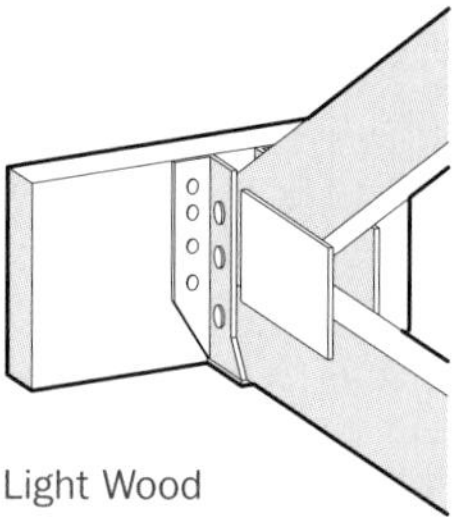

Light Wood

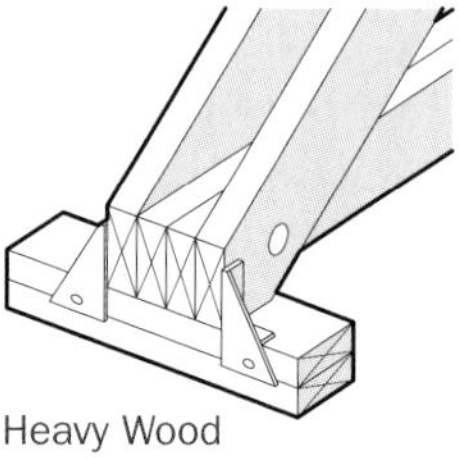

Heavy Wood

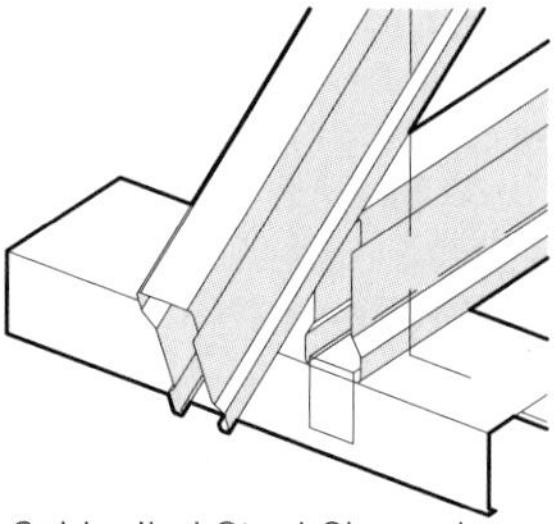

Cold-rolled Steel Channel

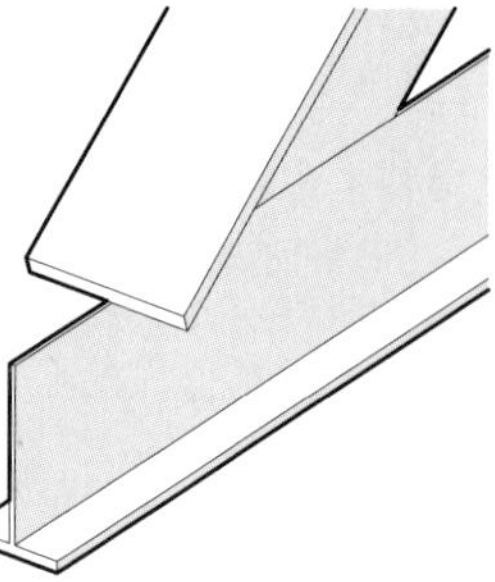

Welded Steel

A truss is a structural framework of triangular units for supporting loads over long spans. The framework of the structural members reduces nonaxial forces to a set of axial forces in the members themselves.

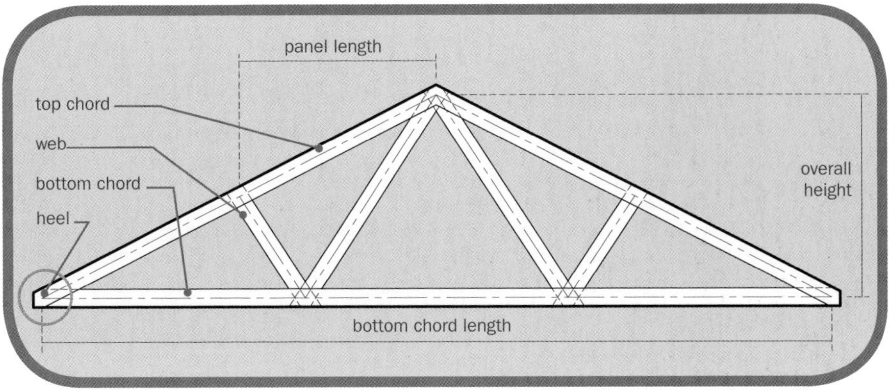
panel length
top chord
web
bottom chord
heel
overall height
bottom chord length

Truss Types

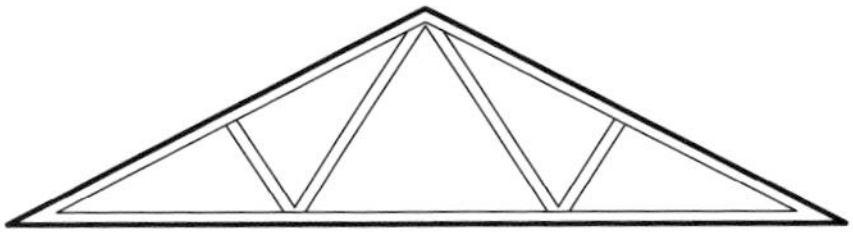
Belgian

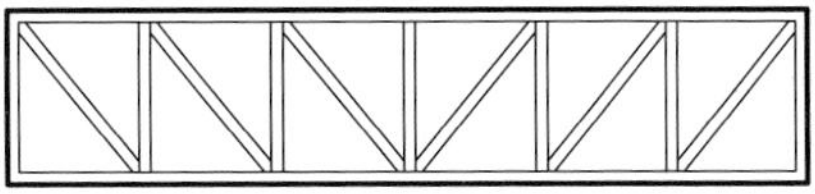
Flat Pratt

Warren

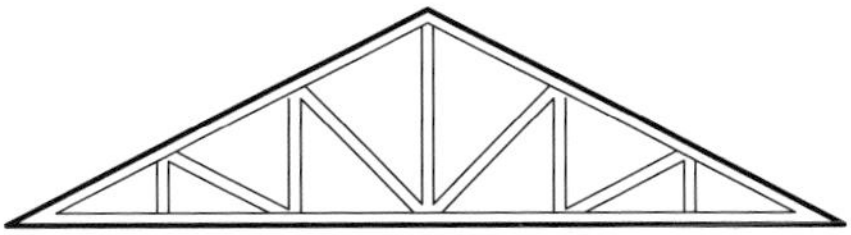
Pitched Howe

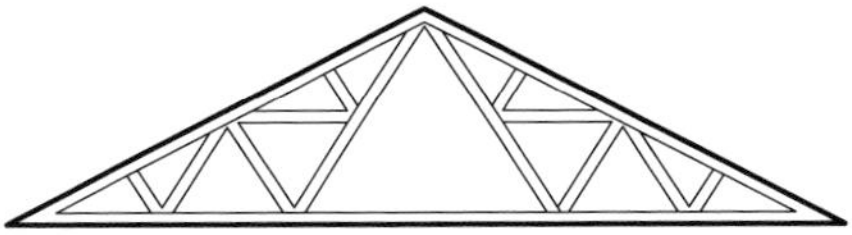
Fink

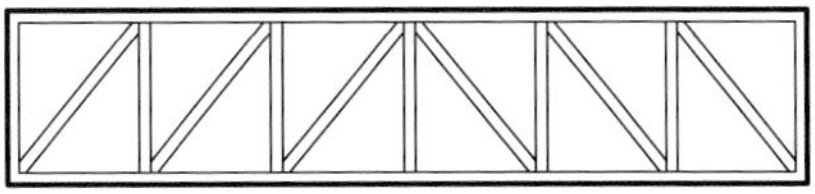
Flat Howe

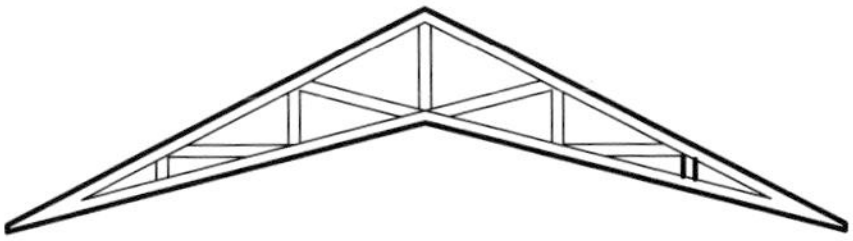
Scissors

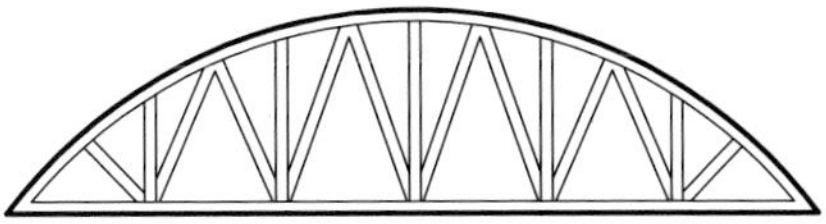
Bowstring

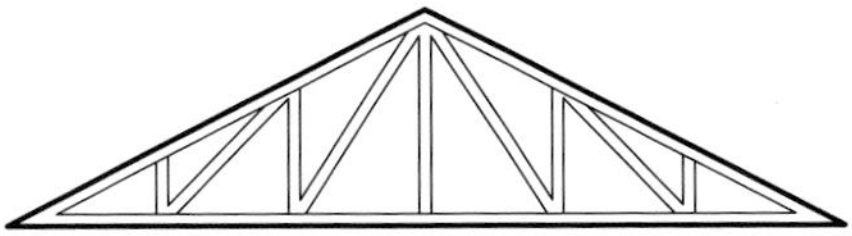
Pitched Pratt

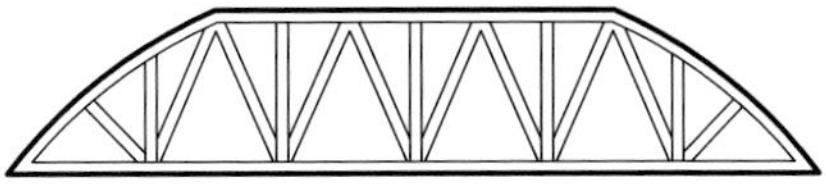
Modified Bowstring

Chapter 7: Mechanical Systems

A building's mechanical systems involve control of heat, ventilation, air-conditioning, refrigeration, plumbing, fire protection, and noise reduction, all of which must be integrated with the architectural, structural, and electrical design.

ENERGY DISTRIBUTION SYSTEMS

All-air Systems: Conditioned air is circulated to and from spaces by central fans that direct it through runs of ductwork.

Air and Water Systems: Conditioned air is ducted to each space, and chilled and heated water are piped to each space to modify the temperature of the air at each outlet.

All-water Systems: No ductwork is used, and air is circulated within each space, not from a central source. Chilled and heated water are furnished to each space. Because water piping is much smaller than ductwork for air, all-water systems are very compact.

Air duct: Pipe that carries warm and cold air to rooms and back to a furnace or air-conditioning system.

ASHRAE: American Society of Heating, Refrigerating, and Air-Conditioning Engineers.

Cavity wall: Hollow wall formed with two layers of masonry, providing an insulating air space between.

Chase wall: Cavity wall containing electrical runs or plumbing pipes in its cavity.

Closed loop: Evaporator side of chiller system, closed to the atmosphere.

Dry bulb: Ambient outside temperature.

Furnace: Device that generates heated air, and is powered by natural gas, fuel oil, or electricity. Most often used in small commercial or residential applications.

Heat pump: A device that warms or cools by transfering thermal energy from a heat source to a heat sink.

HVAC: Heating, ventilating, and air-conditioning.

IAQ: Indoor air quality.

Louver: Opening with horizontal slats that permit passage of air, but not rain, sunlight, or view, into a structure.

Open loop: Condenser/tower side of chiller system; open to the atmosphere.

Plenum: Chamber that serves as a distribution area for heating or cooling systems, usually found between a false ceiling and the actual ceiling.

Radiant heat: Heating system that uses coils of electricity, hot water, or steam pipes embedded in floors, ceilings, or walls to heat rooms.

Shaft: Enclosed vertical space (usually with fire-resistive walls) containing all vertical runs of pipes, ducts, and elevators.

Variable air volume (VAV): Air-handling system that conditions air to a constant temperature and varies airflow to ensure thermal comfort.

Wet bulb: Combination of outside air temperature and relative humidity; higher relative humidity makes it more difficult for a cooling tower to evaporate water into the atmosphere.

HVAC SYSTEMS

The systems for accomplishing heating, ventilation, and air conditioning of indoor spaces vary considerably, based on factors including building type and program, cost, climate, and building size. The basic principals and components of heating, cooling, and circulating are similar across all systems.

Cooling tower: Open recirculating system where heat exchange occurs by evaporation.

Air handling unit (AHU): Equipment including a fan or blower, heating and/or cooling coils, regulator controls, condensate drain pans, and air filters.

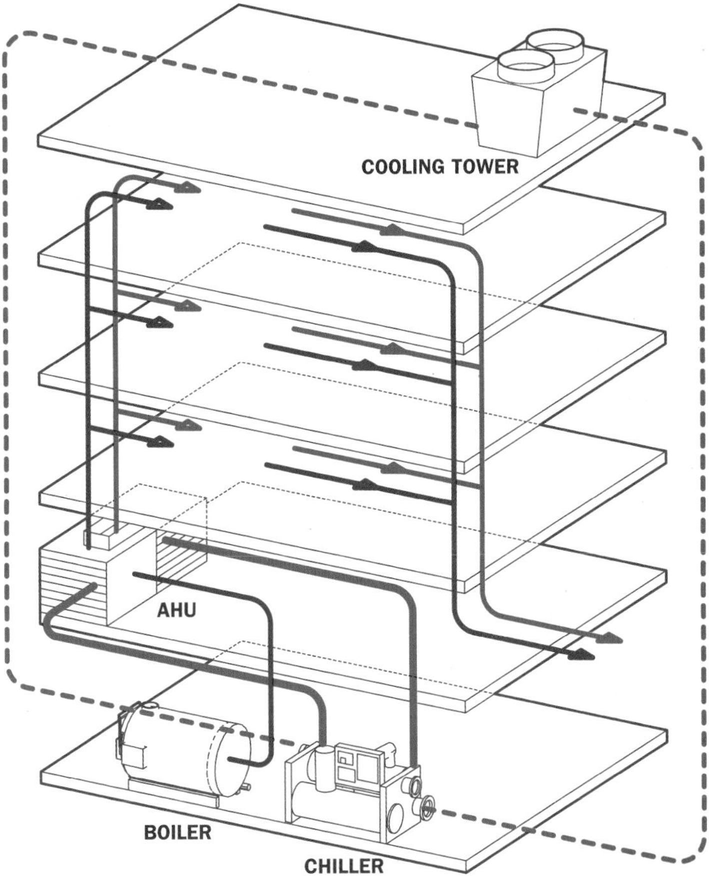

COOLING TOWER
AHU
BOILER
CHILLER

Boiler: Tank where the heat produced from the combustion of fuels (natural gas, fuel oil, wood, or coal) generates hot water or steam for use in heating.

Chiller: Heat exchanger (evaporator, condenser, and compressor system) that uses air, a refrigerant, water, and evaporation to transfer heat and produce air-conditioning.

MECHANICAL DISTRIBUTION TYPES

FAN COIL UNITS

Fan coil units (FCUs) contain cooling or heating coils and a fan. Typically, hot or chilled water is piped to the unit from a central boiler and chiller. Air from the room is drawn into the unit (return air) and blown over the coil by a fan. The air is then heated or cooled and discharged (supply air) to the room. FCUs may be vertical or horizontal, mounted on walls, ceilings, or freestanding.

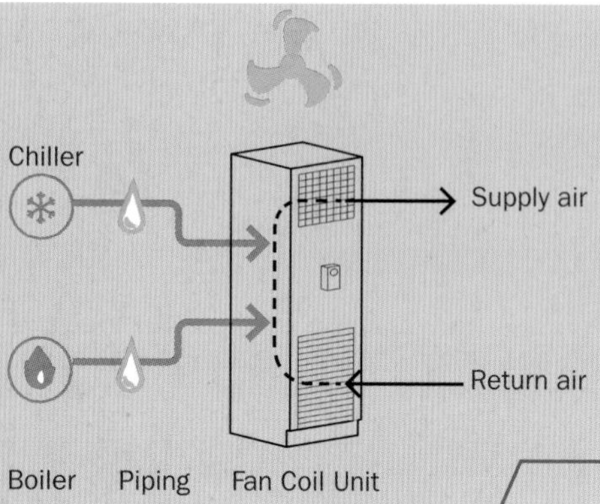
Chiller
Supply air
Return air
Boiler
Piping
Fan Coil Unit

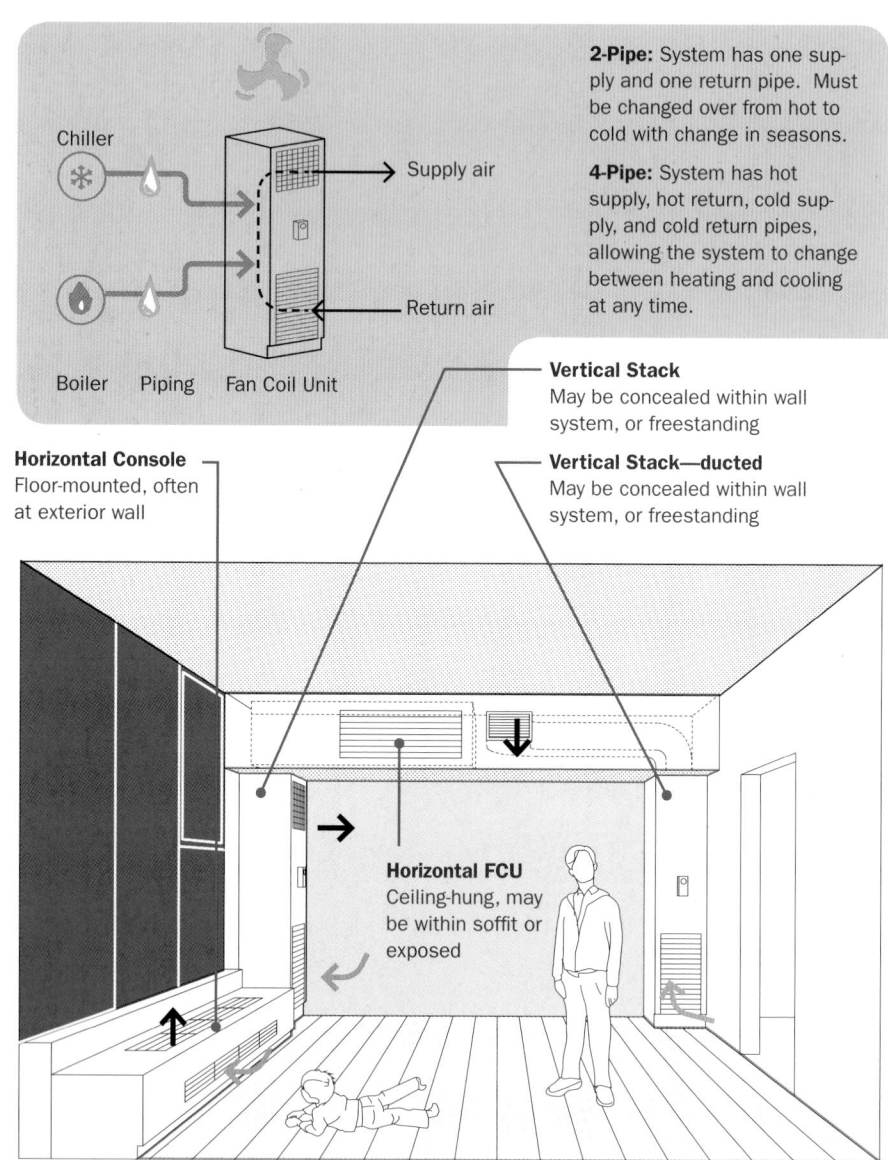

2-Pipe: System has one supply and one return pipe. Must be changed over from hot to cold with change in seasons.

4-Pipe: System has hot supply, hot return, cold supply, and cold return pipes, allowing the system to change between heating and cooling at any time.

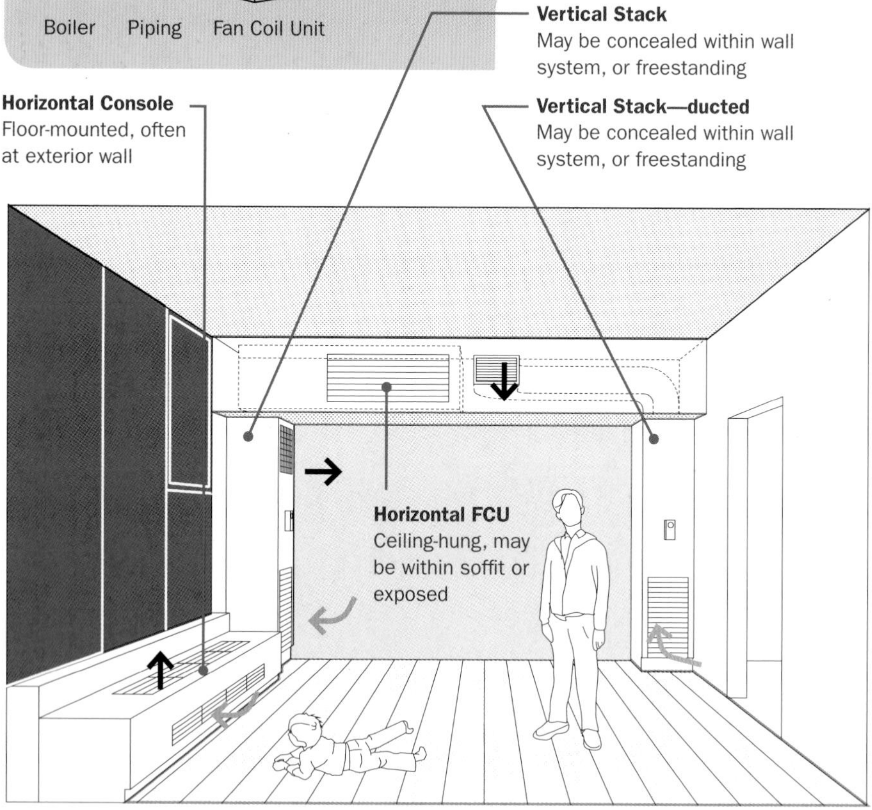
Vertical Stack
May be concealed within wall system, or freestanding
Horizontal Console
Floor-mounted, often at exterior wall
Vertical Stack—ducted
May be concealed within wall system, or freestanding
Horizontal FCU
Ceiling-hung, may be within soffit or exposed

FORCED AIR DUCT SYSTEM
A duct system distributes heated, cooled, and fresh air throughout the building, while also filtering and dehumidifying the air.

HYDRONIC SYSTEMS
Hydronic systems provide heating, but typically not cooling. Hot water is circulated through tubing, from the central heat source to radiators throughout the space to be heated. The radiators may be wall-mounted or floor-mounted. Tubes may also be designed into floor systems, providing consistent radiant heat. Heat sources may include boilers, water heaters, and solar power.

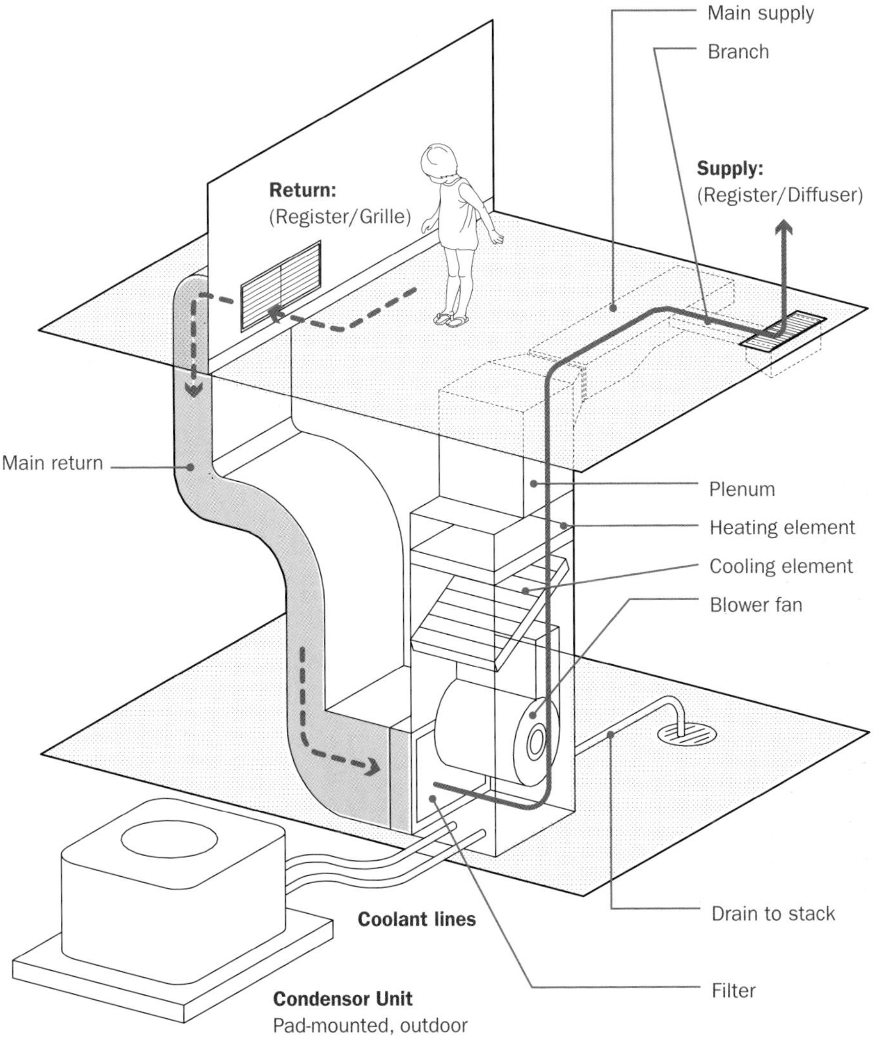
Main supply
Branch
Supply:
(Register/Diffuser)
Return:
(Register/Grille)
Main return
Plenum
Heating element
Cooling element
Blower fan
Coolant lines
Drain to stack
Filter
Condensor Unit
Pad-mounted, outdoor

FORCED AIR FURNACE — Typical residential heating and cooling system

SUSTAINABLE DESIGN

The issue of sustainable design shines a bright light on architecture's need to grow, learn, and adapt to a changing world. By nature, architecture is subject to inertia: buildings take years to design and realize, and architects, engineers, and contractors take years to train. This process once ensured painstaking attention to detail and craftsmanship that resulted in a building that could last forever. Today architecture must too often bend to economic pressures to build quickly and inexpensively. Technological and engineering advances allow for such economy, though often at the risk of producing disposable buildings, ultimately unable to stand the test of time and frequently at odds with the well-being of the environment. Sustainable design proposes using systems that meet present needs without compromising those of future generations. Architects, for their part, are increasingly compelled to understand and implement such new systems and methods as they envision ways in which buildings may work with the environment and the living world. The result is a built world that enhances instead of diminishes its surroundings and resources. Designing sustainably is not just one thing or a static set of rules, but a conscious and informed confluence of many approaches.

KEY TERMS

Adaptive reuse: Changing a building's function in response to the changing needs of its users.

Embodied energy: All of the energy consumed by all of the processes associated with the production of a building, including transportation.

Gray water: Wastewater from baths, showers, washers, and lavatories, which might be appropriate for irrigation or other uses not requiring clean water.

Heat island: Thermal gradient difference between developed and underdeveloped areas.

Passive solar: Technology of heating and cooling a building naturally, through the use of energy-efficient materials and proper site placement.

Renewable: Resource that comes into being through a relatively quick natural process. Bamboo is an excellent example.

Volatile organic compound (VOC): Highly evaporative, carbon-based chemical substance producing noxious fumes and found in many paints, caulks, stains, and adhesives.

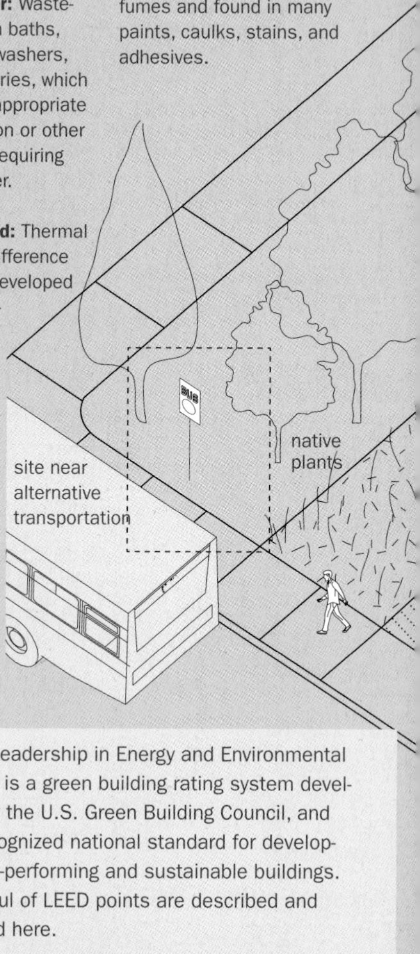
native plants
site near alternative transportation

LEED (Leadership in Energy and Environmental Design) is a green building rating system developed by the U.S. Green Building Council, and is a recognized national standard for developing high-performing and sustainable buildings. A handful of LEED points are described and explored here.

Materials and Resources: Make responsible material choices that privilege salvaged materials and those with recycled content, have low embodied energy, or come from renewable sources.

Indoor Environment: Strive for good ventilation, thermal comfort, use of low-VOC materials that will minimize off-gassing pollutants, and natural daylight and views.

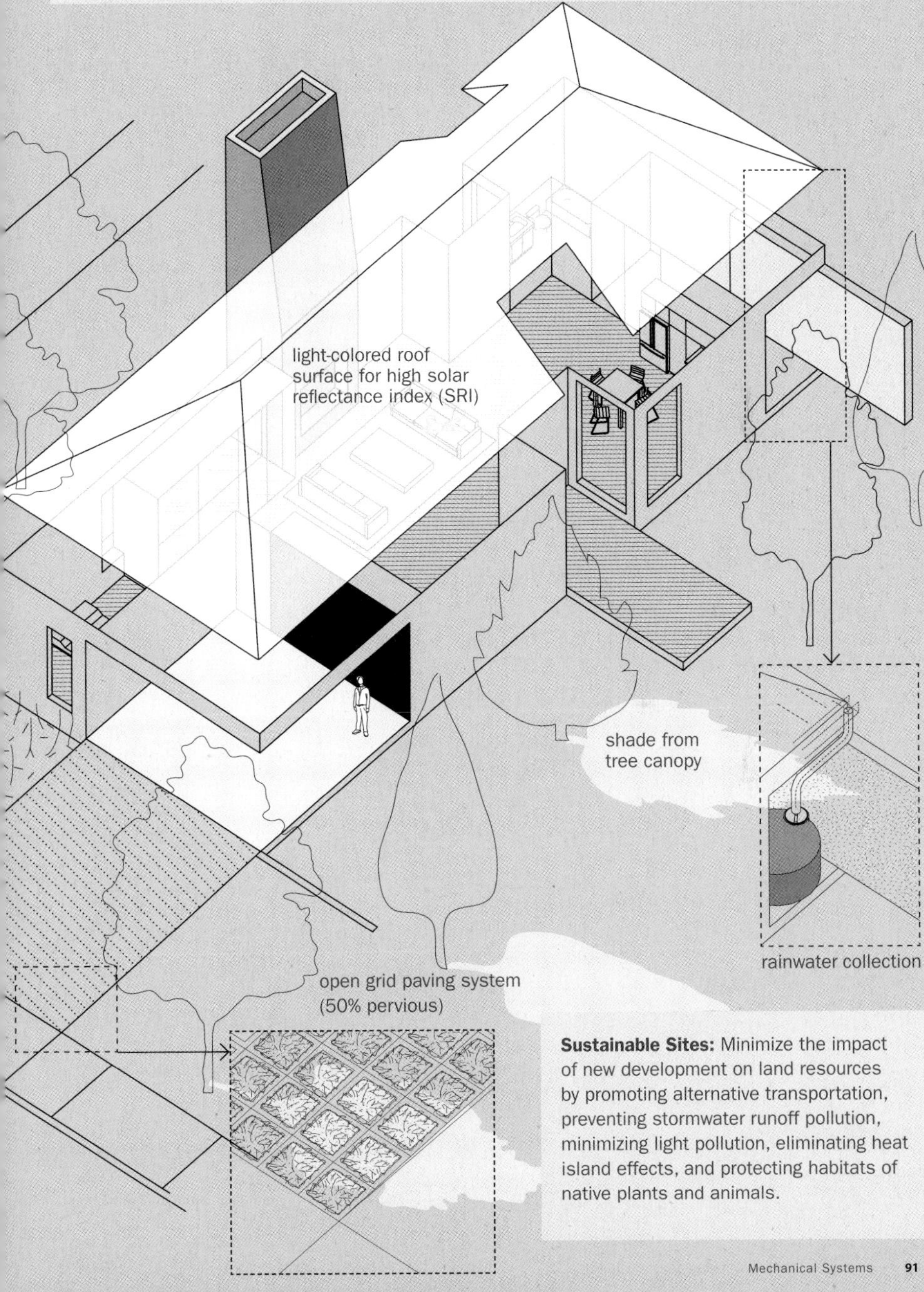
light-colored roof surface for high solar reflectance index (SRI)
shade from tree canopy
rainwater collection
open grid paving system (50% pervious)

Sustainable Sites: Minimize the impact of new development on land resources by promoting alternative transportation, preventing stormwater runoff pollution, minimizing light pollution, eliminating heat island effects, and protecting habitats of native plants and animals.

Chapter 8: Lighting

Lighting has a tremendous effect on the manner in which a space will be experienced and perceived. Architects often work closely with lighting designers, who provide expertise on the technical aspects and effects of lighting and how they can best serve the design and function of a space. Lighting designers provide lighting specifications for the project and coordinate much of their design information with the electrical drawings and reflected ceiling plans.

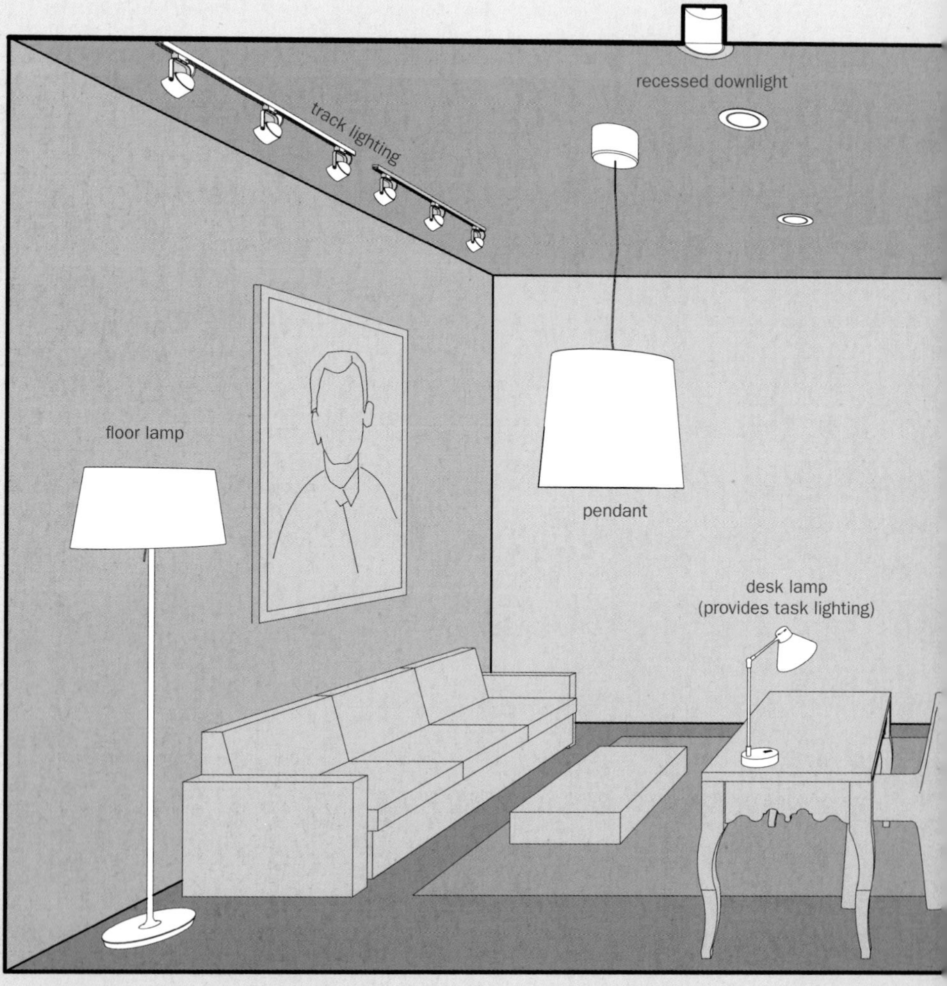
recessed downlight
track lighting
floor lamp
pendant
desk lamp
(provides task lighting)

Ambient lighting: General lighting for an entire space.

Ballast: Device that provides starting voltage for a fluorescent or HID lamp, then limits and regulates the current in the lamp during operation.

Bulb: Decorative glass or plastic housing that diffuses light distribution.

Candela: SI unit of the luminous intensity of a light source in a specific direction. Also called candle.

Candlepower (CP): Measure (in candelas) of the luminous intensity of a light source in a specific direction.

Foot-candle (FC): English unit of measuring the light level on a surface, equal to one lumen per square foot.

IALD: International Association of Lighting Designers.

IESNA: Illuminating Engineering Society of North America.

Optics: Components of a light fixture—reflectors, refractors, lenses, louvers, and so on; or, the light-emitting performance of a luminaire.

Ultraviolet (UV): Invisible radiation of shorter wavelength and higher frequency than visible violet light.

Underwriters' Laboratories (UL): Independent organization that tests the safety of products for public use.

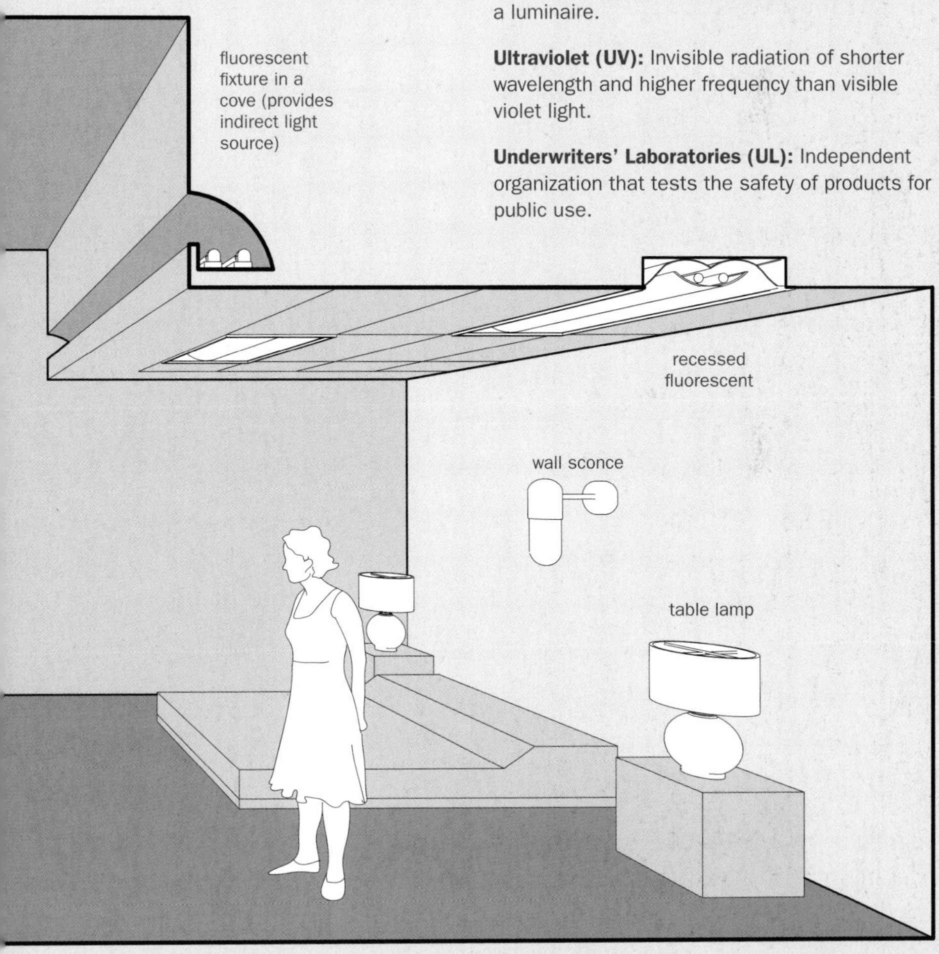
fluorescent fixture in a cove (provides indirect light source)
recessed fluorescent
wall sconce
table lamp

COMMON BULB TYPES

Fluorescent lamps are long, sealed glass tubes, coated inside with a phosphor powder. Fluorescent bulbs contain mercury, which is converted from a liquid to a gas by the energy produced by electrodes at either end.

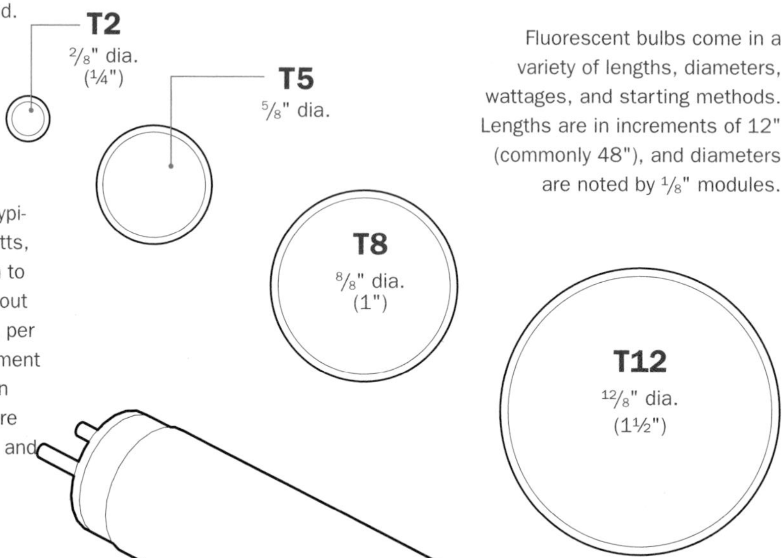
T2
2/8" dia.
(1/4")
T5
5/8" dia.
T8
8/8" dia.
(1")
T12
12/8" dia.
(1½")

Fluorescent bulbs come in a variety of lengths, diameters, wattages, and starting methods. Lengths are in increments of 12" (commonly 48"), and diameters are noted by 1/8" modules.

T12 bulbs, which are typically 40 watts, have begun to be phased out in the U.S., per the Department of Energy, in favor of more efficient T8 and T5 lamps.

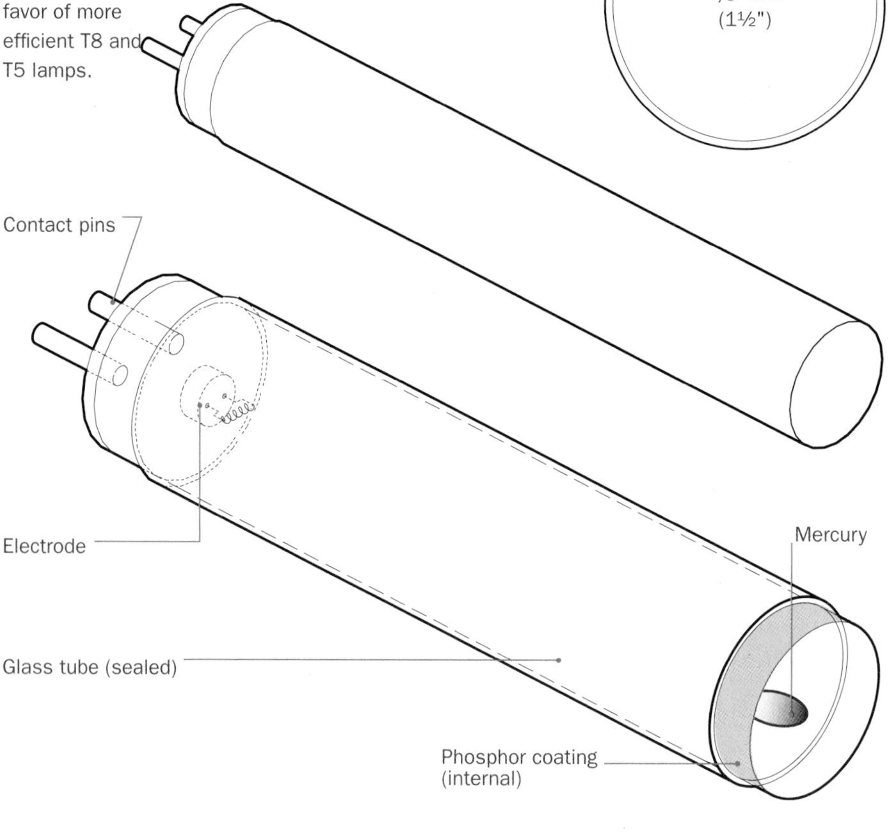
Contact pins
Electrode
Mercury
Glass tube (sealed)
Phosphor coating
(internal)

Bulbs are typically identified by a letter or letters that indicate its type or shape, and a number that indicates the greatest diameter of the bulb in 1/8".

Incandescent

The A-series incandescent light bulb has long been the "classic" multi-purpose bulb type. The most common size is the A19 (2 3/8" dia.)

CFL (Compact Fluorescent Lamp)

CFLs are fluorescent lights designed to replace incandescent bulbs - many screw into the same fixtures, and the fluorescent tube has been folded and curved to fit the same volume as a typical incandescent bulb. CFLs use less power and last longer than incandescent, though their mercury content makes safe disposal difficult.

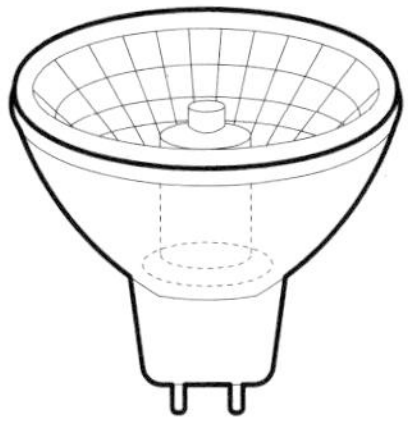

MR (Multi-faceted Reflector)

The inside surface of MR lamps is faceted and covered in a reflective coating. The light is produced by a single-ended quartz halogen filament capsule.

Common sizes are MR16 (2" dia.), MR11 (1 3/8" dia.), and MR8 (1" dia.)

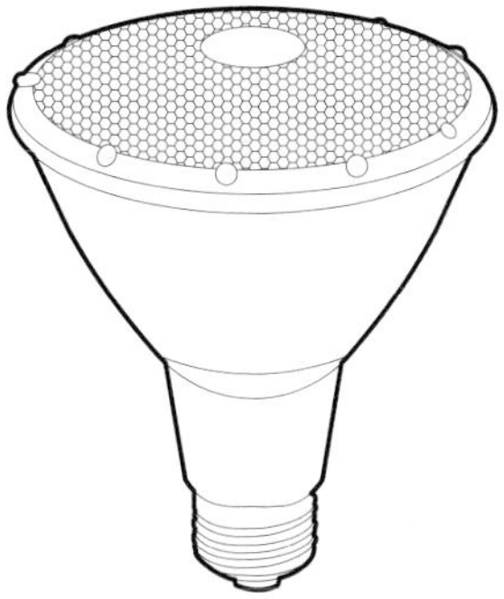

PAR (Parabolic Aluminized Reflector)

PARs contain the light bulb, reflector, and lens within one unit, allowing them to shape and concentrate light for specific tasks and settings. The light is a sealed beam incandescent. Sizes vary, and include PAR 16 (2" dia.), PAR 30 (3¾" dia.), PAR 38 (4¾" dia.), and PAR 64 (8" dia.)

Chapter 9: Plumbing

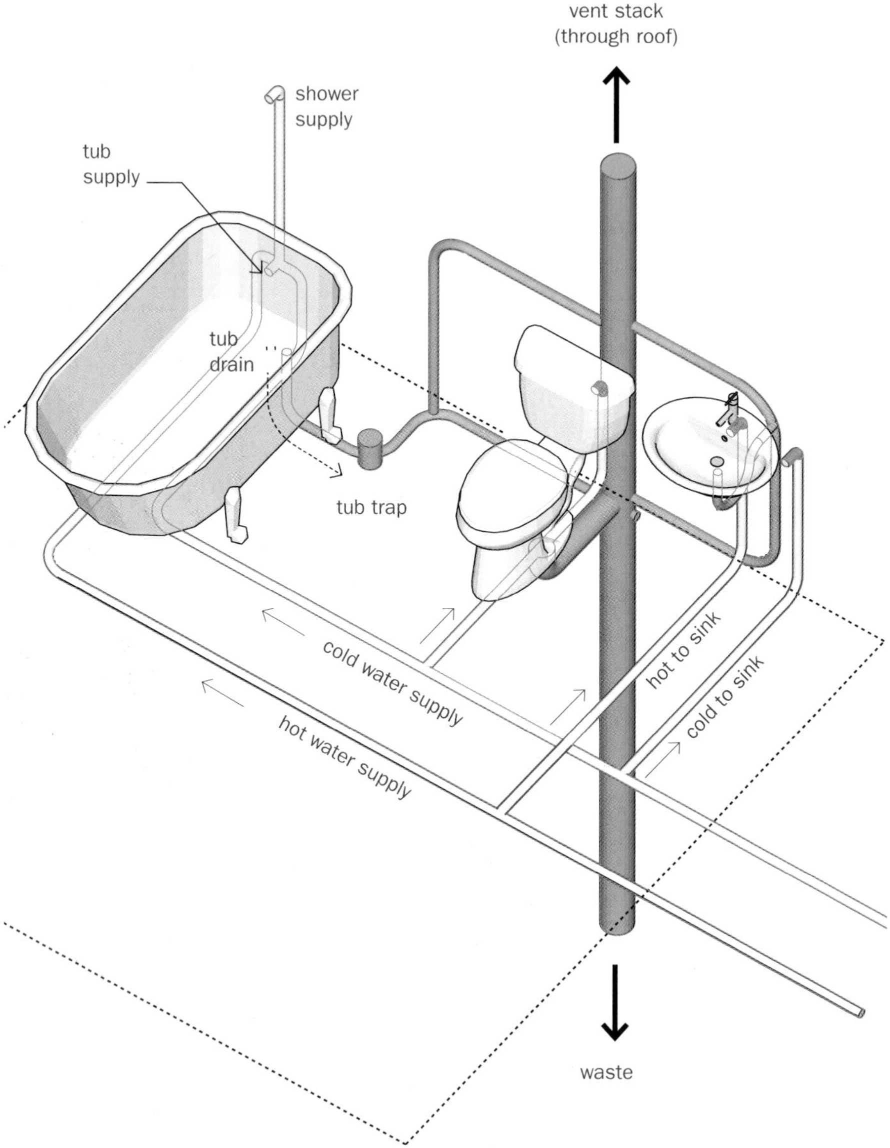
vent stack
(through roof)
shower
supply
tub
supply
tub
drain
tub trap
cold water supply
hot water supply
hot to sink
cold to sink
waste

Common Bathroom Pipe Layout

PIPES

SUPPLY

Water Supply:
white plastic (PVC)
½"–1" dia.

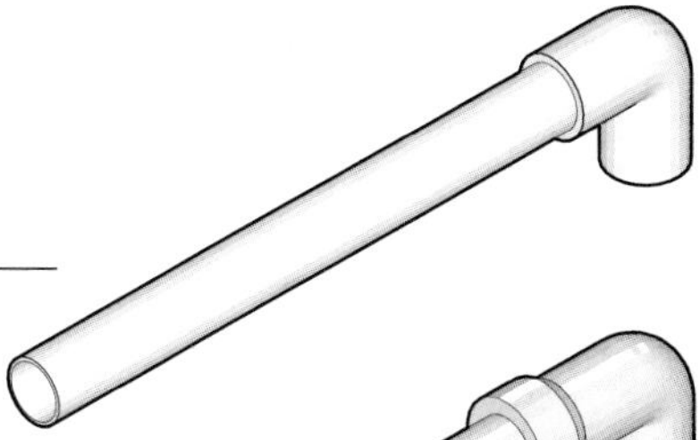

Water or Gas Supply:
copper
½"–1" dia.

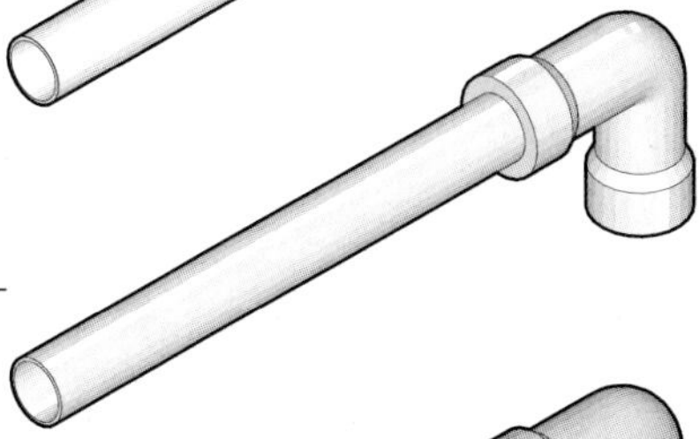

Water Supply:
galvanized iron
½"–1" dia.

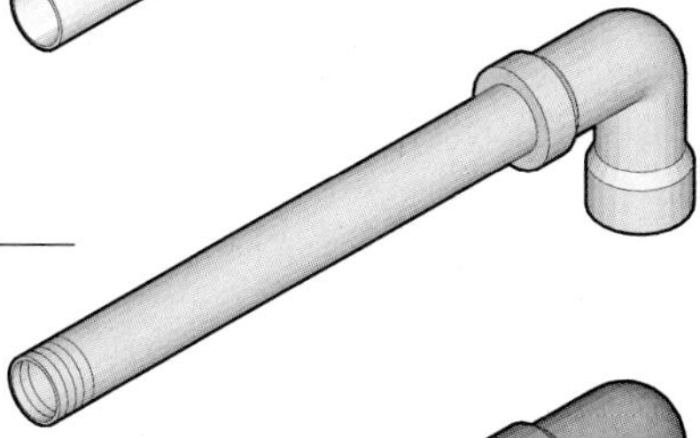

Gas Supply:
black iron
½"–1" dia.

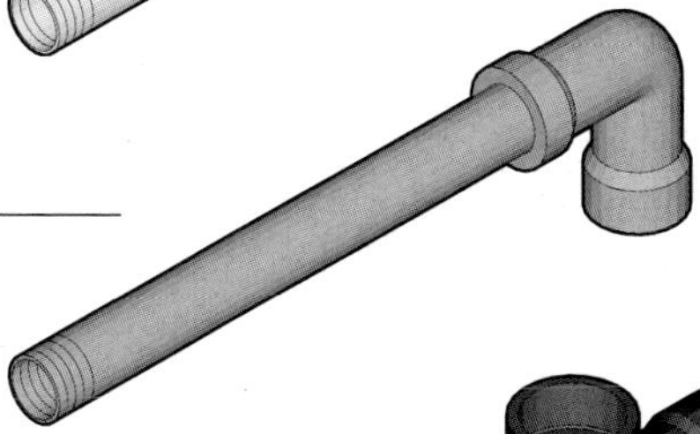

DRAIN

Drain and Vent:
black plastic
1½" + dia.

Drain and Vent:
cast iron
1½" + dia.

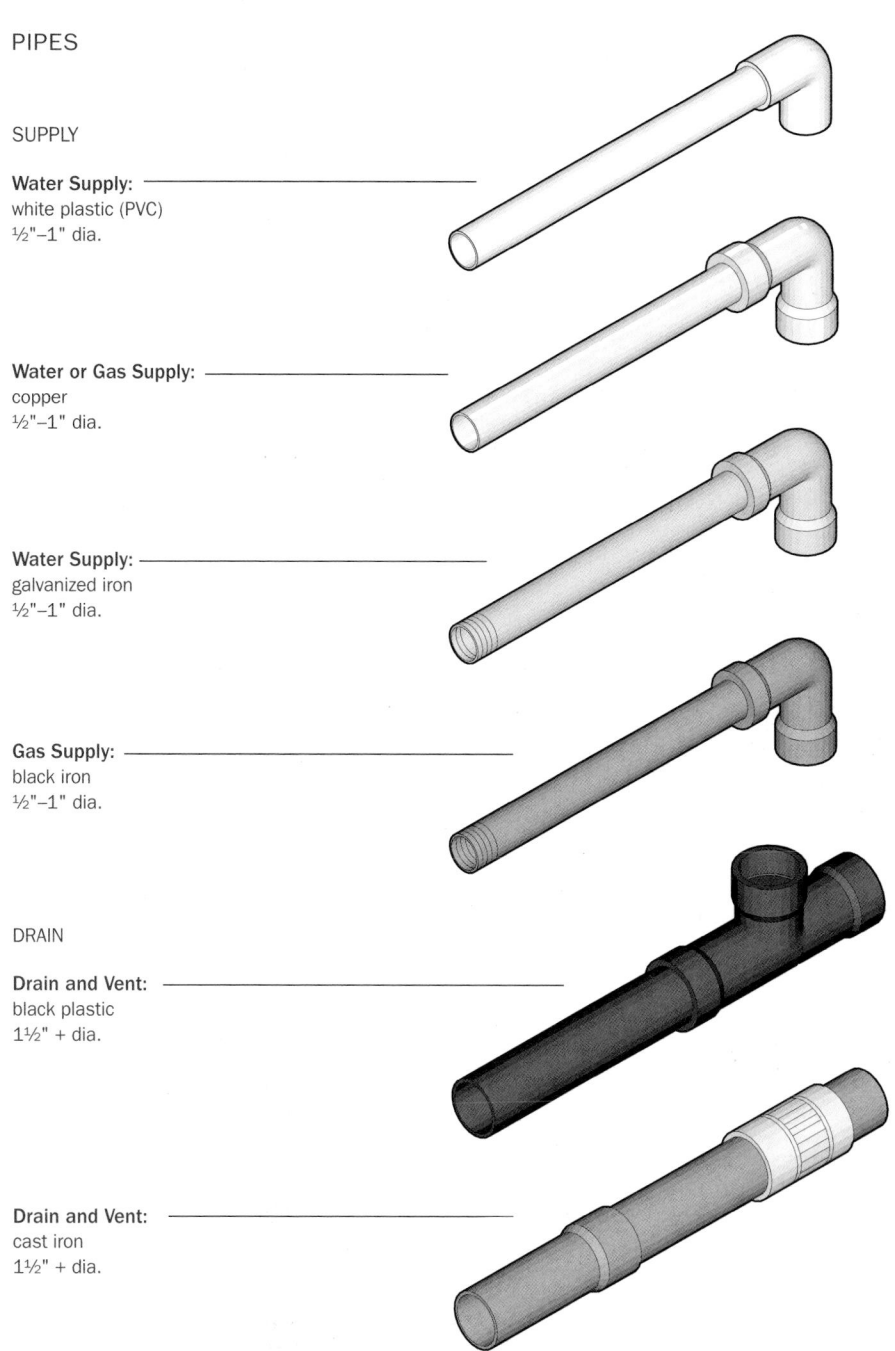

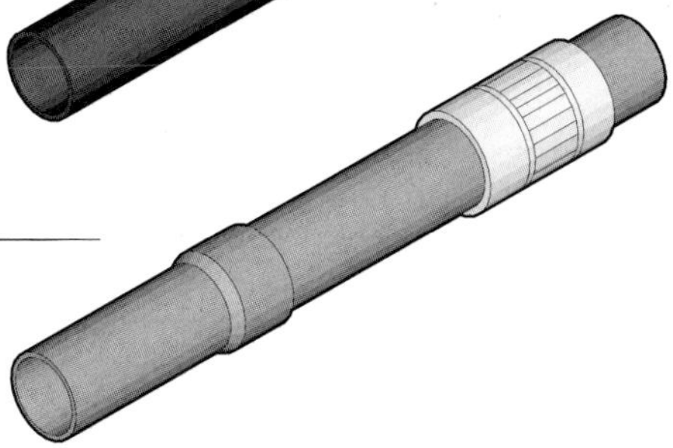

MEASURE AND DRAWING 3.

For an architect's ideas to evolve into fully considered designs, they require constant evaluation, investigation, and experimentation. Scribbled notes and sketches are quickly put to the test as real scales and measures are applied; flat plans grow into volumes, and spaces are examined inside and out. To become built form, ideas must be communicated to the various groups involved in the design process, and so the architect embarks on a cycle of production and presentation.

For presentation to the client whose building this will become, communication can take the form of sketches, cardboard models, computer models, and digital animations—whatever is needed to ensure that the design is understood. In preparing such materials, the architect often discovers new aspects of the design that prompt further study and presentation.

For construction, the architect prepares documents to certain standards. Technical measured drawings describe everything necessary to erect the building. Depending on the size of the project, many other parties will also be involved, from structural and mechanical engineers to electrical engineers and lighting designers. Each of these trades also produces construction documents specific to their work and coordinated with the entire set. In every case, these drawings and written specifications must be clear and precise to ensure a well-built structure.

Chapter 10: Measurement and Geometry

The two primary measurement systems used in the world today are the metric system, also known as the Système International d'Unités and commonly abbreviated to SI in all languages, and the U.S. customary units system, referred to in the United States as English units or standard units. The latter is an irregular system based on imperial units once used in the United Kingdom and the British Commonwealth.

The metric system has become the universally accepted system of units in science, trade, and commerce. In the United States, however, where the Metric Conversion Act of 1975 established SI as the preferred system of weights and measures for trade and commerce, federal laws have yet to mandate SI as the official system, making its use still primarily voluntary. Several U.S. agencies, including the American National Metric Council (ANMC) and the United States Metric Association (USMA), are working to establish SI as the official measurement system, a process known as metrication. Though the architectural, engineering, and building trades have been slow to make a full transition, nearly all federally funded building projects are now required to be in SI units.

UNITS OF MEASURE: CUSTOMARY UNIT DATA

Customary units may be shown in a number of ways, including as fractions (1 1/2") or as decimals (1.5" or 0.125'), depending on the more common usage for a particular situation. It should be noted that, though not the case here, exponents can be used with abbreviations that designate area or volume—for example, 100 $ft.^2$ for area or 100 $ft.^3$ for volume.

Linear Equivalents

Customary Unit of Measure	Relation to Other Customary Units
inch (in. or ")	1/12 ft.
foot (ft. or ')	12 in. 1/3 yd.
yard (yd.)	36 in. 3 ft.
rod (rd.), pole, or perch	16 1/2 ft. 5 1/2 yd.
chain	4 rd. 22 yd.
furlong	220 yd. *or* 40 rd. *or* 10 chains *or* 1/8 mi.
mile (mi.), statute	5,280 ft. *or* 1,760 yd. *or* 8 furlongs
mile (mi.), nautical	2,025 yd.

Area Equivalents

Customary Unit of Measure	Relation to Other Customary Units
square inch (sq. in.)	0.007 (1/142) sq. ft.
square foot (sq. ft.)	144 sq. in.
square yard (sq. yd.)	1,296 sq. in. 9 sq. ft.
square pole	30 1/4 sq. yd.
acre	43,560 sq. ft. 40 rd. (1 furlong) × 4 rd. (1 chain)
square mile (sq. mi.)	640 acres

Fraction to Decimal Equivalents

Fraction	Decimal
1/32	0.03125
1/16	0.0625
3/32	0.0938
1/8	0.1250
5/32	0.1563
3/16	0.1875
7/32	0.2188
1/4	0.2500
9/32	0.2813
5/16	0.3125
11/32	0.3438
3/8	0.3750
13/32	0.4063
7/16	0.4375
15/32	0.4688
1/2	0.5000
17/32	0.5313
9/16	0.5625
19/32	0.5938
5/8	0.6250
21/32	0.6563
11/16	0.6875
23/32	0.7188
3/4	0.7500
25/32	0.7813
13/16	0.8125
27/32	0.8438
7/8	0.8750
29/32	0.9063
15/16	0.9375
31/32	0.9688
1/1	1.0000

METRIC CONVERSION

Conversion Factors for Length

Customary	Metric
1 in.	25.4 mm
1 ft.	0.304 8 m *or* 304.8 mm
1 yd.	0.914 4 m
1 mi.	1.609 344 km

Customary	Metric
1 sq. in.	645.16 mm^2
1 sq. ft.	0.092 903 m^2
1 sq. yd.	0.836 127 m^2
1 acre	0.404 686 ha *or* 4 046.86 m^2
1 sq. mi.	2.590 00 km^2

Conversion Factors for Length

Metric	Customary
1 micrometer (μm)	0.0000394 in. *or* 0.03937 mils
1 mm	0.0393701 in.
1 m	3.28084 ft. *or* 1.09361 yd.
1 km	0.621371 mi.

Conversion Factors for Area

Metric	Customary
1 mm^2	0.001550 sq. in.
1 m^2	10.7639 sq. ft. *or* 1.19599 sq. yd.
1 ha	2.47105 acres
1 km^2	0.368102 sq. mi.

UNITS OF MEASURE: SI METRIC UNIT DATA

The General Conference on Weights and Measures (abbreviated to CGPM from the French Conférence Générale des Poids et Mesures), which meets every four years concerning issues related to the use of the metric system, has established specific rules for use, type style, and punctuation of metric units. The National Institute of Standards and Technology (NIST)—formerly the National Bureau of Standards (NBS)—determines metric usage in the United States. Millimeters are the preferred unit for dimensioning buildings, with no symbol necessary if they are used consistently. Meters and kilometers are reserved for larger dimensions such as land surveying and transportation.

Unit names and symbols employ standard, lowercase type, except for symbols derived from proper names (for example, N for newton). Another exception is L for liter, to avoid confusing the lowercase l with the numeral 1. Prefixes describing multiples and submultiples are also lowercase, except for M, G, and T (mega-, giga-, and tera-), which are capitalized in symbol form to avoid confusion with unit symbols, but which maintain the lowercase standard when spelled out. No space is left between the prefix and the letter for the unit name (mm for millimeter and mL for milliliter). A space is left between the numeral and the unit name or symbol—for example, 300 mm.

Linear Metric Equivalents

Millimeters (mm)	Centimeters (cm)	Decimeters (dm)	Meters (m)	Decameters (dam)	Hectometers (hm)	Kilometers (km)
1	0.1	0.01	0.001	0.000 1	0.000 01	0.000 001
10	1	0.1	0.01	0.001	0.000 1	0.000 01
100	10	1	0.1	0.01	0.001	0.000 1
1 000	100	10	1	0.1	0.01	0.001
10 000	1 000	100	10	1	0.1	0.01
100 000	10 000	1 000	100	10	1	0.1
1 000 000	100 000	10 000	1 000	100	10	1

Area Metric Equivalents

Square Millimeters (mm^2)	Square Centimeters (cm^2)	Square Decimeters (dm^2)	Square Meters (m^2)	Ares	Hectares (ha)	Square Kilometers (km^2)
1	0.01	0.001	0.000 001			
100	1	0.01	0.000 1	0.000 001		
10 000	100	1	0.01	0.000 1	0.000 001	
1 000 000	10 000	100	1	0.01	0.000 1	0.000 001
	1 000 000	10 000	100	1	0.01	0.000 1
		1 000 000	10 000	100	1	0.01
			1 000 000	10 000	100	1

Although the United States and Canada mark the decimal with a point, other countries use a comma (for example: 5,00 vs. 5.00). For this reason, commas should not be used to separate groups of digits. Instead, the digits should be separated into groups of three, both to the left and the right of the decimal point, with a space between each group of three digits (for example, 1,000,000 is written as 1 000 000). This convention for metric units is used throughout the book.

Units with Compound Names

Physical Quantity	Unit	Symbol
Area	square meter	m^2
Volume	cubic meter	m^3
Density	kilogram per cubic meter	kg/m^3
Velocity	meter per second	m/s
Angular velocity	radian per second	rad/s
Acceleration	meter per second squared	m/s^2
Angular acceleration	radian per second squared	rad/s^2
Volume rate of flow	cubic meter per second	m^3/s
Moment of inertia	kilogram meter squared	$kg\ m^2$
Moment of force	newton meter	N m
Intensity of heat flow	watt per square meter	W/m^2
Thermal conductivity	watt per meter kelvin	W/m K
Luminance	candela per square meter	cd/m^2

Area in Metrics

SI metric units for area, like volume, are derived from the base units for length. They are expressed as powers of the base unit: for example, square meter $= m^2 = 10^6\ mm^2$.

The square centimeter is not a recommended unit for construction and should be converted to square millimeters.

The hectare is acceptable only in the measurement of land and water.

When area is expressed by linear dimensions, such as 50 × 100 mm, the width is written first and the depth or height second.

SOFT AND HARD CONVERSIONS

Conversions of customary and SI units can be either "soft" or "hard." In a soft conversion, 12 inches equals 305 millimeters (already rounded up from 304.8). In a hard conversion of this same number, 12 inches would equal 300 millimeters, which makes for a cleaner and more rational equivalency. This is the ultimate goal of total metrication within the building trades. The process, however, is an extensive one, which will require many building products whose planning grid is in customary units to undergo a hard metric conversion of their own, making 6 inches equal 150 millimeters (instead of 152) and 24 inches equal 600 millimeters (instead of 610). Thus, to conform to a rational metric grid, the actual sizes of standard products such as drywall, bricks, and ceiling tiles will need to change.

Every attempt has been made in this book to represent accurately the relationship between customary and SI units. Except where noted, soft conversions are used throughout and, due to constraints of space, are usually written as follows: 1'-6" (457).

METRIC CONVERSION

Inches and Millimeters Scale

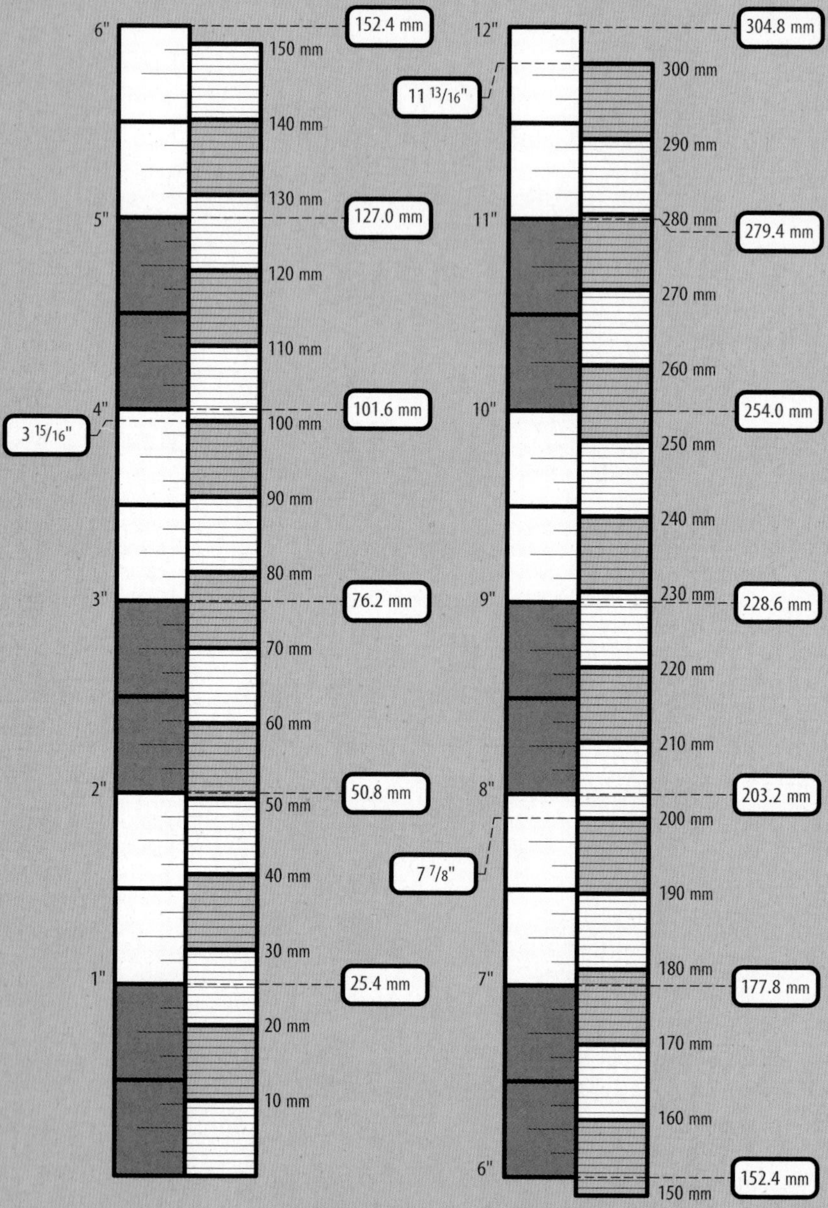
6"
152.4 mm
150 mm
140 mm
130 mm
5"
127.0 mm
120 mm
110 mm
4"
3 15/16"
101.6 mm
100 mm
90 mm
80 mm
3"
76.2 mm
70 mm
60 mm
2"
50.8 mm
50 mm
40 mm
30 mm
1"
25.4 mm
20 mm
10 mm
12"
304.8 mm
11 13/16"
300 mm
290 mm
11"
280 mm
279.4 mm
270 mm
260 mm
10"
254.0 mm
250 mm
240 mm
9"
230 mm
228.6 mm
220 mm
210 mm
8"
203.2 mm
200 mm
7 7/8"
190 mm
180 mm
7"
177.8 mm
170 mm
160 mm
6"
152.4 mm
150 mm

Feet and Meters Scale

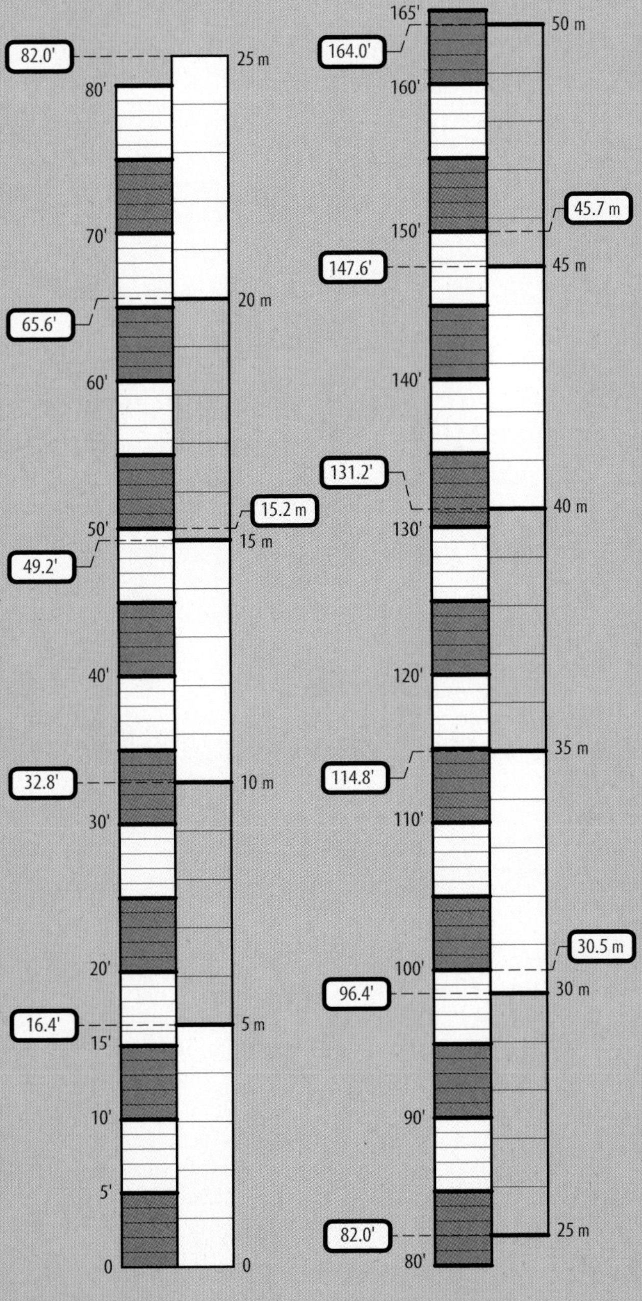

82.0'
25 m
80'
70'
65.6'
20 m
60'
15.2 m
50'
49.2'
15 m
40'
32.8'
10 m
30'
20'
16.4'
5 m
15'
10'
5'
0
0
165'
164.0'
50 m
160'
45.7 m
150'
147.6'
45 m
140'
131.2'
40 m
130'
120'
35 m
114.8'
110'
30.5 m
100'
96.4'
30 m
90'
82.0'
25 m
80'

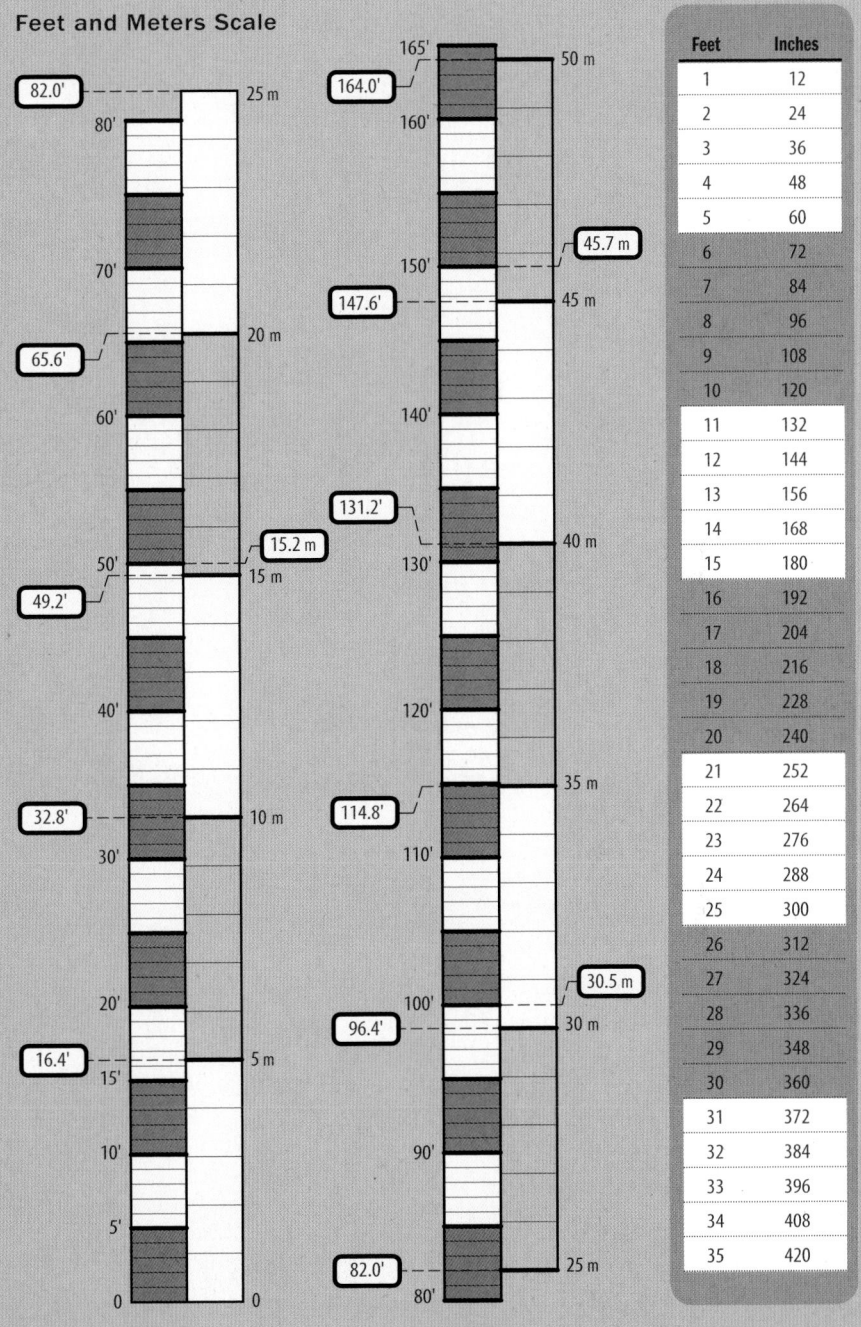

Feet	Inches
1	12
2	24
3	36
4	48
5	60
6	72
7	84
8	96
9	108
10	120
11	132
12	144
13	156
14	168
15	180
16	192
17	204
18	216
19	228
20	240
21	252
22	264
23	276
24	288
25	300
26	312
27	324
28	336
29	348
30	360
31	372
32	384
33	396
34	408
35	420

SLOPES AND PERCENTAGE GRADE

Note: Entries in blue indicate frequently used slopes. Slopes gentler than 1:20 do not require handrails; 1:12 is the maximum ADA-approved slope for ramps and 1:8 is the maximum code-approved slope for ramps (non-ADA).

Degrees	Gradient	% Grade	Degrees	Gradient	% Grade	Degrees	Gradient	% Grade
0.1	1:573.0	0.2	23.0	1:2.4	42.4	57.0	1:0.6	154.0
0.2	1:286.5	0.3	24.0	1:2.2	44.5	58.0	1:0.6	160.0
0.3	1:191.0	0.5	25.0	1:2.1	46.6	59.0	1:0.6	166.4
0.4	1:143.2	0.7	26.0	1:2.1	48.8	60.0	1:0.6	173.2
0.5	1:114.6	0.9	27.0	1:2.0	51.0	61.0	1:0.6	180.4
0.6	1:95.5	1.0	28.0	1:1.9	53.2	62.0	1:0.5	188.1
0.7	1:81.8	1.2	29.0	1:1.8	55.4	63.0	1:0.5	196.2
0.8	1:71.6	1.4	30.0	1:1.7	57.7	64.0	1:0.5	205.0
0.9	1:63.7	1.6	31.0	1:1.7	60.1	65.0	1:0.5	214.5
1.0	1:57.3	1.7	32.0	1:1.6	62.5	66.0	1:0.4	224.6
2.0	1:28.6	3.5	33.0	1:1.5	64.9	67.0	1:0.4	235.6
2.86	1:20.0	5.0	34.0	1:1.5	67.5	68.0	1:0.4	247.5
3.0	1:19.1	5.2	35.0	1:1.4	70.0	69.0	1:0.4	260.5
4.0	1:14.3	7.0	36.0	1:1.4	72.7	70.0	1:0.4	274.7
4.76	1:12.0	8.3	37.0	1:1.3	75.4	71.0	1:0.3	290.4
5.0	1:11.4	8.7	38.0	1:1.3	78.1	72.0	1:0.3	307.8
6.0	1:9.5	10.5	39.0	1:1.2	81.0	73.0	1:0.3	327.1
7.0	1:8.1	12.3	40.0	1:1.2	83.9	74.0	1:0.3	348.7
7.13	1:8.0	12.5	41.0	1:1.2	86.9	75.0	1:0.3	373.2
8.0	1:7.1	14.1	42.0	1:1.1	90.0	76.0	1:0.2	401.1
9.0	1:6.3	15.8	43.0	1:1.1	93.3	77.0	1:0.2	433.1
10.0	1:5.7	17.6	44.0	1:1.0	96.6	78.0	1:0.2	470.5
11.0	1:5.1	19.4	45.0	1:1.0	100.0	79.0	1:0.2	514.5
12.0	1:4.7	21.3	46.0	1:1.0	103.6	80.0	1:0.2	567.1
13.0	1:4.3	23.1	47.0	1:0.9	107.2	81.0	1:0.2	631.4
14.0	1:4.0	24.9	48.0	1:0.9	111.1	82.0	1:0.1	711.5
15.0	1:3.7	26.8	49.0	1:0.9	115.0	83.0	1:0.1	814.4
16.0	1:3.5	28.7	50.0	1:0.8	119.2	84.0	1:0.1	951.4
17.0	1:3.3	30.6	51.0	1:0.8	123.5	85.0	1:0.1	1,143.0
18.0	1:3.1	32.5	52.0	1:0.8	128.0	86.0	1:0.1	1,430.1
19.0	1:2.9	34.4	53.0	1:0.8	132.7	87.0	1:0.1	1,908.1
20.0	1:2.7	36.4	54.0	1:0.7	137.6	88.0	1:0.0	2,863.6
21.0	1:2.6	38.4	55.0	1:0.7	142.8	89.0	1:0.0	5,729.0
22.0	1:2.5	40.4	56.0	1:0.7	148.3	90.0	1:0.0	∞

Calculating Slope Degrees:

$$\text{Slope} = \frac{\text{Vertical Rise Distance (V)}}{\text{Horizontal Distance (H)}} = \text{tangent m}$$

Slope Angle = tangent m

Calculating Gradient:

$$= 1 \text{ unit in } \frac{\text{Horizontal Distance (H)}}{\text{Vertical Distance (V)}}$$

Calculating % Grade:

= 100 × Tangent (Slope) or 100 × V/H

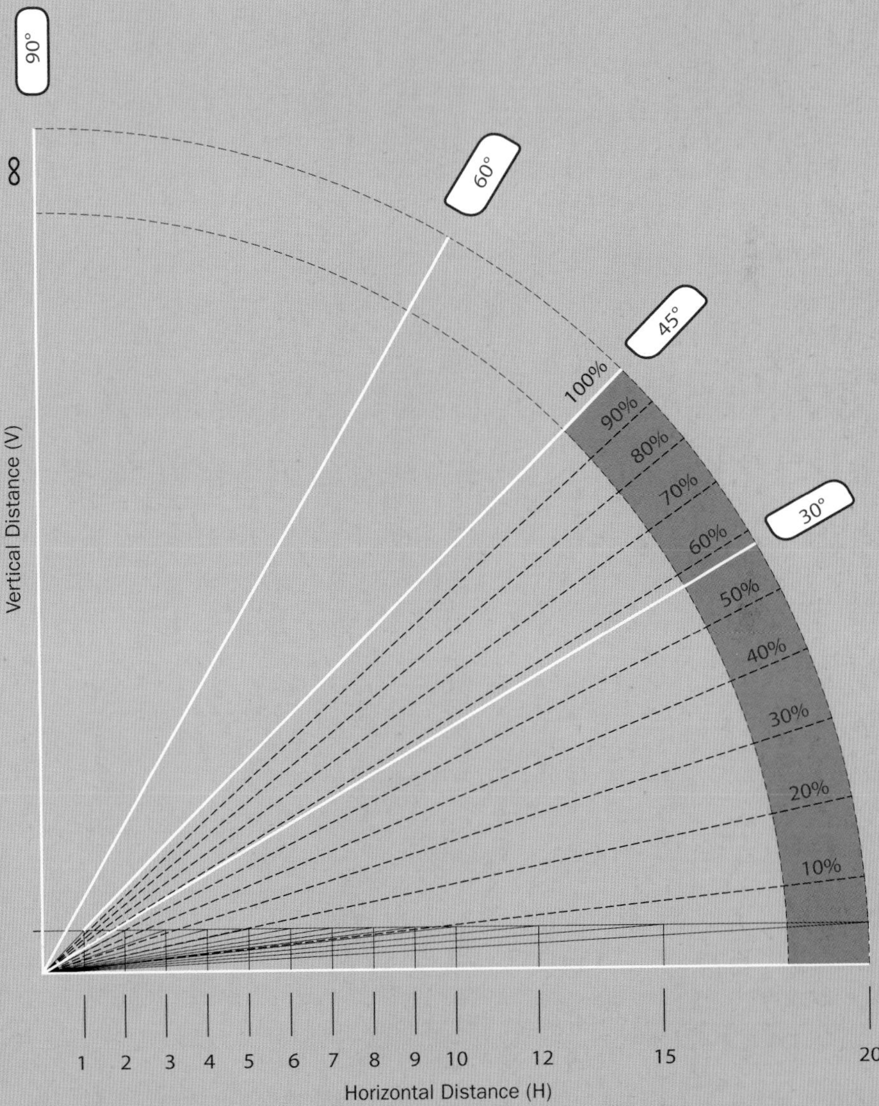

90°
∞
60°
45°
30°
100%
90%
80%
70%
60%
50%
40%
30%
20%
10%
Vertical Distance (V)
1
2
3
4
5
6
7
8
9
10
12
15
20
Horizontal Distance (H)

PLANE FIGURE FORMULAS

Rectangle

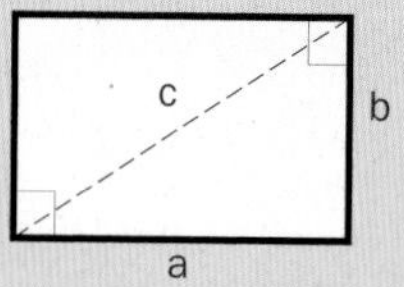
c
b
a

area = ab

perimeter = $2(a+b)$

$a^2 + b^2 = c^2$

Equilateral Triangle

(all sides equal)

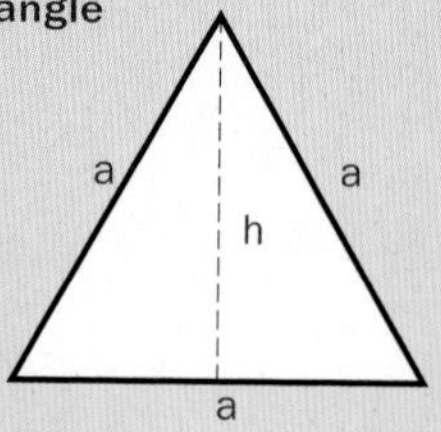
a
a
h
a

area = $a^2\frac{\sqrt{3}}{4} = 0.433\ a^2$

perimeter = $3a$

$h = \frac{a}{2}\sqrt{3} = 0.866a$

Parallelogram

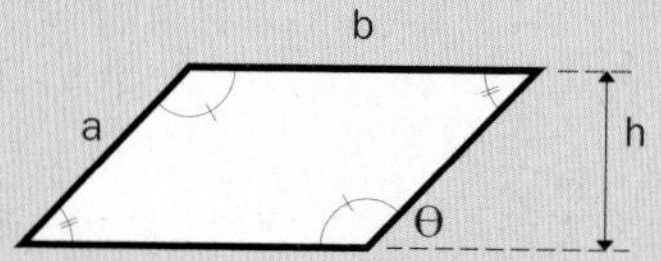
b
a
h
Θ

area = $ah = ab\ \sin\Theta$

perimeter = $2(a+b)$

Triangle

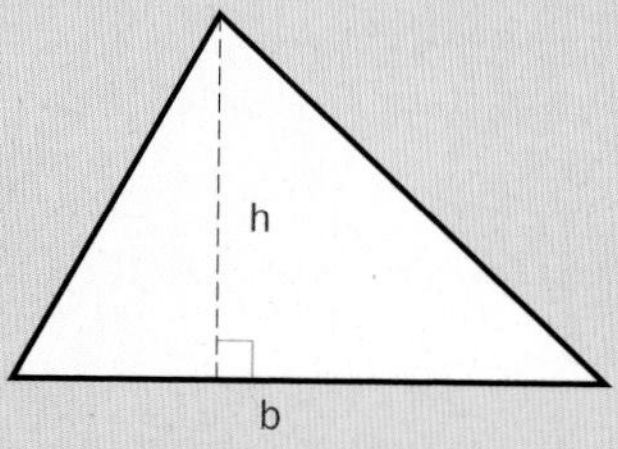
h
b

area = $\frac{bh}{2}$

perimeter = sum of length of all sides

Trapezoid

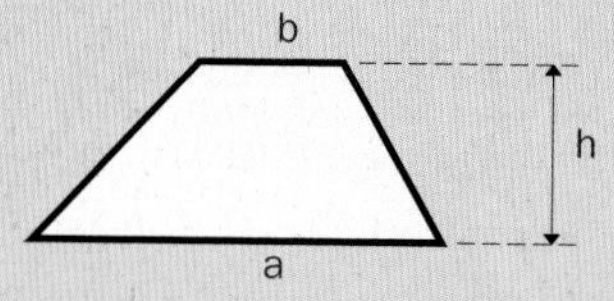
b
h
a

area = $\frac{(a+b)}{2}h$

perimeter = sum of length of sides

Trapezium

(irregular quadrilateral)

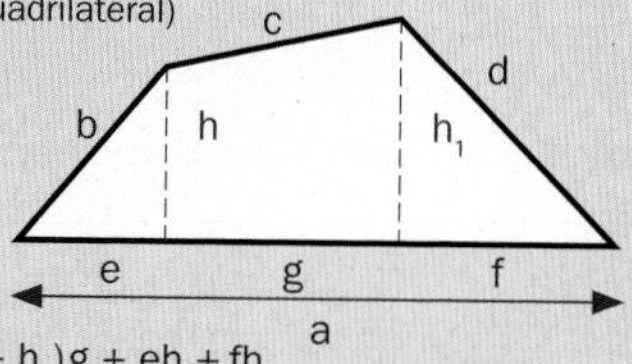
c
d
b
h
h1
e
g
f
a

area = $\frac{(h + h_1)g + eh + fh_1}{2}$

perimeter = sum of length of all sides

or

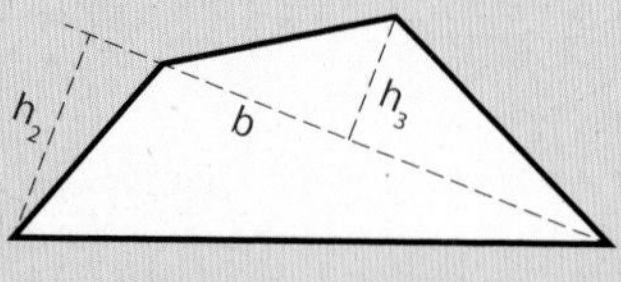
h2
b
h3

area = $\frac{bh_2}{2} + \frac{bh_3}{2}$

(Divide figure into two triangles and add their areas together.)

Quadrilateral

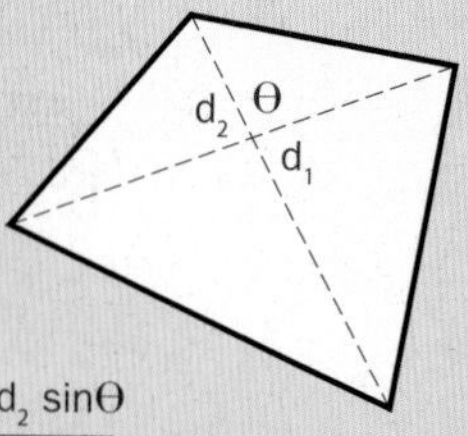
d2
Θ
d1

area = $\frac{d_1 d_2\ \sin\Theta}{2}$

Regular Polygons

(all sides equal)

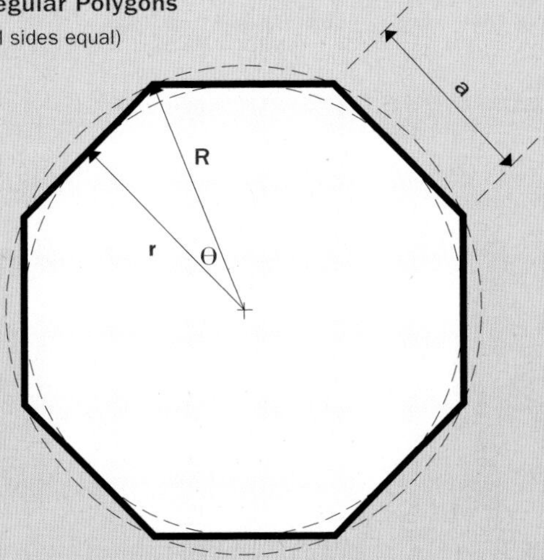
a
R
r
Θ

n = number of sides

$$\text{area} = \frac{nar}{2} = nr^2$$

$$\tan \Theta = \frac{nR^2}{2} \sin 2\Theta$$

perimeter = n a

Polygon	Sides	Area
Triangle (equilateral)	3	0.4330 a^2
Square	4	1.0000 a^2
Pentagon	5	1.7205 a^2
Hexagon	6	2.5981 a^2
Heptagon	7	3.6339 a^2
Octagon	8	4.8284 a^2
Nonagon	9	6.1818 a^2
Decagon	10	7.6942 a^2
Undecagon	11	9.3656 a^2
Dodecagon	12	11.1962 a^2

VOLUMES

Prism or Cylinder (right or oblique, regular or irregular)

volume = area of base × altitude

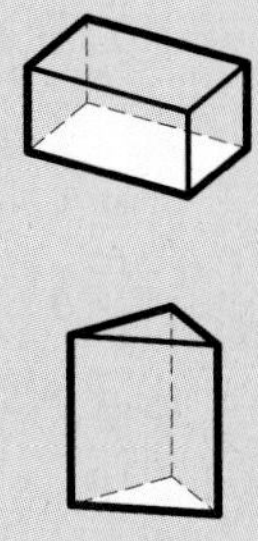

Altitude (h) = distance between parallel bases, measured perpendicular to the bases. When bases are not parallel, then altitude = perpendicular distance from one base to the center of the other.

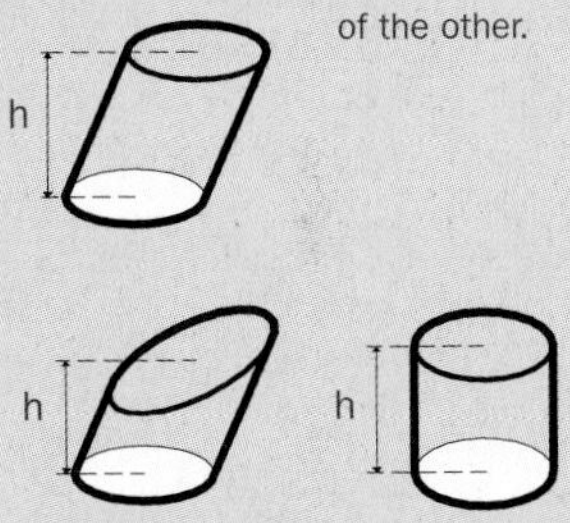
h
h
h

Pyramid or Cone (right or oblique, regular or irregular)

volume = area of base × 1/3 altitude

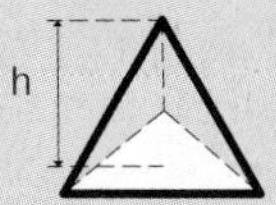
h

Altitude (h) = distance from base to apex, measured perpendicular to base.

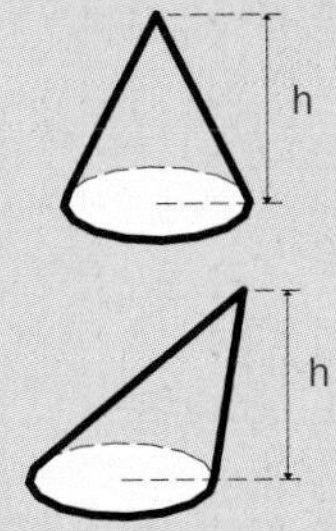
h
h

CIRCLE

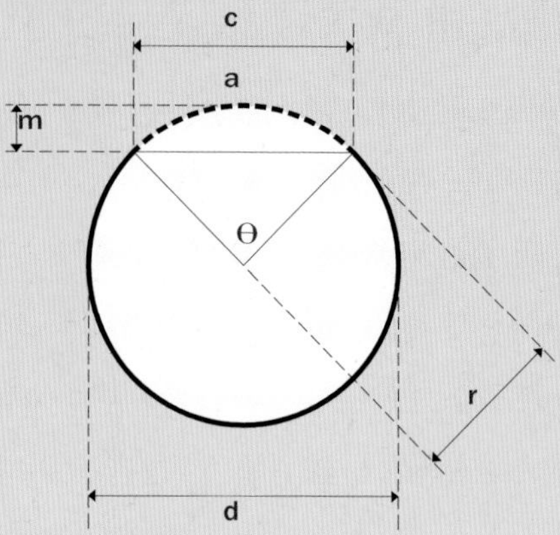
c
a
m
Θ
r
d

a = arc
r = radius
d = diameter
c = cord
m = distance
Θ = degrees
π = 3.14159

circumference = $2\pi r = \pi d = 3.14159\,d$

area = $\pi r^2 = \pi \dfrac{d^2}{4} = 0.78539 d^2$

length of arc a = $\Theta \dfrac{\pi}{180} r = 0.017453\,\Theta\, r$

$r = \dfrac{m^2 + c^2/4}{2m} = \dfrac{c/2}{\sin \frac{1}{2}\Theta}$

$c = 2\sqrt{2mr - m^2} = 2r \sin \frac{1}{2}\Theta$

$m = r \pm \sqrt{r^2 - \dfrac{c^2}{4}}$ use + if arc ≥ *180°* use – if arc < *180°*

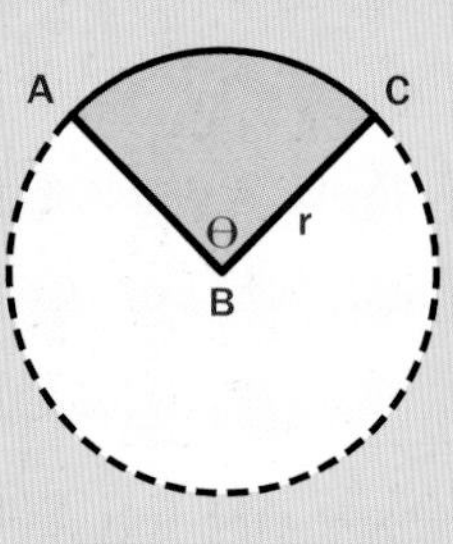
A
C
Θ
r
B

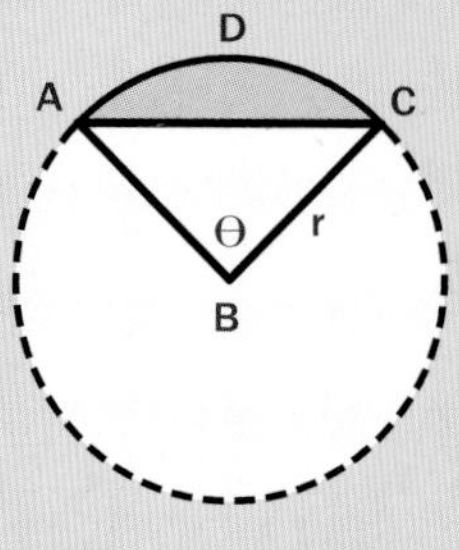
D
A
C
Θ
r
B

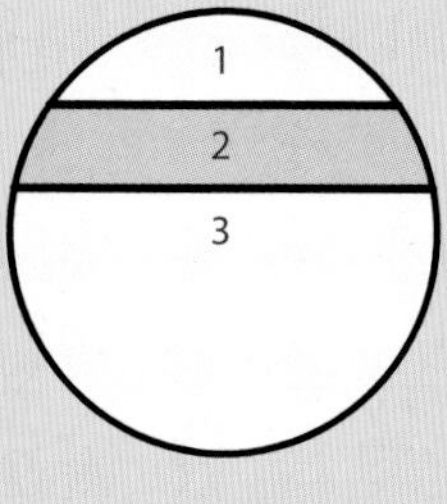
1
2
3

Sector of Circle

arc length AC = $\dfrac{\pi r \Theta}{180}$

area ABCA = $\dfrac{\pi \Theta r^2}{360}$

or

area ABCA = $\dfrac{\text{arc length AC} \times r}{2}$

Segment of Circle

area ACDA =

$\dfrac{r^2}{2} \times \left(\dfrac{\pi\Theta}{180} - \sin\Theta\right)$

r = radius
Θ = degrees
A, B, C, D = points
π = 3.14159

Circular Zone

area 2 =
circle area – area 1
– area 3

1 = segment
2 = zone
3 = segment

ELLIPSE

perimeter (approximate) =

$\pi\,[1.5\,(x + y) - \sqrt{x\,y}]$

(Assume point G is the center point of the ellipse, with x,y coordinates of 0,0, and point B coordinates of B_x and B_y.)

area ABFEA =
$(B_x \times B_y) + ab\,\sin^{-1}(B_x/a)$

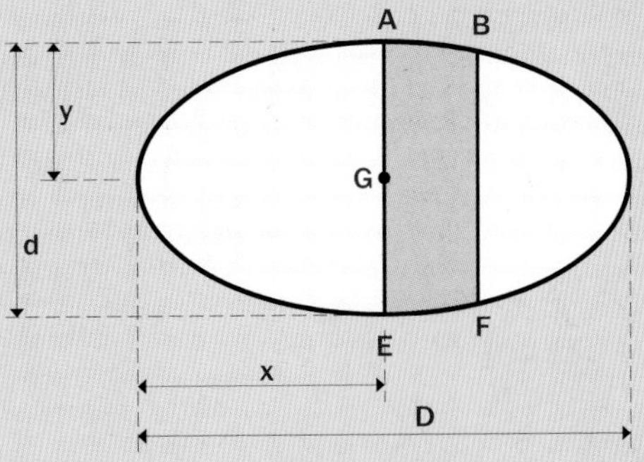
A
B
y
G
d
F
E
x
D

DOUBLE-CURVED SOLIDS

Sphere

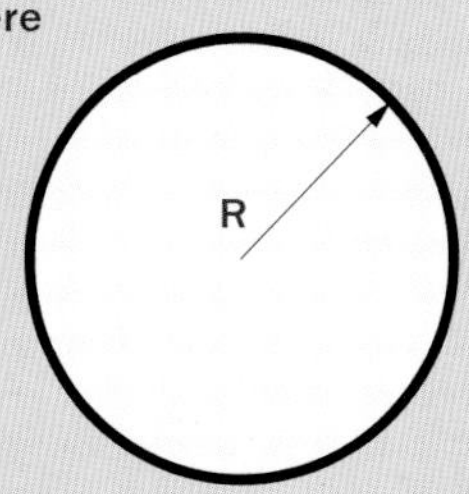
R

volume = $\dfrac{4\,\pi\,R^3}{3}$

surface = $4\,\pi\,R^2$

Segment of Sphere

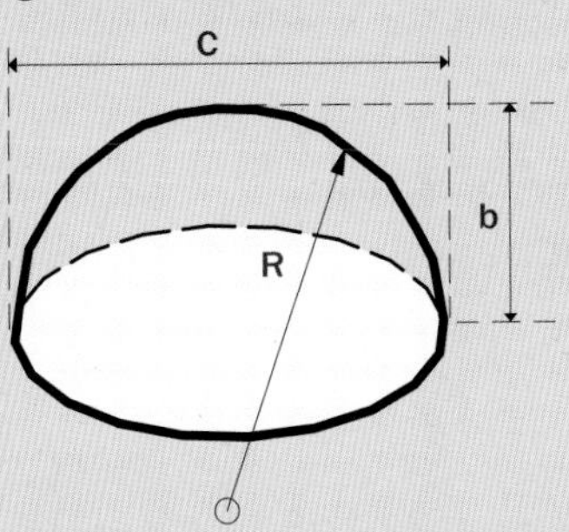
C
b
R

volume = $\dfrac{\pi\,b^2\,(3R-b)}{3}$

(sector – cone)

surface = $2\pi R b$

Sector of Sphere

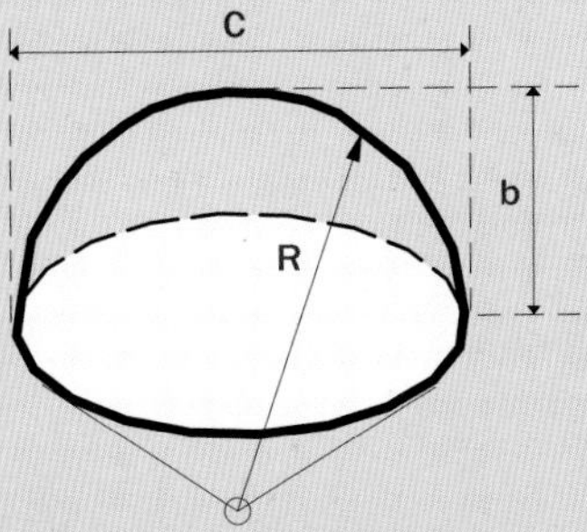
C
b
R

volume = $\dfrac{2\pi\,R^2\,b}{3}$

surface = $\dfrac{\pi\,R(4b + C)}{2}$

(segment + cone)

Ellipsoid

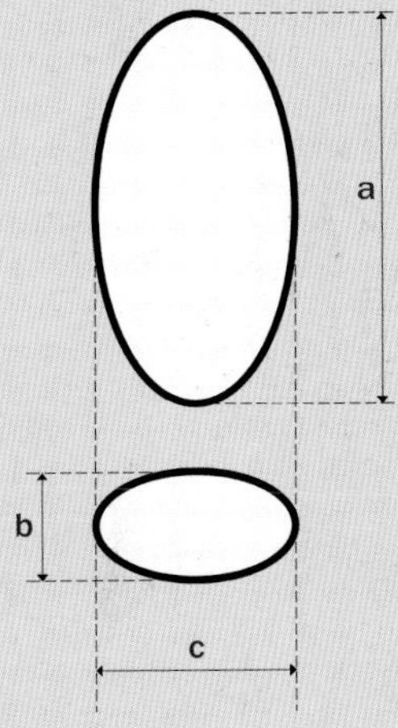
a
b
c

volume = $\dfrac{\pi\,abc}{6}$

surface = no simple equation

Chapter 11: Architectural Drawing Types

An architect uses eight basic drawing types within the drawing set to most completely describe the design of a building.

PLAN

View of the horizontal planes of the building, showing their relationship to each other. A plan is a horizontal section, typically depicting the building as though cut approximately 3'-0" (915) from its floor.

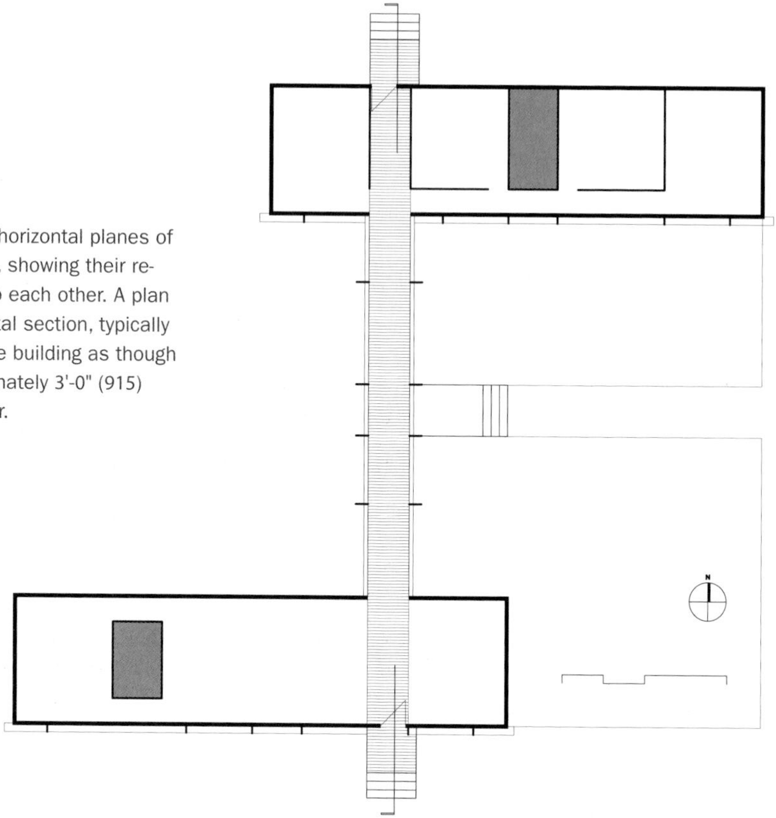

N

SECTION

View of a vertical cut through the building's components. A section acts as a vertical plan and often contains elevational information, such as doors and windows. This information is shown with a lighter line weight than the section cuts.

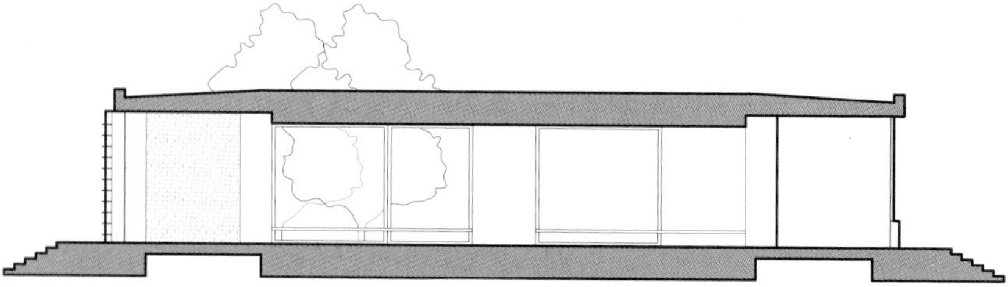

ELEVATION

View of the vertical planes of the building, showing their relationship to each other. An elevation is viewed perpendicularly from a selected plane.

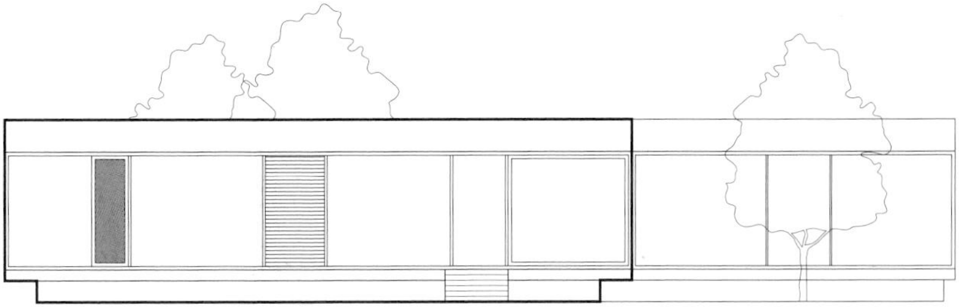

THREE-DIMENSIONAL REPRESENTATIONS

Perspectives (not scaled), axonometrics, and isometrics describe the building or space in a way that conventional plans, elevations, and sections cannot. Perspectives are particularly effective in producing a view that would actually be experienced by being in the space designed.

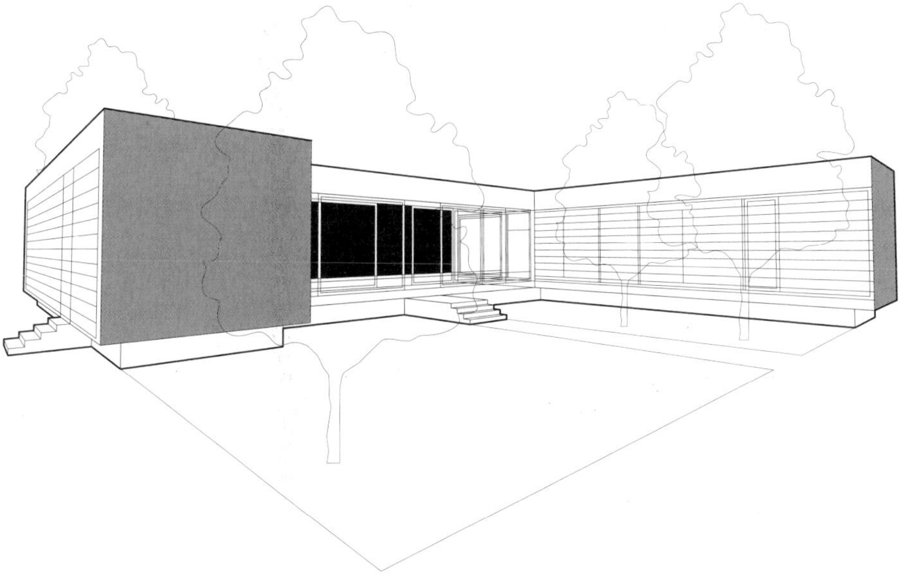

READING THE DRAWING SET

Drawing Symbols

Symbols and reference markers are necessary for navigating the drawing set. They tell whoever is looking at a drawing where to go to find out more information about certain elements.

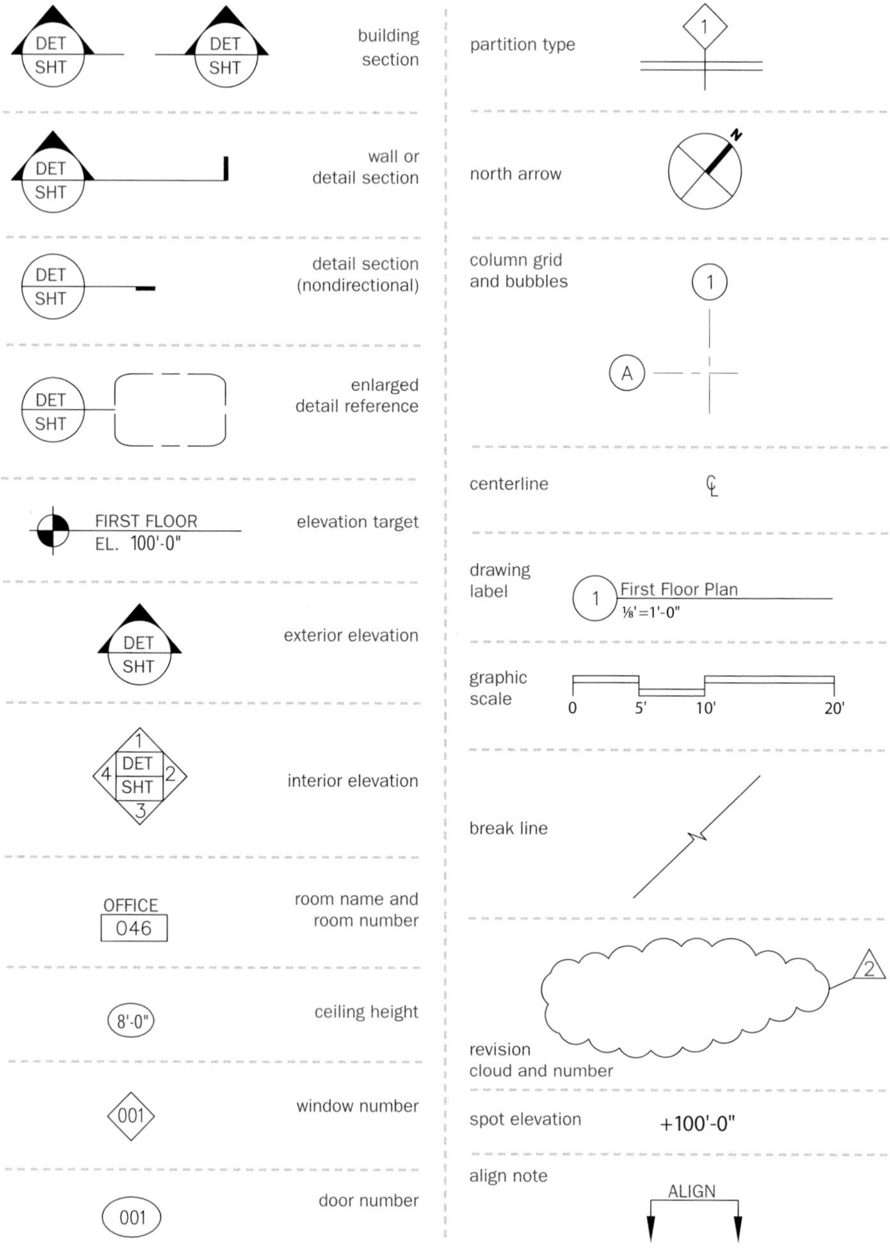
DET
SHT
DET
SHT
building section
DET
SHT
wall or detail section
DET
SHT
detail section (nondirectional)
DET
SHT
enlarged detail reference
FIRST FLOOR
EL. 100'-0"
elevation target
DET
SHT
exterior elevation
1
DET
SHT
2
3
4
interior elevation
OFFICE
046
room name and room number
8'-0"
ceiling height
001
window number
001
door number
partition type
1
north arrow
N
column grid and bubbles
1
A
centerline
℄
drawing label
1
First Floor Plan
⅛" = 1'-0"
graphic scale
0
5'
10'
20'
break line
revision cloud and number
2
spot elevation
+100'-0"
align note
ALIGN

Floor Plans

Overall building plans are usually drawn at a scale that enables one to see the whole plan. Most elements of the overall plan are keyed to other drawings in the set, as in the case of larger-scale plans, details, sections, and elevations. Some information may be keyed and cross-referenced among multiple drawings. Keys shown on the plan below reappear on the drawings to follow.

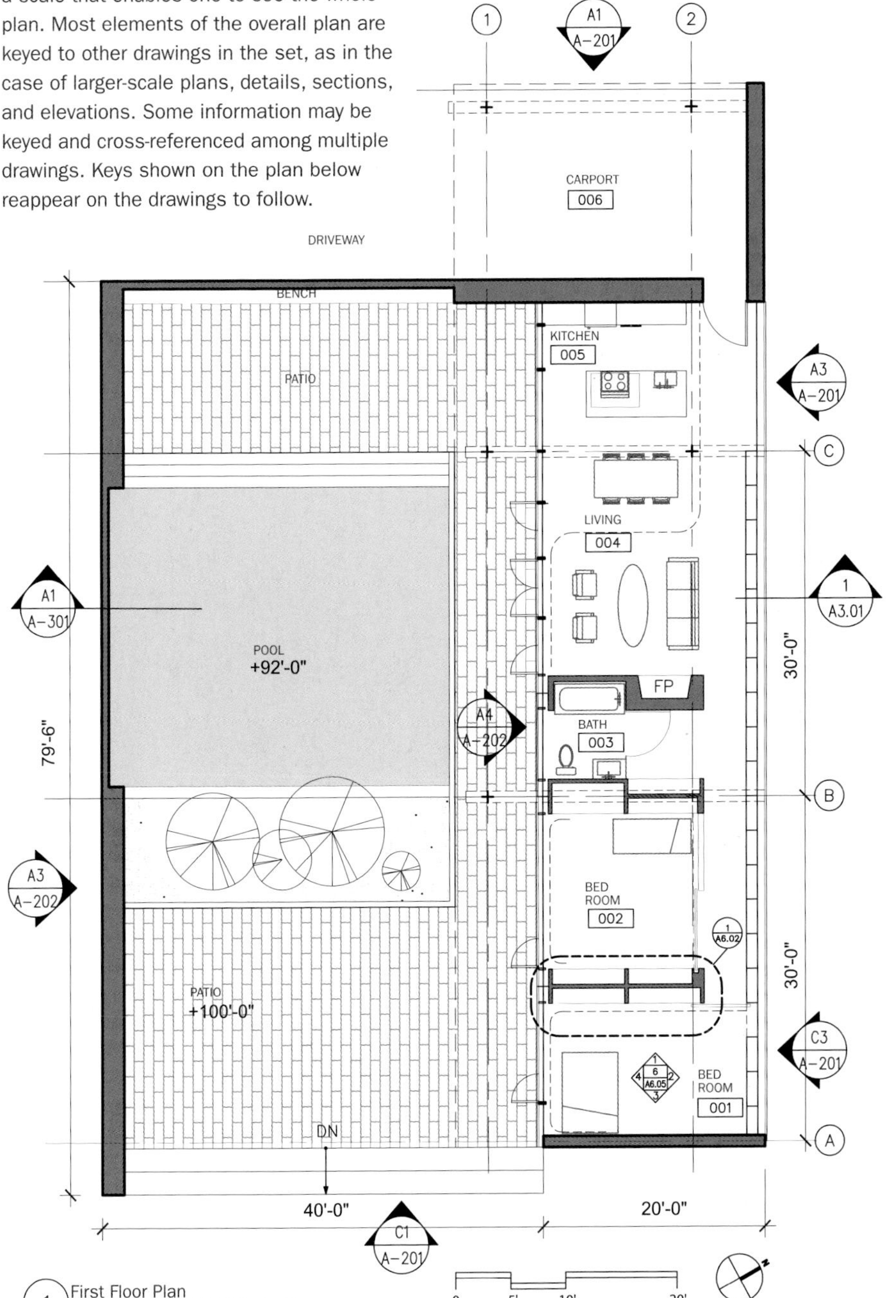

1
2
A1
A–201
CARPORT
006
DRIVEWAY
BENCH
KITCHEN
005
PATIO
A3
A–201
C
LIVING
004
A1
A–301
1
A3.01
POOL
+92'-0"
30'-0"
FP
A4
A–202
BATH
003
79'-6"
B
A3
A–202
BED
ROOM
002
1
A6.02
30'-0"
PATIO
+100'-0"
C3
A–201
6
4
2
3
A6.05
BED
ROOM
001
A
DN
40'-0"
20'-0"
C1
A–201
0
5'
10'
20'

1 First Floor Plan
¼"=1'-0"

Building Elevations

Building elevations depict the exterior conditions of the building, describing materials and important vertical dimensions. In instances where a drawing is too large to fit on a standard sheet, it must be broken apart and continued on the same sheet or another sheet, requiring the use of match lines for alignment.

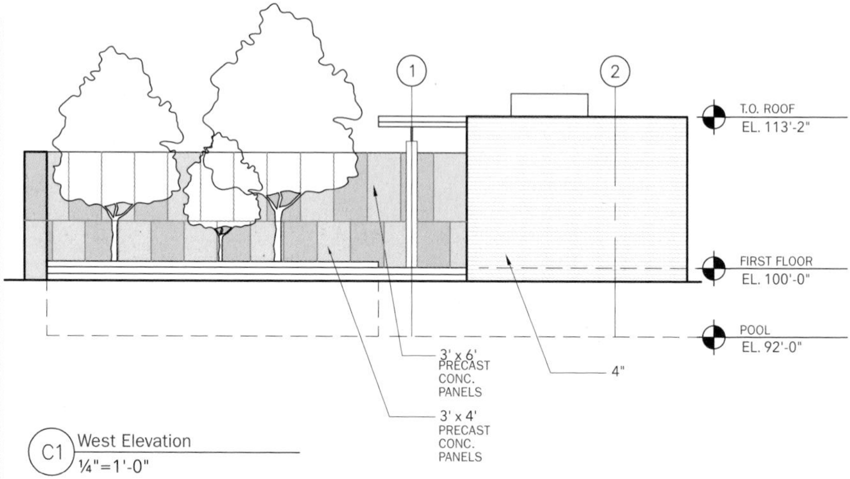
1
2
T.O. ROOF
EL. 113'-2"
FIRST FLOOR
EL. 100'-0"
POOL
EL. 92'-0"
3' x 6'
PRECAST
CONC.
PANELS
4"
3' x 4'
PRECAST
CONC.
PANELS

C1 West Elevation
¼"=1'-0"

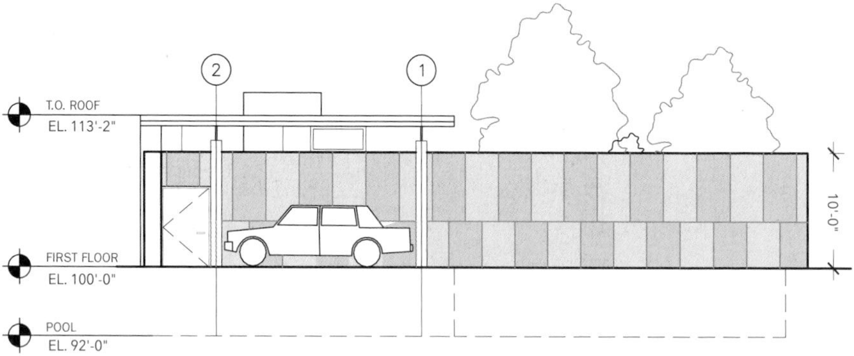
2
1
T.O. ROOF
EL. 113'-2"
FIRST FLOOR
EL. 100'-0"
POOL
EL. 92'-0"
10'-0"

A1 East Elevation
¼"=1'-0"

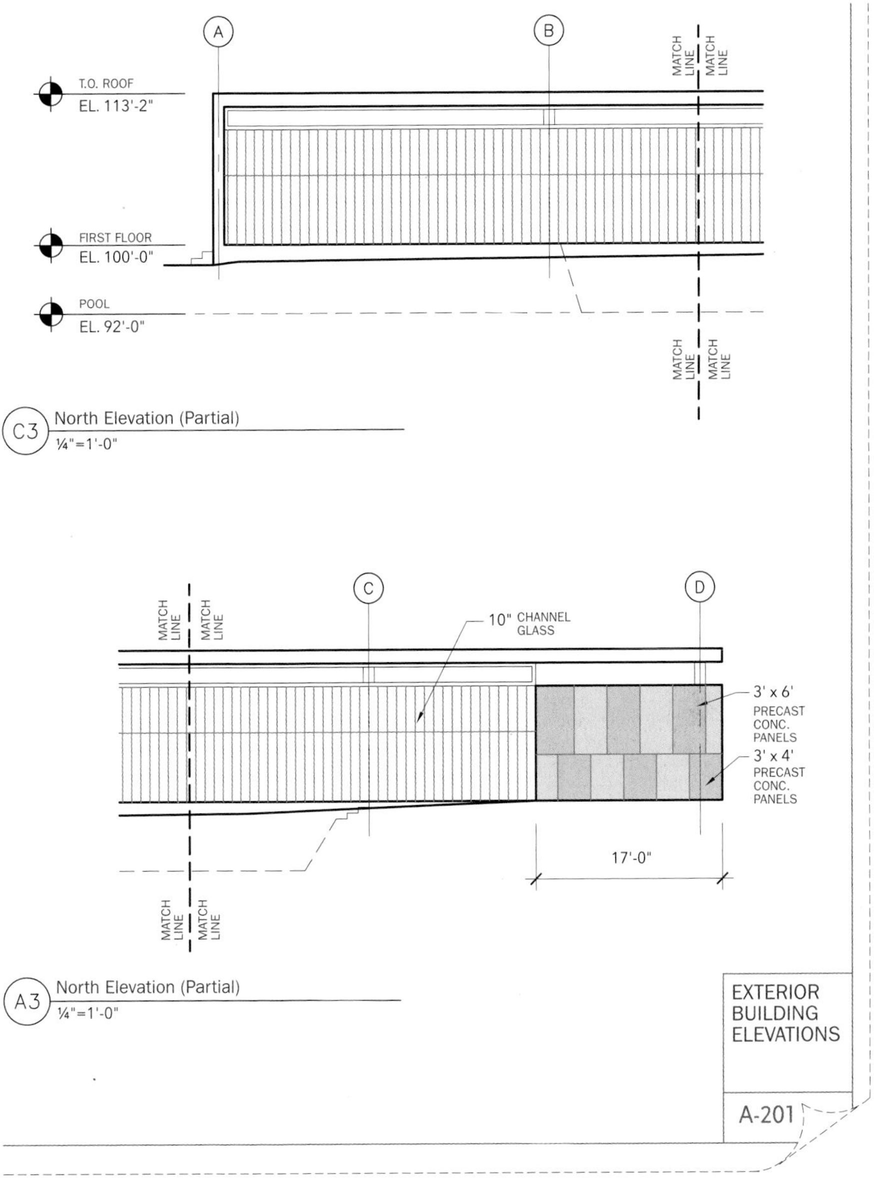
A
B
MATCH LINE
T.O. ROOF
EL. 113'-2"
FIRST FLOOR
EL. 100'-0"
POOL
EL. 92'-0"
C3
North Elevation (Partial)
¼"=1'-0"
C
D
10" CHANNEL GLASS
3' x 6' PRECAST CONC. PANELS
3' x 4' PRECAST CONC. PANELS
17'-0"
A3
North Elevation (Partial)
¼"=1'-0"
EXTERIOR BUILDING ELEVATIONS
A-201

Reflected Ceiling Plans

Reflected ceiling plans (RCPs) may be thought of as upside-down floor plans, for they are literally a plan of the ceiling. They are used to describe light fixture placement and types, ceiling heights and materials, and anything else found on the ceiling plane. RCPs employ standard keys and symbols as well as some specific to the ceiling plan.

Light fixtures often bear tags that refer to their descriptions in the lighting specifications.

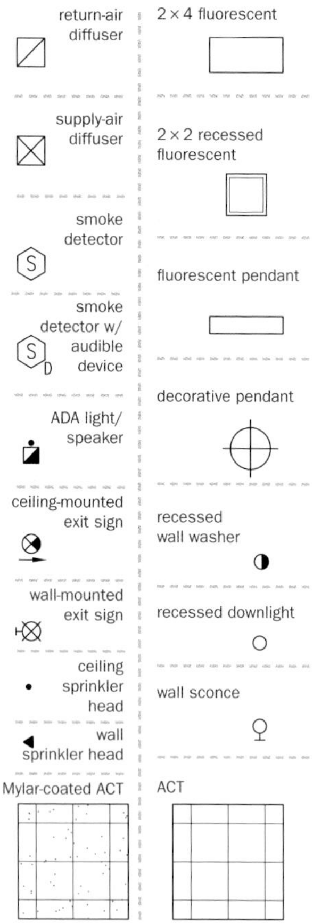

return-air diffuser
supply-air diffuser
smoke detector
smoke detector w/ audible device
ADA light/ speaker
ceiling-mounted exit sign
wall-mounted exit sign
ceiling sprinkler head
wall sprinkler head
Mylar-coated ACT
2 × 4 fluorescent
2 × 2 recessed fluorescent
fluorescent pendant
decorative pendant
recessed wall washer
recessed downlight
wall sconce
ACT

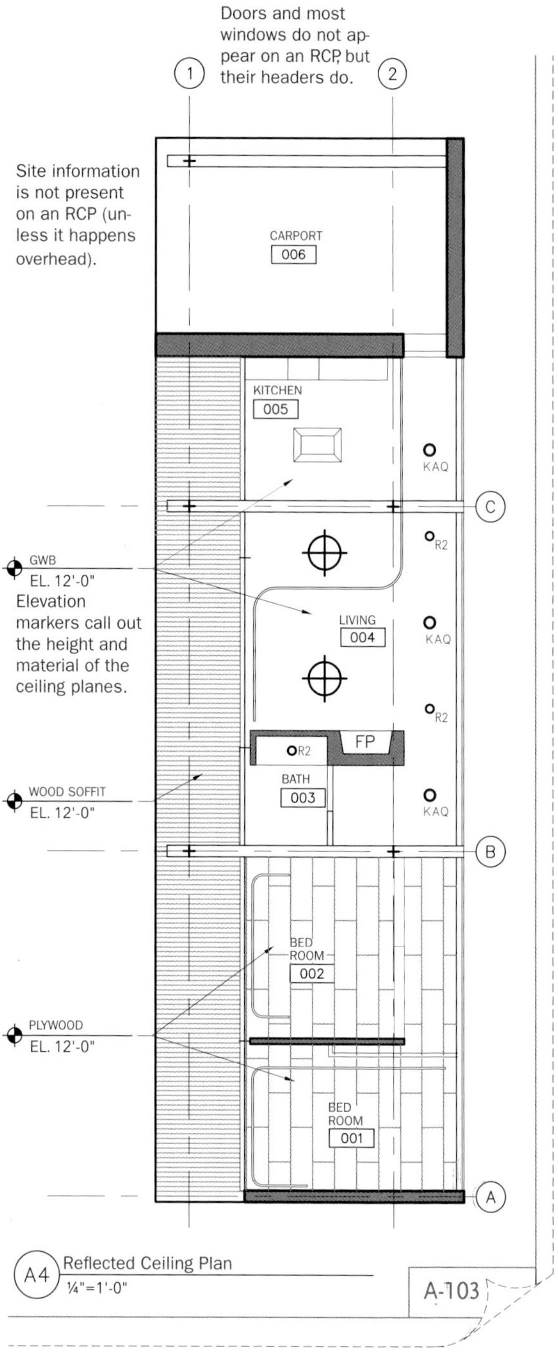

Doors and most windows do not appear on an RCP, but their headers do.
Site information is not present on an RCP (unless it happens overhead).
Elevation markers call out the height and material of the ceiling planes.
1
2
CARPORT
006
KITCHEN
005
KAQ
C
GWB
EL. 12'-0"
R2
LIVING
004
KAQ
R2
FP
R2
BATH
003
WOOD SOFFIT
EL. 12'-0"
KAQ
B
BED ROOM
002
PLYWOOD
EL. 12'-0"
BED ROOM
001
A
A4
Reflected Ceiling Plan
¼"=1'-0"
A-103

Interior Elevations

Interior elevations are drawn at a larger scale than the overall building plans, allowing for more details, notes, and dimensions to be represented. Keyed from the building plan, interior elevations are, in turn, keyed to other, larger-scale views, such as section and plan details of cabinetry construction and wall sections.

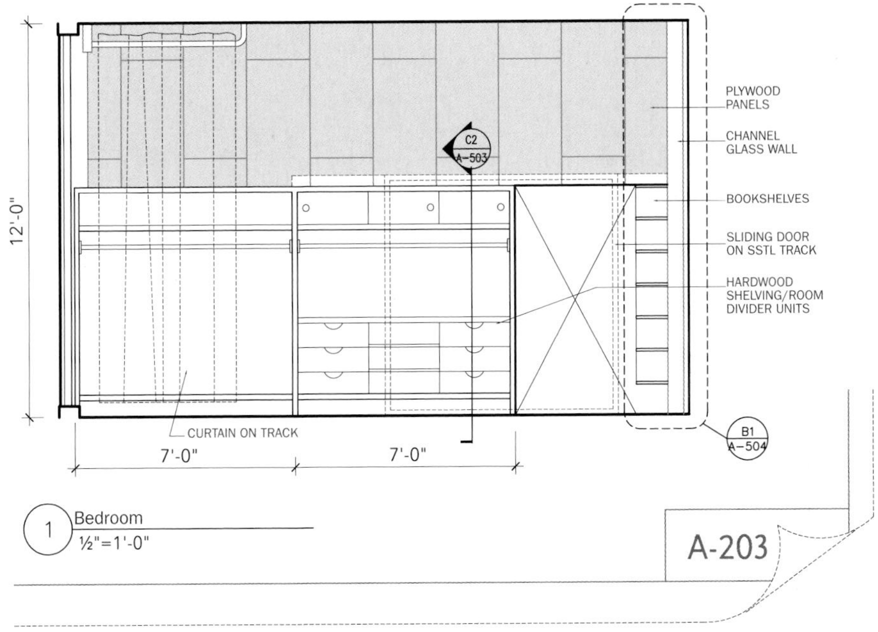
12'-0"
PLYWOOD PANELS
CHANNEL GLASS WALL
BOOKSHELVES
SLIDING DOOR ON SSTL TRACK
HARDWOOD SHELVING/ROOM DIVIDER UNITS
C2
A-503
B1
A-504
CURTAIN ON TRACK
7'-0"
7'-0"
1
Bedroom
½"=1'-0"
A-203

Details

Details are drawn at scales such as 1½" = 1'-0", 3"= 1'-0", 6"= 1'-0", and sometimes even at full scale, and are keyed from and to numerous other drawings.

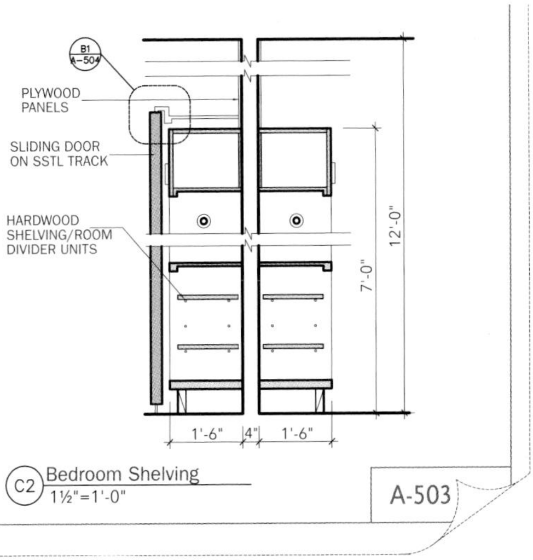
B1
A-504
PLYWOOD PANELS
SLIDING DOOR ON SSTL TRACK
HARDWOOD SHELVING/ROOM DIVIDER UNITS
12'-0"
7'-0"
1'-6"
4"
1'-6"
C2
Bedroom Shelving
1½"=1'-0"
A-503

THREE-DIMENSIONAL DRAWINGS

Paraline Drawings

Paraline drawings are projected pictorial representations of the three-dimensional qualities of an object. Unlike in perspective drawings, the projection lines in a paraline drawing remain parallel instead of converging to a point on the horizon.

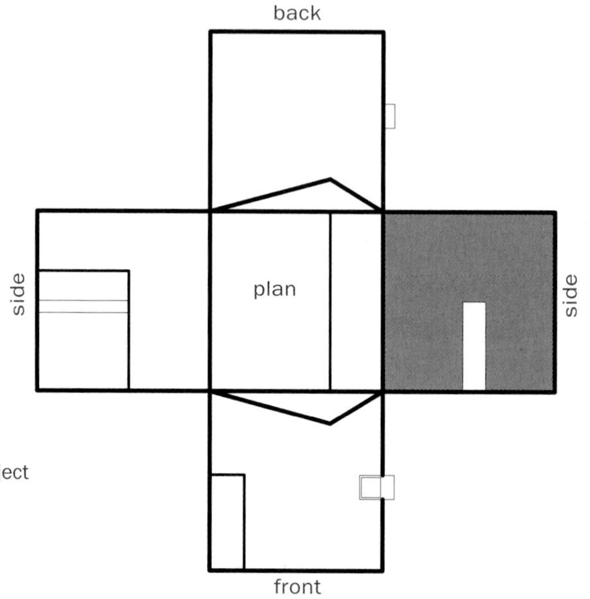
back
side
plan
side
front

Unfolded Object

OBLIQUES

One face of the object (either the plan or elevation) is drawn directly on the picture plane. From this, projected lines are drawn at an angle to the picture plane. The length of the projecting lines can vary (examples are shown opposite).

AXONOMETRICS

Dimetric

In a dimetric drawing, the object is rotated so that only one corner touches the picture plane.

Isometric

An isometric drawing is a dimetric drawing where all axes of the object are simultaneously rotated away from the picture plane and kept at 30 degrees of projection. All legs are equally distorted in length and maintain an exact 1:1:1 proportion.

Trimetric

A trimetric drawing is similar to a dimetric drawing, except that the plan of the object is rotated so that the scales of all three axes are varied.

Oblique Projections

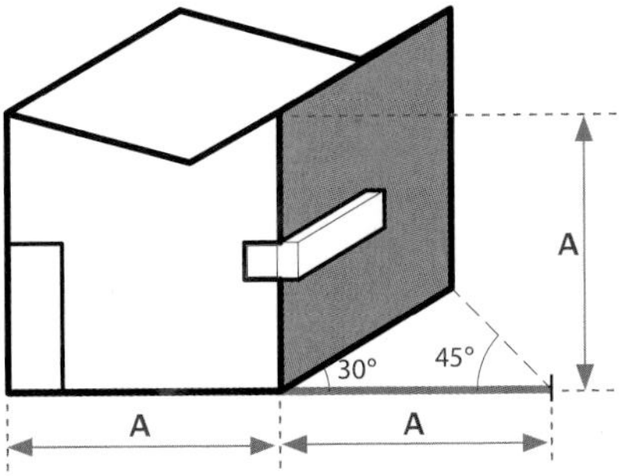
A
30°
45°
A
A

30° Oblique

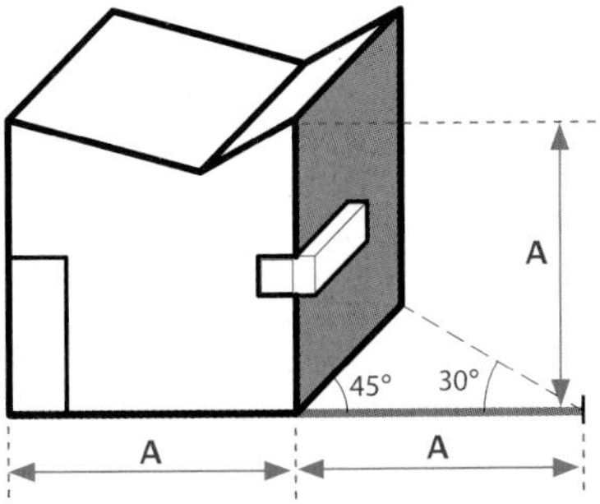
A
45°
30°
A
A

45° Oblique

Orthographic Projections

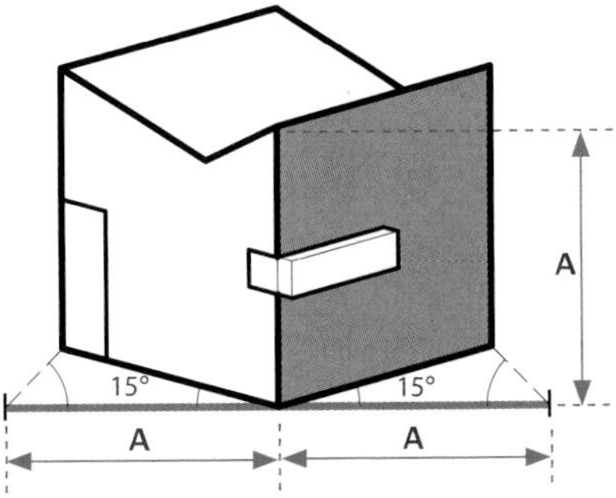
A
15°
15°
A
A

15° Dimetric Axonometric

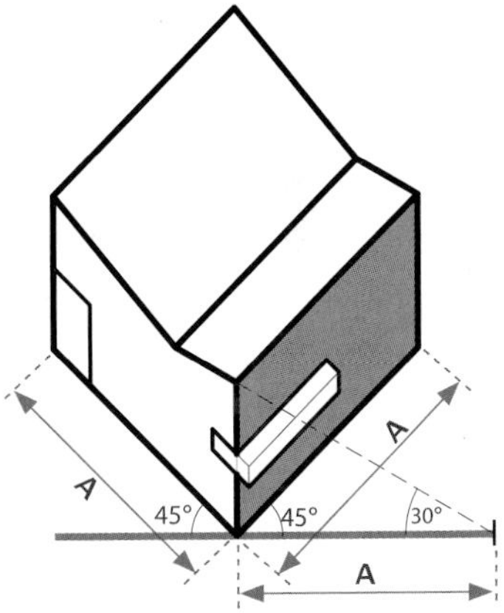
A
A
45°
45°
30°
A

45° Dimetric Axonometric

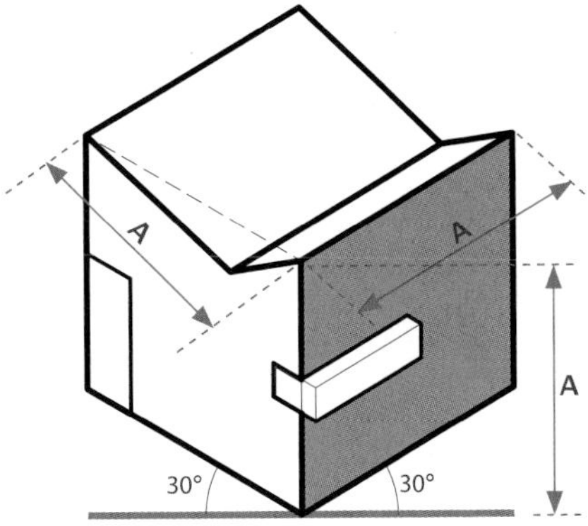
A
A
A
30°
30°

Isometric
(30° Dimetric)

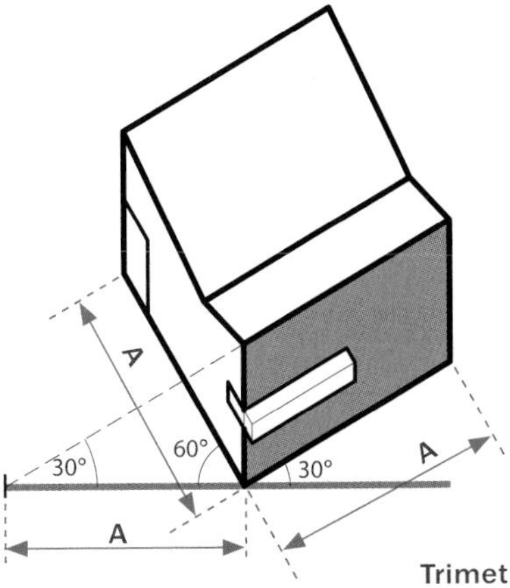
A
30°
60°
30°
A
A

Trimetric

Two-Point Common Method Perspective

Station Point (SP): Locates the fixed position of the viewer.

Picture Plane (PP): Flat, two-dimensional surface that records the projected perspective image and aligns perpendicular to the viewer's center of vision. The picture plane is the only true-size plane in the perspective field: Objects behind the picture plane project to its surface smaller than true scale, whereas those between the viewer and the picture plane project to its surface larger than true scale.

Measuring Line (ML): Located on the picture plane, the measuring line is the only true-scale line in a perspective drawing. Most commonly, this is a vertical line from which can be projected the key vertical dimensions of the object.

Horizon Line (HL): Lies at the intersection of the picture plane and a horizontal plane through the eye of the viewer.

Vanishing Point: Point at which parallel lines appear to meet in perspective. The left (vpL) and right (vpR) vanishing points for an object are determined by the points at which a set of lines originating from the station point and parallel to the object lines intersect the picture plane.

Ground Line (GL): Lies at the intersection of the picture plane and the ground plane.

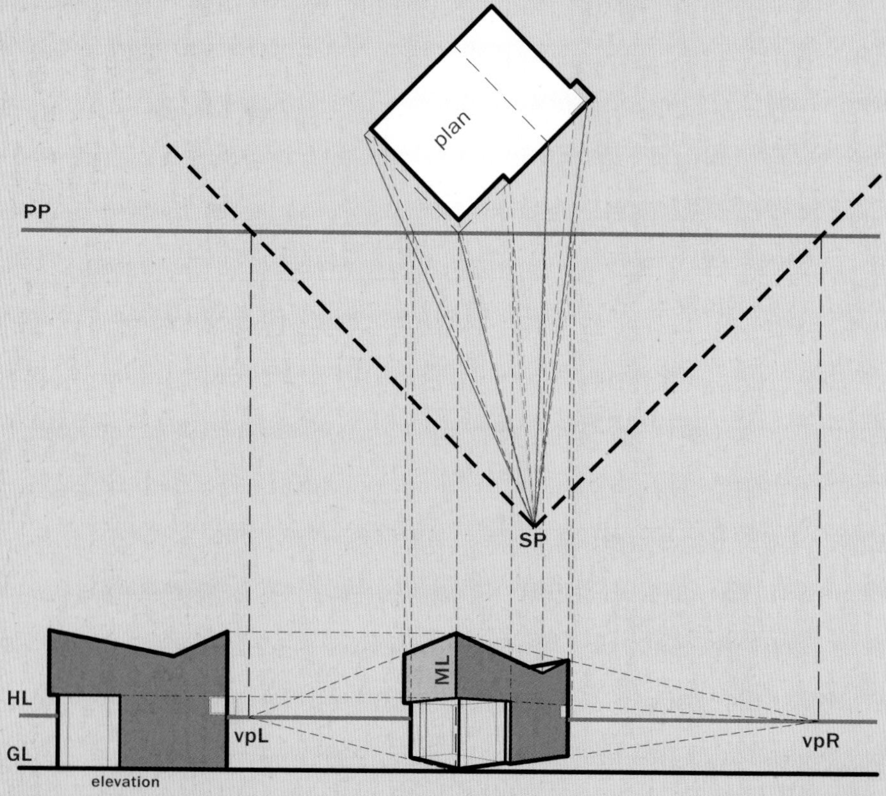
plan
PP
SP
ML
HL
vpL
vpR
GL
elevation

One-Point Common Method Perspective

One-point perspectives use a single vanishing point, and all edges and planes that are perpendicular to the picture plane vanish toward this point. To locate this point (C), draw a vertical line from the station point to the horizon line. Building edges that are parallel to the picture plane appear as parallel lines in perspective, with no vanishing point.

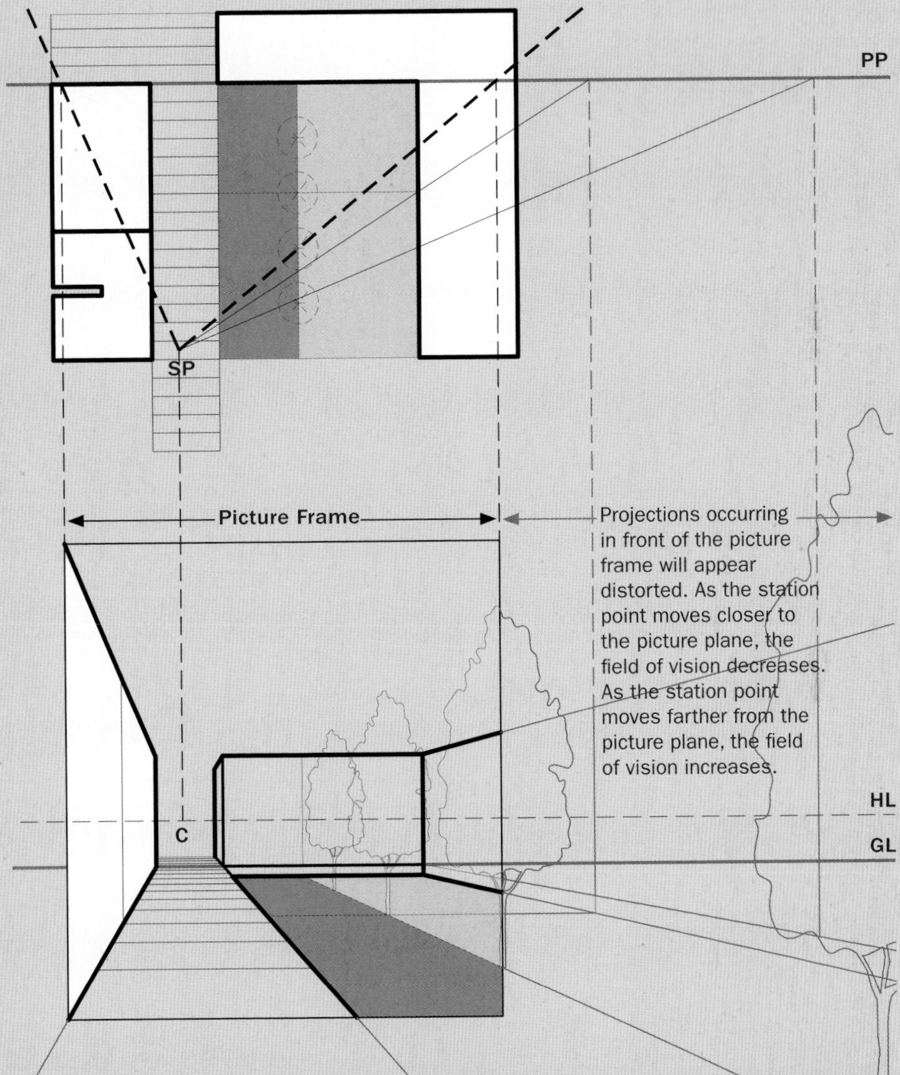
PP
SP
Picture Frame
Projections occurring in front of the picture frame will appear distorted. As the station point moves closer to the picture plane, the field of vision decreases. As the station point moves farther from the picture plane, the field of vision increases.
HL
C
GL

Chapter 12: Architectural Documents

THE PRACTICE OF ARCHITECTURE

To speak an architectural language is to do many things: It could involve the art of form and style or the more prosaic aspects of contract administration. Architecture and its practice move, sometimes with effort, among realms not only of art, science, and engineering, but also of business, economics, and sociology. All professional groups speak their own language to some extent. To their written and spoken language architects add drawings and symbols, organizing them into accepted standards of presentation and legibility. As with good manners, the point of these standards is not to complicate but to ease communication and interaction.

Most countries have a governing body in architectural practice—in the United States it is the American Institute of Architects (AIA)—which oversees ethics and professional conduct and establishes guidelines for issues ranging from project delivery schedules to contracts and legal documents. The architect who has complete mastery of every aspect of the multiple personalities of architectural practice may be rare. However, all responsible practicing architects are compelled to understand the business of the profession, because the art of architecture depends on the practice of getting it built.

COMMON PROJECT TERMS

Addendum: Written information that clarifies or modifies the bidding documents, often issued during the bidding process.

Alternate: Additional design or material options added to the construction documents and/or specifications to obtain multiple possible cost estimates for a project. "Add-alternates" imply added material and cost; "deduct-alternates" imply removal of certain elements to lower the project cost, as necessary.

ANSI: American National Standards Institute.

As-built drawings: Contract drawings that have been marked up to reflect any changes to a project during construction, differentiating them from the bid documents. Also known as record drawings.

Bid: Offer of a proposal or a price. When a project is "put out to bid," contractors are asked to submit their estimates as to the time and the cost of a project.

Building permit: Written document issued by the appropriate government authority permitting the construction of a specific project in accordance with the drawings and specifications that the authority has approved.

Certificate of occupancy: Document issued by the appropriate local governmental agency, stating that a building or property meets local standards for occupancy and is in compliance with public health and building codes.

Change order: Written document between and signed by the owner and the contractor authorizing a change in the work, or an adjustment in the contract sum or length of time. Architects and engineers may also sign a change order, but only if authorized (in writing) by the owner to do so.

Charrette: Intensive design process for solving an architectural problem quickly; often undertaken by students of architecture, but also employed by professionals in various stages of the design process. The instructors of the École des Beaux Arts in Paris would use a *charrette*, French for "small wooden cart," for collecting the design work of the students after such a process.

Construction cost: Direct contractor costs for labor, material, equipment, and services, as well as overhead and profit. Excluded from construction cost are fees for architects, engineers, consultants, costs of land, or any other items that, by definition of the contract, are the responsibility of the owner.

Construction management: Organization and direction of the labor force, materials, and equipment to build the project as designed by the architect.

Construction management contract: Written agreement giving responsibility for coordination and accomplishment of overall project planning, design, and construction to a construction management firm or individual, called the construction manager (CM).

Consultant: Professional hired by the owner or architect to provide information and to advise the project in the area of his or her expertise.

Contract administration: Contractual duties and responsibilities of the architect and engineer during a project's construction.

Contract over- (or under-) run: Difference between the original contract price and the final completed cost, including all change order adjustments.

Contractor: Licensed individual or company that agrees to perform the work as specified, with the appropriate labor, equipment, and materials.

Date of substantial completion: Date certified by the architect when the work is to be completed.

Design-build construction: Arrangement wherein a contractor bids or negotiates to provide design and construction services for the entire project.

Estimating: Calculation of the amount of material, labor, and equipment needed to complete a given project.

Fast-track construction: Method of construction management in which construction work begins before completion of the construction documents, resulting in a continuous design-construction situation.

FF&E: Moveable furniture, fixtures, or equipment that do not require permanent connection to the structure or utilities of a building.

Field order: Written order calling for a clarification or minor change in the construction work and not involving any adjustment to the terms of the contract.

General contractor: Licensed individual or company with prime responsibility for the work.

Indirect cost: Expenses that are not chargeable to a specific project or task, such as overhead.

Inspection list: List prepared by the owner or authorized owner's representative of work items requiring correction or completion by the contractor; generally done at the end of construction. Also called a punch list.

NIBS: National Institute of Building Sciences.

Owner-architect agreement: Written contract between the architect and client for professional architectural services.

Parti: Central idea governing and organizing a work of architecture, from the French *partir* "to depart with the intention of going somewhere."

Program: Desired list of spaces, rooms, and elements, as well as their sizes, for use in designing the building.

Progress schedule: Line diagram showing proposed and actual starting and completion times in a project.

Project cost: All costs for a specific project, including those for land, professionals, construction, furnishings, fixtures, equipment, financing, and any other project-related expenses.

Project directory: Written list of names and addresses of all parties involved in a project, including the owner, architect, engineer, and contractor.

Project manager: Qualified individual or firm authorized by the owner to be responsible for coordinating time, equipment, money, tasks, and people for all or portions of a project.

Project manual: Detailed written specifications describing acceptable construction materials and methods.

Request for Information (RFI): Written request from a contractor to the owner or architect for clarification of the contract documents.

Request for Proposal (RFP): Written request to a contractor, architect, or subcontractor for an estimate or cost proposal.

Schedule: Plan for performing work; also, a chart or table within the drawing set.

Scheme: Chart, diagram, or outline of a system being proposed.

Scope of work: Written range of view or action for a specific project.

Shop drawings: Drawings, diagrams, schedules, and other data specially prepared by the contractor or a subcontractor, sub-subcontractor, manufacturer, supplier, or distributor to illustrate some portion of the work being done. These drawings show the specific way in which the particular contractor or shop intends to furnish, fabricate, assemble, or install its products. The architect is obligated by the owner-architect agreement to review and approve these drawings or to take other appropriate action.

Site: Location of a structure or group of structures.

Soft costs: Expenses in addition to the direct construction cost, including architectural and engineering fees, permits, legal and financing fees, construction interest and operating expenses, leasing and real estate commissions, advertising and promotion, and supervision. Soft costs and construction costs add up to the project cost.

Standards of professional practice: Listing of minimum acceptable ethical principals and practices adopted by qualified and recognized professional organizations to guide their members in the conduct of specific professional practice.

Structural systems: Load-bearing assembly of beams and columns on a foundation.

Subcontractor: Specialized contractor who is subordinate to the prime or main contractor.

Substitution: Proposed replacement or alternate for a material or process of equivalent cost and quality.

Tenant improvements (TIs): Interior improvements of a project after the building envelope is complete.

Time and materials (T&M): Written agreement wherein payment is based on actual costs for labor, equipment, materials, and services rendered, in addition to overhead.

Value engineering (VE): Process of analyzing the cost versus the value of alternative materials, equipment, and systems, usually in the interest of achieving the lowest total cost for a project.

Zoning: Restrictions of areas or regions of land within specific areas based on permitted building size, character, and uses as established by governing urban authorities.

Zoning permit: Document issued by a governing urban authority that permits land to be used for a specific purpose.

COMMON PAPER SIZES

ANSI (American National Standards Institute)

Paper Size	Inches	Millimeters
ANSI-A	8 1/2 × 11	216 × 279
ANSI-B	11 × 17	279 × 432
ANSI-C	17 × 22	432 × 559
ANSI-D	22 × 34	559 × 864
ANSI-E	34 × 44	864 × 1 118

Architectural

Paper Size	Inches	Millimeters
Arch-A	9 × 12	229 × 305
Arch-B	12 × 18	305 × 457
Arch-C	18 × 24	457 × 610
Arch-D	24 × 36	610 × 914
Arch-E	36 × 48	914 × 1 219

ISO (International Organization for Standardization)—based on one square meter

Paper Size	Inches	Millimeters
4A0	66 1/4 × 93 3/8	1 682 × 2 378
2A0	46 3/4 × 66 1/4	1 189 × 1 682
A0	33 1/8 × 46 3/4	841 × 1 189
A1	23 3/8 × 33 1/8	594 × 841
A2	16 1/2 × 23 3/8	420 × 594
A3	11 3/4 × 16 1/2	297 × 420
A4	8 1/4 × 11 3/4	210 × 297

Paper Size	Inches	Millimeters
B0	39 3/8 × 55 5/8	1 000 × 1 414
B1	27 7/8 × 39 3/8	707 × 1 000
B2	19 5/8 × 27 7/8	500 × 707
B3	13 7/8 × 19 5/8	353 × 500
B4	9 7/8 × 13 7/8	250 × 353

Paper Size	Inches	Millimeters
C0	36 1/8 × 51	917 × 1 297
C1	25 1/2 × 36 1/8	648 × 917
C2	18 × 25 1/2	458 × 648
C3	12 3/4 × 18	324 × 458
C4	9 × 12 1/2	229 × 324

SHEET FOLDING

Individual sheets that must be folded (for reasons of file storage or mailing) should be folded in a logical and consistent manner that allows the title and sheet number information to be visible in the bottom-right corner of the folded sheet. Large numbers of sheets are best bound into sets and rolled for shipping or laid flat for storage.

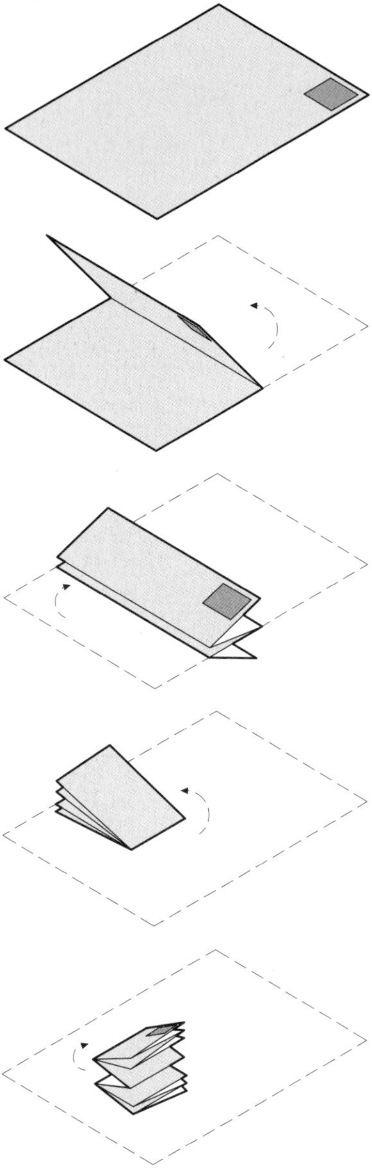

DRAWING SHEET LAYOUT AND SET ASSEMBLY

In the NIBS Standard sheet layout (in accordance with the National CAD Standard), drawings within a sheet are numbered by coordinate system modules as described below. The graphic or text information modules are known as drawing blocks and their numbers are established by the coordinates for the bottom-left corner of their module. This system enables new drawing blocks to be added to a sheet without having to renumber the existing blocks, saving considerable time once drawings begin to be keyed to other drawings and schedules.

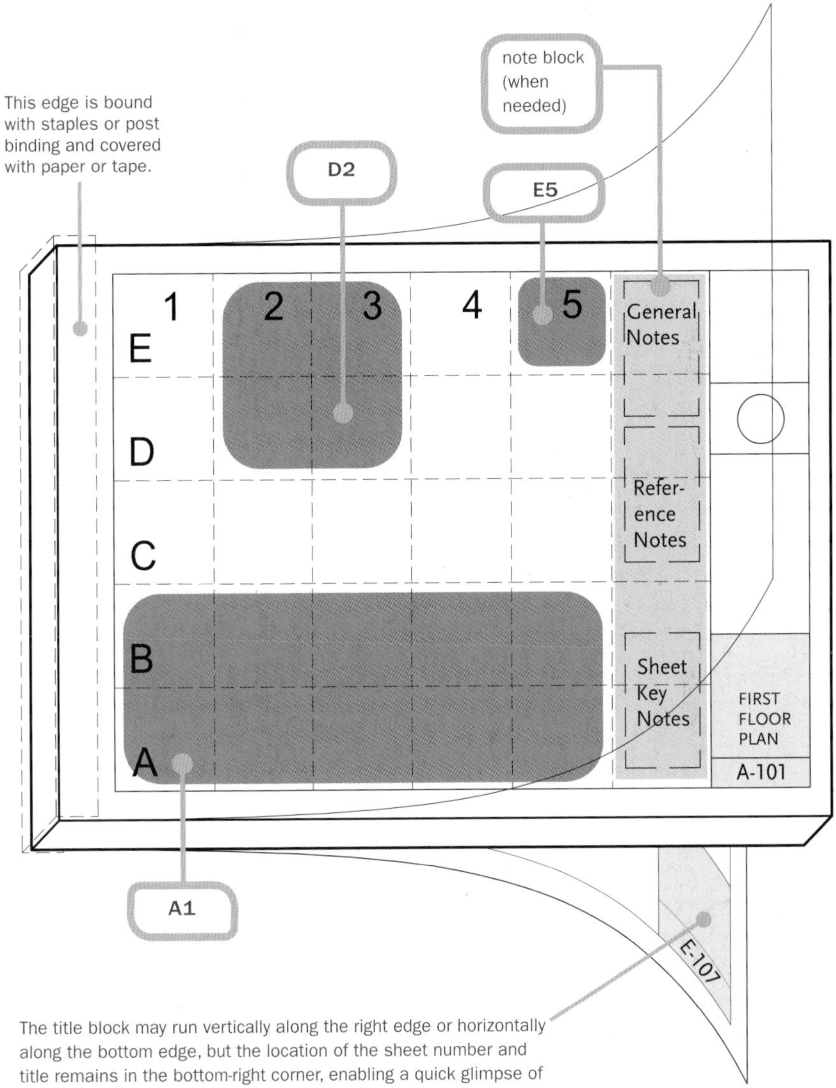
note block (when needed)
This edge is bound with staples or post binding and covered with paper or tape.
D2
E5
1
2
3
4
5
E
D
C
B
A
General Notes
Refer-ence Notes
Sheet Key Notes
FIRST FLOOR PLAN
A-101
A1
E-107

The title block may run vertically along the right edge or horizontally along the bottom edge, but the location of the sheet number and title remains in the bottom-right corner, enabling a quick glimpse of all sheets when flipping through the set.

DRAWING SET ORDER

Typical Order for Disciplines

Standards for the order of disciplines in the drawing set may vary within different offices. The order below is recommended by the Uniform Drawing System (UDS) to minimize confusion among the many trades that will use the set. Note that most projects will not contain all the disciplines listed here, and others might have need for additional, project-specific disciplines.

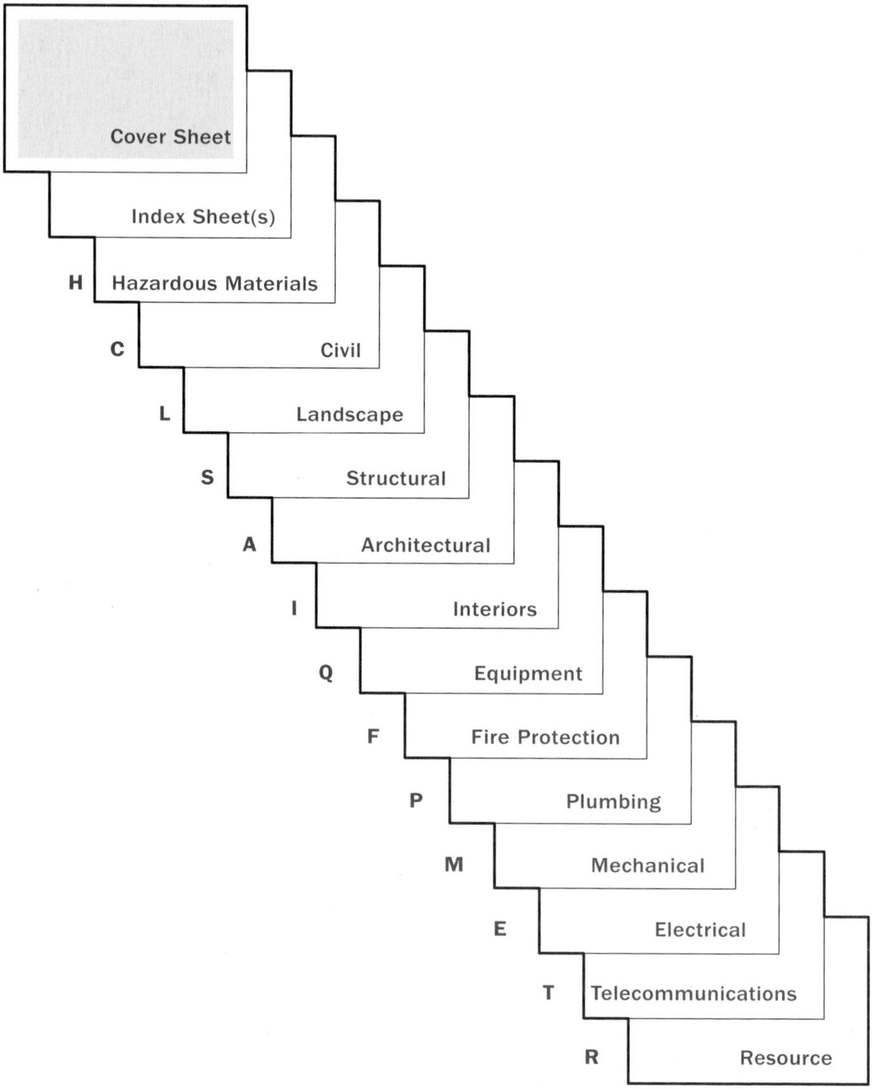
Cover Sheet
Index Sheet(s)
H Hazardous Materials
C Civil
L Landscape
S Structural
A Architectural
I Interiors
Q Equipment
F Fire Protection
P Plumbing
M Mechanical
E Electrical
T Telecommunications
R Resource

Typical Order for Sheets within the Architecture Discipline

A-0:	**General**
A-001	Notes and Symbols
A-1:	**Architectural Floor Plans**
A-101	First-Floor Plan
A-102	Second-Floor Plan
A-103	Third-Floor Plan
A-104	First-Floor RCP
A-105	Second-Floor RCP
A-106	Third-Floor RCP
A-107	Roof Plan
A-2:	**Architectural Elevations**
A-201	Exterior Elevations
A-202	Exterior Elevations
A-203	Interior Elevations
A-3:	**Architectural Sections**
A-301	Building Sections
A-302	Building Sections
A-303	Wall Sections
A-4:	**Large-Scale Views**
A-401	Enlarged Toilet Plans
A-402	Enlarged Plans
A-403	Stair and Elevator Plans and Sections
A-5:	**Architectural Details**
A-501	Exterior Details
A-502	Exterior Details
A-503	Interior Details
A-504	Interior Details
A-6:	**Schedules and Diagrams**
A-601	Partition Types
A-602	Room Finish Schedule
A-603	Door and Window Schedules

DRAWING SET ABBREVIATIONS

When all drawings were done by hand, architectural lettering—an art form of its own—could be tedious and time-consuming. As a result, architects and draftspersons abbreviated words. Though many standards were created, they have not always been consistent and historically have led to interpretive errors by contractors. CAD technology makes much shorter work of text production and arrangement and enables less frequent use of abbreviations. If space dictates that abbreviations must be used, omit spaces or periods and capitalize all letters. Though variations still exist, the following is a widely accepted list.

ACT: acoustical ceiling tile
ADD: additional
ADJ: adjustable
AFF: above finish floor
ALUM: aluminum
APPX: approximately

BC: brick course
BD: board
BIT: bituminous
BLDG: building
BLK: block
BLKG: blocking
BM: beam
BOT: bottom
BUR: built-up roofing

CB: catch basin
CBD: chalkboard
CEM: cement
CI: cast iron
CIP: cast-in-place
CJ: control joint
CLG: ceiling
CLR: clearance
CLO: closet
CMU: concrete masonry unit
COL: column
COMP: compressible
CONC: concrete
CONST: construction
CONT: continuous

CPT: carpet
CRS: courses
CT: ceramic tile
CUB: column utility box

DET: detail
DF: drinking fountain
DIA: diameter
DN: down
DR: door
DWG: drawing

EA: each
EJ: expansion joint
EL: elevation or electrical
ELEV: elevator
ENC: enclosure
EQ: equal
EQUIP: equipment
ERD: emergency roof drain
EWC: electric water cooler
EXIST: existing
EXP: expansion
EXT: exterior

FD: floor drain
FDN: foundation
FE: fire extinguisher
FEC: fire extinguisher cabinet

FFT: finished floor transition
FHC: fire hose cabinet
FIN: finish
FIXT: fixture
FLR: floor
FLUOR: fluorescent
FOC: face of concrete
FOF: face of finish
FOM: face of masonry
FR: fire-rated
FT: feet
FTG: footing
FUB: floor utility box

GA: gauge
GALV: galvanized
GC: general contractor
GL: glass
GWB: gypsum wallboard
GYP: gypsum

HC: hollow core or handicap accessible
HDW: hardware
HGT: height
HM: hollow metal
HORIZ: horizontal
HP: high point
HTR: heater
HVAC: heating, ventilating, and air conditioning

IN: inch
INCAN: incandescent
INCL: including
INS: insulation
INT: interior

JAN: janitor
JC: janitor's closet
JT: joint

LAM: laminated
LAV: lavatory
LINO: linoleum
LP: low point
LTG: lighting

MAT: material
MAX: maximum
MECH: mechanical
MEMB: member
MFR: manufacturer
MIN: minimum
MISC: miscellaneous
MO: masonry opening
MTL: metal

NIC: not in contract
NO: number
NTS: not to scale

OC: on center
OD: outside diameter or overflow drain
OHD: overhead door
OHG: overhead grille
OPNG: opening
OPP: opposite
OPPH: opposite hand

PC: precast
PGL: plate glass
PL: plate
PLAM: plastic laminate
PLUM: plumber

PT: paint
PTD: painted
PTN: partition
PVC: polyvinyl chloride

QT: quarry tile
QTY: quantity

R: radius or riser
RA: return air
RD: roof drain
REG: register
REV: revision or reverse
REINF: reinforcing
REQD: required
RM: room
RO: rough opening
RSL: resilient flooring

SC: solid core
SECT: section
SHT: sheet
SIM: similar
SPEC: specifications
SQ: square
SSTL: stainless steel
STA: station
STD: standard
STL: steel
STOR: storage
STRUC: structural
SUSP: suspended

T: tread
TBD: tackboard
TD: trench drain
TEL: telephone
THK: thickness
TO: top of
TOC: top of concrete
TOF: top of footing
TOR: top of rail
TOS: top of steel
TOW: top of wall

TRT: treated
TYP: typical

UNO: unless noted otherwise

VCT: vinyl composition tile
VERT: vertical
VIF: verify in field
VP: veneer plaster
VWC: vinyl wall covering

W/: with
WC: water closet
WD: wood
WDW: window
WF: wide flange
W/O: without
WPR: waterproofing
WUB: wall utility box
WWF: welded wire fabric

&: and
<: angle
": inch
': foot
@: at
CL: centerline
[: channel
#: number
Ø: diameter

PROJECT TIMELINE

The information presented here is a generalization of the phases and events within a typical architectural project. It does not attempt to account for all project sizes and client types. The length of each phase is a rough estimation for a medium-sized project, but the timeframes can vary wildly. The expectations and duration of any of these phases are subject to the stipulations of the project's owner-architect agreement.

Pre-design

Even before beginning the actual design of a project, the architect may be asked to perform the following tasks, alone or in conjunction with other consultants: site selection and evaluation, environmental analysis, community participation, feasi-bility studies, programming, cost analysis, and conceptual design. It is not unusual for the architect to do many of these services as a (paid or unpaid) marketing effort, in anticipation of being awarded the project.

varies

Marketing

In the competitive environment of architecture, procuring a project can be more time- and labor-intensive than getting it built. Marketing takes many forms, but common modes of obtaining work are:

Competitions: Firms or individuals submit a design for a specified program and site, for which a winner is chosen. Competitions vary in form—they may be paid or unpaid, open or invited—and do not always result in a project being built.

Requests for Qualifications (RFQs): A potential client asks architects to submit their qualifications, sometimes to a specified format.

Requests for Proposal (RFPs): Similar to RFQs, though often firms are specifically asked to supply information about other relevant projects they have completed. Proposals may include a wide variety of information types, including proposed budget and schedule, and sometimes may require a design for the project.

Interviews: A potential client will want to meet the architect, sometimes with his or her prospective consultants. At this meeting, the design team may be asked to present a proposal for the project in question.

SD Schematic Design

Major design ideas are proposed and explored, including alternate schemes. Drawings produced in this phase include site plan, plans, elevations, and sections sufficient for cost estimation. SD often requires multiple presentations to the client for review and approval and can encompass the production of perspectives, renderings, and models to describe the design concept.

3 months

DD Design Development

The detailed development of the design (as established in SD) results in a drawing set suitable for a more accurate cost estimate. Coordination with consultants is key in this phase to identify and address potential problems before the design has proceeded too far. Presentations to the client turn more to these issues of coordination and cost control and take into account more specific feedback about the nature of rooms and spaces. The design is documented inside and out, including construction details, interior elevations, schedules, and specifications, all of which will be further refined in the CD phase.

6 months

CD Construction Documents

The "working drawing" phase of the project, in which every aspect of the design is drawn to scale and appropriately specified, is time- and energy-intensive, and project teams usually grow larger to accommodate the work involved. The design of the project must be well established by this point, and most owner-architect agreements stipulate that any requests for major design changes made after DD must be part of an "Additional Services" agreement, to make up for the time it has taken to document the project to date.

The CD set is the official documentation of the project and is distributed to contractors for bids as well as to the building department and other officials for all necessary permits. The architect is responsible for assisting the client in this process.

A CD set contains, at a minimum, a site plan, floor plans, reflected ceiling plans, exterior and interior building elevations, building sections, wall sections depicting construction detailing, interior details, door and window schedules, equipment schedules (if applicable), finishes schedules, and written specifications, as well as the drawings of engineers and other consultants.

9 months

CA Construction Administration

Though the project is under construction, the architect must still maintain control over its outcome, both through regular site visits, in which construction quality is observed for its conformance with the CD set, and by overseeing solutions to unanticipated problems as they arise. The architect must review shop drawings, change orders, and requests for information from the contractor, always acting in the best interest of the client and the budget. At the end of construction, the architect prepares the punch list and assists in obtaining a Certificate of Occupancy.

duration of construction

Marketing

Once completed, the project is photographed and documented. The architect may submit it for publication in any number of professional magazines, include it in the firm's brochure, or post it on the firm's website. It now serves as a marketing tool for obtaining more projects, and the process continues.

SPECIFICATIONS

Architectural specifications act as written instructions to the contractor and all parties involved in the construction of a building. Specifications are part of the construction document set, usually as a separate project manual. They provide detailed descriptions of the acceptable construction materials for all aspects of a building, from the type and color of paint to the type and method of structural fireproofing. Specification writing is time-consuming and exacting work; it is most often undertaken by specification writers or architects who specialize in the writing of specifications. Certified spec writers list the suffix CCS (Certified Construction Specifier) after their name. A well-written set of specs is imperative to keeping a project safe and on budget and to ensure that the needs of both architect and owner have been met.

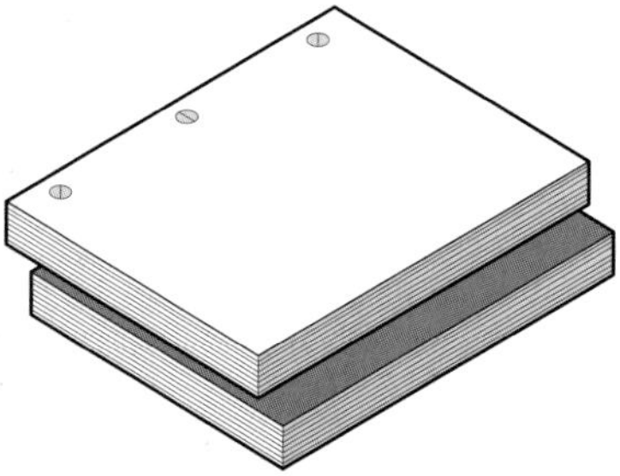

CSI MASTERFORMAT SYSTEM

The Construction Specifications Institute (CSI) was established in 1948 to bring order to the post–World War II building boom. CSI governs standardization of specification writing and formatting, and its Project Resource Manual (formerly the Manual of Practice, or MOP) is the industry reference. Spec writers might avail themselves of prewritten master guide specs that serve as a basis for many projects, or they might begin a set of specs entirely from scratch.

The CSI MasterFormat system has become the standard formatting system for nonresidential building projects in the United States and Canada. It consists of a list of numbers and titles that organize the information contained in the specification project manual.

Division Numbering

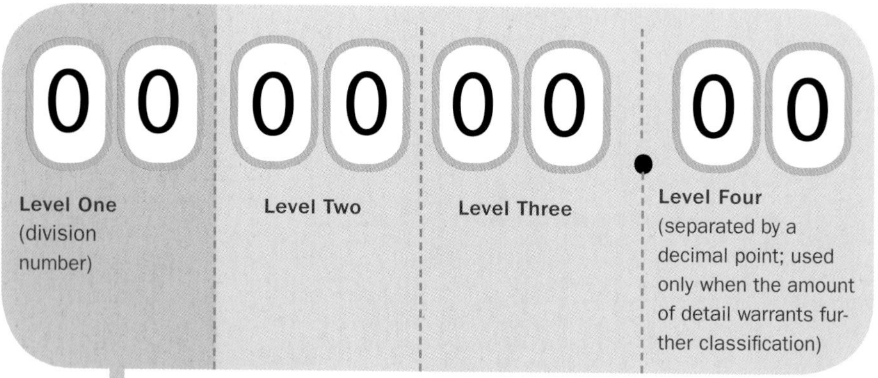
00 00 00.00
Level One (division number)
Level Two
Level Three
Level Four (separated by a decimal point; used only when the amount of detail warrants further classification)

CSI MasterFormat Division Titles

Reserved divisions provide space for future development and expansion, and CSI recommends that users not appropriate these divisions for their own use.

PROCUREMENT AND CONTRACTING REQUIREMENTS GROUP

00—Procurement and Contracting

SPECIFICATIONS GROUP

General Requirements

01—General Requirements

Facility Construction

02—Existing Conditions
03—Concrete
04—Masonry
05—Metals
06—Wood, Plastics, and Composites
07—Thermal and Moisture Protection
08—Openings
09—Finishes
10—Specialties
11—Equipment
12—Furnishings
13—Special Construction
14—Conveying Equipment
15—Reserved for future expansion
16—Reserved for future expansion
17—Reserved for future expansion
18—Reserved for future expansion
19—Reserved for future expansion

Facility Services

20—Reserved
21—Fire Suppression
22—Plumbing
23—Heating, Ventilating, and Air-Conditioning
24—Reserved
25—Integrated Automation
26—Electrical
27—Communications
28—Electronic Safety and Security
29—Reserved for future expansion

Site and Infrastructure

30—Reserved for future expansion
31—Earthwork
32—Exterior Improvements
33—Utilities
34—Transportation
35—Waterway and Marine Construction
36—Reserved
37—Reserved
38—Reserved
39—Reserved

Process Equipment

40—Process Interconnections
41—Material Processing and Handling Equipment
42—Process Heating, Cooling, and Drying Equipment
43—Process Gas and Liquid Handling, Purification and Storage Equipment
44—Pollution and Waste Control Equipment
45—Industry-Specific Manufacturing Equipment
46—Water and Wastewater Equipment
47—Reserved for future expansion
48—Electrical Power Generation
49—Reserved for future expansion

Chapter 13: Hand Drawing

Though rapidly being replaced by computer-aided drafting, hand drafting continues to be used by some practitioners, and its principles can still be applied to computer drawing. The practice of hand drafting employs a number of key instruments.

WORK SURFACE

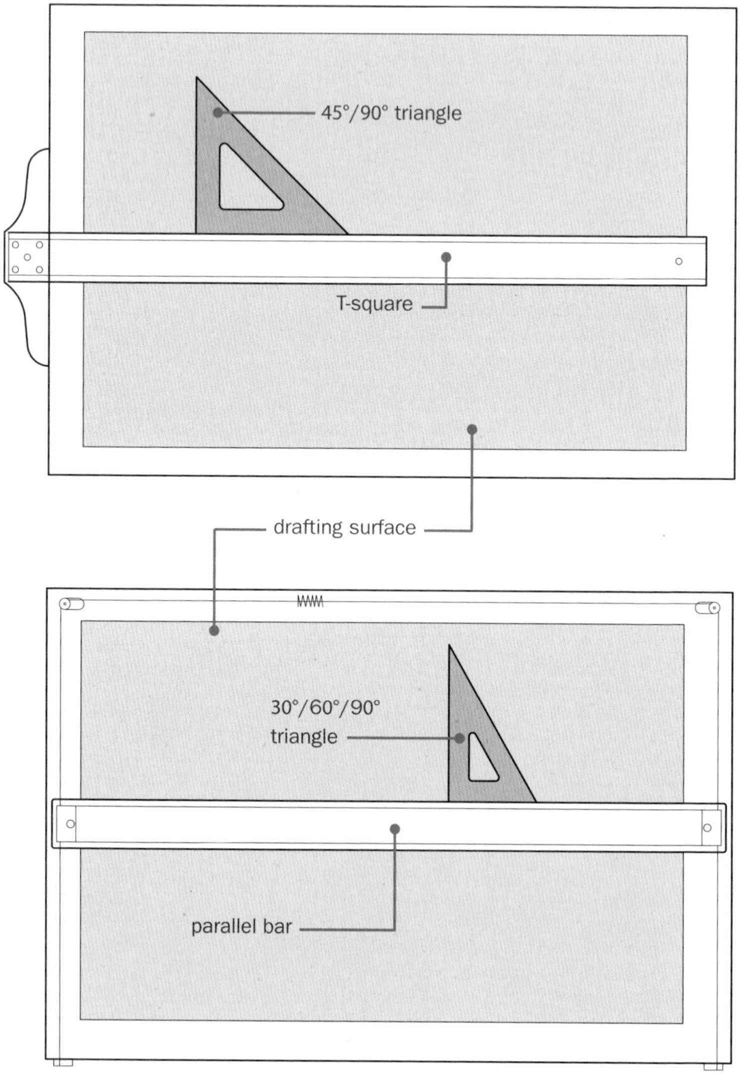
45°/90° triangle
T-square
drafting surface
30°/60°/90°
triangle
parallel bar

PAPERS AND BOARDS

Paper Type	Qualities	Format	Best Uses	Use for Overlay
Tracing paper	white, buff or yellow; inexpensive	Rolls in multiple sizes (12", 18", 24", 36", 48"); pads	sketch overlay; layouts	yes
Vellum	oil-treated to achieve transparency	rolls, sheets, and pads	pencil and technical pen work; overlay work	yes
Mylar (drafting film)	nonabsorbent polyester film (1- and 2-sided)	rolls and sheets	pencil and technical pen work; ideal for archival work	yes
Bond and drawing papers	variety of weights, textures, and colors	rolls and sheets	smooth best for pens; textured best for pencils	no
Illustration board	high-quality white rag affixed to board	large-scale sheet sizes	finished work in watercolor, pencil, chalk, or pen	no
Chip board	variety of plies; mostly gray	large-scale sheet sizes	model making; some dry mounting	no
Foam board	polystyrene foam between paper liners; white/black	large-scale boards; 1/8", 3/16", 1/4", 1/2" thick	model making; dry-mounting sheets	no

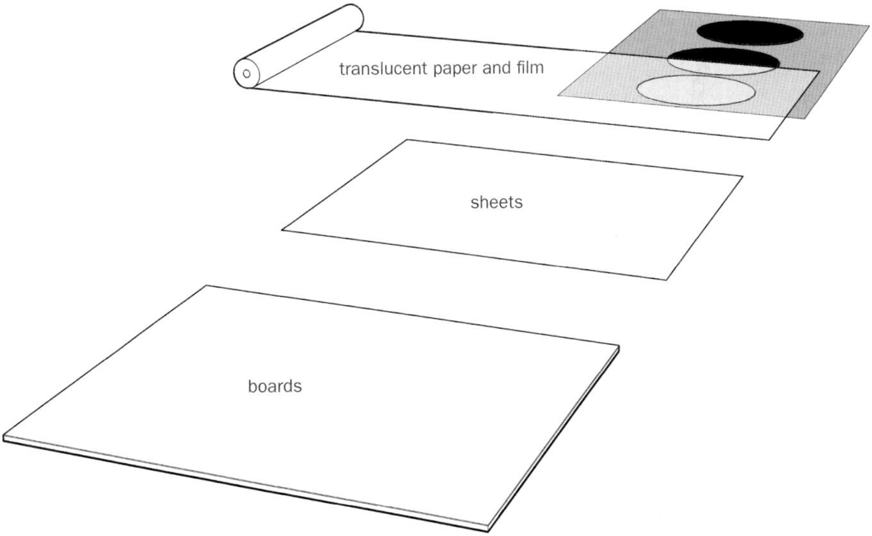
translucent paper and film
sheets
boards

DRAFTING SUPPLIES

1. Drafting brush:
Implement used to brush away erasures and drafting powder.

2. Drafting powder:
Finely ground white compound that prevents dust, dirt, and smudges from being ground into the drafting media.

3. French curve:
Template used as guide to draw smoothly most desired curvatures.

4. X-Acto knife:
Cutting tool used in model making and in Letratone application.

5. Erasing shield:
Device used to erase specific lines and areas without affecting others.

6. Adjustable triangle:
Tool used alone or in combination with other triangles to achieve any angle.

7. Template:
Pattern guides available in a wide variety of types (lettering, toilets, people) and scales.

8. Compass:
Hinge-legged instrument that accommodates a pen or pencil to describe precise circles or circular arcs.

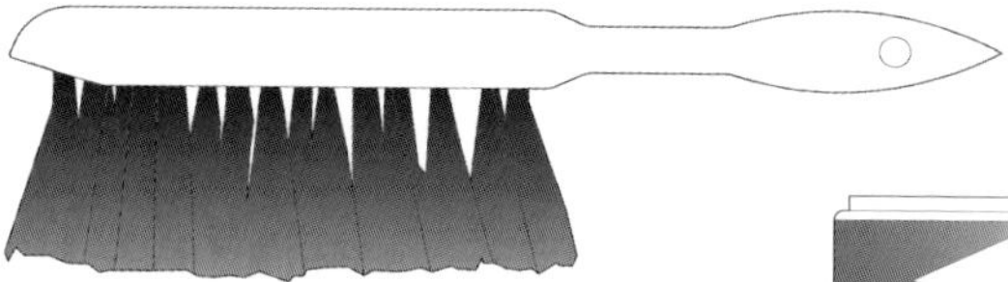

1

Quic Kleen
DRAFTING
POWDER

2

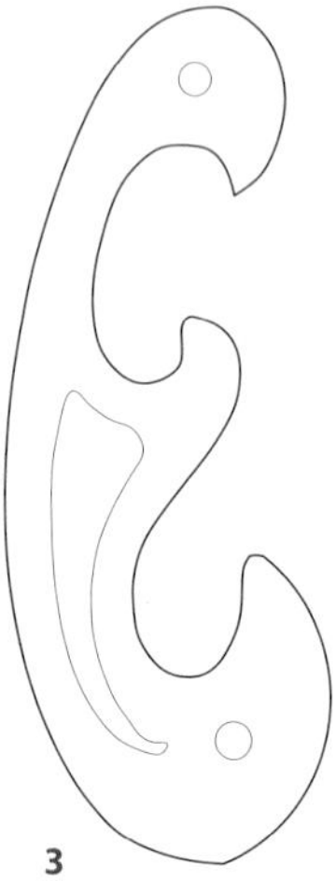

3

4

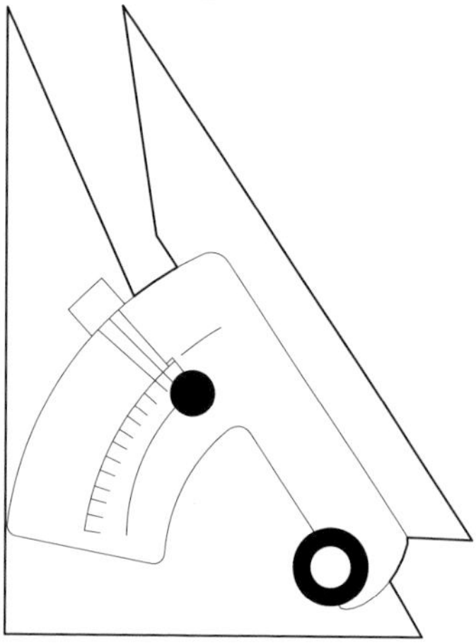

6

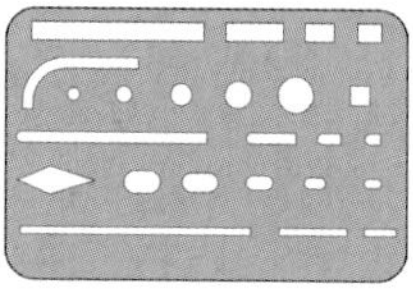

5

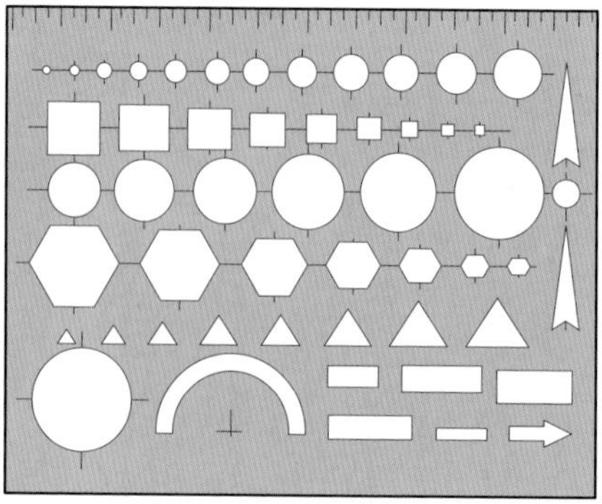

7

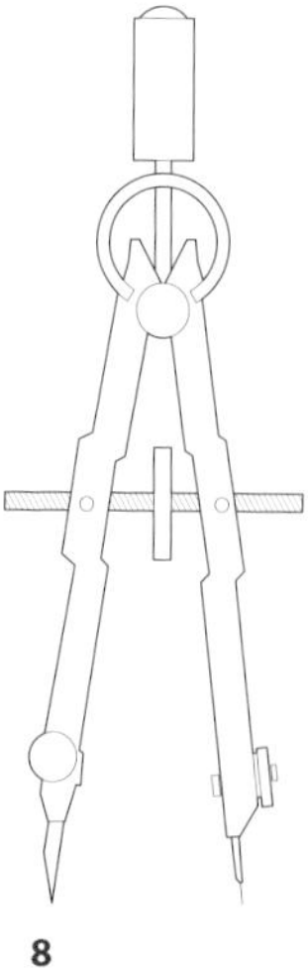

8

PENCILS

Harder leads contain more clay, whereas softer leads contain more graphite. Lead holders employ a push-button that advances the 2 mm lead, which comes in a wide array of hardnesses, colors, and nonphoto blue (does not appear on reproductions). Leads are sharpened in lead pointers or with simple emery paper or sandpaper blocks.

Pencil Hardness Range

Grade		Range
9H	very hard and dense	ideal range for guidelines and underlay work
8H		
7H		
6H		
5H		
4H		
3H		
2H		best range for finished drawings
H		
F		
HB		
B		range for bold lines and shading, less suitable for drafting purposes
2B		
3B		
4B		
5B		
6B	very soft	

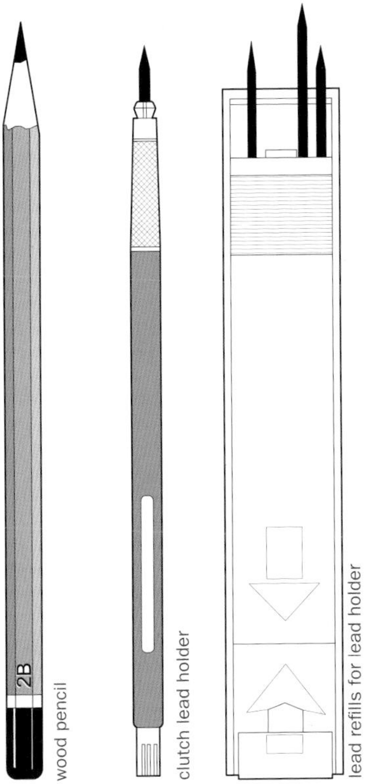
2B
wood pencil
clutch lead holder
lead refills for lead holder

TECHNICAL INK PENS

Technical pens, which use an ink flow–regulating wire with a tubular point (the pen nib), can produce very precise line widths. The ink may come in a prepackaged cartridge or the barrel of the pen may be filled with ink as needed. Ink pens are ideal for vellum and Mylar; they can even be erased from Mylar film with a nonabrasive drafting eraser or electric eraser.

Technical Pen Line Weights

Pen size	Line width
7	2.0
6	1.4
4	1.2
3 1/2	1.0
3	.80
2 1/2	.70
2	.60
1	.50
0	.35
00	.30
3x0	.25
4x0	.18
6x0	.13

technical pen body
pen nib

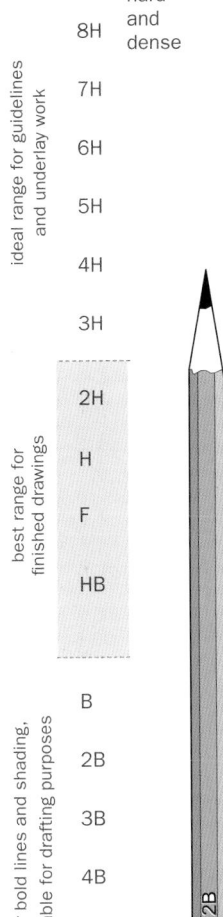

WORKING TO SCALE

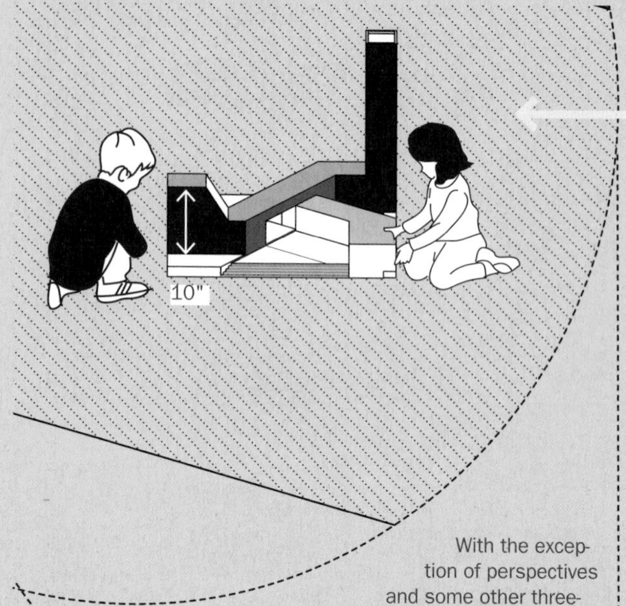
10"

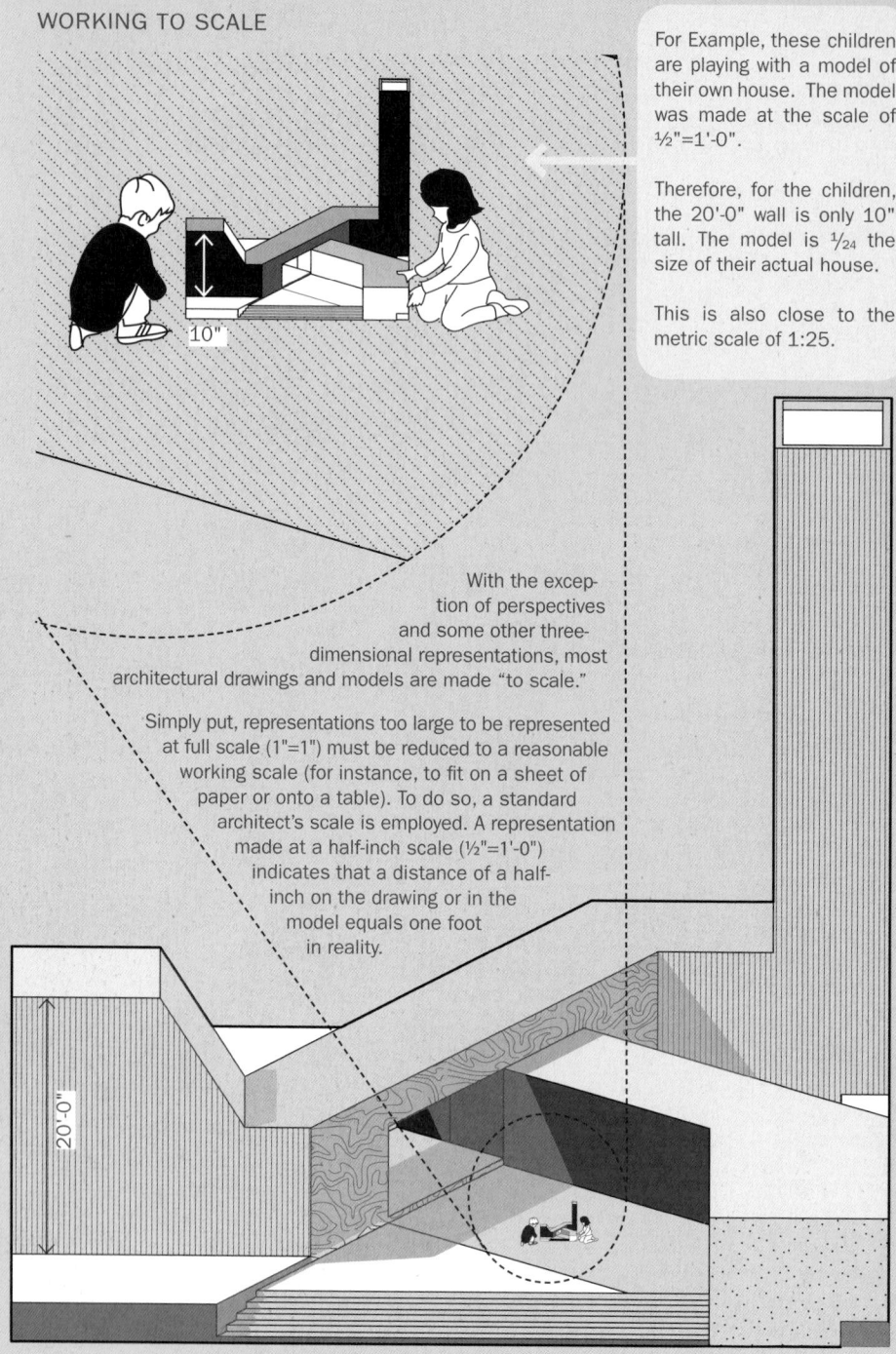

For Example, these children are playing with a model of their own house. The model was made at the scale of ½"=1'-0".

Therefore, for the children, the 20'-0" wall is only 10" tall. The model is 1⁄24 the size of their actual house.

This is also close to the metric scale of 1:25.

With the exception of perspectives and some other three-dimensional representations, most architectural drawings and models are made "to scale."

Simply put, representations too large to be represented at full scale (1"=1") must be reduced to a reasonable working scale (for instance, to fit on a sheet of paper or onto a table). To do so, a standard architect's scale is employed. A representation made at a half-inch scale (½"=1'-0") indicates that a distance of a half-inch on the drawing or in the model equals one foot in reality.

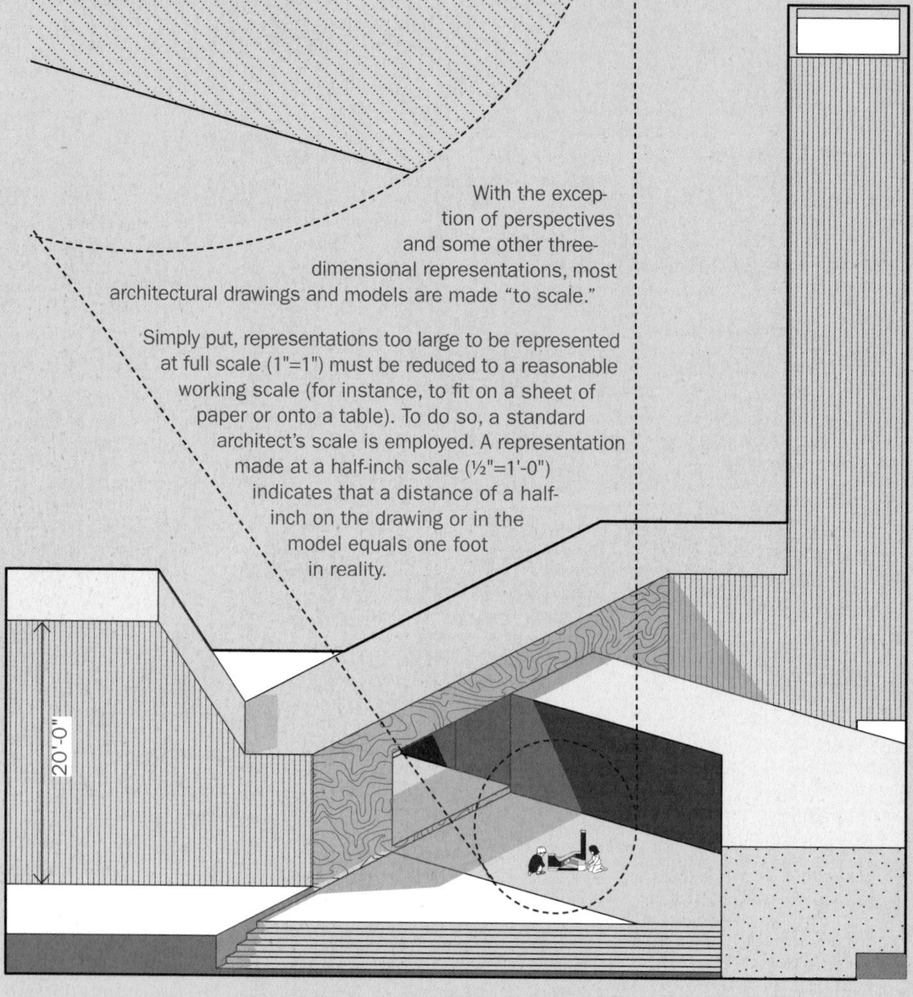
20'-0"

The three sides of a triangular architect's scale provide a total of eleven scales (plus full scale), which are written as follows:

- 1/16"=1'-0"
- 3/32"=1'-0"
- 1/8"=1'-0"
- 3/16"=1'-0"
- 1/4"=1'-0"
- 3/8"=1'-0"
- 1/2"=1'-0"
- 3/4"=1'-0"
- 1"=1'-0"
- 1 1/2"=1'-0"
- 3"=1'-0"

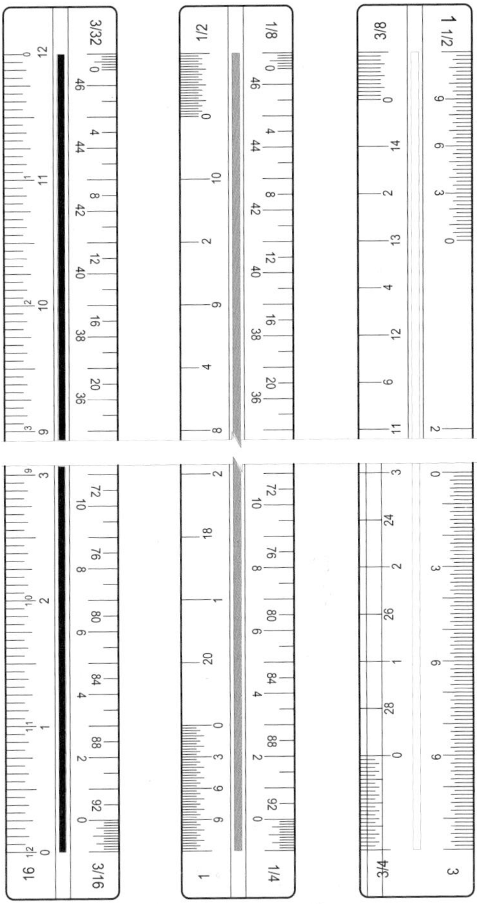
3/32
16
3/16
1/2
1
1/8
1/4
3/8
1 1/2
3/4
3

Engineer's scales are often used for larger-scale drawings such as site plans; they follow the same principle as architect's scales but with larger increments of ten (1"=10', 1"=50', 1"=100', and so forth). Scales are also available in metric units.

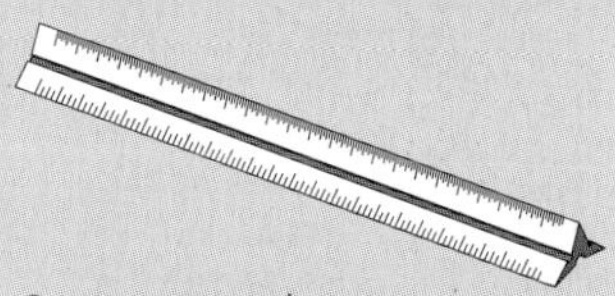

Customary scales are understood by their relationship to one foot (i.e., 1/4"=1'-0"). Metric scales operate as ratios (i.e., 1:1 is full scale, 1:50 is 1/50th of full scale, etc.). Though easy to confuse the two systems, it's important to note that 1/4"=1'-0" is NOT the same as 1/4th of full scale. Instead, its ratio is determined as follows:

$\frac{1}{4} \times \frac{1}{12} = \frac{1}{48}$, or 1:48

Comparable scales

CUSTOMARY	METRIC
1/16" = 1'-0" (1:192)	1:200
3/32" = 1'-0" (1:128)	1:125
1/8" = 1'-0" (1:96)	1:100
3/16" = 1'-0" (1:64)	
1/4" = 1'-0" (1:48)	1:50
3/8" = 1'-0" (1:32)	
1/2" = 1'-0" (1:24)	1:25
3/4" = 1'-0" (1:16)	
1" = 1'-0" (1:12)	1:10
1 1/2" = 1'-0" (1:8)	
3" = 1'-0" (1:4)	1:5

Chapter 14: Digital Production

Building design and construction involves enormous amounts of information in need of organization and dissemination among numerous groups of interested and active parties. The introduction of computers into this process has understandably changed the way in which buildings are conceived, designed, and documented. Truly, many things can now be done faster and with more ease, but computers have given rise to new issues involving management of computer files, quality standards for deliverable materials, and the constant need to stay current with rapidly evolving technologies. The prospect of documenting computer standards and guidelines as static and absolute is therefore neither productive nor possible—the only thing that is certain is that things will change. With this in mind, this chapter focuses on elements common to many types of digital architectural work.

Digital Model: In the virtual space of the compter, this is a "full scale" spatial representation of an object. A digital model can be the basis for numerous forms of output, including orthogaphic projection drawings, renderings, animations, and fabrication.

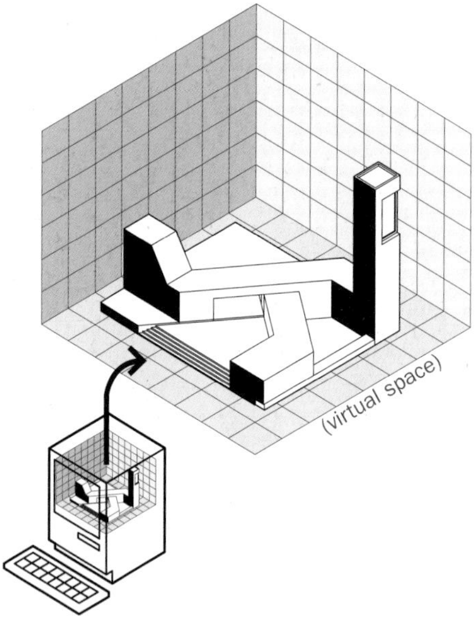
(virtual space)

Physical Model: A tangible, three-dimensional replica of a design, usually at a scale much smaller than full size. Such models used to be made exclusively by hand, of materials such as chip board, wood, and foam core. With the increasing dominance of digital production, a physical model is also easily created from a digital model, through methods such as laser cutting and 3D printing.

COMPUTER MODELING

Computers allow for efficient, precise, and easily modifiable architectural output. Within practice, commonly used programs for modeling and drafting deliverable drawing sets include AutoCAD and Revit, though digital modeling and rendering programs are numerous and varied. Often, the more sophisticated the intended product, the more expensive the digital tool.

Digital programs are not limited to the production of static drawings. Many are employed extensively to design complex forms that would simply be impossible otherwise, often with the ability to interface with digital fabrication.

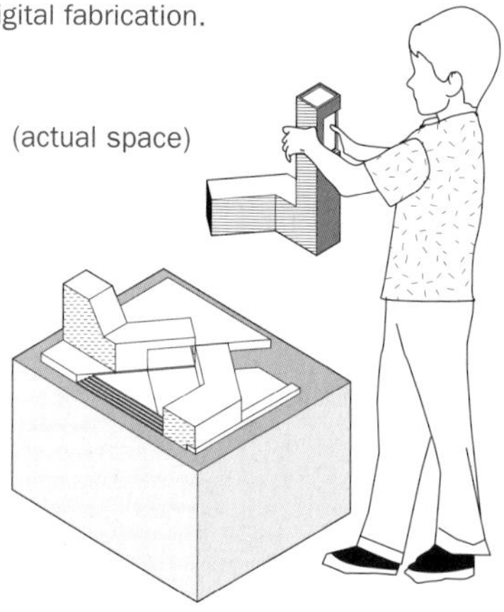
(actual space)

DIGITAL TERMS

Aspect ratio: Ratio of display width to height.

BIM: (Building Information Modeling) Modeling in which a model's three-dimensional information can be shared among multiple users via a database linking models and assemblies.

Block: Grouping of one or more objects combined to form a single object. On creation, blocks are given a name and an insertion point.

CAD: Computer-aided design or computer-aided drafting. Also CADD, for computer-aided design and drafting.

Command line: Text area reserved for keyboard input, messages, and prompts.

Coordinates: X, y, and z location relevant to a model's origin (0,0,0).

Crosshairs: Type of cursor.

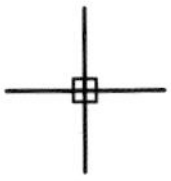

Cursor: Active object on a video display that enables the user to place graphic information or text.

Drawing file: Electronic representation of a building or an object.

Drawing interchange format (DXF): ASCII or binary file format of an AutoCAD drawing, for exporting AutoCAD drawings to other applications or importing those from other applications into AutoCAD.

DWG: File format for saving vector graphics from within AutoCAD.

Entity: Geometric element or piece of data in a digital drawing, such as a line, a point, a circle, a polyline, a symbol, or a piece of text.

External reference: In AutoCAD, a file or drawing that is used as background in another drawing but cannot be edited, except in its original drawing. Examples include building grids and site information. Also called X-Ref.

Polyline: Object made up of one or more connected segments or arcs, treated as a single object.

Raster graphic: Image comprised of a grid of pixels (as bitmap). More pixels create higher resolution and a larger digital file. When scaled up from its original size, a raster image will lose quality and become jagged in appearance, looking pixelated.

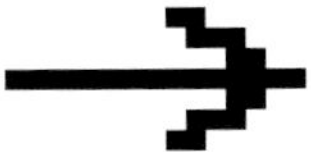

Sheet file: Print- or plot-ready electronic representation of a presentation sheet, containing a view or views of the model, text, symbols, and a title block.

Vector graphic: Graphic composed of paths displayed and stored as geometric primitives (points, lines, curves, and polygons). Made of paths instead of pixels, vectors can remain crisp and sharp even when scaled up or down.

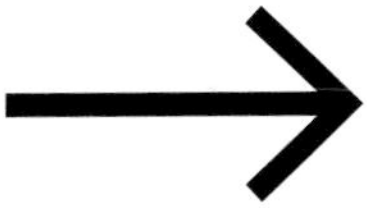

X, y, and z axes: The three directions of the Cartesian coordinate system. x and y establish the two-dimensional plane, and z establishes the third dimension.

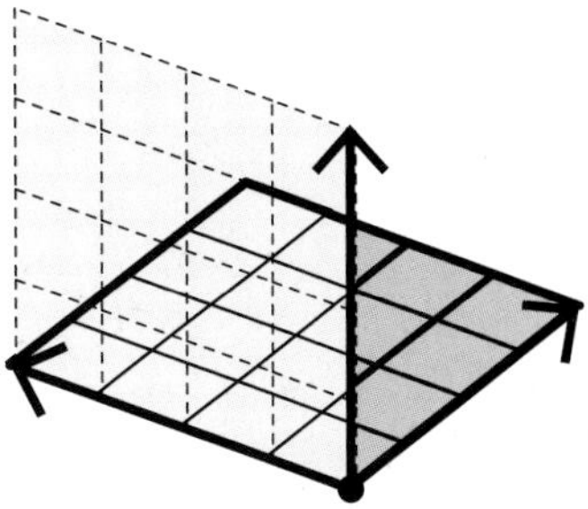

MODEL SPACE AND PAPER SPACE SCALES IN AUTOCAD

All AutoCAD models and drawings, from detailed wall sections to expansive site plans, are drawn in model space at full scale (1:1). Paper space is used to set up print- and plot-worthy sheets (often with the use of a title block) that enable the information in model space to be printed to a specific and accurate scale. Such a system allows the architect considerable flexibility when designing and drawing, because one drawing can be used at many different scales and for many different purposes and need not be drawn "to scale."

A simple way to envision the relationship between model and paper space is to think of the paper space title block as an actual piece of paper, with a hole cut out (the viewport). Through this hole model space is visible. Using XP factors (see following page), the model in the viewport is scaled in relation to the paper space title block.

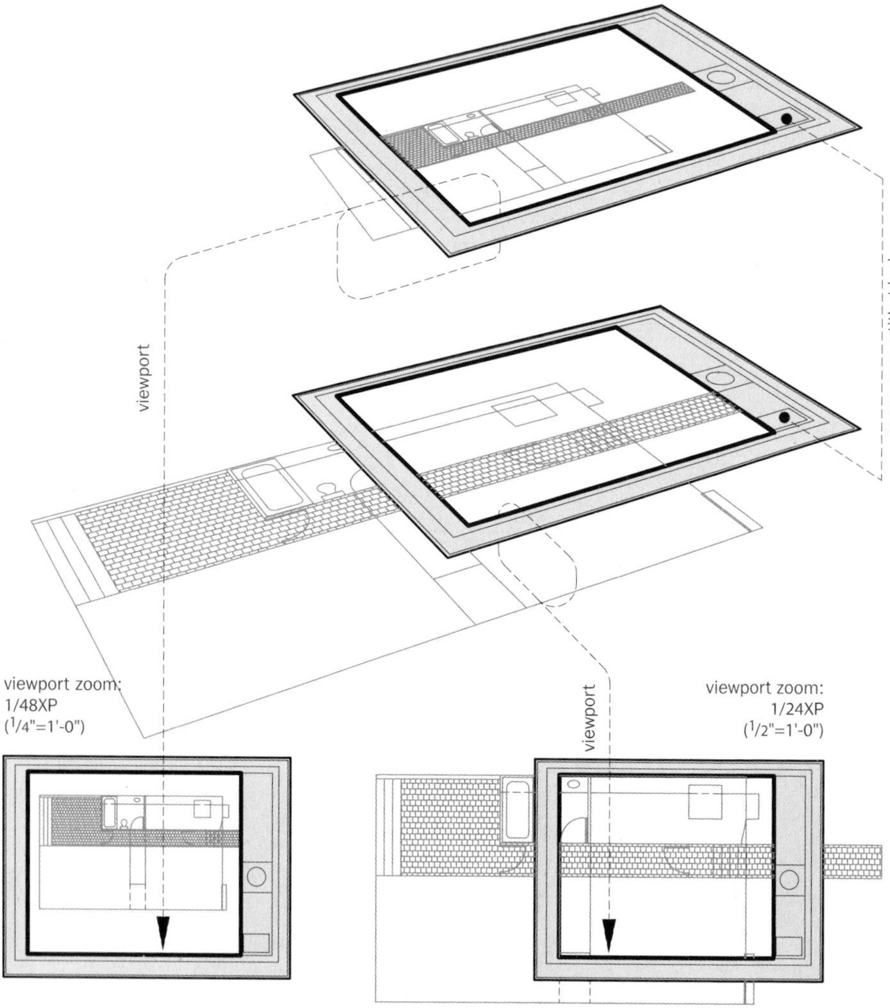
paper space title blocks
viewport
viewport
viewport zoom:
1/48XP
(1/4"=1'-0")
viewport zoom:
1/24XP
(1/2"=1'-0")

AutoCAD Text Scale Chart (in inches)

DWG Scale	Scale Factor	XP Factor	Desired Text Height 1/16"	3/32"	1/8"	3/16"	1/4"	5/16"	3/8"	1/2"	3/4"	1"
Full	1	1	.0625	.09375	.125	.1875	.25	.3125	.375	.5	.75	1
6"=1'	.5	1/2	.125	.1875	.25	.375	.5	.625	.75	1	1.5	2
3"=1'	.25	1/4	.25	.375	.5	.75	1	1.25	1.5	2	3	4
1 1/2"=1'	.125	1/8	.5	.75	1	1.5	2	2.5	3	4	6	8
1"=1'	.08333	1/12	.75	1.125	1.5	2.25	3	3.75	4.5	6	9	12
3/4"=1'	.0625	1/16	1	1.5	2	3	4	5	6	8	12	16
1/2"=1'	.04167	1/24	1.5	2.25	3	4.5	6	7.5	9	12	18	24
3/8"=1'	.03125	1/32	2	3	4	6	8	10	12	16	24	32
1/4"=1'	.02083	1/48	3	4.5	6	9	12	15	18	24	36	48
3/16"=1'	.015625	1/64	4	6	8	12	16	20	24	32	48	64
1/8"=1'	.01042	1/96	6	9	12	18	24	30	36	48	72	96
1/16"=1'	.005208	1/192	12	18	24	36	48	60	72	96	144	192
1"=10'	.0083	1/120	7.5	11.25	15	22.5	30	37.5	45	60	90	120
1"=20'	.004167	1/240	15	22.5	30	45	60	75	90	120	180	240
1"=30'	.002778	1/360	22.5	33.75	45	67.5	90	112.5	135	180	270	360

Using This Chart

Because all work done in AutoCAD models should be at 1:1, text and labels must be adjusted to appropriate sizes based on the scale at which they will be printed.

For example, if a detail drawing will be printed at 3"=1'-0", and the desired height of the text when printed is 1/8", the text in the model must be set to 0.5". If the same drawing will be printed at 1/4" = 1'-0", and that text also needs to be 1/8" high, any text related to the 1/4" scale output would be set to 6" in the model. Many clients, including government agencies, will require a minimum text size for legibility.

Using Paper Space Scales (XP)

The XP scale is the relationship between the desired plotted scale and the sheet of paper on which it will be plotted. With hand drafting, one would typically use an architect's or engineer's scale to assist in correctly making a drawing "to scale." On such a scale, if using 1/4" = 1'-0", 1' is shown on the scale as 1/4" in length; 2' is shown as 1/2", and so on. In reality, the scale has already done much of the calculation necessary to draw at the desired scale. To describe this process accurately, one could say that, for the drawing to fit on a certain sheet of paper, the drawing has been made at 1/48th its full scale (if 1/4"=12", 1/4 x 1/12 =X, therefore x =1/48).

In AutoCAD the process is much the same. To set the scale of a viewport while inside the viewport (ms) in paper space, zoom to 1/48XP (also equal to 0.02083XP). XP literally means "times paper space." This action will zoom the viewport window to 1/4"=1'-0" in relation to the paper space title block, which is printed at 1:1.

CODES AND GUIDELINES 4.

Codes, laws, and regulations can carry with them a certain off-putting suggestion of bureaucratic obfuscation. To run afoul of them would never be recommended, but attempts to understand them can be frustrating. Certainly, there exist standards that appear senseless or unnecessarily restrictive, but as the world changes and populations expand, the built environment is subject to an increasing number of forces that dictate its use and forms.

As we open doors, turn on lights, and navigate stairs, we all experience firsthand standards within design practice. Ideally, codes and standards allow us to use buildings safely. Constraints brought by code restrictions may also provide an opportunity to let good design solve difficult problems.

As the very real design needs of people with disabilities receive official and widespread acknowledgment and the concept of accessibility becomes more naturally integrated with architecture—for younger designers this is the norm—it can be difficult to imagine how recently it was viewed as an impediment to good design.

Acceptance of the aesthetic possibilities of sustainable design is even more recent. In fact, new standards that accommodate all types of users and a growing recognition of architecture's responsibility to the environment and its future can provide fresh takes on old forms and strong incentives to try new processes.

Chapter 15: Building Codes

The fundamental purpose of building codes is to protect the health, safety, and welfare of all people through the construction of safe buildings and environments. Building practices have long been regulated in various ways, and regulations have existed in America since the early colonies, but it was the 1871 Chicago fire that emphasized the need for effective and enforceable building codes. In the early years since, most building codes in the United States were written and administered by local city, county, or state jurisdictions, eventually producing three major model codes: the National Codes of the Building Officials and Code Administrators International (BOCA), the Uniform Codes of the International Conference of Building Officials (ICBO), and Standard Codes of the Southern Building Code Congress International (SBCCI). With a few exceptions, each of the fifty states has adopted one of these models for its primary building code, in addition to supplemental codes for fire, mechanical, electrical, plumbing, and residential.

INTERNATIONAL BUILDING CODE

The first International Building Code (IBC) was established by the International Code Council in 2000, and with it, the development of the National Codes, Uniform Codes, and Standard Codes was discontinued.

Currently, most U.S. states have adopted or are making efforts to adopt the IBC as their primary building code, though the process continues to differ for each state. The current status of the applicable codes for any given state or local jurisdiction should be verified with local building departments or by visiting the ICC website at www.iccsafe.org. Any code information cited in this book is from the IBC, unless stated otherwise.

NOTE OF DISCLAIMER
The code information contained in this chapter is for general information only and is here to provide the reader with an introductory overview of the purposes and organization of building codes, and simple "rules of thumb" to follow when beginning design work.

It is not intended to replace any codes discussed, to present interpretations or analyses of said codes, or to address any specific project. It also does not try to address all aspects of any one code in such a small number of pages; rather, the information touches on topics of general interest to most users of this book. All attempts have been made to present information as accurately as possible, with the understanding that code content may change after the book's publication.

EVOLUTION OF THE IBC

To address a changing world, the IBC codes are evolving through continual review by almost any party that comes in contact with them, including code enforcing officials, various code development committees, and design professionals. Changes occur, for instance, to address new materials, emerging technologies, and shifts in use types. They even occur to clarify interpretations of language and the intent of the codes as written. As a result, the IBC has been designed to be updated every three years. The 2015 edition, for example, exhibits the 2012 code with ICC-approved changes included.

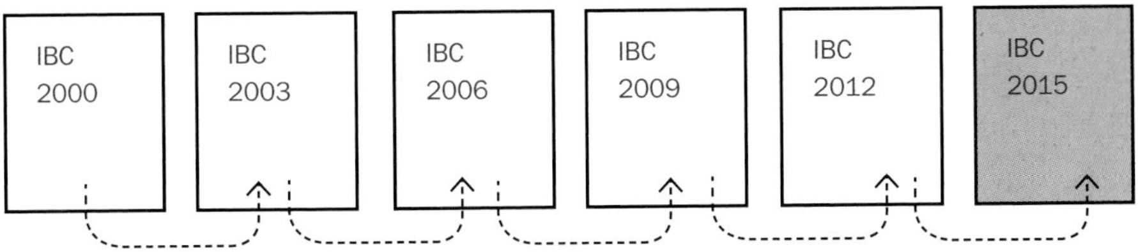
IBC 2000
IBC 2003
IBC 2006
IBC 2009
IBC 2012
IBC 2015

For any project, the applicable codes must be interpreted by the appropriate Authority Having Jurisdiction (AHJ), which could include, among others, local building and fire officials. The use and interpretation of codes can be daunting, and differences of interpretation may occur among designers and building officials. For this reason, it is beneficial to a project to establish contact with the local building department early enough in the design process to address any questions of interpretation.

Even with the help of consultants and the interpretations of others, architects must make every effort to familiarize themselves with pertinent codes, which puts them in a position of greater authority when issues of interpretation do arise. It is never recommended to memorize passages of the code, however, because these will change over time and memory may fail. What is important is to have a thorough working knowledge of the table of contents and to be able to navigate the code with a confident efficiency that, like all aspects of the practice of architecture, comes with experience.

All codes are structured around protection of human life and of property, including both prevention and reaction. Code analysis is performed based on the following sets of data:

- Occupancy Type
- Construction Type
- Building or Floor Area
- Building Height
- Exits and Egress
- Building Separations and Shafts
- Fire Protection
- Fire Extinguishing Systems
- Engineering Requirements

OCCUPANCY TYPE AND USE GROUPS

A building's use and occupancy are primary criteria for determining many aspects of how codes will affect a building, including the height, area, and type of construction allowed. Within each occupancy use group are further subdivisions. It is not unusual for a building to fall under more than one category of occupancy type, which is known as a mixed-use occupancy. It may then be handled either as a "separated use," by providing complete fire separation between occupancies, or as a "nonseparated use," by subjecting each occupancy type to the most stringent requirements for its respective use group.

Occupancy Use Groups

A	Assembly
B	Business
E	Educational
F	Factory and Industrial
H	High Hazard
I	Institutional
M	Mercantile
R	Residential
S	Storage
U	Utility and Miscellaneous

In addition, other building types exist that do not fall into the above categories, and/or contain elements requiring additional code requirements.

Group A: Assembly
(50 or more occupants)

A-1: Assembly areas usually with fixed seats, usually for viewing movies or performances (may or may not have a stage).

A-2: Assembly areas involving serving and consumption of food and drink, as in a restaurant or bar. Loose seating and possible patron alcohol impairment are key factors in this group.

A-3: Other assembly groups that don't fit A-1 or A-2. May include houses of worship, art galleries, and libraries.

A-4: Assembly areas for indoor sporting events.

A-5: Assembly areas for outdoor sporting events.

Group B: Business

Most office buildings fall into this category, including their storage areas (unless they exceed the amount of hazardous materials allowable, in which case they become Use Group H).

Also included are educational facilities after grade 12 (colleges and universities), ambulatory care facilities, and research laboratories.

Any assembly area, including a lecture hall, may fall into Group A and should be treated as such.

Group E: Educational

More than 6 people, for classes up to the 12th grade

Daycare facilities for 5 or more children over age $2^1/2$ (daycare in a dwelling unit for fewer than 5 people is classified as R-3).

Group F: Factory and Industrial

F-1: Moderate-hazard factory occupancy that has established that the relative hazards of fabrication operations do not put them in Group H (Hazardous) or in category F-2.

F-2: Low-hazard factory industrial occupancy where the materials of manufacture are considered to be noncombustible.

Group H: High Hazard

A range in high-hazard occupancies from H-1 to H-5, addressing the quantities and nature of use of the hazardous materials.

Group I: Institutional

I-1: More than 16 people in a 24-hour residential environment and under supervised conditions. May include group homes, assisted-living facilities, and halfway houses whose residents require custodial care, but are capable of self-preservation.

I-2: More than 5 people in a 24-hour residential environment and under supervised conditions and receiving medical care. May include hospitals and nursing homes whose residents are unable to respond to emergency situations without the aid of staff members.

I-3: More than 5 people in a 24-hour supervised environment under full-time restraint and security. Because of security measures, occupants cannot respond to emergencies without the aid of a staff member. May include prisons, detention centers, and reformatories, which may be further subdivided into five categories based on the amount of freedom of movement of residents inside the facility.

I-4: More than 5 people under supervised conditions or custodial care for less than 24 hours a day. May include adult and child daycare. For facilities with children over age $2^1/2$, Group E may apply.

Group M: Mercantile

Department stores, drugstores, markets, gas stations, sales rooms, and retail or wholesale stores.

Group R: Residential

R-1: Residences with sleeping units serving transient occupants. May include hotels and boarding houses.

R-2: Permanent dwellings with more than two units. May include apartments, dormitories, and longer term boarding houses.

R-3: Permanent single-family or duplex residences. May also include care facilities for 5 or fewer people, boarding houses with 10 or fewer occupants, and (nontransient) congregate living facilities with 16 or fewer occupants. Includes many residential occupancies not included in R-1, R-2, R-4, or I.

R-4: Between 5 and 16 occupants of a residential care or assisted-living facility, in which the residents receive custodial care on a 24-hour basis, but are capable of self-preservation. Types include alcohol and drug centers and social rehabilitation facilities.

Group S: Storage

S-1: Moderate-hazard storage occupancy for materials not considered hazardous enough for Group H but that do not qualify as S-2.

S-2: Low-hazard storage occupancy for materials considered to be noncombustible.

Group U: Utility and Miscellaneous

Used for accessory buildings and nonbuildings (such as fences or retaining walls) that are generally not occupied for long periods of time and may serve a secondary function to other occupancies.

CONSTRUCTION TYPES AND FIRE RESISTANCE

Construction types are categorized by their material content and the resistance to fire of the structural system. The IBC assigns five broad categories to all buildings, based on the predominant materials in the building's construction. These categories are I, II, III, IV, and V, with Type I being most fire resistive and Type V being least fire resistive. The five types are divided into A and B categories, reflecting the level of fire-resistance rating for each.

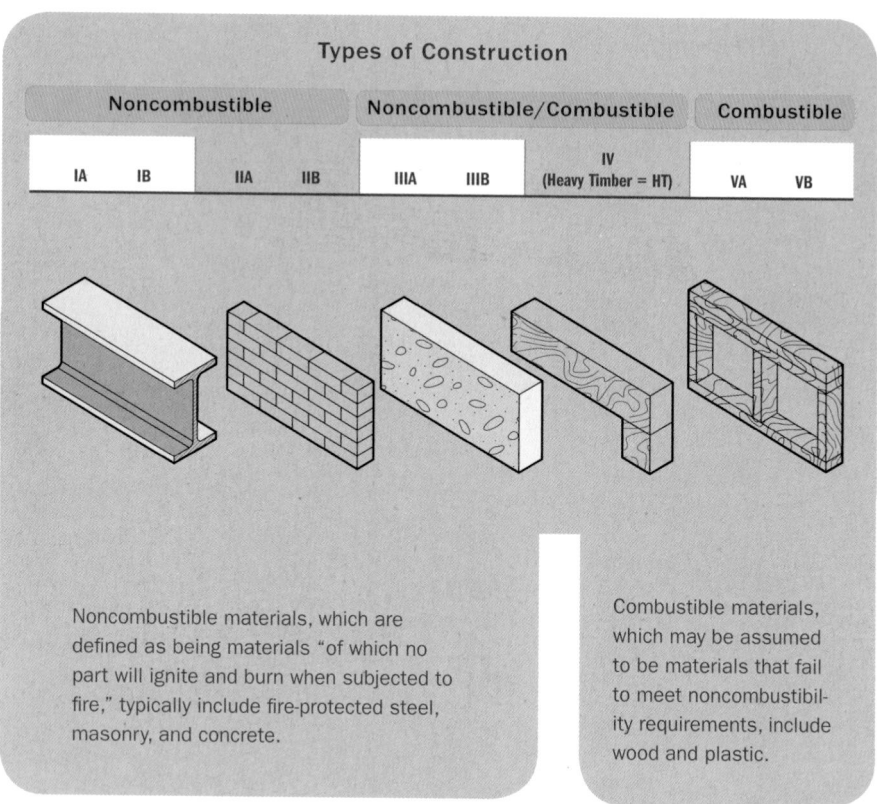

Types of Construction

Noncombustible				Noncombustible/Combustible			Combustible	
IA	IB	IIA	IIB	IIIA	IIIB	IV (Heavy Timber = HT)	VA	VB

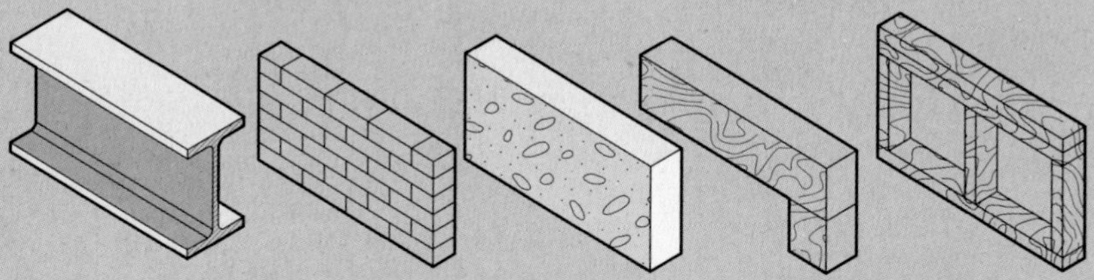

Noncombustible materials, which are defined as being materials "of which no part will ignite and burn when subjected to fire," typically include fire-protected steel, masonry, and concrete.

Combustible materials, which may be assumed to be materials that fail to meet noncombustibility requirements, include wood and plastic.

Fire-Resistance Ratings

Fire-resistance ratings are measured in hours or fractions of an hour and reflect the amount of time that a material or assembly of materials will resist fire exposure, as set forth in ASTM E119 (American Society for Testing and Materials Standard for Fire Tests of Building Constructions). When beginning design of a building, the initial code analysis must consider the desired occupancy and the desired height and area to determine the minimum allowable construction type for fire ratings.

EGRESS

Means of Egress Diagram

An **exit** is an enclosed, protected way of travel from an exit access to an exit discharge. When the exit access is above or below the grade of the exit discharge, an enclosed stair or ramp is required.

The number of means out of an occupied space is determined by size, occupancy type, and occupant load.

An **exit access** leads an occupant from an occupied part of the building to an exit (commonly, this is a corridor).

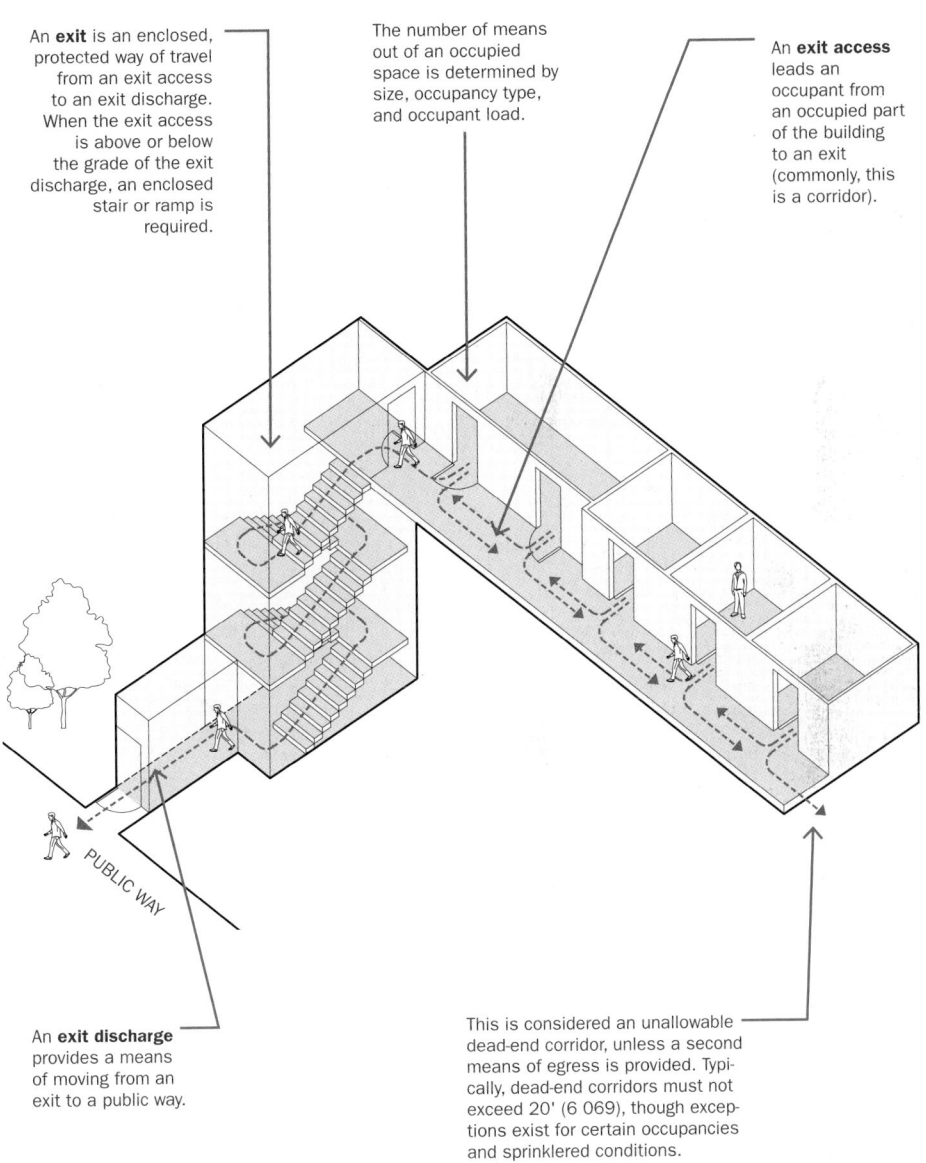

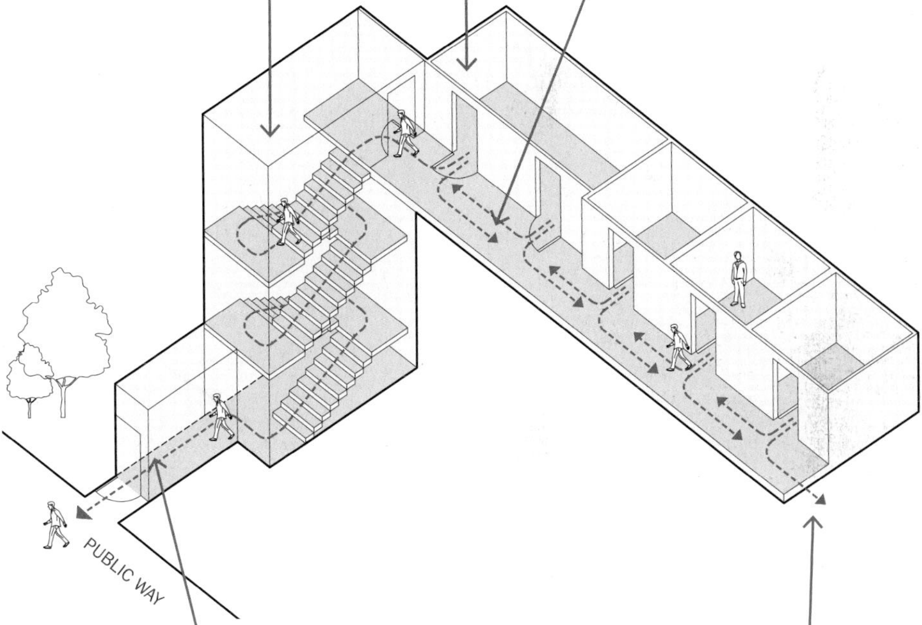
PUBLIC WAY

An **exit discharge** provides a means of moving from an exit to a public way.

This is considered an unallowable dead-end corridor, unless a second means of egress is provided. Typically, dead-end corridors must not exceed 20' (6 069), though exceptions exist for certain occupancies and sprinklered conditions.

MEANS OF EGRESS

IBC 202 defines a means of egress as "a continuous and unobstructed path of vertical and horizontal egress travel from any occupied portion of a building or structure to a public way." It consists of the exit access, the exit, and the exit discharge. Simply put, means of egress provide conditions for getting all occupants to a safe place (usually an outdoor public way) in the event of fire or other emergency.

Number of Means of Egress

Per IBC 1006, occupancies (per story) that require more than one means of egress are (other restrictions may apply relative to the level above or below grade):

A, B, E, F, M, and U, with occupant loads 50 and over

H-2, H-3, with occupant loads over 3

H-4, H-5, I, and R-1, R-2, R-4 with occupant loads over 10

S with occupant loads 30 and over

Any occupancy between 501 and 1,000 requires three exits, and occupancies over 1,000 require four.

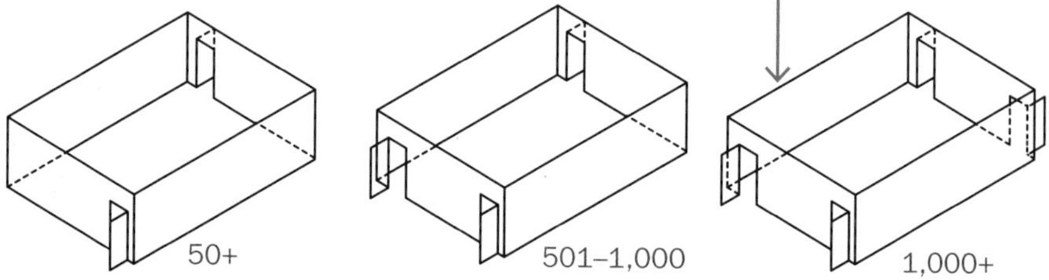
50+
501–1,000
1,000+

MEANS OF EGRESS SIZING

Egress Stairs

Minimum width is determined by IBC 1005, but must not be less than 44" (1 118), except for passageways serving occupant loads of fewer than 50, which must be no less than 36" (914) (IBC 1011).

Ramps

Ramps in an egress system should have a width no less than the corridors that serve them, and no less than 36" (914) between handrails (IBC 1012).

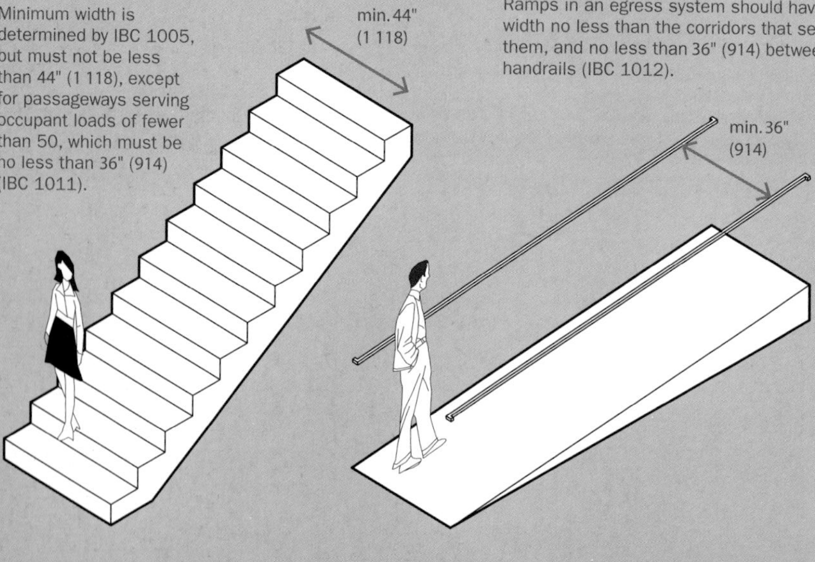
min. 44"
(1 118)
min. 36"
(914)

Required Egress Widths

Sizes are determined by coordinating IBC 1004 (Floor Area per Occupant) with IBC 1005 (Means of Egress Sizing), and comparing to the minimum allowable sizing, taking the higher option.

Exit Passageways

Minimum passageway width is determined by IBC 1005, but must not be less than 44" (1 118), except for (IBC 1020):

Within a dwelling unit or in an occupancy of less than 50: 36" (914)

Group E with 100+ occupant load: 72" (1 829)

Group 1-2 areas with required bed movement: 96" (2 438)

Egress Doors

In areas with an egress load of more than 50 occupants, or any Group H occupancy, exit access doors should swing in the direction of travel (IBC 1010). If they swing into a required egress path, they may not reduce the required width by more than one half while swinging open, and once opened 180º, the door may not project into the required width more than 7" (178).

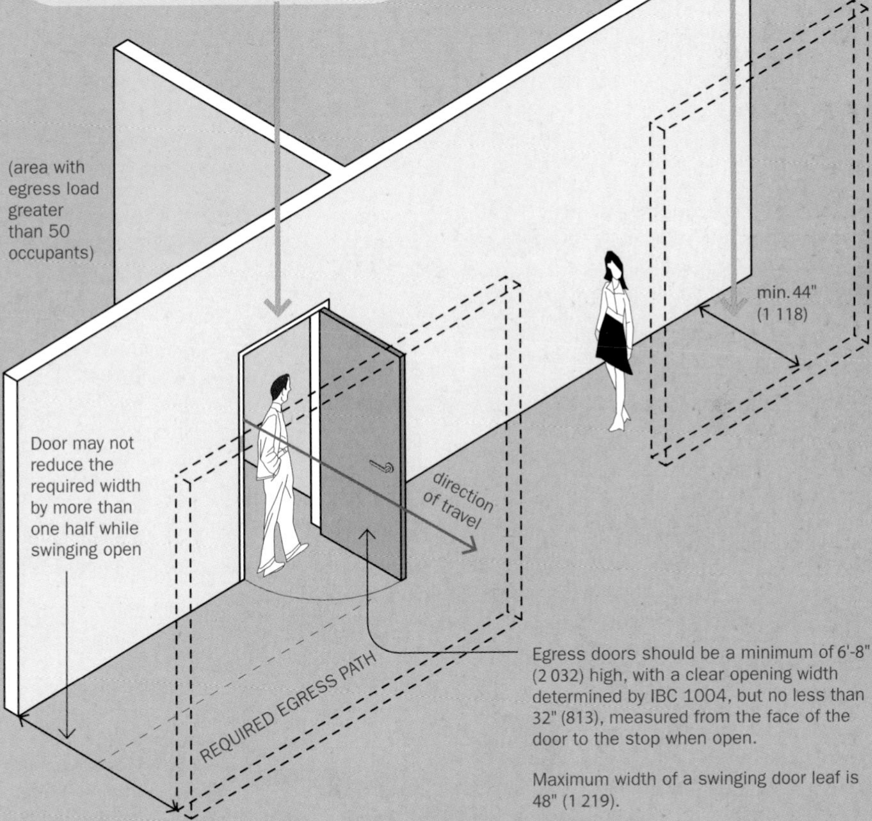
(area with egress load greater than 50 occupants)
Door may not reduce the required width by more than one half while swinging open
direction of travel
REQUIRED EGRESS PATH
min. 44" (1 118)

Egress doors should be a minimum of 6'-8" (2 032) high, with a clear opening width determined by IBC 1004, but no less than 32" (813), measured from the face of the door to the stop when open.

Maximum width of a swinging door leaf is 48" (1 219).

FIRE PROTECTION SYSTEMS

Limitations on building area and height may be lessened when fire-protection systems such as automatic sprinklers are in place. Active fire-protection systems are defined by IBC 202 as "approved devices, equipment and systems or combinations of systems used to detect a fire, activate an alarm, extinguish or control a fire, control or manage smoke and products of a fire, or any combination thereof." They are meant to work in conjunction with the building's passive systems (fire-resistive construction) to provide necessary protection for the occupants of any building type. Higher levels of stringency in one system might mean lessened requirements in the other, though neither should be compromised for the sake of cost or convenience.

The IBC requires active systems for buildings above certain sizes and occupant loads, regardless of the type of construction. IBC Section 903 establishes these requirements based on use groups and fire areas ("the aggregate floor area enclosed and bounded by fire walls, fire barriers, exterior walls, or fire-resistance-rated horizontal assemblies of a building"). Alternative fire-extinguishing systems may be used when necessary, in compliance with IBC 904. Examples of reasons to use alternative systems might include libraries and museums or telecommunications facilities, whose contents would sustain water damage from standard water sprinkler systems. Until recently, Halon 1301 gas was widely preferred as a fire-suppression option; however, it has proven to be harmful to the ozone layer and is being replaced by other options.

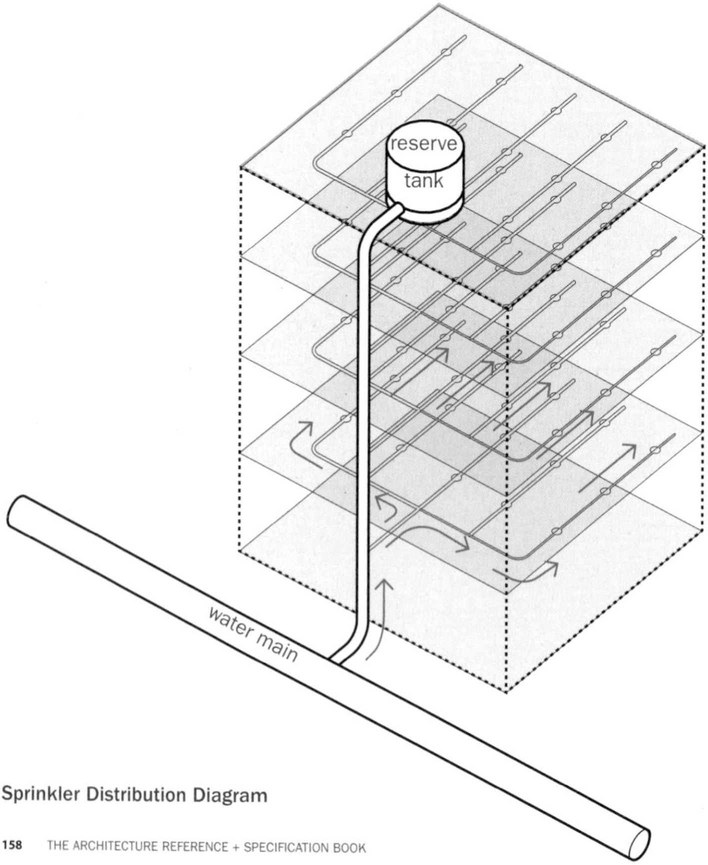
reserve
tank
water main

Sprinkler Distribution Diagram

Sprinkler Head Distribution Types

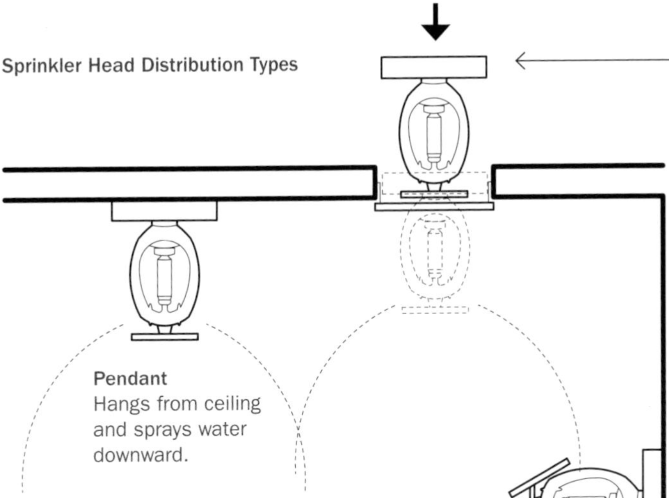

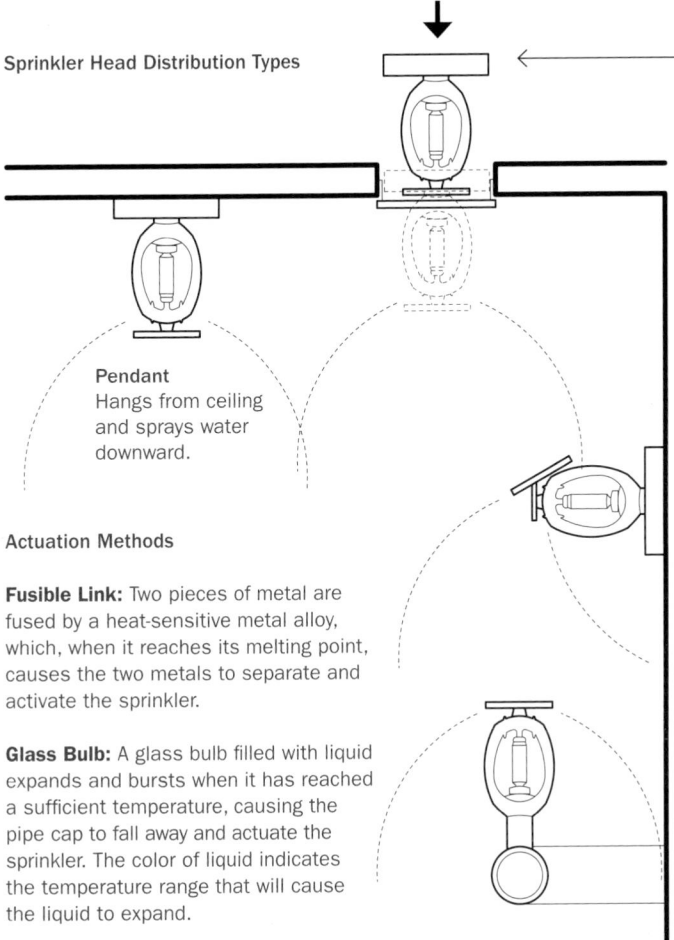

Concealed Pendant
Sprinkler head is recessed in ceiling and covered with a decorative cap, which falls off once ambient air temperatures reach a temperature of 20˚F lower than the sprinkler activation temperature, prior to sprinkler activation. Water sprays downward in a circular pattern.

Pendant
Hangs from ceiling and sprays water downward.

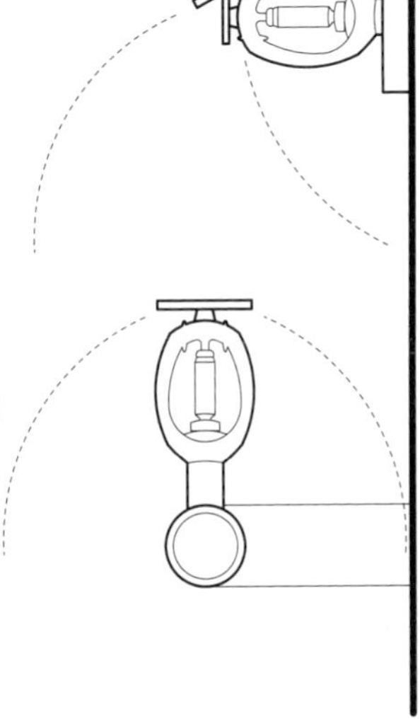

Side Wall
When mounting sprinklers to ceiling is not possible, they may be mounted to walls. Two deflectors spray water out and back toward the wall.

Upright
Mounted atop supply pipe, upright sprinkler heads are used in locations where ceiling mounting is not possible, or obstructions prevent adequate coverage (such as mechanical or storage rooms).

Actuation Methods

Fusible Link: Two pieces of metal are fused by a heat-sensitive metal alloy, which, when it reaches its melting point, causes the two metals to separate and activate the sprinkler.

Glass Bulb: A glass bulb filled with liquid expands and bursts when it has reached a sufficient temperature, causing the pipe cap to fall away and actuate the sprinkler. The color of liquid indicates the temperature range that will cause the liquid to expand.

Chapter 16: ADA and Accessibility

The Americans with Disabilities Act (ADA) was passed by Congress in 1990 to protect and honor the civil rights of people with disabilities, including conditions affecting mobility, sight, hearing, stamina, speech, and learning disorders. Modeled on earlier landmark laws prohibiting discrimination based on race and gender, the ADA provides equal access for all people to housing, public accommodations, employment, government services, transportation, and telecommunications. Similar to building codes, accessibility guidelines and standards are continually subject to improvement and revision, and in 2010 the Department of Justice adopted a revised set of standards, published as the 2010 Standards for Accessible Design. Included among the revisions are accommodation for children, and ambulatory (in addition to wheelchair) accessibility.

KEY TERMS AS DEFINED BY ADA

Access aisle: Accessible pedestrian space between elements such as parking spaces, seating, or desks that provides clearances appropriate for use of the elements.

Accessible: Of a site, building, facility, or portion thereof, in compliance with ADA guidelines.

Accessible element: Element (telephone, controls, and the like) specified by ADA guidelines as in compliance.

Accessible route: Continuous unobstructed path connecting all accessible elements and spaces of a building or facility. Interior accessible routes may include corridors, floors, ramps, elevators, lifts, and clear floor space at fixtures. Exterior accessible routes may include parking access aisles, curb ramps, crosswalks at vehicular ways, walks, ramps, and lifts.

Accessible space: Space that complies with ADA guidelines.

Adaptability: Ability of certain building spaces and elements, such as kitchen counters, sinks, and grab bars, to be added or altered so as to accommodate the needs of individuals with or without disabilities or with different types or degrees of disability.

Addition: Expansion, extension, or increase in the gross floor area of a building or facility.

Administrative authority: Governmental agency that adopts or enforces regulations and guidelines for the design, construction, or alteration of buildings and facilities.

Area of rescue assistance: Area that has direct access to an exit, where people who cannot use stairs may remain temporarily in safety to await further instructions or assistance during emergency evacuation.

Assembly area: Room or space accommodating a group of individuals for recreational, educational, political, social, or amusement purposes, or for the consumption of food and drink.

Automatic door: Door equipped with a power-operated mechanism and controls that open and close the door automatically on receipt of a momentary actuating signal. The switch that begins the automatic cycle may be a photoelectric device, floor mat, or manual switch. See power-assisted door.

Building: Any structure used and intended for supporting or sheltering any use or occupancy.

Circulation path: Exterior or interior way of passage from one place to another for pedestrians, including, but not limited to, walks, hallways, courtyards, stairways, and stair landings.

Clear: Unobstructed.

Clear floor space: Minimum unobstructed floor or ground space required to accommodate a single, stationary wheelchair and occupant.

Common use: Describes interior and exterior rooms, spaces, or elements that are made available for the use of a restricted group of people (for example, the occupants of a homeless shelter, the occupants of an office building, or the guests of such occupants).

Cross slope: Slope that is perpendicular to the direction of travel.

Curb ramp: Short ramp cutting through a curb or built up to it.

Detectable warning: Standardized surface feature built in or applied to a walking surface or other elements to warn visually impaired people of hazards on a circulation path.

Egress, means of: Continuous and unobstructed way of exit travel from any point in a building or facility to a public way. A means of egress comprises vertical and horizontal travel and may include intervening room spaces, doorways, hallways, corridors, passageways, balconies, ramps, stairs, enclosures, lobbies, horizontal exits, courts, and yards. An accessible means of egress is one that complies with ADA guidelines and does not include stairs, steps, or escalators. Areas of rescue assistance or evacuation elevators may be included as part of accessible means of egress.

Elements: Architectural or mechanical component of a building, facility, space, or site (for example, a telephone, curb ramp, door, drinking fountain, seating, or water closet).

Entrance: Any access point to a building or portion of a building or facility used for the purpose of entering. An entrance includes the approach walk, the vertical access leading to the entrance platform, the entrance platform itself, vestibules if provided, the entry door(s) or gate(s), and the hardware of the entry door(s) or gate(s).

Marked crossing: Crosswalk or other identified path intended for pedestrian use in crossing a vehicular way.

Operable part: Part of a piece of equipment or appliance used to insert or withdraw objects, or to activate, deactivate, or adjust the equipment or appliance (for example, a coin slot, push button, or handle).

Power-assisted door: Door used for human passage with a mechanism that helps to open the door, or relieves the opening resistance of a door, on the activation of a switch or a continued force applied to the door itself.

Public use: Describes interior or exterior rooms or spaces that are made available to the general public. Public use may be provided at a building or facility that is privately or publicly owned.

Ramp: Walking surface that has a running slope greater than 1:20.

Running slope: Slope that is parallel to the direction of travel.

Signage: Displayed verbal, symbolic, tactile, and pictorial information.

Space: Definable area (for example, a room, toilet room, hall, assembly area, entrance, storage room, alcove, courtyard, or lobby).

Tactile: Of an object, perceptible using the sense of touch.

Text telephone: Machinery or equipment that employs interactive graphic (that is, typed) communications through the transmission of coded signals across the standard telephone network. Text telephones can include devices known as TDDs (telecommunication display devices or telecommunication devices for deaf persons) or computers.

Walk: Exterior pathway with a prepared surface intended for pedestrian use, including general pedestrian areas such as plazas and courts.

SIGNAGE

Elevator Control Panel

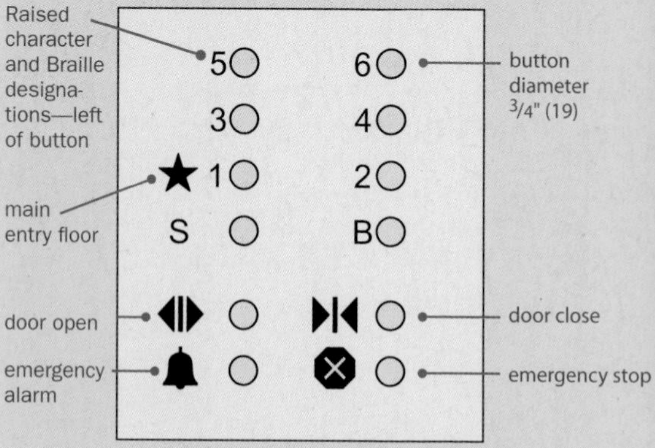
Raised character and Braille designa-tions—left of button
5
6
3
4
1
2
S
B
button diameter 3/4" (19)
main entry floor
door open
door close
emergency alarm
emergency stop

Emergency controls should be grouped at the bottom, with centerlines no less than 35" (889) AFF.

Raised and Tactile Characters

Characters should be raised 1/32" (0.8) and in uppercase with sans serif font. Characters shall not be italic, oblique, decorative or unusual.

Characters must be accompanied by Grade 2 Braille.

Raised characters must be a minimum of 5/8" (16) and maximum of 2" (51) high based on an uppercase I.

Braille shall be positioned below the corresponding text, and shall be separated by 3/8" (10) minimum from any other tactile characters or raised borders.

Tactile characters on signs shall be located 48" (1 220) min. AFF, measured from the baseline of the lowest character, and 60" (1 525) max. AFF, measured from the baseline of the highest tactile character.

Visual Characters

Characters and background must be eggshell, matte, or another nonglare finish and must contrast with background (either light on dark or dark on light).

Characters may be uppercase or lowercase, or a combination of both, and shall not be italic, oblique, decorative or unusual.

Minimum character height shall be determined by the horizontal viewing distance (per 2010 Standard 703).

Pictograms

Text descriptors (if any) must be placed directly below pictogram field.

Pictograms can be any size within a minimum field of 6" (153) in height.

RESTROOMS

ACCESSIBLE MEANS OF EGRESS

Any space that is considered to be accessible must have at least one accessible means of egress.

Elevators that comply with ASME A17.1, Safety Code for Elevators and Escalators, may be allowed as part of an accessible egress route. Primarily, they must be equipped with standby power and emergency operation and signaling devices, and most must be accessed from an area of refuge.

Areas of refuge, where those unable to use stairways remain temporarily in an evacuation, should be in an egress stairway or have direct access to one, or to an elevator with emergency power. Two-way communications systems should be provided in the area of refuge, connecting it to a central control point.

One 30" × 48" (762 × 1 219) wheelchair space must be provided for every 200 occupants of the space served. Generally these spaces are alcoves within an enclosed stair, because they must not reduce the egress width.

Except in sprinklered buildings, accessible egress stairways should be a minimum of 48" (1 219) wide clear between handrails. This provides a space wide enough for two people to carry a disabled person down or up to safety.

ACCESSIBLE PARKING SPACES

The length of accessible parking spaces must be in accordance with local building codes. Accessible spaces should be marked by high-contrast painted lines or other high-contrast delineation. Access aisles should be a part of an accessible route to the building or facility entrance. Two accessible parking spaces may share a common access aisle. Access aisles should be marked clearly by means of diagonal stripes.

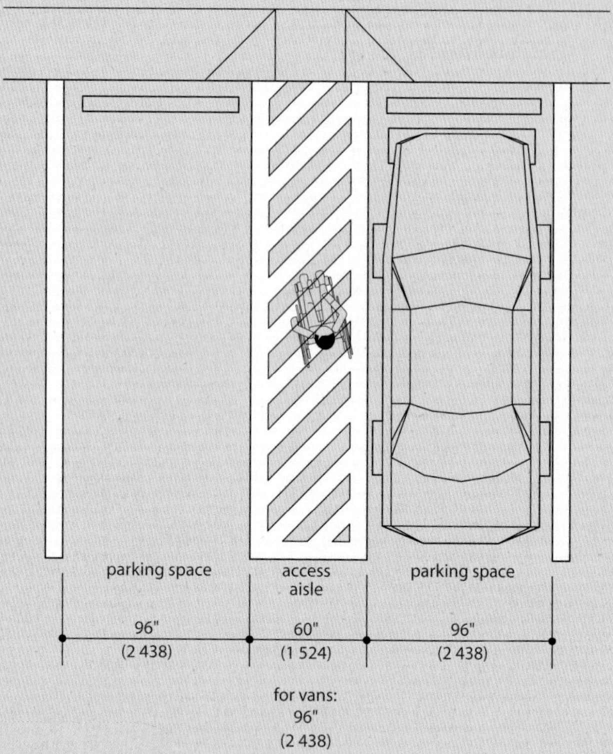
parking space
access aisle
parking space
96" (2 438)
60" (1 524)
96" (2 438)
for vans: 96" (2 438)

Number of Accessible Spaces Required

1–25	1
26–50	2
51–75	3
76–100	4
101–150	5
151–200	6
201–300	7
301–400	8
401–500	9
501–1,000	2% of total
1,001 and over	20 plus 1 for each 100 over 1,000

Surface slopes should not exceed 1:50 (2%) in any direction on accessible parking spaces and access aisles.

Accessible parking spaces serving a particular building should be located on the shortest accessible route of travel from the adjacent parking to an accessible entrance.

In buildings with multiple accessible entrances with adjacent parking, accessible parking spaces should be dispersed and located closest to the accessible entrances.

WHEELCHAIR SPACE ALLOWANCES

Clear floor or ground space is defined as the minimum clear area required to accommodate a single, stationary wheelchair and occupant. This applies to both forward and parallel approaches to an element or object. Clear floor space may be part of the knee space required under objects such as sinks and counters.

Wheelchair Passage Widths

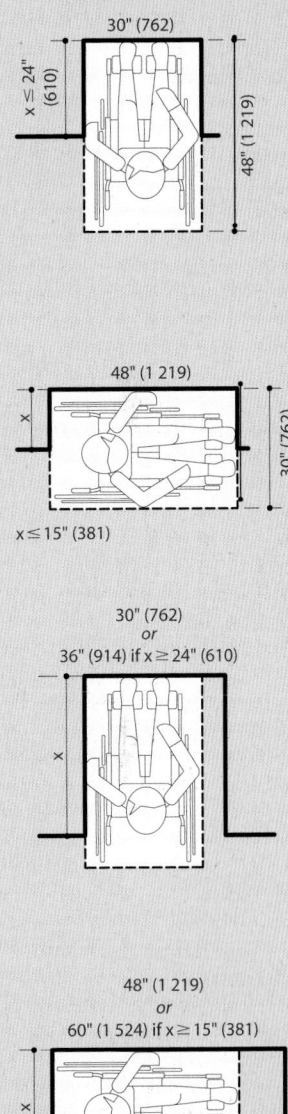

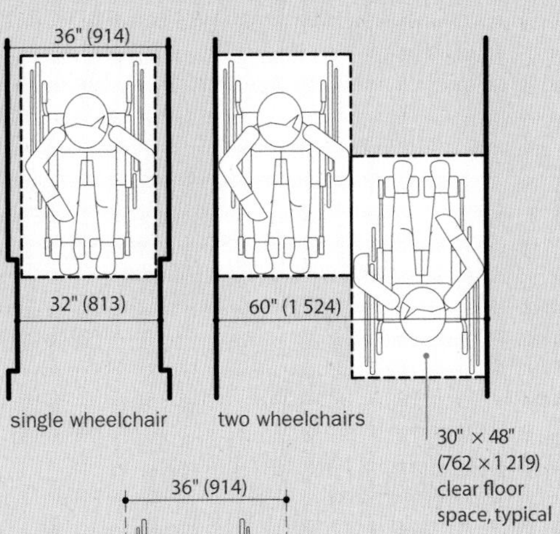
36" (914)
32" (813)
60" (1 524)
single wheelchair
two wheelchairs
30" × 48"
(762 × 1 219)
clear floor
space, typical

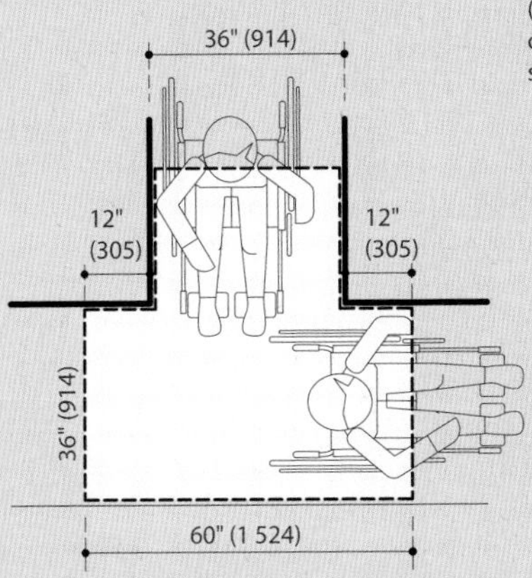
36" (914)
12"
(305)
12"
(305)
36" (914)
60" (1 524)

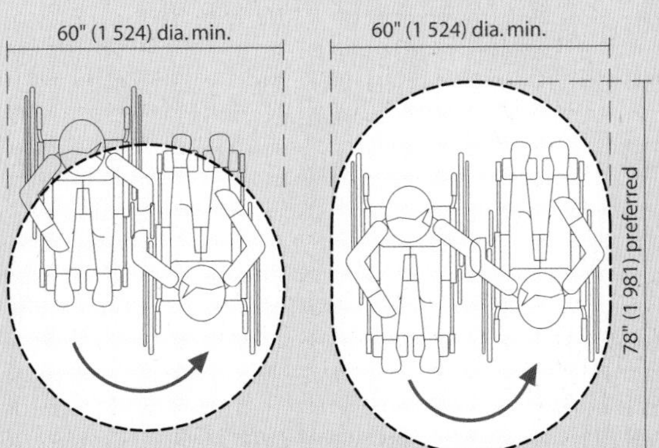
60" (1 524) dia. min.
60" (1 524) dia. min.
78" (1 981) preferred

Clear Floor Space at Alcoves

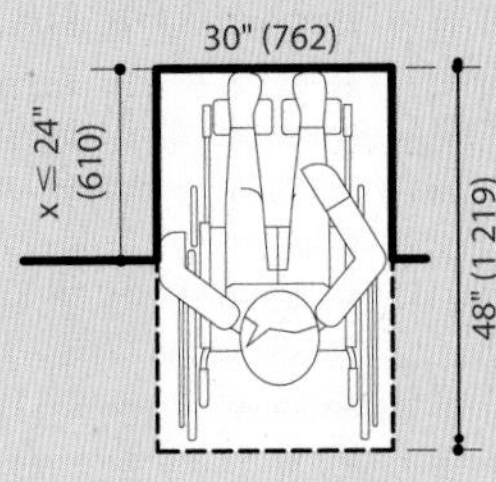
30" (762)
x ≤ 24"
(610)
48" (1 219)

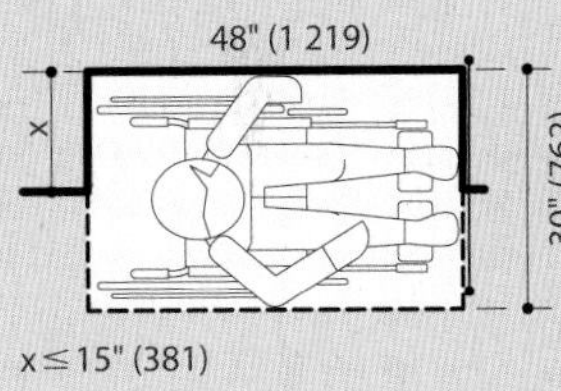
48" (1 219)
x
30" (762)
x ≤ 15" (381)

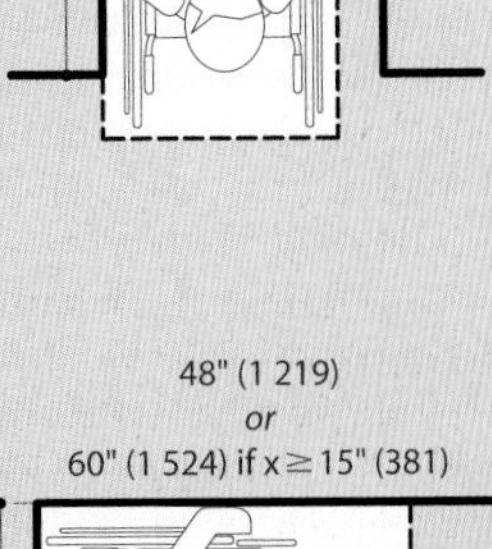
30" (762)
or
36" (914) if x ≥ 24" (610)
x

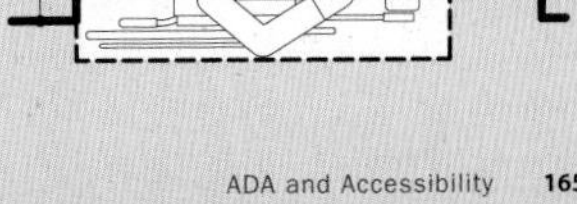
48" (1 219)
or
60" (1 524) if x ≥ 15" (381)
x

DOORS

Clear Doorway Width and Depth

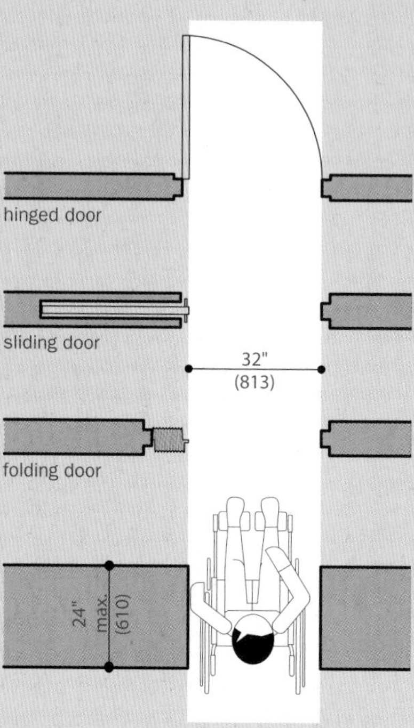
hinged door
sliding door
32"
(813)
folding door
24"
max.
(610)

Maneuvering Clearances at Doors

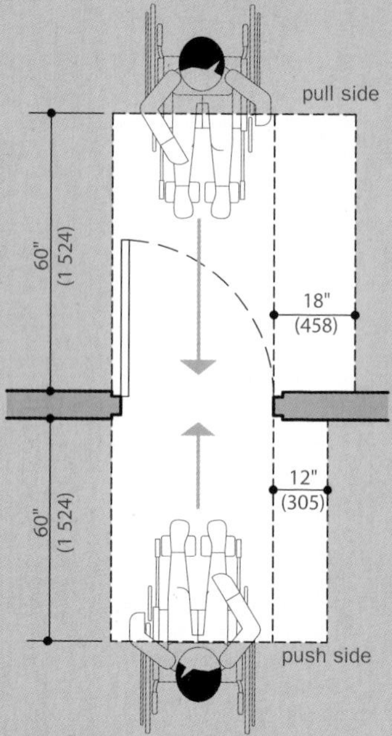
pull side
60"
(1 524)
18"
(458)
12"
(305)
60"
(1 524)
push side

Swinging Doors
(front approaches)

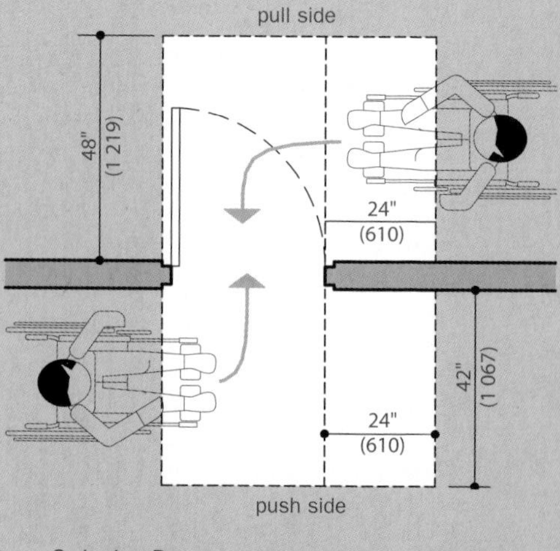
pull side
48"
(1 219)
24"
(610)
42"
(1 067)
24"
(610)
push side

Swinging Doors
(latch-side approaches)

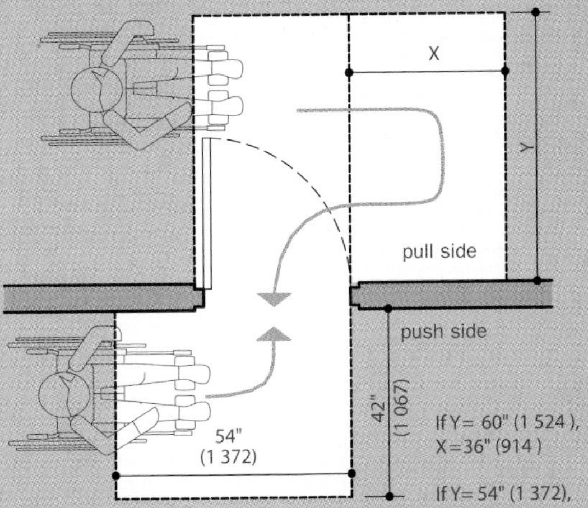
X
Y
pull side
push side
42"
(1 067)
54"
(1 372)
If Y= 60" (1 524),
X=36" (914)
If Y= 54" (1 372),
X=42" (1 067)

Swinging Doors
(hinge-side approaches)

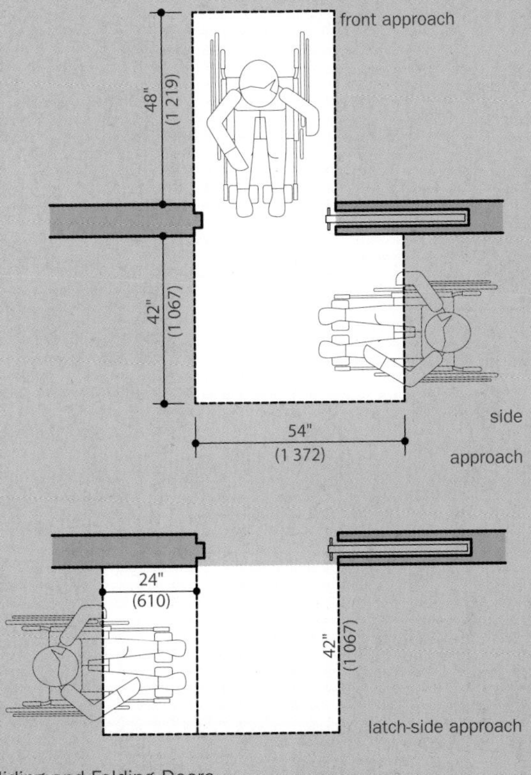
front approach
48"
(1 219)
42"
(1 067)
54"
(1 372)
side
approach
24"
(610)
42"
(1 067)
latch-side approach

Sliding and Folding Doors

Two Hinged Doors in a Series

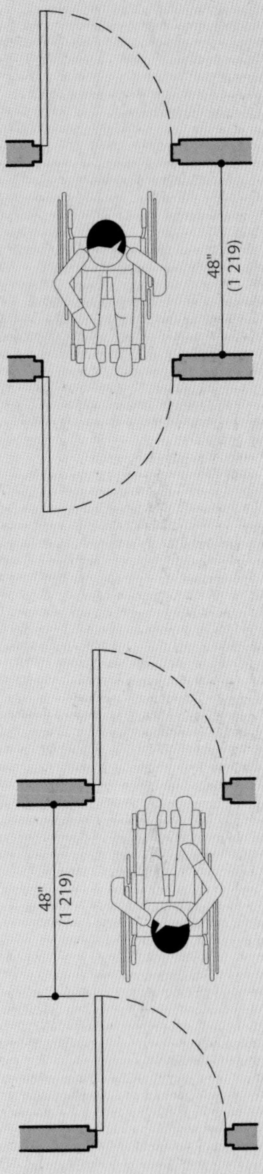
48"
(1 219)
48"
(1 219)

TOILETS AND BATHROOMS

Clear Floor Space at Water Closets - Adult

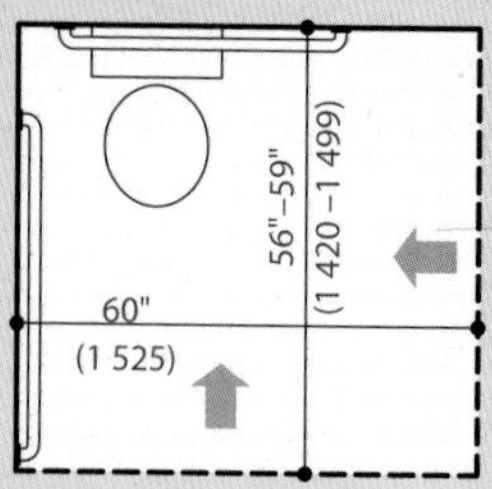
56"–59"
(1 420 –1 499)
60"
(1 525)

Toilet Stalls

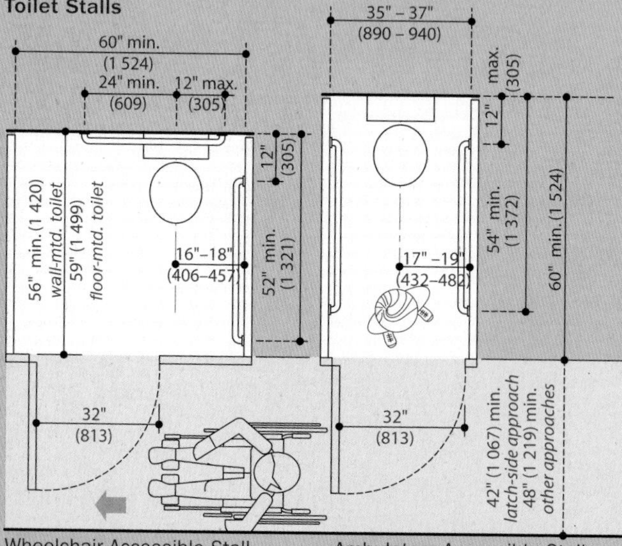
60" min.
(1 524)
24" min.
(609)
12" max.
(305)
12"
(305)
56" min.(1 420)
wall-mtd. toilet
59" (1 499)
floor-mtd. toilet
16"–18"
(406–457)
52" min.
(1 321)
32"
(813)
35" – 37"
(890 – 940)
max.
(305)
12"
17" –19"
(432–482)
54" min.
(1 372)
60" min.(1 524)
32"
(813)
42" (1 067) min.
latch-side approach
48" (1 219) min.
other approaches

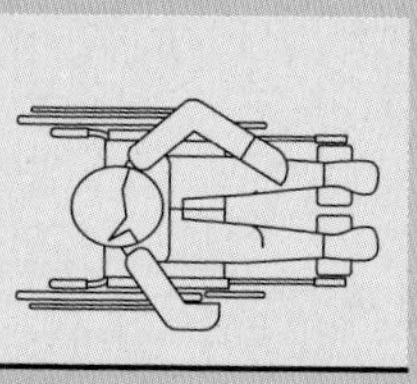

Wheelchair Accessible Stall

Ambulatory Accessible Stall

Grab bars:

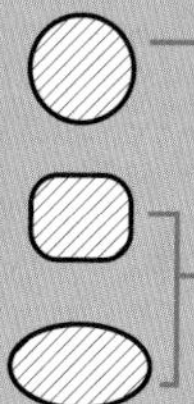

circular cross section should be 1 1/4"–2" (32–5 in diameter, with a clear- ance of 1 1/2" (38) from wa

non-circular cross sectior shall have a cross- sectional dimension of 2 (51) max, and a perimete dimension between 4" a 4.8" (100–120)

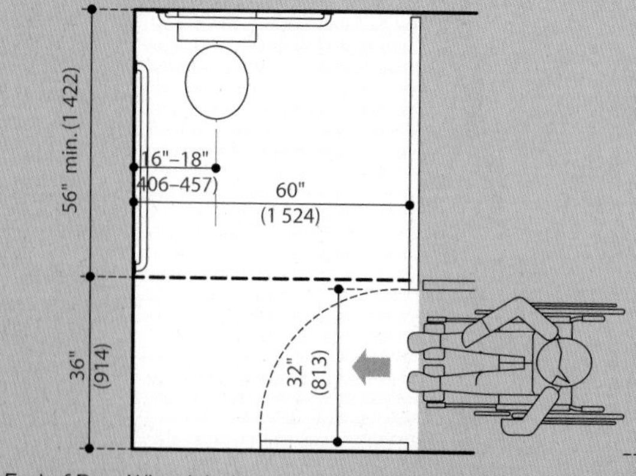
56" min.(1 422)
16"–18"
406–457)
60"
(1 524)
36"
(914)
32"
(813)

End-of-Row Wheelchair Accessible Stall

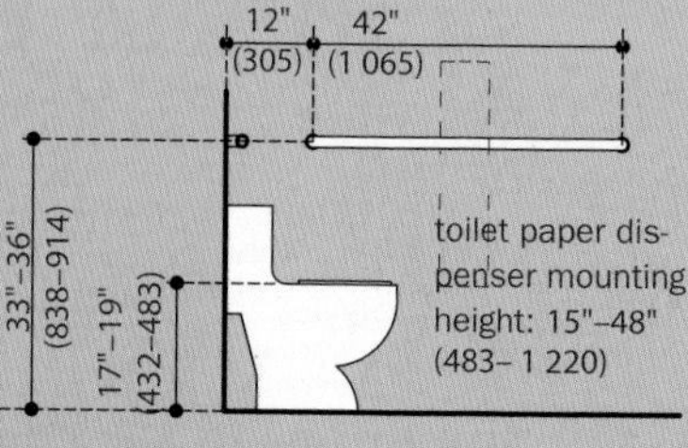
12"
(305)
42"
(1 065)
33"–36"
(838–914)
17"–19"
(432–483)
toilet paper dis-
penser mounting
height: 15"–48"
(483– 1 220)

Side-wall Elevation

Lavatories

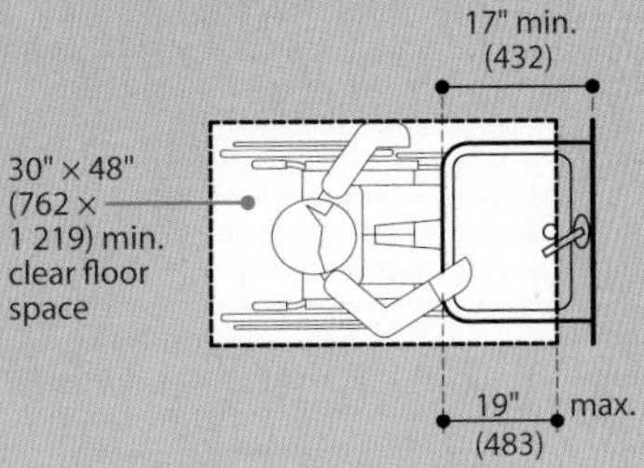
17" min.
(432)
30" × 48"
(762 ×
1 219) min.
clear floor
space
19"
(483)
max.

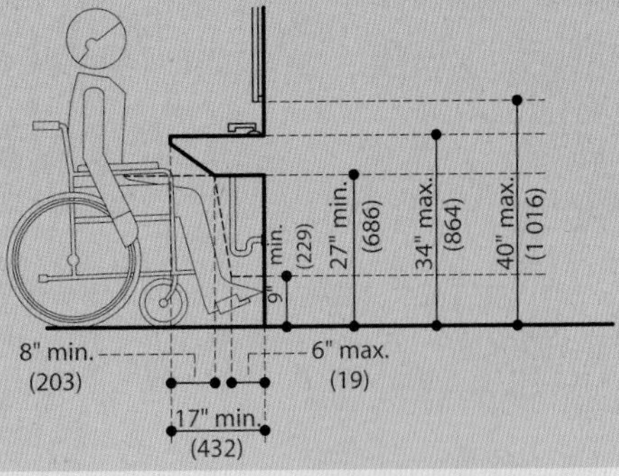
8" min.
(203)
17" min.
(432)
6" max.
(19)
9" min.
(229)
27" min.
(686)
34" max.
(864)
40" max.
(1 016)

Showers

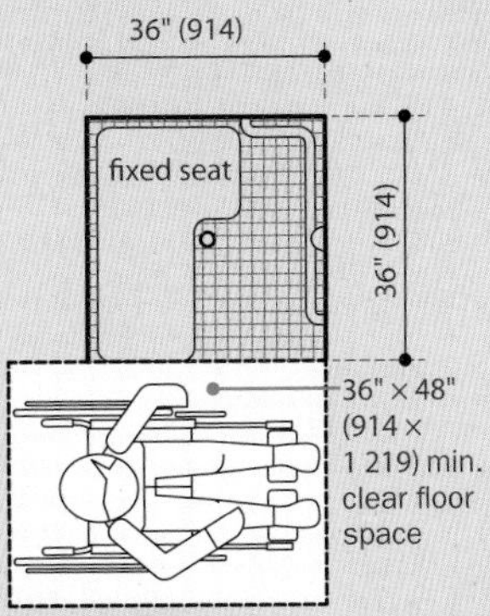
36" (914)
fixed seat
36" (914)
36" × 48"
(914 ×
1 219) min.
clear floor
space

Transfer Type

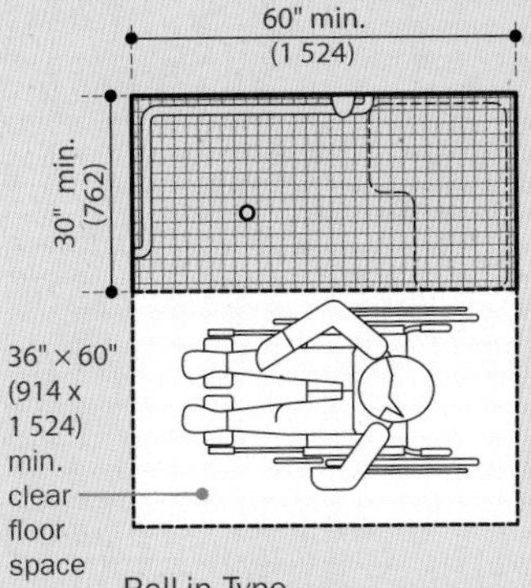
60" min.
(1 524)
30" min.
(762)
36" × 60"
(914 x
1 524)
min.
clear
floor
space

Roll-in Type

A seat must be provided in shower stalls 36" × 36" (914 × 914), mounted 17"–19" (432–83) from the bathroom floor and extending from the back wall to a point within 3" (76) of the compartment entry.

Fixed seats in 30" × 60" (762 × 1 524) shower stalls should be of a folding type mounted on the wall adjacent to the controls.

Bathtubs

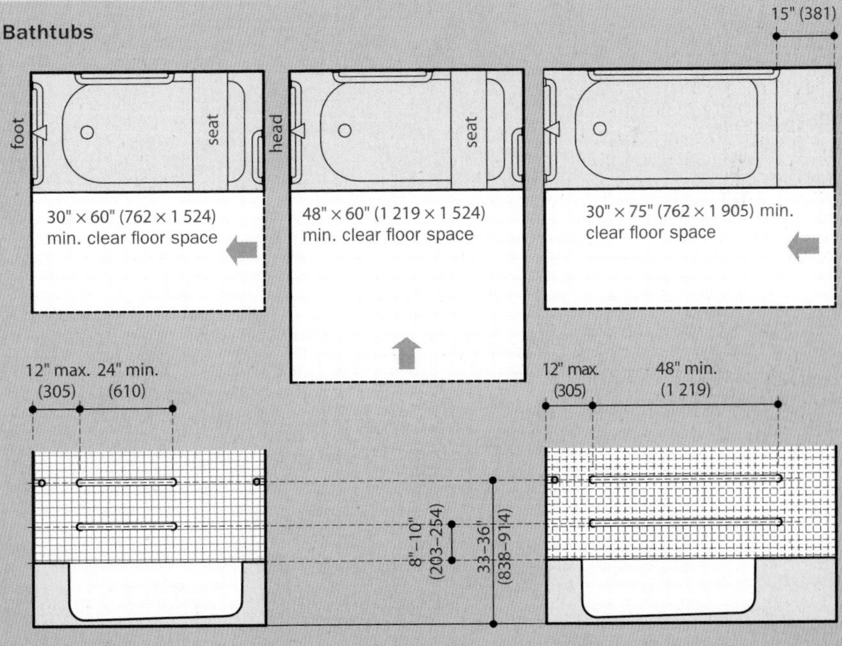
15" (381)
foot
seat
head
seat
30" × 60" (762 × 1 524)
min. clear floor space
48" × 60" (1 219 × 1 524)
min. clear floor space
30" × 75" (762 × 1 905) min.
clear floor space
12" max.
(305)
24" min.
(610)
12" max.
(305)
48" min.
(1 219)
8"–10"
(203–254)
33–36"
(838–914)

ELEVATORS

Hall lantern fixtures at each hoistway entrance must indicate visibly and audibly which car is answering a call.

Door jambs should have raised and Braille floor designation markings.

Call buttons must be a minimum 3/4" (19) in the smallest direction.

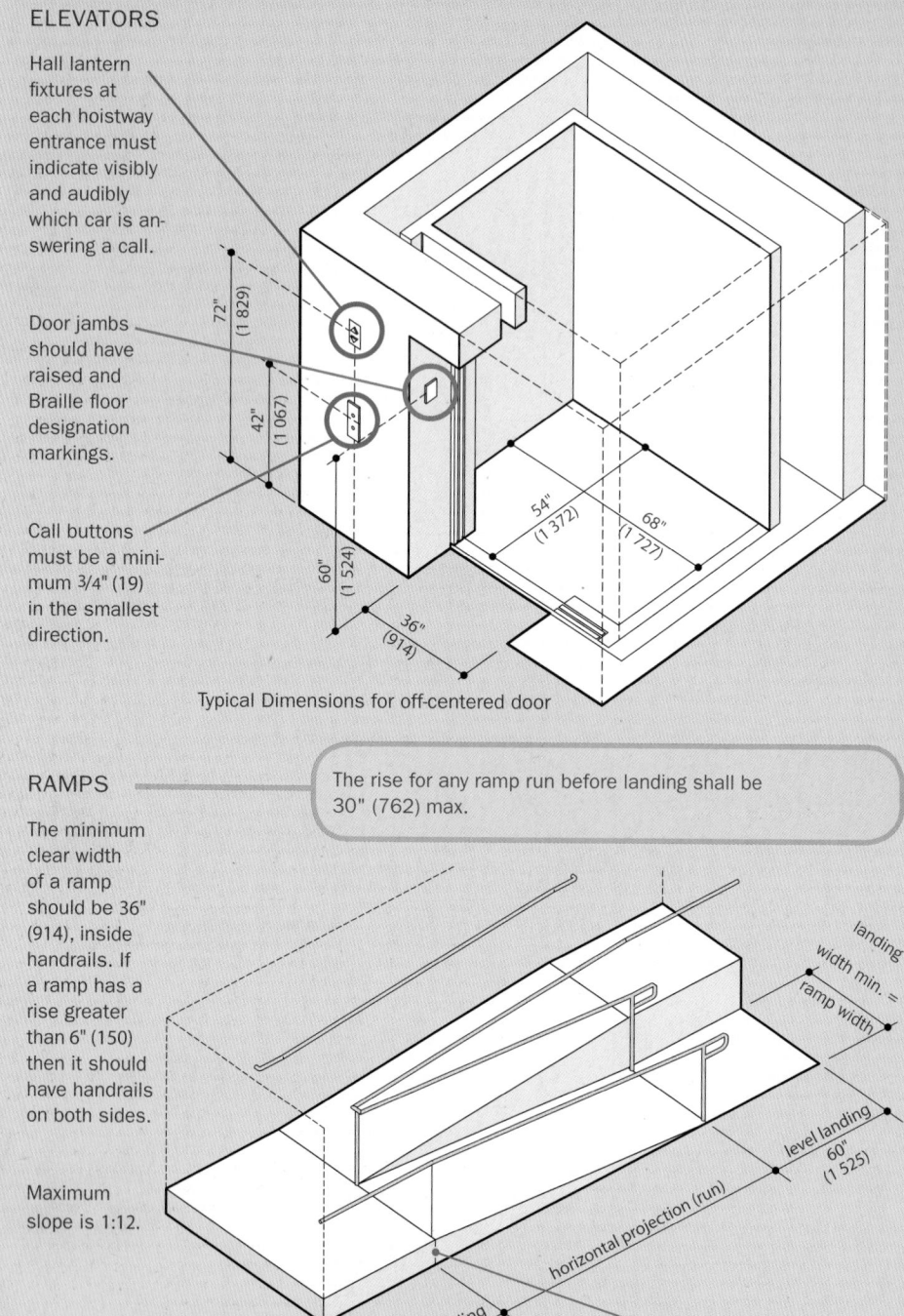

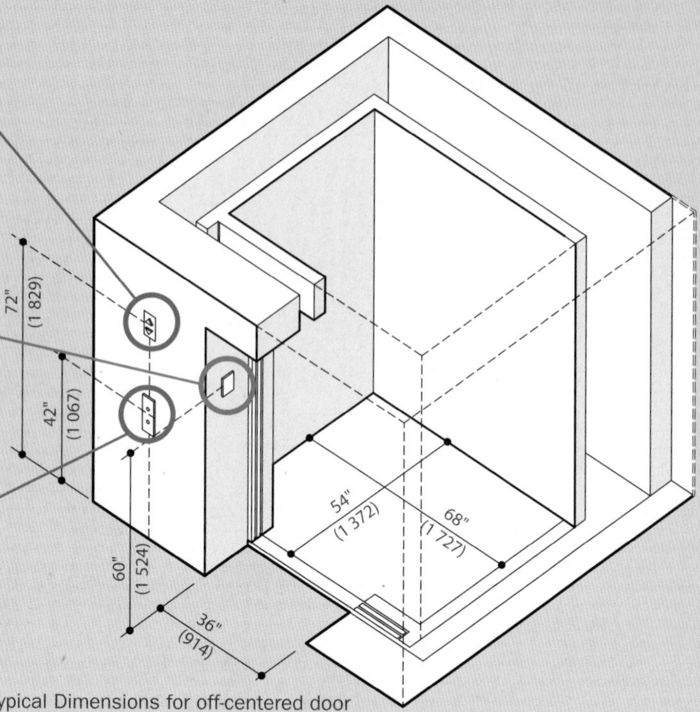
72"
(1 829)
42"
(1 067)
60"
(1 524)
36"
(914)
54"
(1 372)
68"
(1 727)

Typical Dimensions for off-centered door

RAMPS

The rise for any ramp run before landing shall be 30" (762) max.

The minimum clear width of a ramp should be 36" (914), inside handrails. If a ramp has a rise greater than 6" (150) then it should have handrails on both sides.

Maximum slope is 1:12.

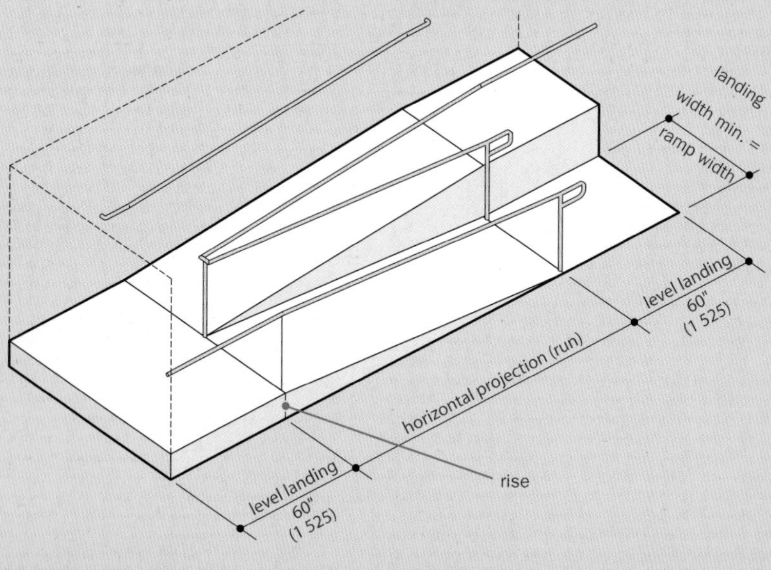
landing width min. = ramp width
level landing
60"
(1 525)
horizontal projection (run)
rise
level landing
60"
(1 525)

STAIRS

Nosings

Risers should be sloped, or the underside of nosings should have an angle not less than 60° from the horizontal.

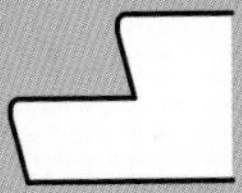

flush riser

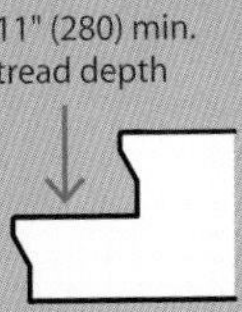
11" (280) min.
tread depth

angled nosing

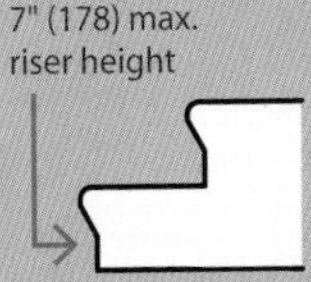
7" (178) max.
riser height

rounded nosing

Handrail Extension (min.)at Bottom of Run

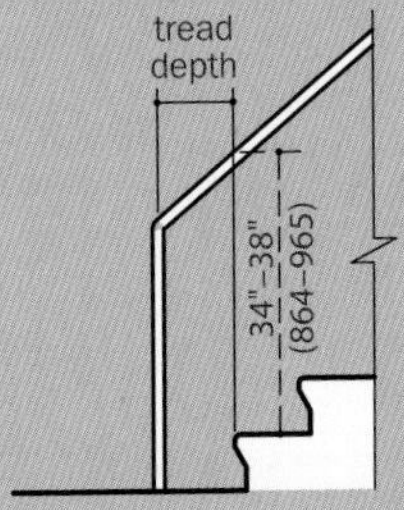
tread
depth
34"–38"
(864–965)

Handrails

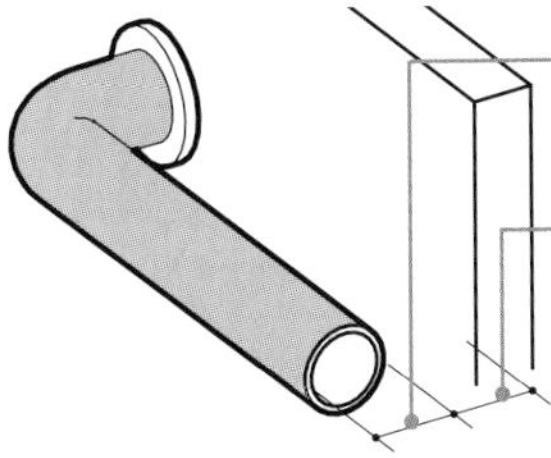
1 1/4" –2"
(32–51) dia.
1 1/2" (38) min.
from wall

at wall: handrail returns to wall

at switchback: handrail is continuous

where no wall: handrail returns smoothly to the floor

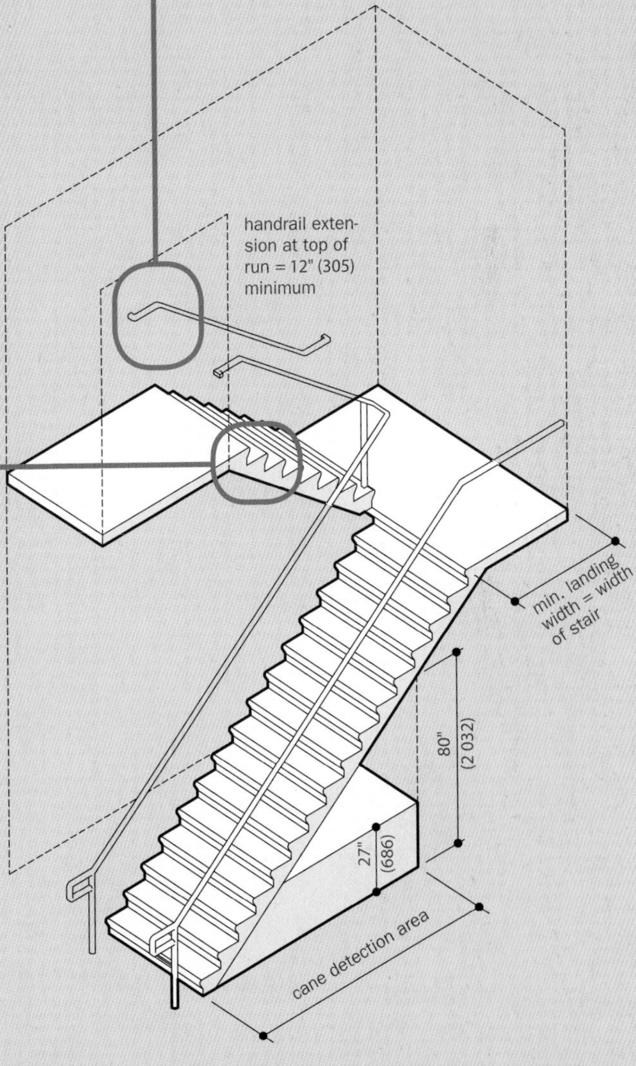
handrail extension at top of run = 12" (305) minimum
min. landing width = width of stair
80"
(2 032)
27"
(686)
cane detection area

Chapter 17: Parking

Almost everywhere, parking is often a person's first and last interface with a building and should be designed with this in mind. Primarily, parking should be safe, efficient, well-marked, and able to accommodate users of all kinds. Because vehicle sizes fluctuate, parking areas must be flexible enough to respond to future scenarios.

PARKING LOTS

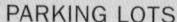

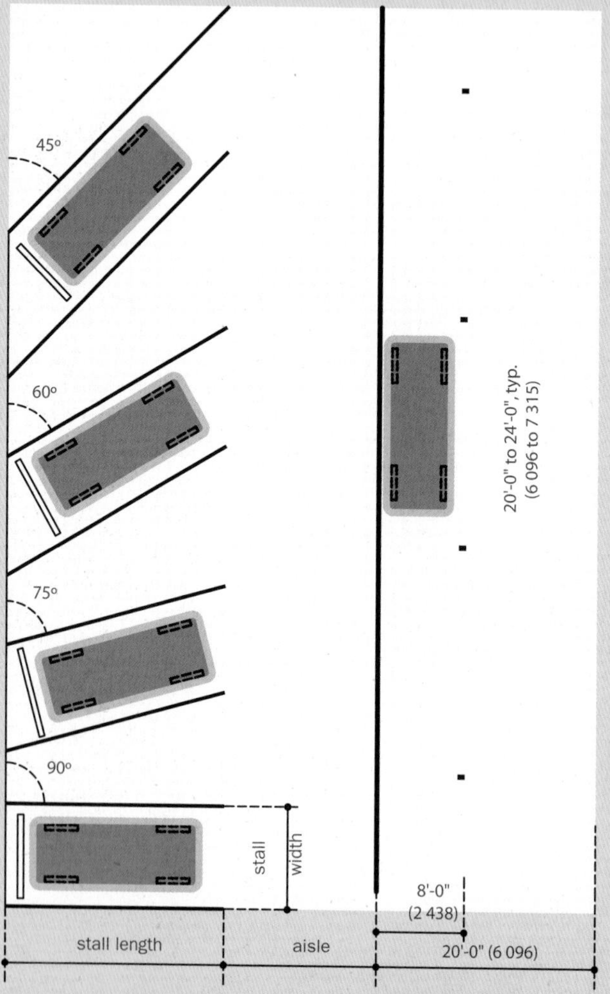
45°
60°
75°
90°
stall
width
stall length
aisle
20'-0" to 24'-0", typ.
(6 096 to 7 315)
8'-0"
(2 438)
20'-0" (6 096)

Parking Stalls

Parallel Parking

General Guidelines

Pavement striping should be 4" (102) wide, in white or yellow paint.

Parking area surfaces should have a minimum slope of 2 percent (a ¼" per foot or 6 mm per 305 mm) for drainage purposes.

Lots are laid out with modules. One complete module includes one access aisle and the parking it serves on either side.

The most common angle for parking is the 60° stall, which provides for ease of entering and exiting spaces while still allowing for an efficiently sized module. Stalls of 45° reduce the total number of parking spaces for a given area but do not require a wide access aisle. They are the only acceptable angle for a herringbone parking lot pattern. Stalls of 90° provide the most parking spaces for a given area, though they are unsuitable for in-and-out traffic, due to the higher degree of difficulty entering and exiting the stalls. They are ideal for all-day parking, such as for employees.

COMMON PARKING STALL LAYOUTS

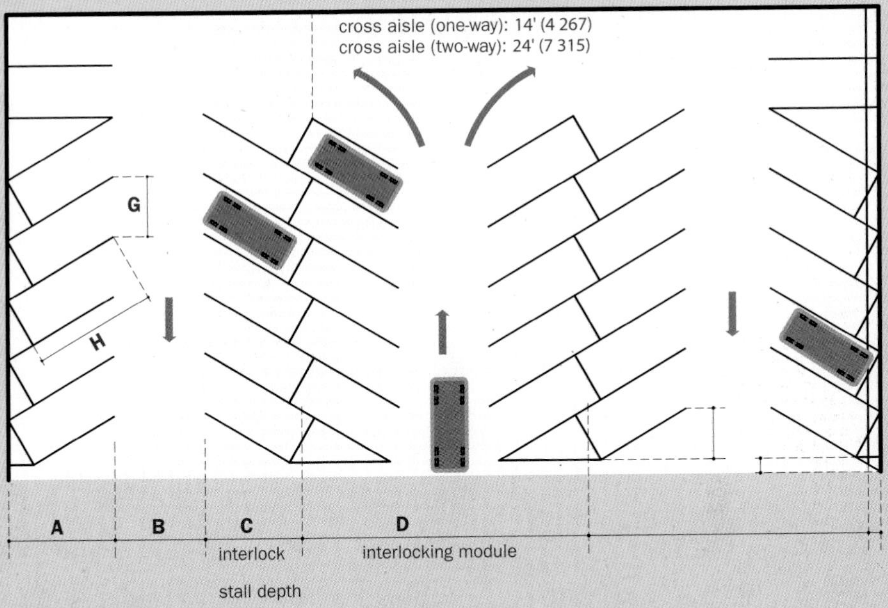
cross aisle (one-way): 14' (4 267)
cross aisle (two-way): 24' (7 315)
G
H
A
B
C
D
interlock
interlocking module
stall depth

	A	B	C	D
45°	17.5' (5 334)	12.0' (3 658)	15.3' (4 663)	42.6' (12 984)
60°	19.0' (5 791)	16.0' (4 877)	17.5' (5 334)	51.0' (15 549)
75°	19.5' (5 944)	23.0' (7 010)	18.8' (5 730)	61.0' (18 593)
90°	18.5' (5 639)	26.0' (7 925)	18.5' (5 639)	63.0' (19 202)

Recommended parking layouts and stall dimensions vary and are most often determined by local or state zoning provisions (which should *always* be consulted). Commonly accepted minimum stall sizes are 9' (2 743) × 18.5'–19.5' (5 639–944), though sizes and layouts should best accommodate their situation; for instance, stalls at hardware or grocery stores should be wide enough to accommodate easy loading and unloading of large packages, and may be up to 10' (3 048) wide. Compact car spaces may be as small as 7'-6" × 15' (2 286 × 4 572) and should be well marked and logically grouped.

Parking Lot Flows

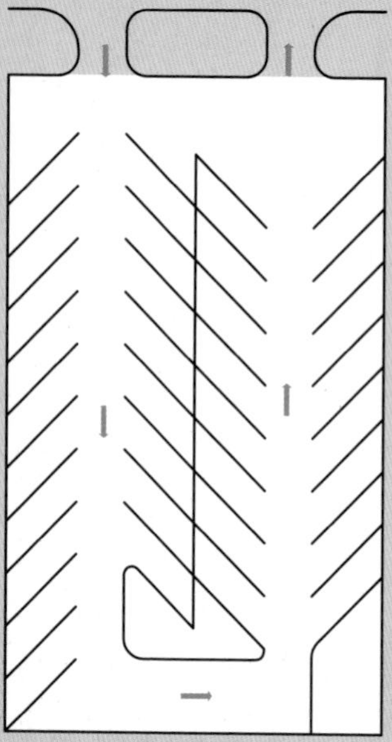

One-way Angled

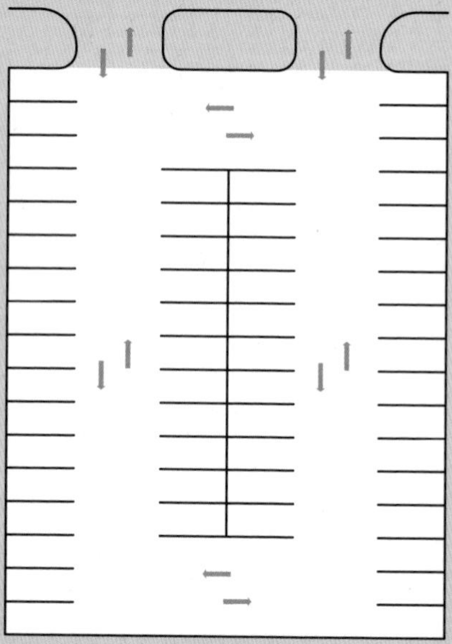

Two-way 90 Degrees

Common Parking Space Allocations

Hospital	1.2 per bed
Auditorium/theater/stadium	0.3 per seat
Restaurant	0.3 per seat
Industrial	0.6 per employee
Church	0.3 per seat
Retail	4.0 per 1000' gross floor area
Office	3.3 per 1000' gross floor area
Shopping center	5.5 per 1000' gross leasable area
Hotels/motel	1.0 per room/0.5 per employee
Senior high schools	0.2 per student/1.0 per staff member
Elementary schools	1.0 per classroom

PARKING GARAGES

Ramp Design

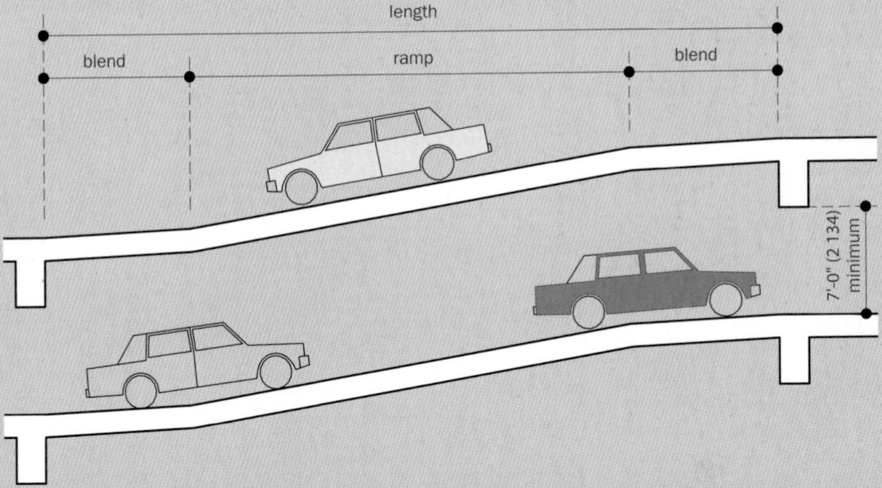
length
blend
ramp
blend
7'-0" (2 134) minimum

Straight Ramps

Length	< 65'-0" (19 812)	> 65'-0" (19 812)
Blend length	10'-0" (3 048)	8'-0" (2 438)
Blend slope	8%	6%
Ramp slope	16%	12%

Helical Ramps

width = 15'-0" (4 572)
for counterclockwise travel

width = 20'-0" (6 096)
for clockwise travel

slope = 12% maximum
(4% in transverse direction)

General Considerations

Parking garage stalls should be well-marked and use clear signage to direct drivers, especially in one-way traffic situations.

Express helical exit ramps are recommended to avoid congestion inside garage.

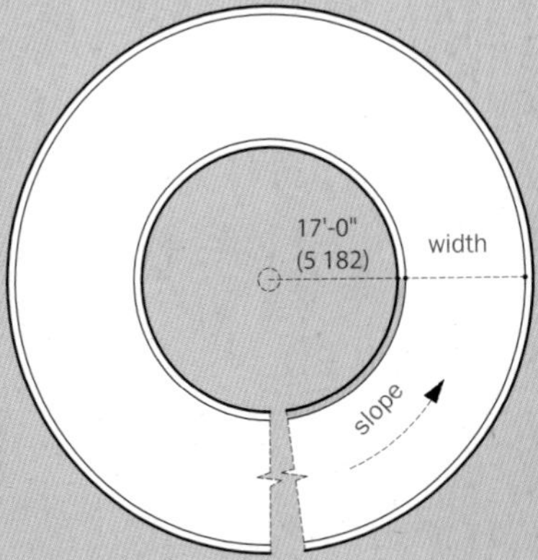
17'-0"
(5 182)
width
slope

Chapter 18: Stairs

Stairs are a primary method of vertical circulation in most private residences and even in public places where elevators or escalators are present. In elevatored buildings, building codes will require a minimum number of enclosed exit stairs. Stair construction is typically of wood, metal, or concrete, or a combination of all three.

STAIR TYPES

Straight Run Stair

Fire codes generally restrict the total rise of a straight stair to 12'-0" (3 658) before an intermediate landing is required. Landing depth should equal the stair width.

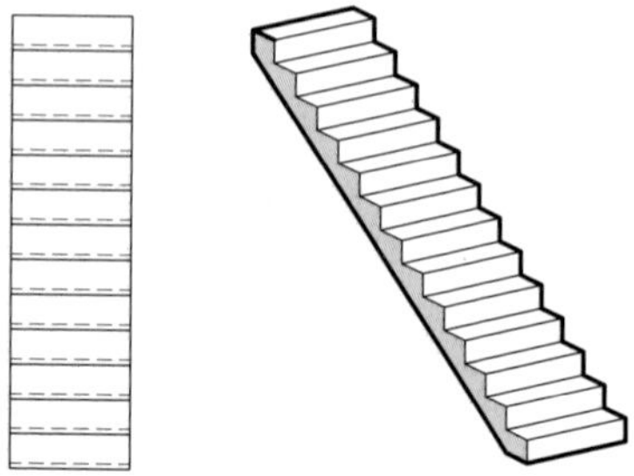

L-shaped Stair with Landing

L-shaped stairs may contain long or short legs, with a landing at any change in direction.

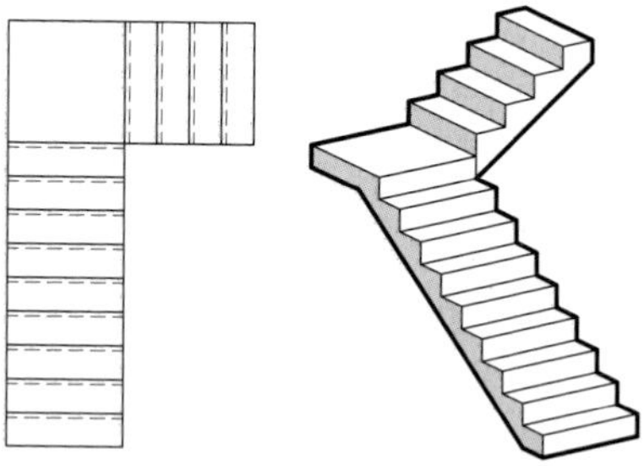

U-shaped Stair with Landing

U-shaped stairs, which switch back as they ascend, are useful in tight floor plans and as one component in a stacking multilevel circulation system (such as an egress stair core).

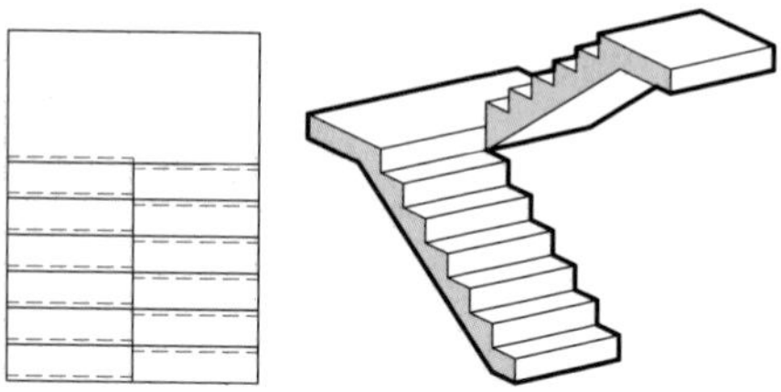

L-shaped Stair with Winders

Winders may help to compress the area needed for a stair by adding angled treads where a landing might go in a typical L-shaped stair. Most winders do not comply with local codes.

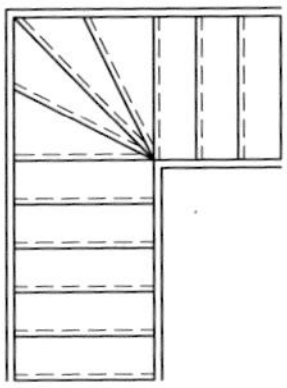

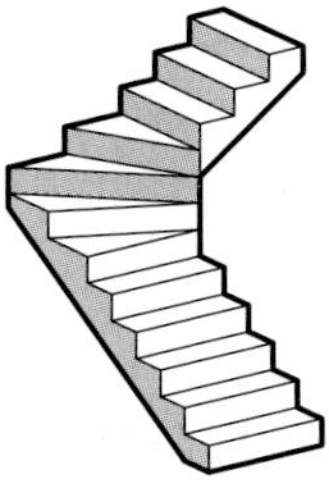

L-shaped Stair with Offset Winders

Offset winder treads are more generous in proportion and, therefore, may comply with applicable codes.

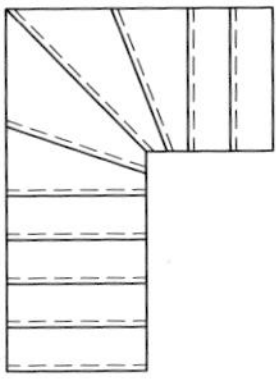

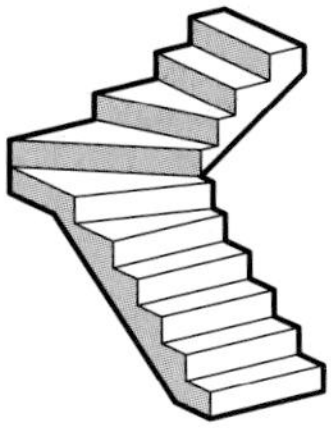

Spiral Stair

Spiral stairs occupy a minimum amount of plan space and are often used in private residences. Most spiral stairs are not acceptable as egress stairs, except in residences and in spaces of five or fewer occupants in 250 sq. ft. (23 m^2) or less.

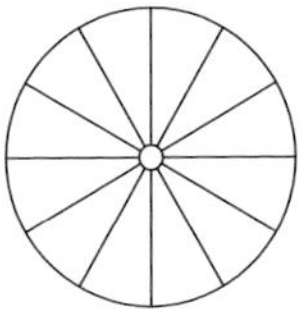

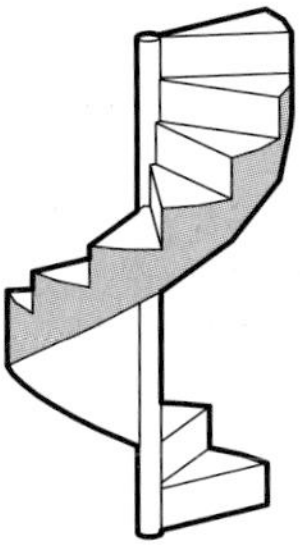

Curved Stair

Curved stairs follow the same layout principles of spiral stairs, though with a sufficient open center diameter, the treads may be dimensioned to legal code standards for egress.

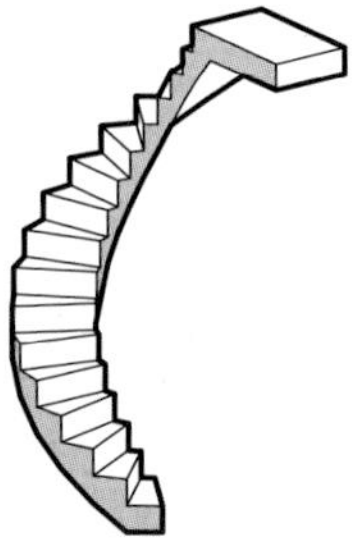

STAIR COMPONENTS

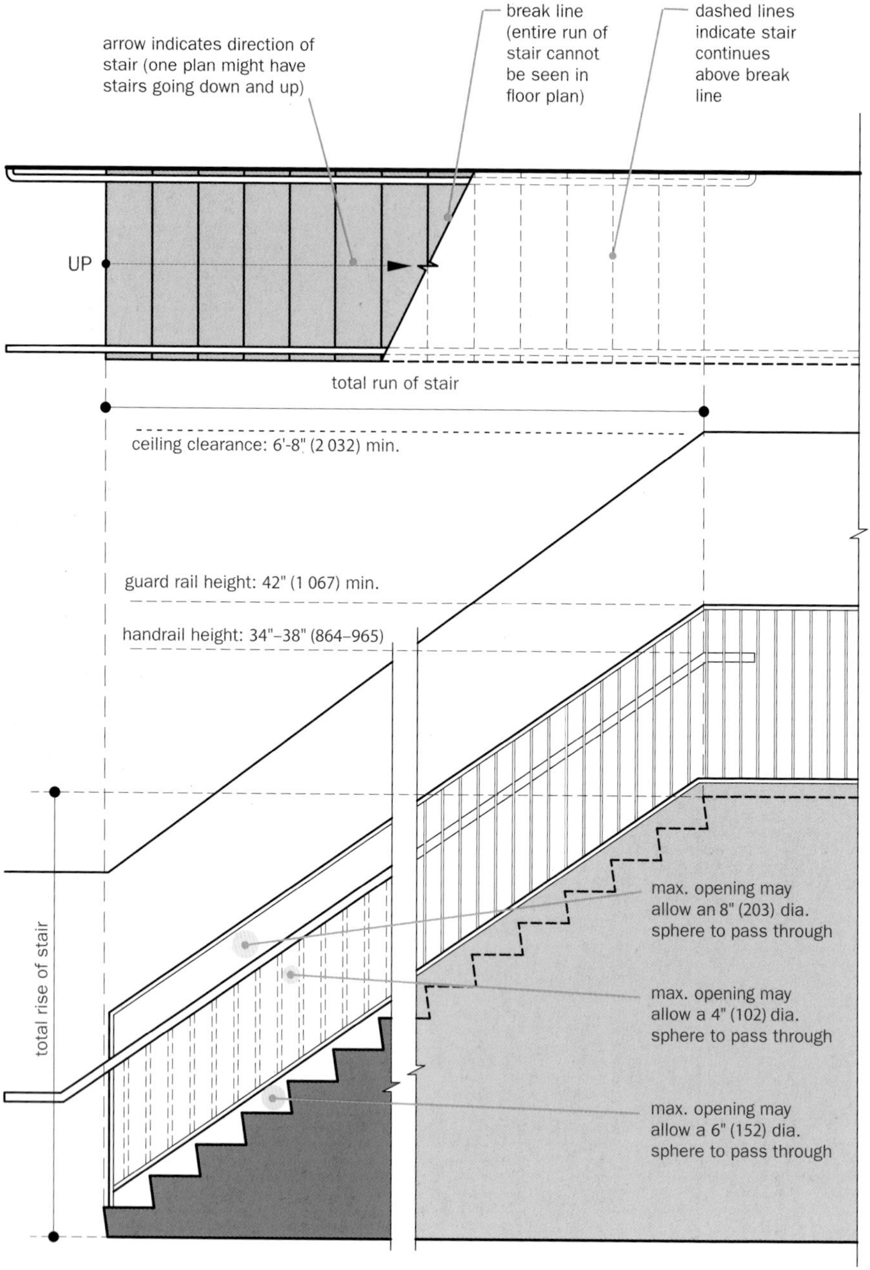
arrow indicates direction of stair (one plan might have stairs going down and up)
break line (entire run of stair cannot be seen in floor plan)
dashed lines indicate stair continues above break line
UP
total run of stair
ceiling clearance: 6'-8" (2 032) min.
guard rail height: 42" (1 067) min.
handrail height: 34"–38" (864–965)
total rise of stair
max. opening may allow an 8" (203) dia. sphere to pass through
max. opening may allow a 4" (102) dia. sphere to pass through
max. opening may allow a 6" (152) dia. sphere to pass through

Plan and Elevation of Stair

TREADS AND RISERS

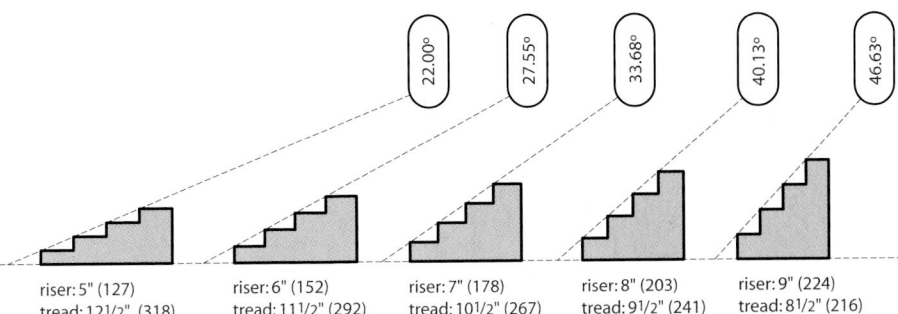

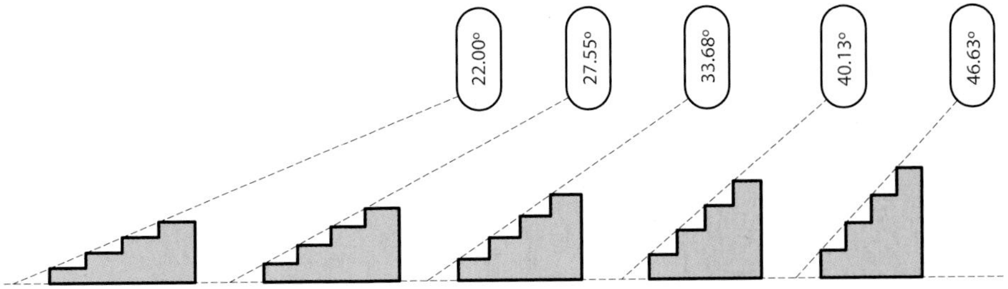
22.00°
27.55°
33.68°
40.13°
46.63°
riser: 5" (127)
tread: 12 1/2" (318)
riser: 6" (152)
tread: 11 1/2" (292)
riser: 7" (178)
tread: 10 1/2" (267)
riser: 8" (203)
tread: 9 1/2" (241)
riser: 9" (224)
tread: 8 1/2" (216)

Riser and Tread Dimensions

Angle	Riser inches (mm)	Tread inches (mm)
22.00°	5 (127)	12 1/2 (318)
23.23°	5 1/4 (133)	12 1/4 (311)
24.63°	5 1/2 (140)	12 (305)
26.00°	5 3/4 (146)	11 3/4 (299)
27.55°	6 (152)	11 1/2 (292)
29.05°	6 1/4 (159)	11 1/4 (286)
30.58°	6 1/2 (165)	11 (279)
32.13°	6 3/4 (172)	10 3/4 (273)
33.68°	7 (178)	10 1/2 (267)
35.26°	7 1/4 (184)	10 1/4 (260)
36.87°	7 1/2 (191)	10 (254)
38.48°	7 3/4 (197)	9 3/4 (248)
40.13°	8 (203)	9 1/2 (241)
41.73°	8 1/4 (210)	9 1/4 (235)
43.36°	8 1/2 (216)	9 (229)
45.00°	8 3/4 (222)	8 3/4 (222)
46.63°	9 (229)	8 1/2 (216)
48.27°	9 1/4 (235)	8 1/4 (210)
49.90°	9 1/2 (241)	8 (203)

Blue band indicates preferred proportions for comfort and safety.

General Guidelines

The following are rules of thumb for calculating limits; always check appropriate local codes:

riser × run = 72"–75" (1 829–905)

riser + run = 17"–17 1/2" (432–445)

2(riser) + run = 24"–25" (610–635)

exterior stairs: 2(riser) + run = 26" (660)

Nonresidential:
minimum width = 44" (1 120)
maximum riser = 7 1/2" (191)

minimum tread = 11" (279)

Residential:
minimum width = 36" (915)
maximum riser = 8 1/4" (210)
minimum tread = 9" (229)

Chapter 19: Doors

Interior and exterior doors may be of many combinations of wood, metal, and glass, and mounted in wood or metal frames. Interior doors may require various levels of fire ratings; exterior doors must be well constructed and tightly weather-stripped to avoid excessive leakage of air and moisture.

Widths

2'-0"	2'-4"	2'-6"	2'-8"	2'-10"	3'-0"	3'-4"	3'-6"	3'-8"	3'-10"	4'-0"
(610)	(711)	(762)	(813)	(864)	(914)	(1 016)	(1 067)	(1 118)	(1 168)	(1 219)

Preferred SI Dimensions

single widths:
700 mm, 800 mm, 900 mm, 1 000 mm

double widths:
1 200 mm, 1 500 mm, 1 800 mm

heights:
2 100 mm, 2 200 mm, 2 400 mm

Thicknesses

1 3/8" (35)
1 3/4" (44)
2 1/4" (54)

Heights

6'-8"	(2 032)
7'-0"	(2 134)
7'-2"	(2 184)
7'-10"*	(2 388)
8'-0"*	(2 438)

*1 3/4" thick doors only

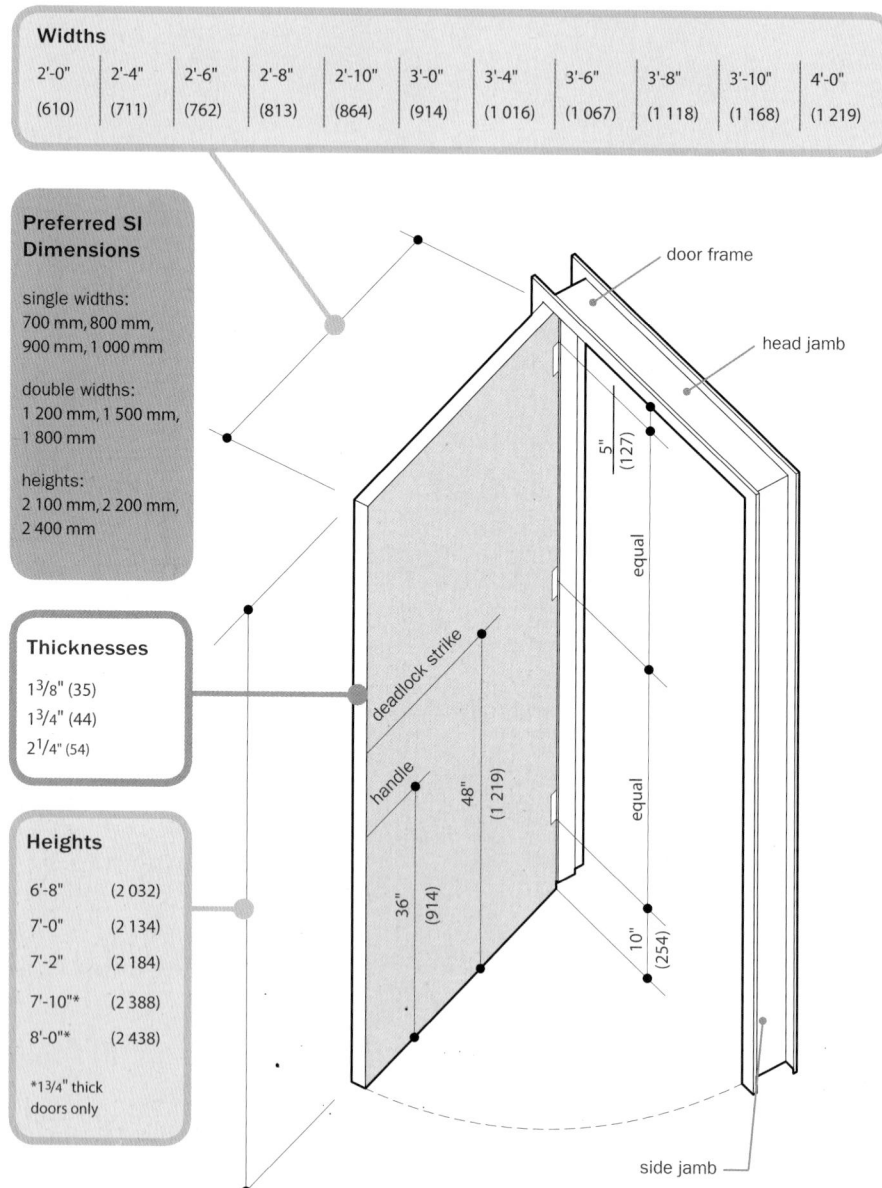

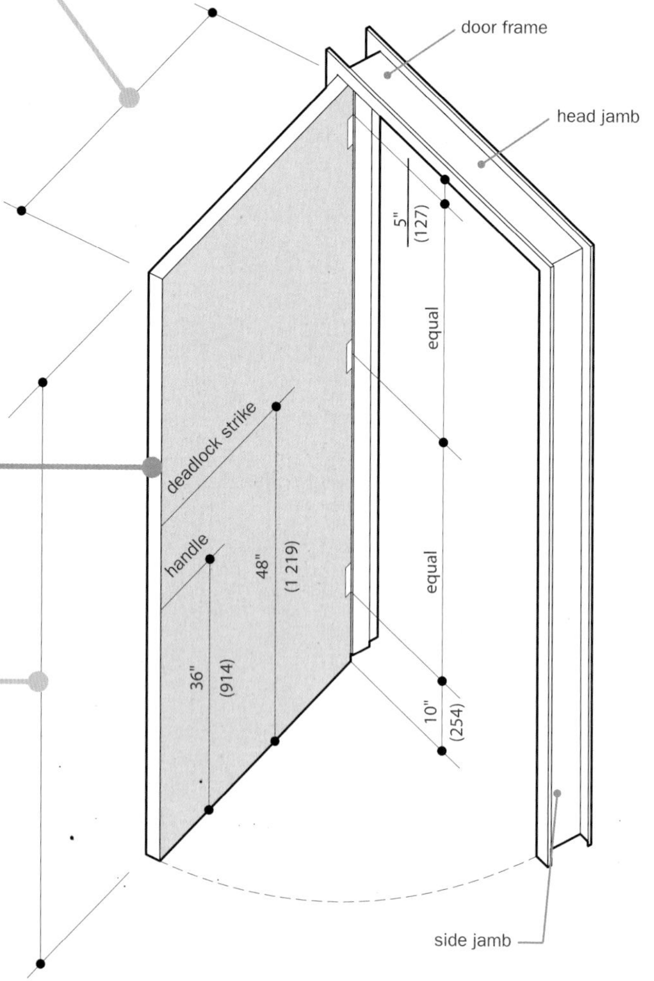
door frame
head jamb
5"
(127)
equal
deadlock strike
handle
48"
(1 219)
36"
(914)
equal
10"
(254)
side jamb

DOOR TYPES

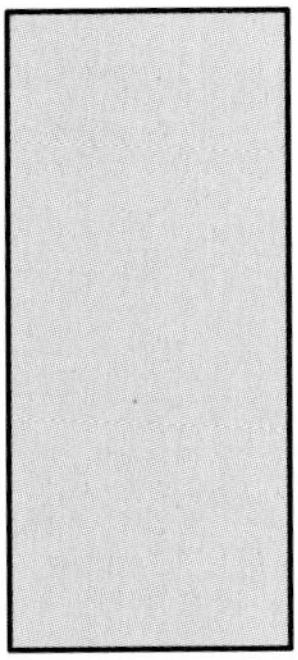

Flush

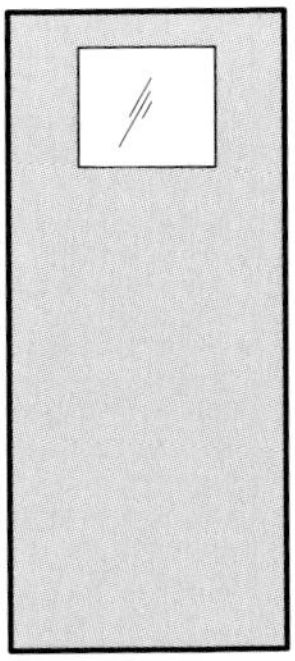

Vision Panel

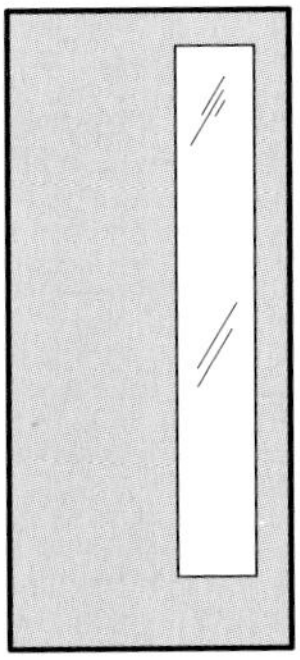

Narrow Lite

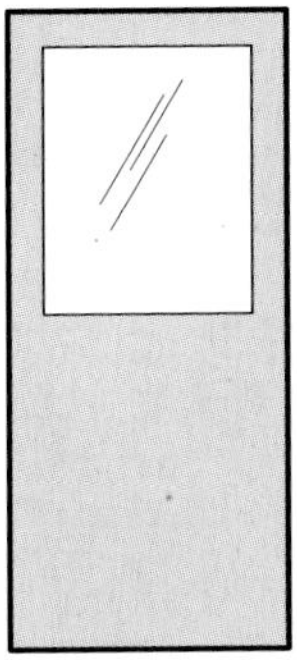

Glass

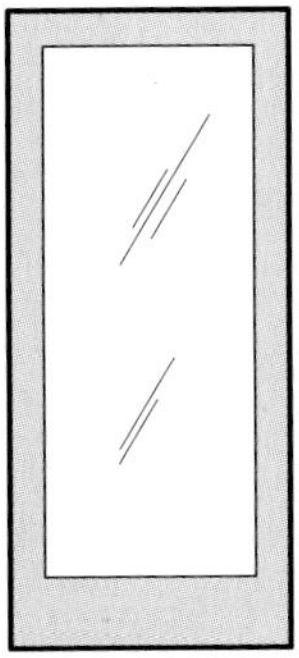

Glass

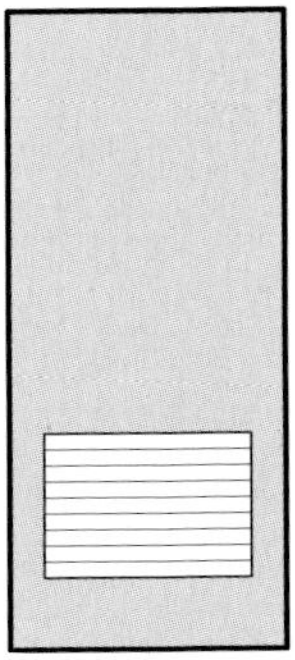

Louvered

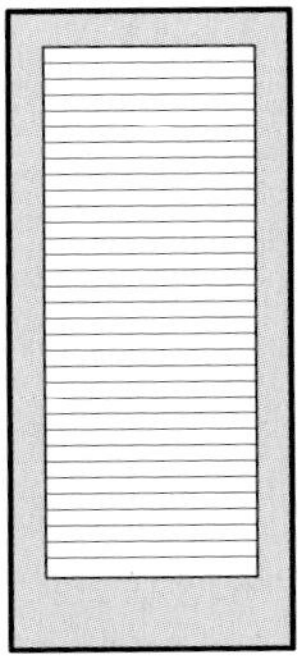

Louvered

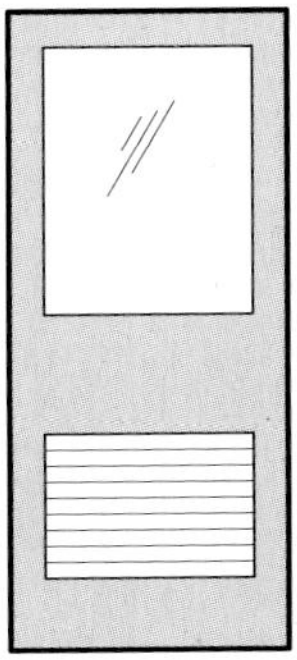

Glass and Louvered

Fire Doors

U.L. Label	Rating	Glazing Permitted: 1/4" (6.4) Wire Glass
A	3 hour	no glazing permitted
B	1 1/2 hour	100 sq. in. (64 516 mm^2) per leaf
C	3/4 hour	1 296 sq. in. (836 179 mm^2) per light; 54" (1 372) max. dimension
D	1 1/2 hour	no glazing permitted
E	3/4 hour	720 sq. in. (464 544 mm^2) per light; 54" (1 372) max. dimension

Max. door size: 4' × 10' (1 219 × 3 048); door frame and hardware must have same rating as door; door must be self-latching and equipped with closers; louvers with fusible links are permitted for B and C label doors; no louver and glass light combinations are allowed.

WOOD DOORS

Flush Solid Core

Used primarily for exterior conditions and wherever increased fire resistance, sound insulation, and dimensional stability are required.

Door Elevation

Detail Section

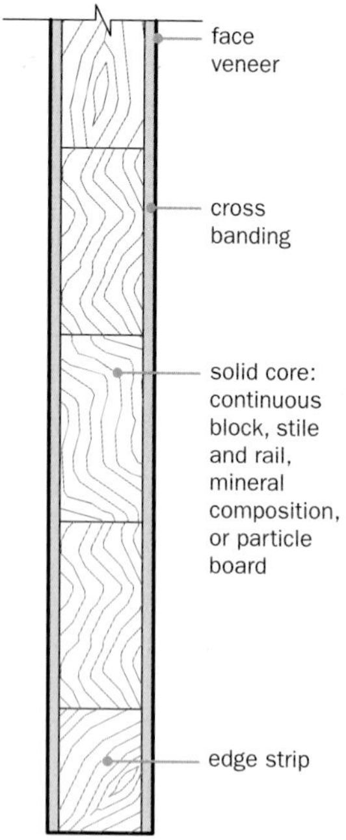
face veneer
cross banding
solid core: continuous block, stile and rail, mineral composition, or particle board
edge strip

Flush Hollow Core

Lightweight and inexpensive, used primarily for interior applications, though may be used on the exterior if bonded with a waterproof adhesive. Low sound and heat insulation value.

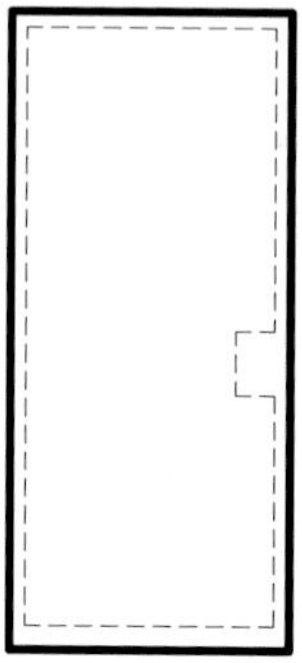

Door Elevation

Detail Section

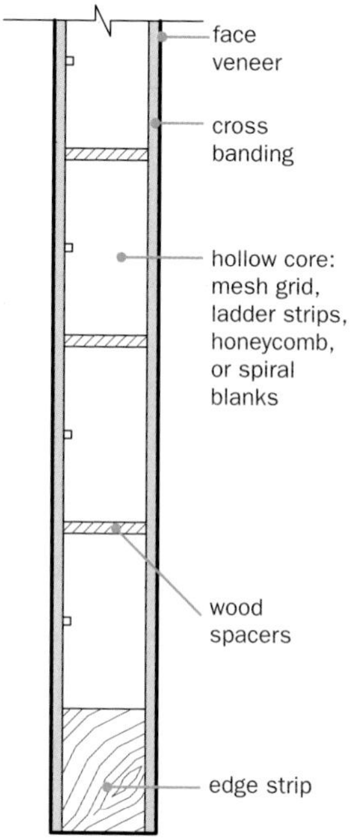
face veneer
cross banding
hollow core: mesh grid, ladder strips, honeycomb, or spiral blanks
wood spacers
edge strip

Panel

Supporting framework of rails and stiles may hold panels of wood, glass, or louvers. Makeup of doors minimizes dimensional changes brought on by fluctuating moisture content of the wood.

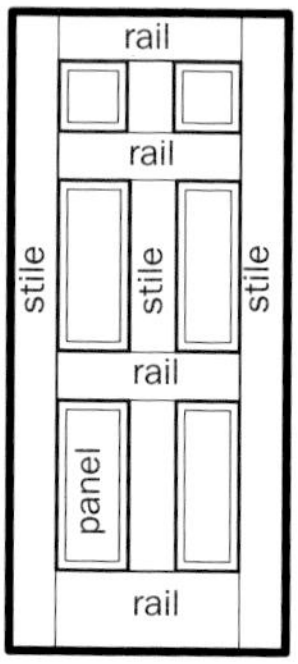
rail
rail
stile
stile
stile
rail
panel
rail

Door Elevation

Detail Section

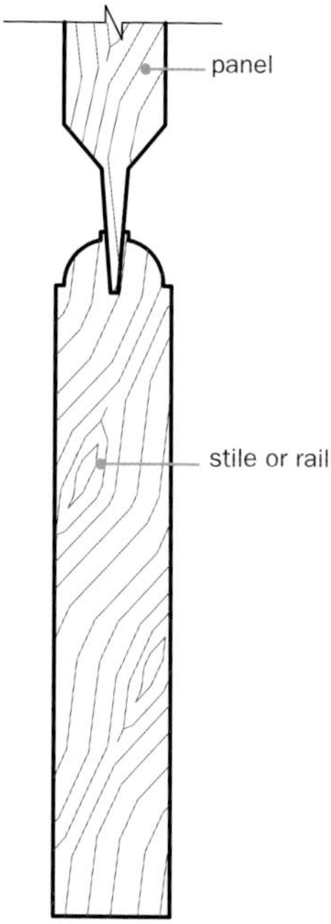
panel
stile or rail

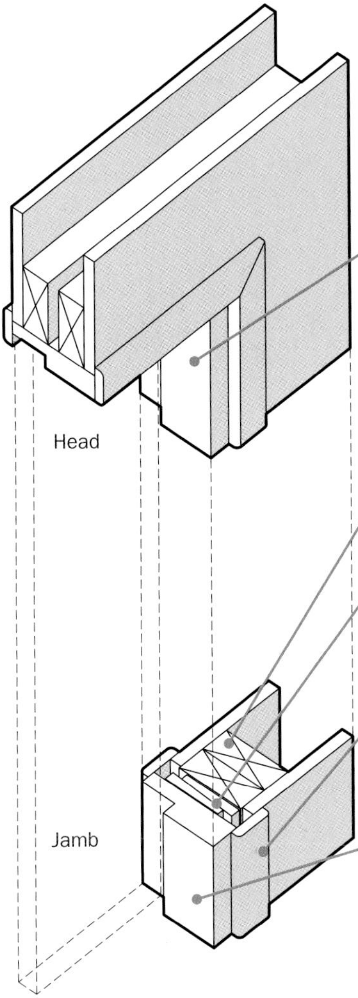

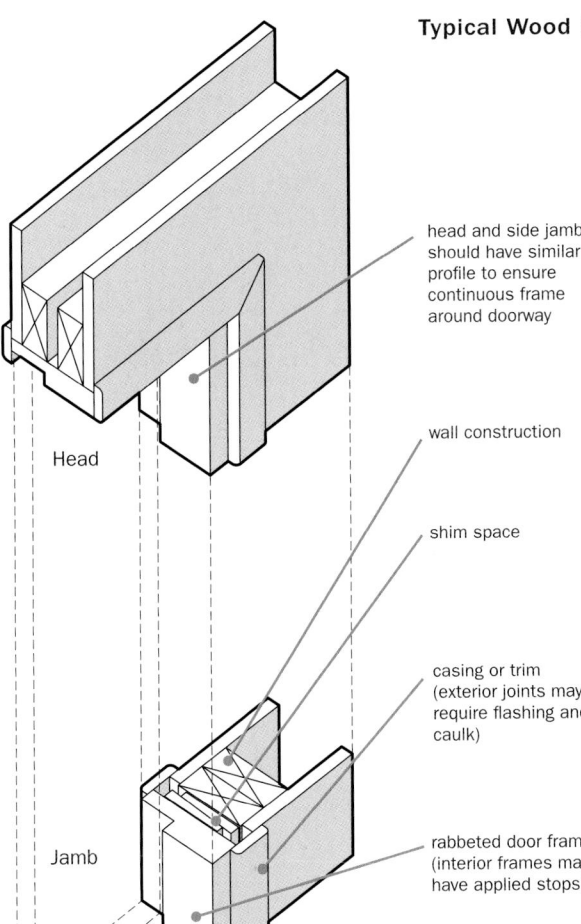

head and side jamb should have similar profile to ensure continuous frame around doorway
wall construction
shim space
casing or trim (exterior joints may require flashing and caulk)
rabbeted door frame (interior frames may have applied stops)
Head
Jamb

Typical Wood Door Framing

In the interest of speed and economy, many wood doors have been prehung (hinged and fitted to their frames at the mill). When they arrive on site, the carpenter may tilt the frame into the rough opening, carefully plumbing the frame and shimming as necessary before nailing the frame in place.

In the prehung method, shims help assure that the door and frame will fit cleanly in the rough opening provided. The resulting gap between the frame and the wall finish is generally covered with a casing. Detailing of this condition may take many forms, depending on the desired result, though a common approach is shown at left.

Wood Face Veneer Types

Standard: 1/32" –1/16" (0.08–1.6), bonded to hardwood; crossband of 1/16" –1/10" (1.6–2.5). Economical and widely used; for all types of cores. Difficult to refinish or repair face damage.

Sawn veneers: 1/8" (3.2), bonded to crossband. Easily refinished and repaired.

Sawn veneers: 1/4" (6.4), no crossband on stile and rail. Face depth allows for decorative grooves.

Wood Grades

Premium:
For natural, clear, or stained finishes

Standard:
For opaque (painted) finishes

HOLLOW METAL DOORS

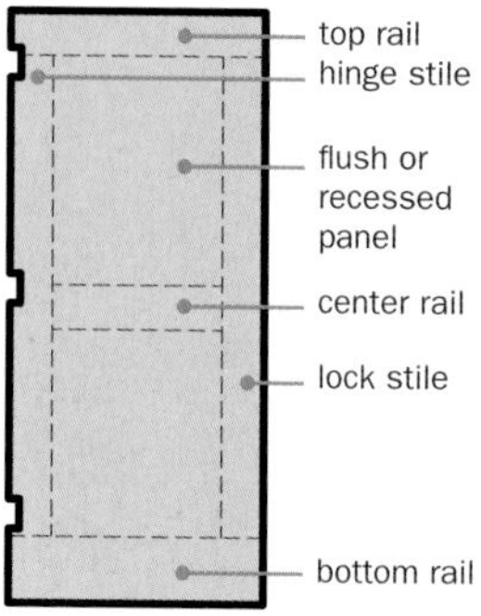
top rail
hinge stile
flush or recessed panel
center rail
lock stile
bottom rail

Meeting Stiles

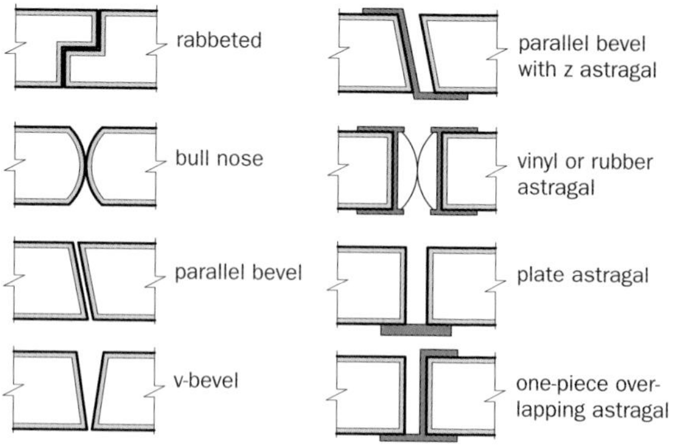
rabbeted
bull nose
parallel bevel
v-bevel
parallel bevel with z astragal
vinyl or rubber astragal
plate astragal
one-piece over-lapping astragal

Standard Double Rabbet Frame

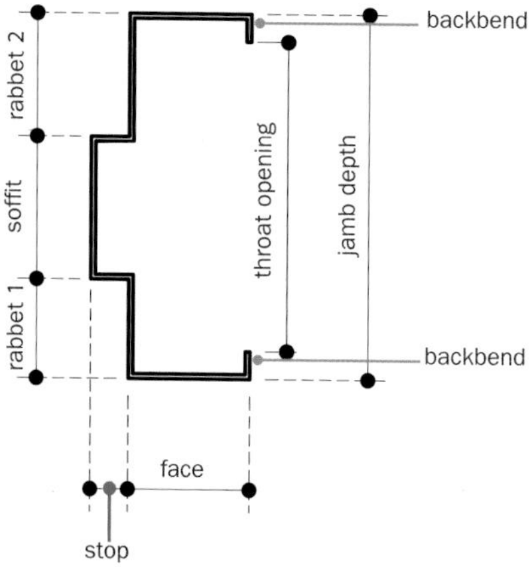
rabbet 2
soffit
rabbet 1
backbend
throat opening
jamb depth
backbend
face
stop

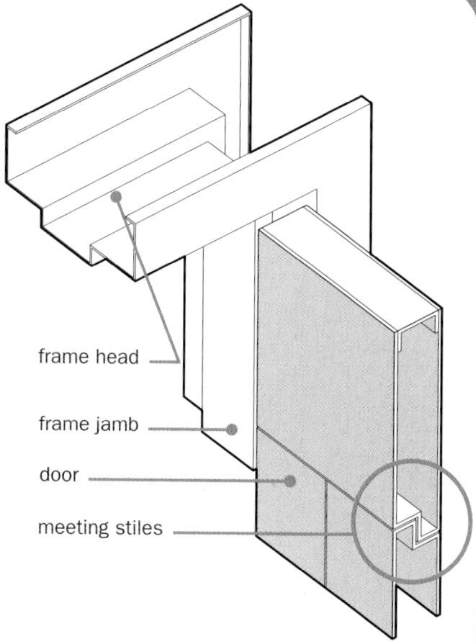
frame head
frame jamb
door
meeting stiles

Jamb Depth	4 3/4" (121)	5 1/2" (140)	5 3/4" (146)	6 3/4" (171)	7 3/4" (197)	8 3/4" (222)	12 3/4" (324)
Rabbet 1	1 9/16" (40) standard for 1 3/8" (35) door						
Rabbet 2	1 15/16" (49) standard for 1 3/4" (44) door						
Backbend	1/2" (13)	3/4" (19)	1/2" (13)	1/2" (13)	1/2" (13)	1/2" (13)	1/2" (13)
Throat	3 3/4" (95)	4" (102)	4 3/4" (121)	5 3/4" (146)	6 3/4" (171)	7 3/4" (197)	11 3/4" (298)

Hollow Metal Door Gauges

GRADE	GAUGE
Residential	20 and lighter
Commercial	16 and 18
Institutional	12 and 14
High Security	steel plate

FRAME ANCHORS

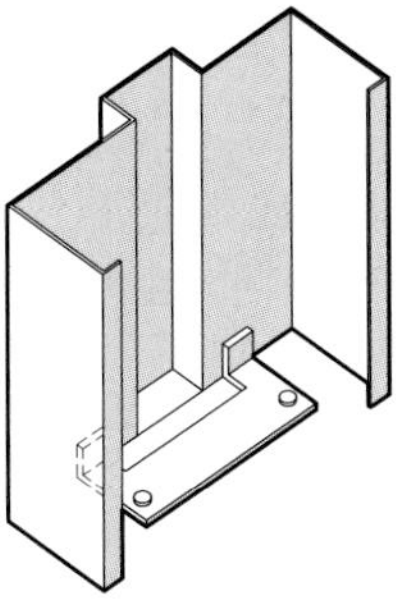

Standard Floor Knee
Jambs are attached to the floor with powder-driven fasteners.

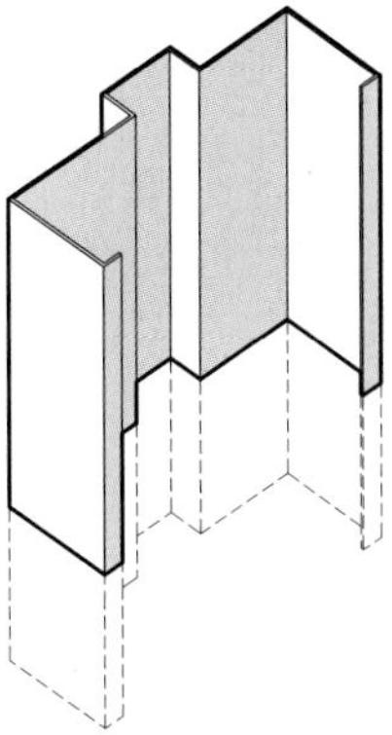

Extended Frame with Base Anchor
Floor-topping concrete is poured around the door frame.

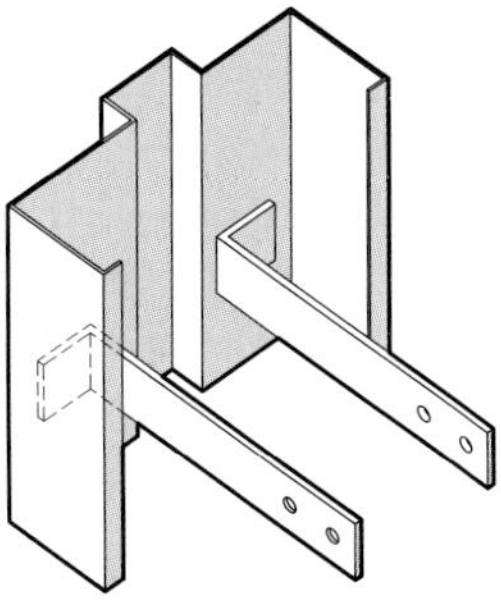

Wood Stud Anchor
Jambs are anchored to wood studs by nailing through holes in jamb inserts.

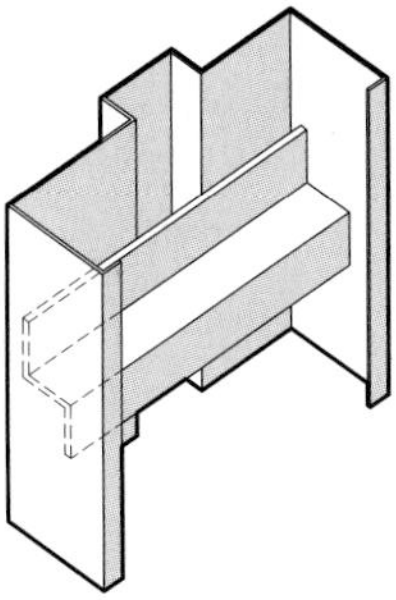

Steel Channel Anchor
Jambs are anchored to steel studs; sheet metal zees are welded to jambs, and receive screws driven through studs.

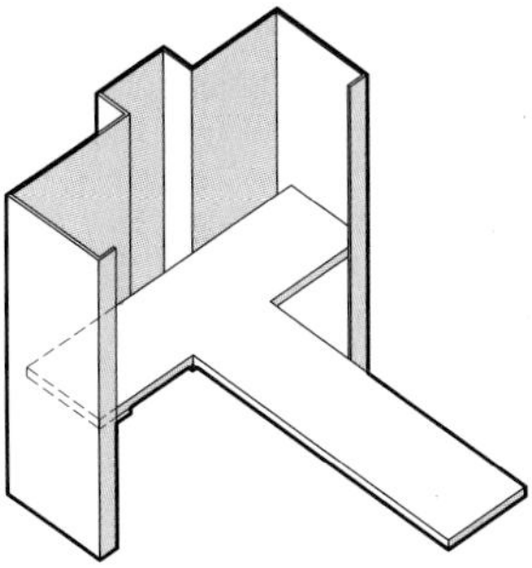

Masonry T Anchor
Jambs are anchored to masonry walls: loose sheet metal tees are inserted into the frame and built into the mortar joints.

OTHER CORES

treated fibrous material formed into honeycomb

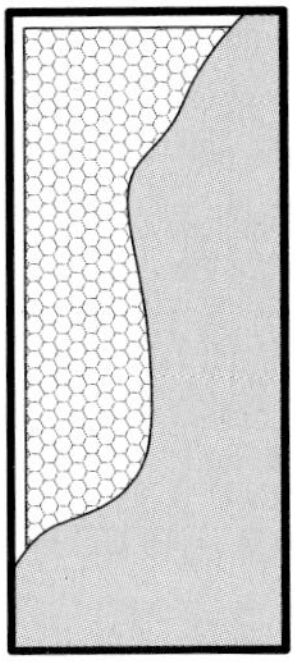

anhydrous mineral, foam, or fiber core

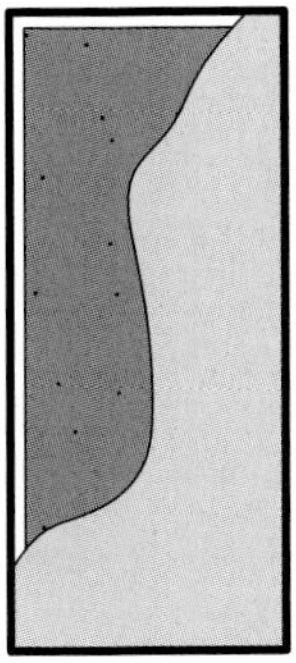

kiln-dried structural wood core

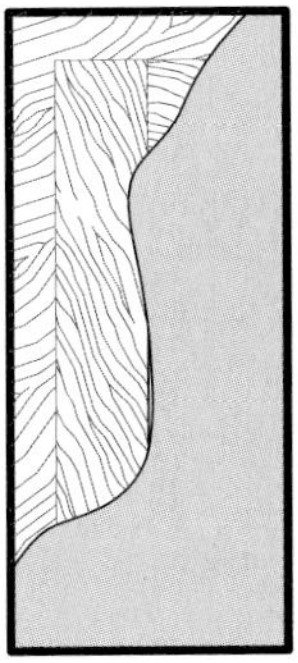

z-member or channel stiffeners (vertical, horizontal, or gridded)

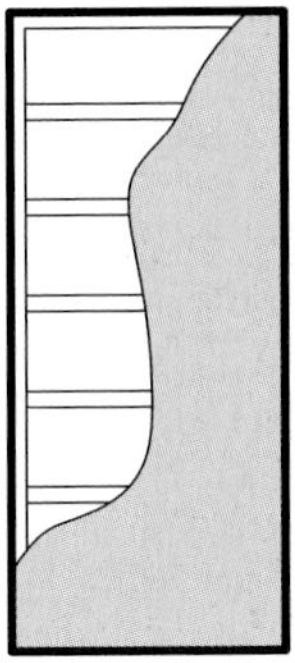

PROPORTION AND FORM 5.

Since most architecture, even that designed for a large-scale use (such as an airplane hangar or an elephant barn), requires some human interface, our own bodies serve as useful reference points for inhabiting space. Similarly, no matter how complicated structures may be, most are reducible to the point, line, or plane that evolved into the more complex combinations of forms and spaces that constitute a design.

Throughout history, architects have devised and employed ordering and proportioning systems for architecture based on the logics of harmonics, arithmetic, geometry, and the human body, often producing a visual and physical order that is apparent to the observer even if the organizing logic is not known or understood.

Daily life brings us into contact with endless numbers of systems of arrangement and order, much of it centered on how our bodies and our cars (extensions of our bodies) use and navigate our immediate surroundings and share them with others. The standards presented here describe the basic clearances demanded of an assortment of programs that architects regularly encounter. They do not propose specific designs, but give a better understanding of how different bodies occupy different spaces.

Chapter 20: The Human Scale

The scale of the human body informs almost every aspect of architectural design. The dimensions in this chapter represent an average range (the lower number denotes the 2.5th percentile, while the upper number denotes the 97.5th percentile).

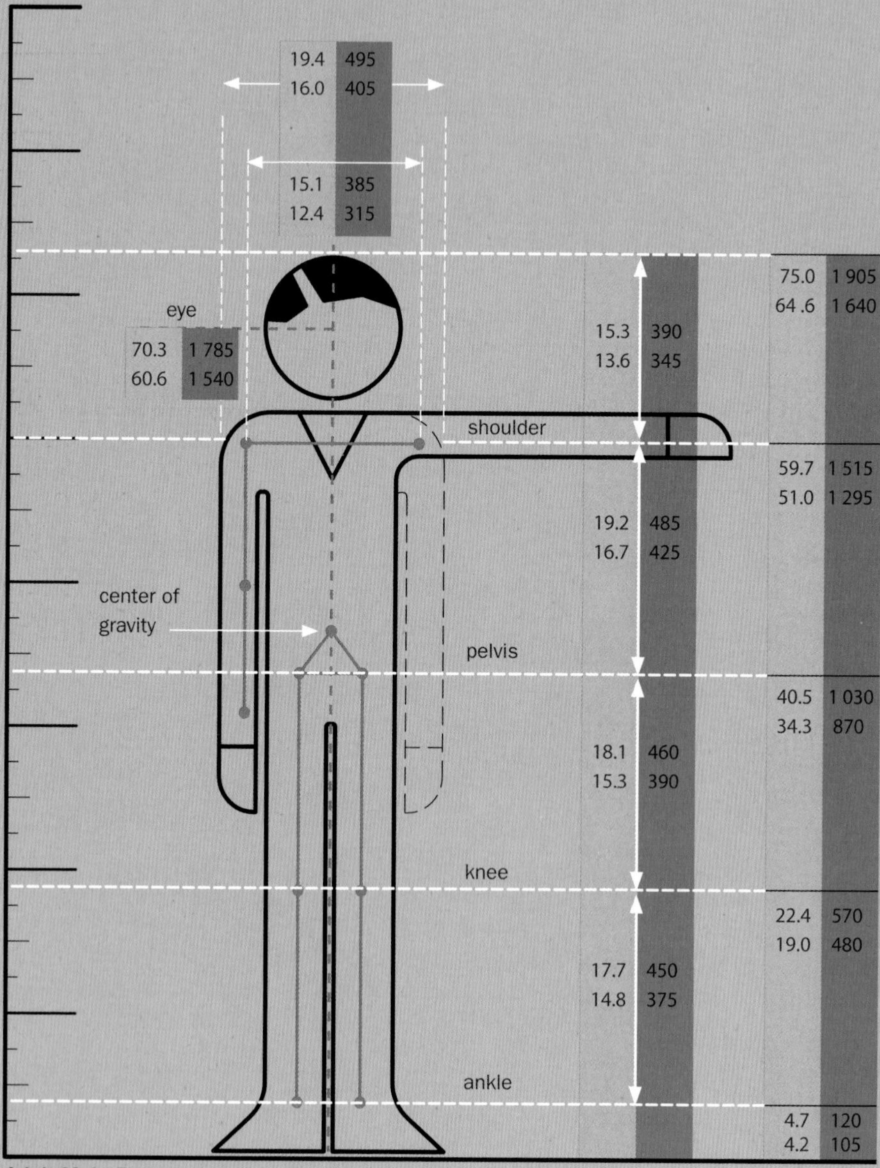
19.4 495
16.0 405
15.1 385
12.4 315
eye
70.3 1 785
60.6 1 540
15.3 390
13.6 345
75.0 1 905
64 .6 1 640
shoulder
59.7 1 515
51.0 1 295
19.2 485
16.7 425
center of gravity
pelvis
40.5 1 030
34.3 870
18.1 460
15.3 390
knee
22.4 570
19.0 480
17.7 450
14.8 375
ankle
4.7 120
4.2 105

Adult Male Figure

On the drawings below, the gray bars indicate inches and the blue bars indicate millimeters.

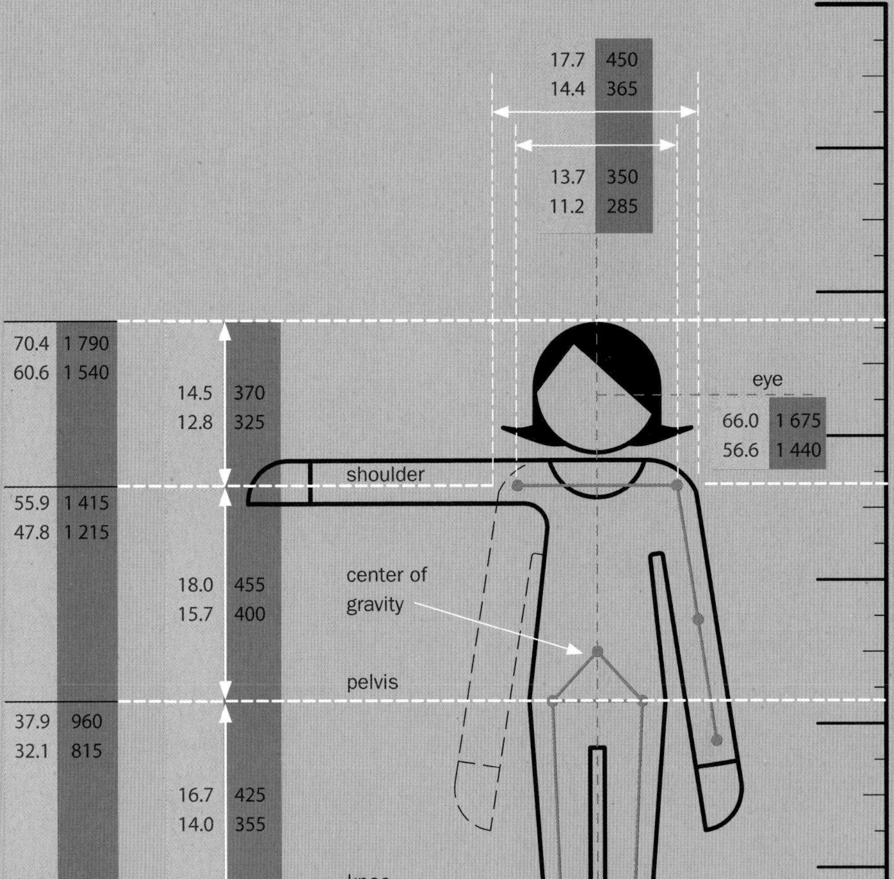
17.7 450
14.4 365
13.7 350
11.2 285
70.4 1 790
60.6 1 540
14.5 370
12.8 325
eye
66.0 1 675
56.6 1 440
shoulder
55.9 1 415
47.8 1 215
18.0 455
15.7 400
center of gravity
pelvis
37.9 960
32.1 815
16.7 425
14.0 355
knee
21.2 535
18.1 460
16.2 410
13.6 345
ankle
5.0 125
4.5 115

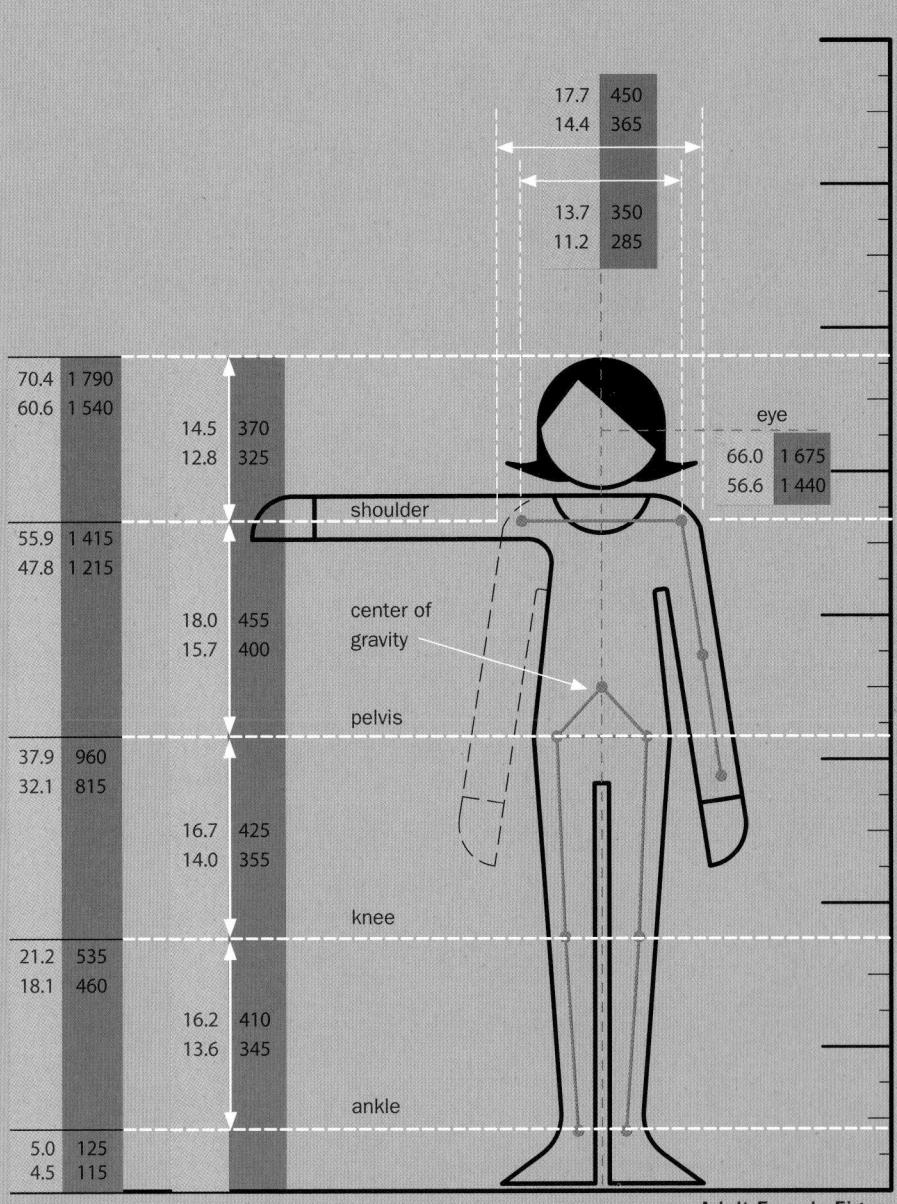

Adult Female Figure

ACCESSIBLE DESIGN DIMENSIONS

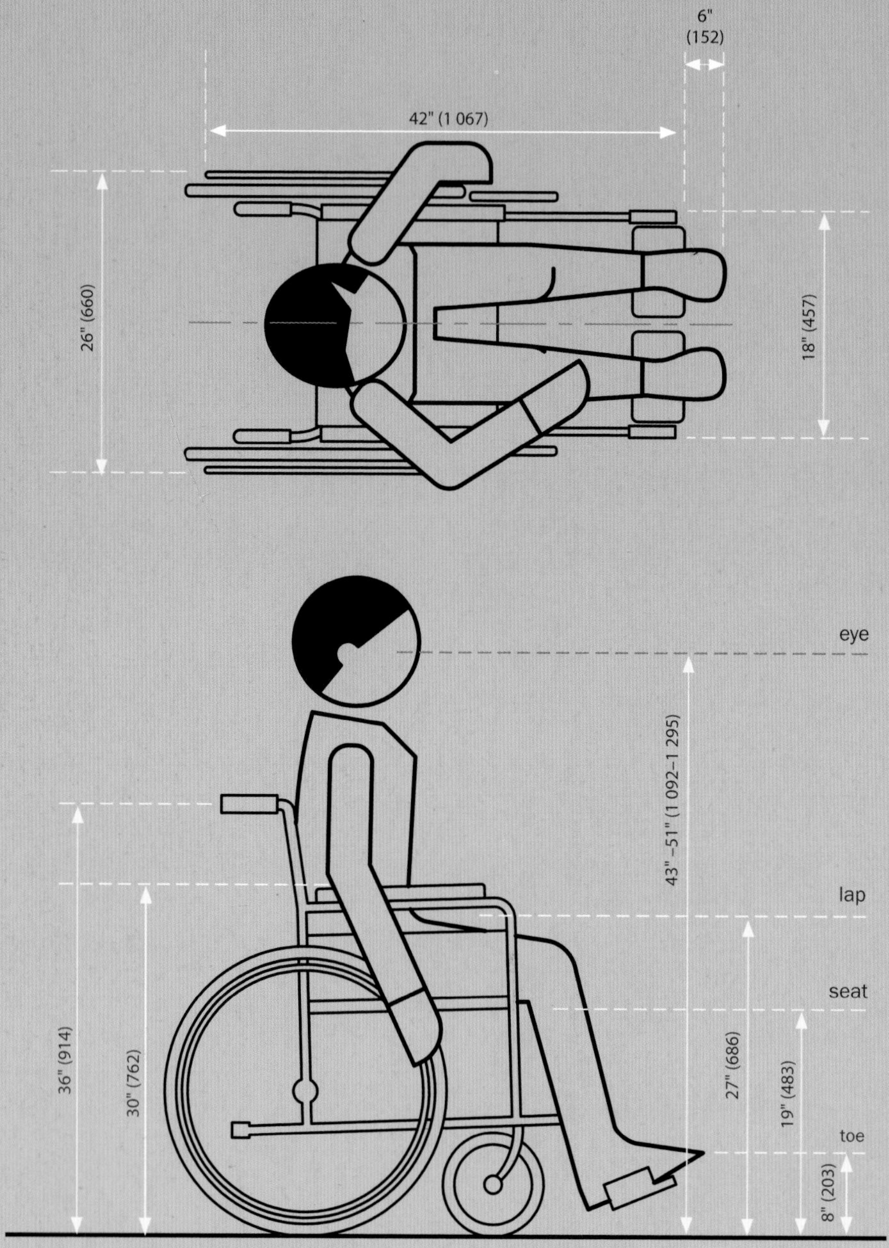
6"
(152)
42" (1 067)
26" (660)
18" (457)
eye
43"–51" (1 092–1 295)
lap
seat
toe
36" (914)
30" (762)
27" (686)
19" (483)
8" (203)

Overall Dimensions for Adult Wheelchairs

Architects must equally be familiar with the dimensions of those with special needs, specifically the constraints posed by wheelchair use. Design to accommodate wheelchairs and other special needs is increasingly the rule rather than the exception, particularly as the concept of universal design gains more prominence. Universal design suggests making all elements and spaces accessible to and usable by all people to the greatest extent possible—a goal that, through thoughtful planning and design, need not add to the cost of production.

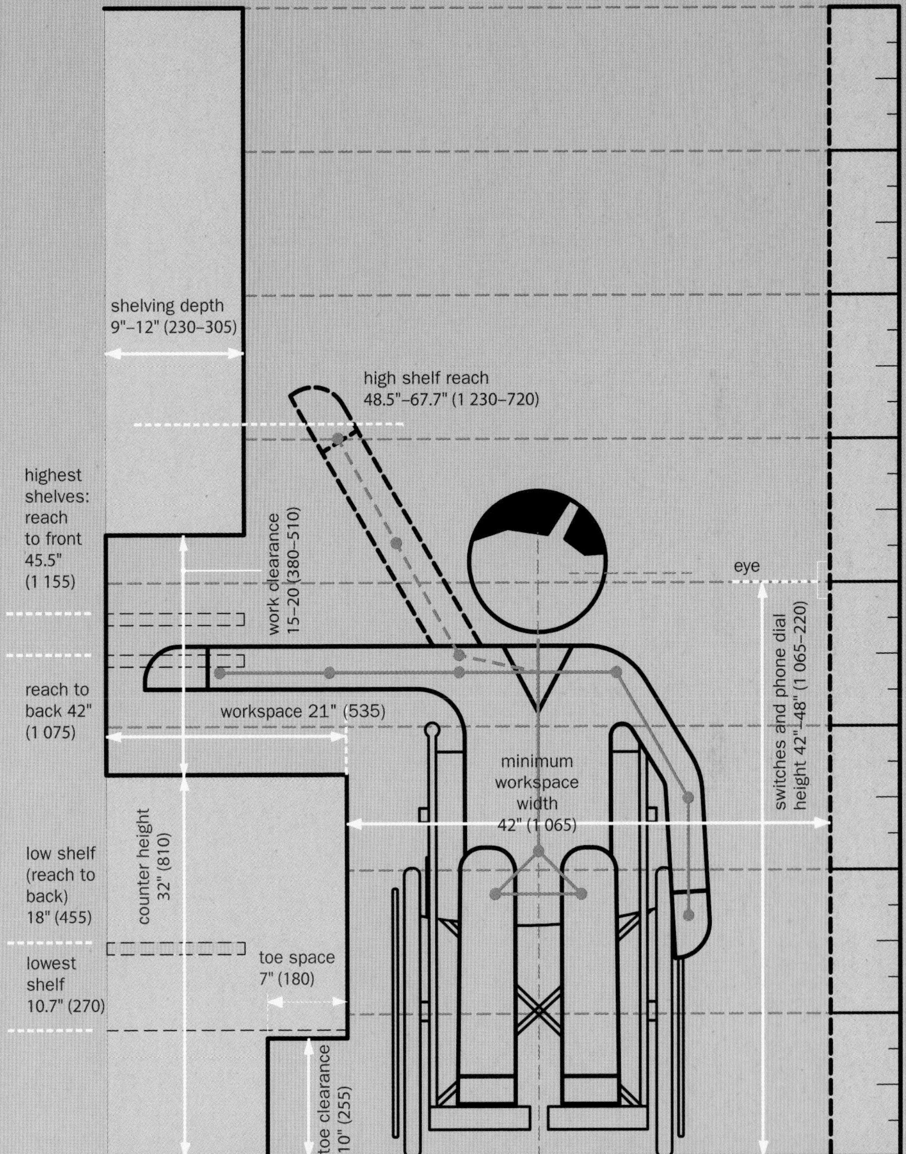
shelving depth 9"–12" (230–305)
high shelf reach 48.5"–67.7" (1 230–720)
highest shelves: reach to front 45.5" (1 155)
work clearance 15–20 (380–510)
eye
switches and phone dial height 42"–48" (1 065–220)
reach to back 42" (1 075)
workspace 21" (535)
minimum workspace width 42" (1 065)
counter height 32" (810)
low shelf (reach to back) 18" (455)
toe space 7" (180)
lowest shelf 10.7" (270)
toe clearance 10" (255)

Side Approach Work Station Clearances

SEATED DIMENSIONS

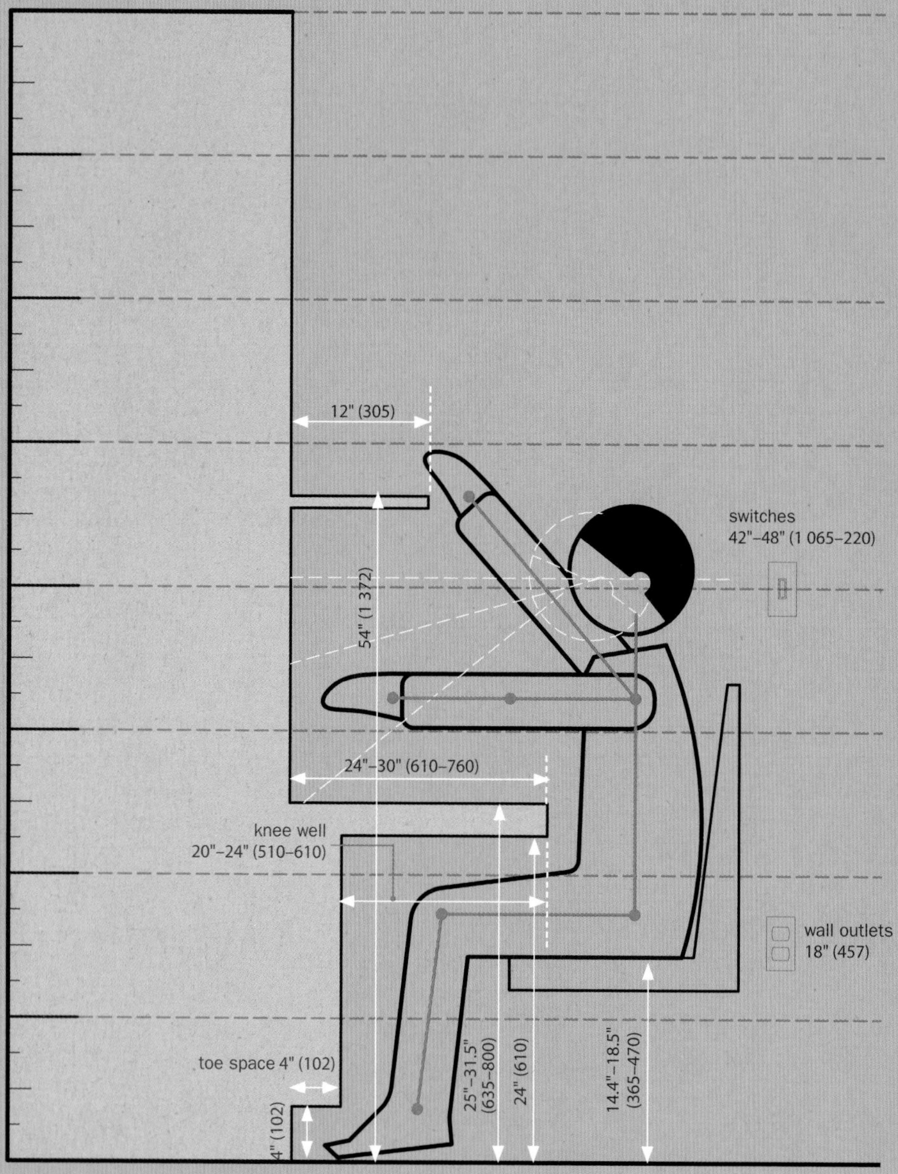
12" (305)
switches
42"–48" (1 065–220)
54" (1 372)
24"–30" (610–760)
knee well
20"–24" (510–610)
wall outlets
18" (457)
toe space 4" (102)
4" (102)
25"–31.5"
(635–800)
24" (610)
14.4"–18.5"
(365–470)

Work Station Clearances

25" (625)
35" (875)
30" (750)
35" (875)
38" (950)
35" (875)
25" (625)
39" (1 000)
35" (875)
73" (1 875)
12" (300)
35" (875)

Lounging Position General Space Considerations

Chapter 21: Interior Spaces

KITCHENS

Typical Dimensions

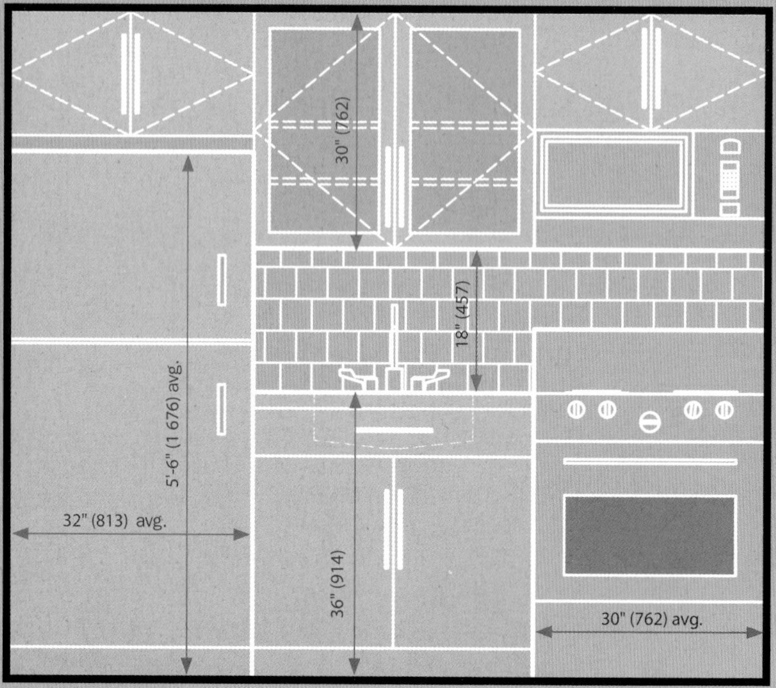
30" (762)
18" (457)
5'-6" (1 676) avg.
32" (813) avg.
36" (914)
30" (762) avg.

Typical Layout Types

Storage guidelines: minimum 18 sq. ft. (1.67 m^2) basic storage, plus 6 sq. ft. (0.56 m^2) per person served.

The total distance of all three sides of the work triangle should average between 12 lineal feet (3 660) and 22 lineal feet (6 705).

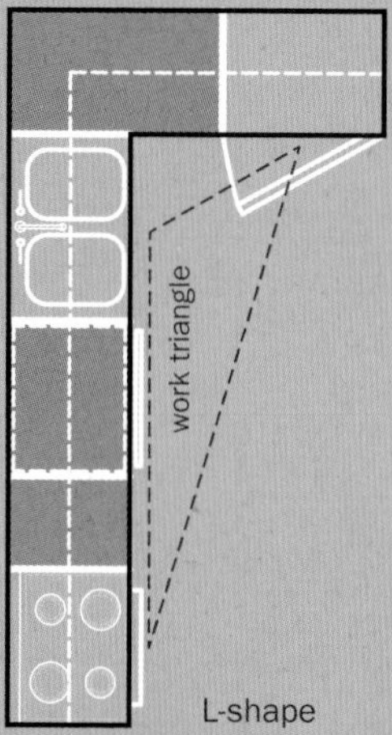
work triangle

L-shape

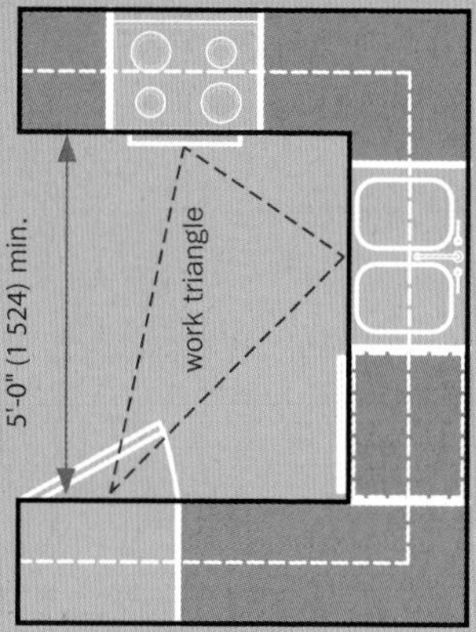
5'-0" (1 524) min.
work triangle

U-shape

Cabinetry Components

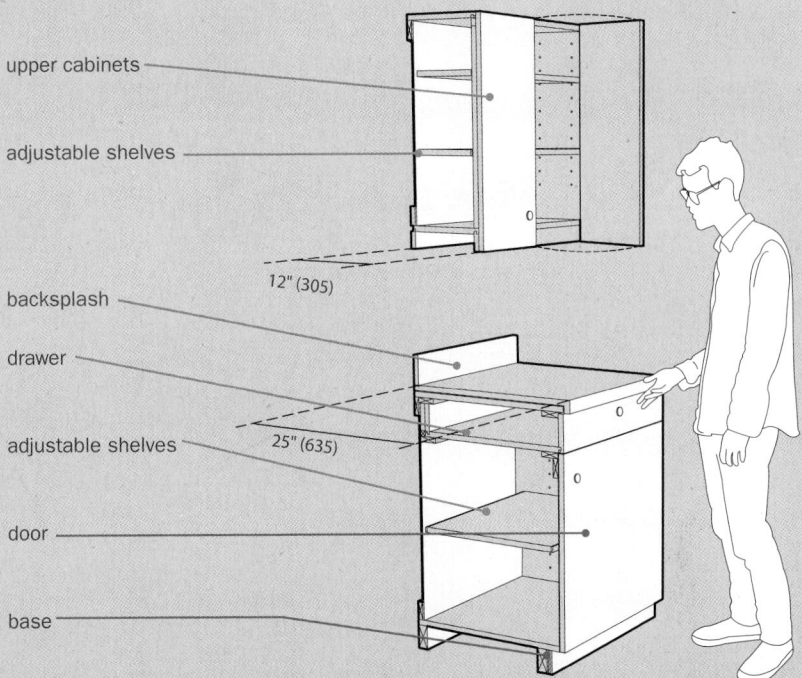

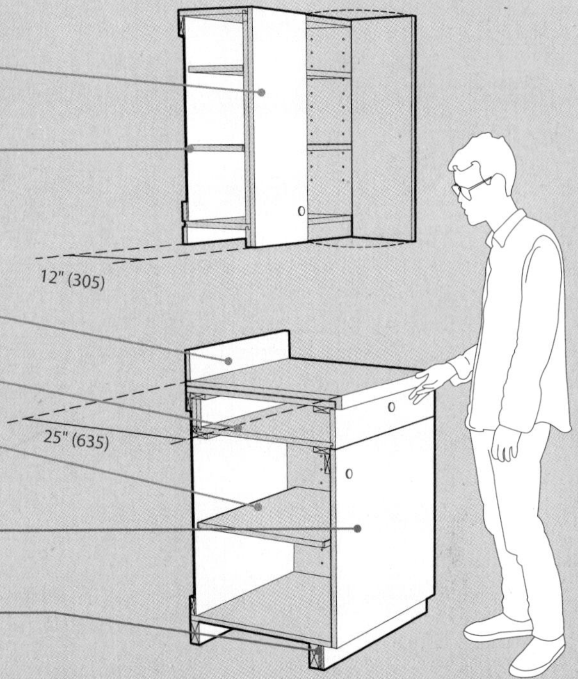
upper cabinets
adjustable shelves
12" (305)
backsplash
drawer
25" (635)
adjustable shelves
door
base

Appliances
Many appliances have become modular in width, and fit within a 3" system (ex. 9", 12", 15", 18", 21", 24"... 48")

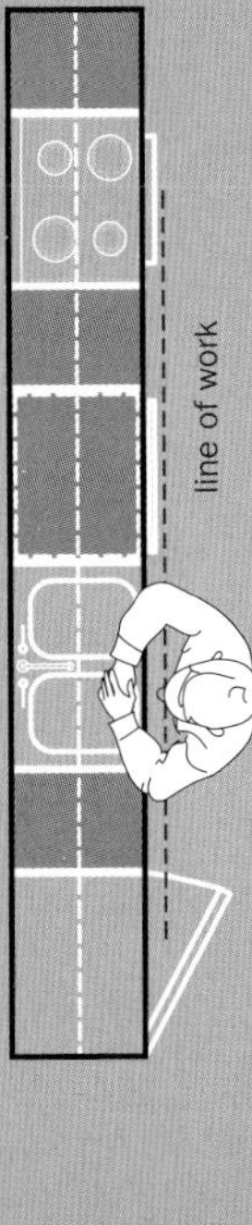
line of work

Single Wall

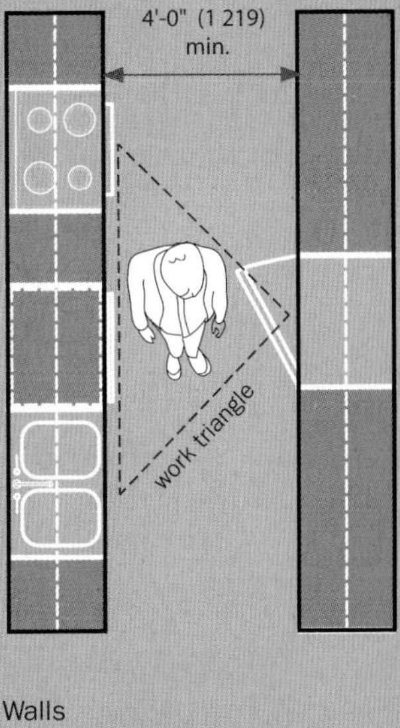
4'-0" (1 219)
min.
work triangle

Parallel Walls

BATHROOMS

General Guidelines (Subject to Local Codes)

Wall area above a tub or shower pan should be covered in a waterproof material to a height of not less than 72" (1 829) AFF.

Minimum ceiling height = 6'-8" (2 032)

Minimum ventilation should be a window of at least 3 sq. ft. (0.28 m²), of which 50 percent is operable, or a mechanical ventilation system of at least 50 cu. ft. per minute (cfm) ducted to the outside.

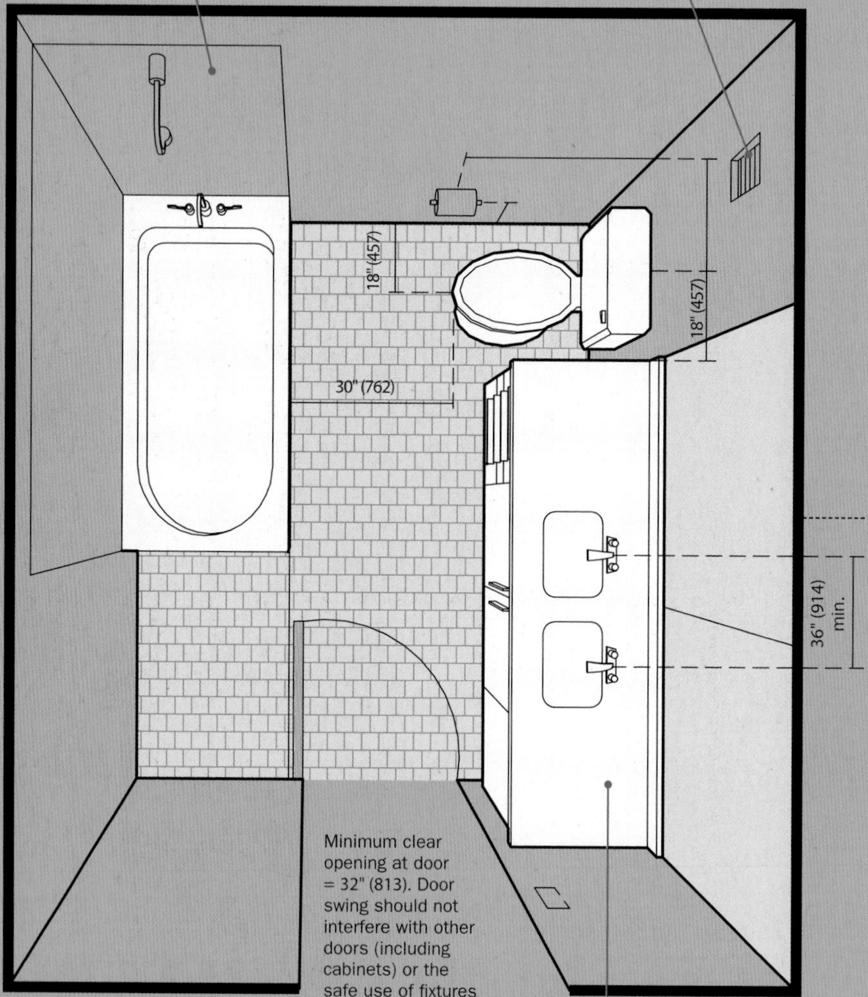

18" (457)
18" (457)
30" (762)
36" (914) min.

Minimum clear opening at door = 32" (813). Door swing should not interfere with other doors (including cabinets) or the safe use of fixtures and cabinets.

Vanity height = 32"–43" (813–1 092), as it suits the user

Glazing

Tempered glass or an approved equal should be used in the following conditions: shower doors or other glass in tub or shower enclosures; tub or shower surrounds with glass windows or walls that are less than 60" (1 524) above any standing surface; and any glazing such as windows or doors whose bottom edge is less than 18" (458) AFF.

Floors

Bathroom floors and tub and shower floors should have slip-resistant surfaces.

Electrical Outlets

All electrical receptacles should be protected by GFCI (ground-fault circuit interrupter) protectors, and at least one GFCI receptacle should be installed within 36" (914) of the outside edge of the lavatory. No receptacles of any kind should be installed in a shower or bathtub space, nor should switches be installed in wet locations in tub and shower spaces (unless installed as part of a UL-listed tub or shower assembly).

Lighting

In addition to general lighting, task lighting should be installed at each functional area of the bathroom, and at least one light must be provided that is controlled by a wall switch located at the entry. Any light fixture installed at a tub or shower must be marked as suitable for damp/wet locations.

Typical Arrangements

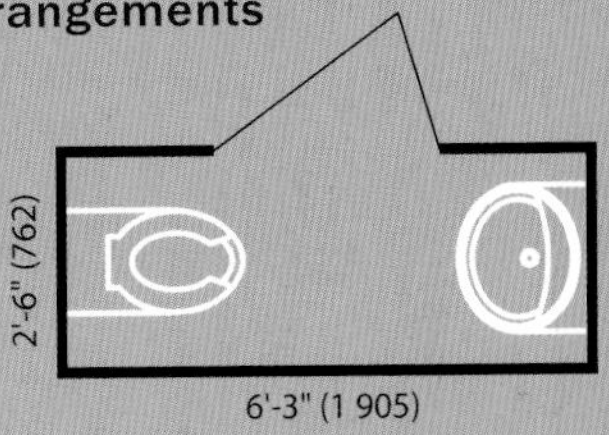
2'-6" (762)
6'-3" (1 905)

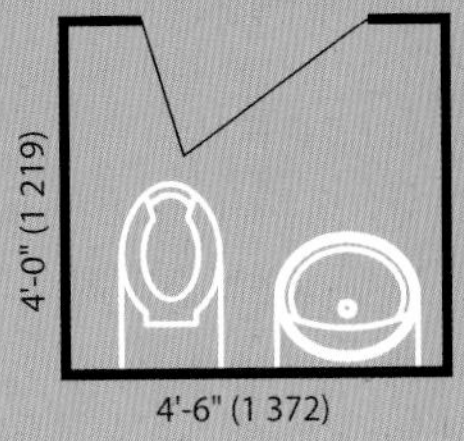
4'-0" (1 219)
4'-6" (1 372)

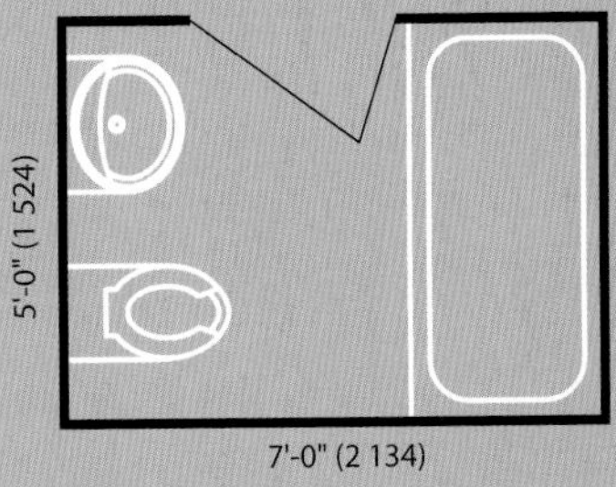
5'-0" (1 524)
7'-0" (2 134)

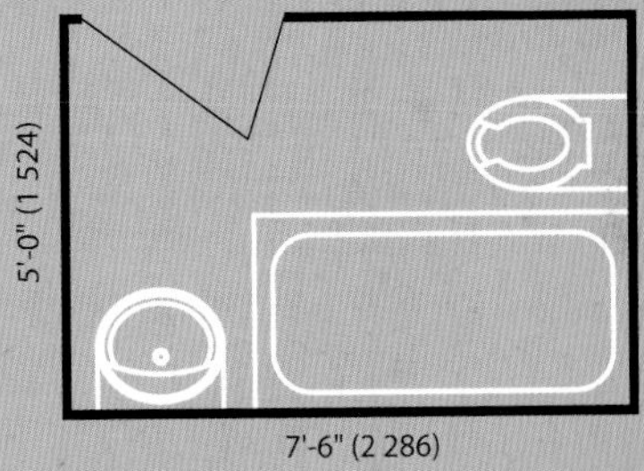
5'-0" (1 524)
7'-6" (2 286)

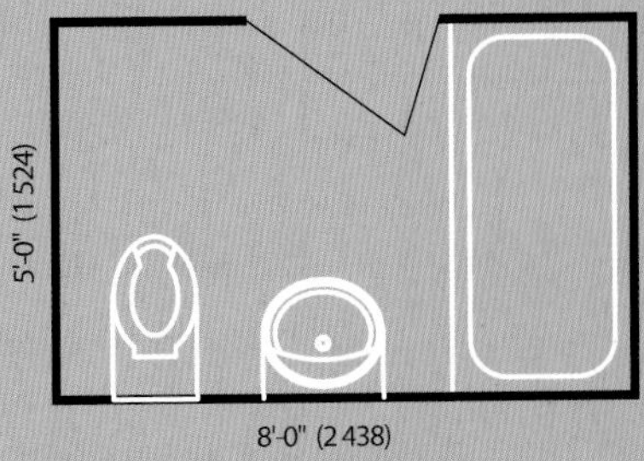
5'-0" (1 524)
8'-0" (2 438)

HABITABLE ROOMS

Beds (mattress sizes)

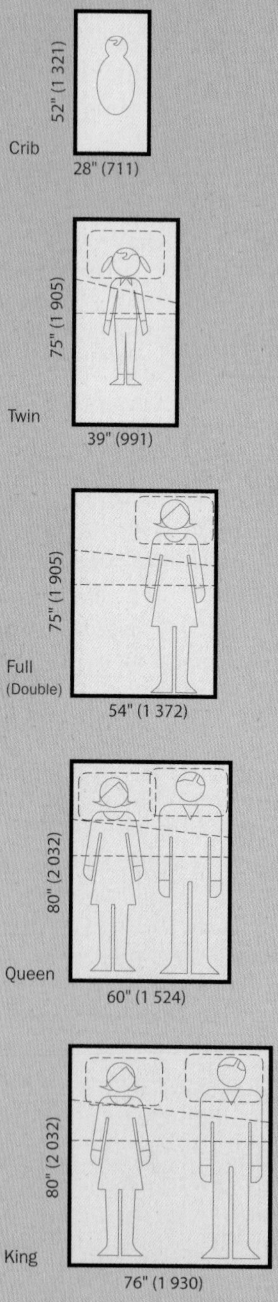
52" (1 321)
Crib
28" (711)
75" (1 905)
Twin
39" (991)
75" (1 905)
Full
(Double)
54" (1 372)
80" (2 032)
Queen
60" (1 524)
80" (2 032)
King
76" (1 930)

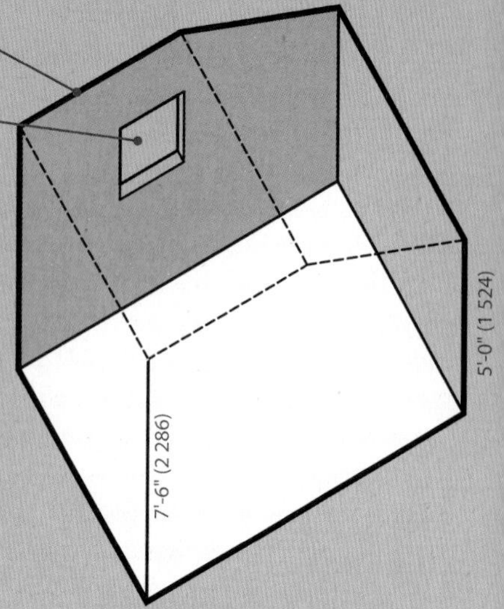
Ceiling height should not be less than 7'-6" (2 286) for at least 50 percent of the required area; 50 percent may be sloped to a minimum height of 5' (1 524).
In most residential projects, sleeping rooms should have at least one means of egress to the exterior, which can be in the form of an operable window of not less than 3.3 sq. ft. (0.307 m²), and with a minimum clear opening of 20" × 24" (508 × 610), with a sill height no higher than 44" (1 118).
7'-6" (2 286)
5'-0" (1 524)

Seating

Table Size (in.)	Maximum Seats
24 × 48	4
30 × 48	4 (2 wch.)
30 × 60	6 (4 wch.)
36 × 72	6 (6 wch.)
36 × 84	8 (6 wch.)
30 × 30	2
36 × 36	4
42 × 42	4 (2 wch.)
48 × 48	8 (2 wch.)
54 × 54	8 (4 wch.)
30 dia.	2
36 dia.	4
42 dia.	4–5
48 dia.	6 (2 wch.)
54 dia.	6 (4 wch.)

wch. = wheelchair

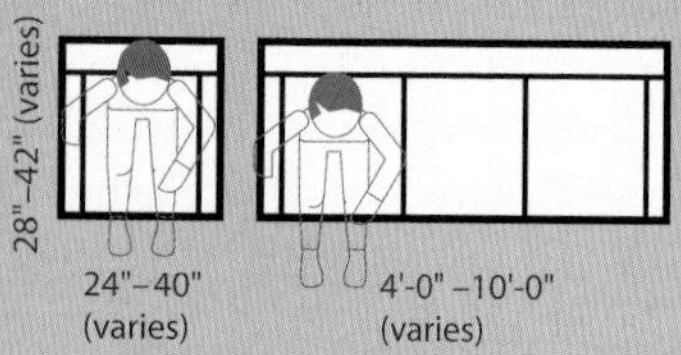
28"–42" (varies)
24"–40"
(varies)
4'-0" –10'-0"
(varies)

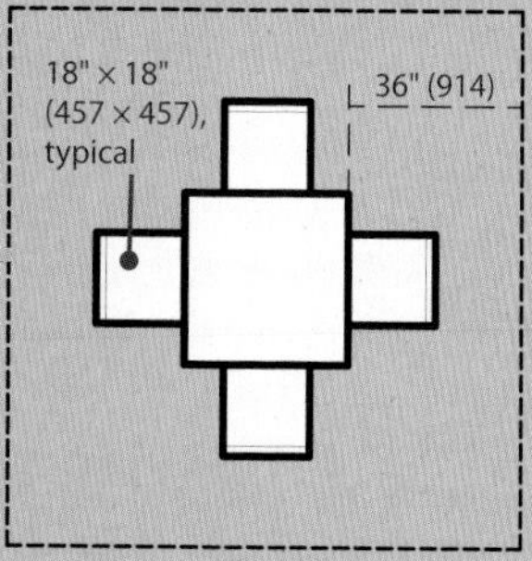
18" × 18"
(457 × 457),
typical
36" (914)

in.	24	30	36	42	48	54	60	72	84
mm	610	762	914	1067	1 219	1 372	1 524	1 829	2 134

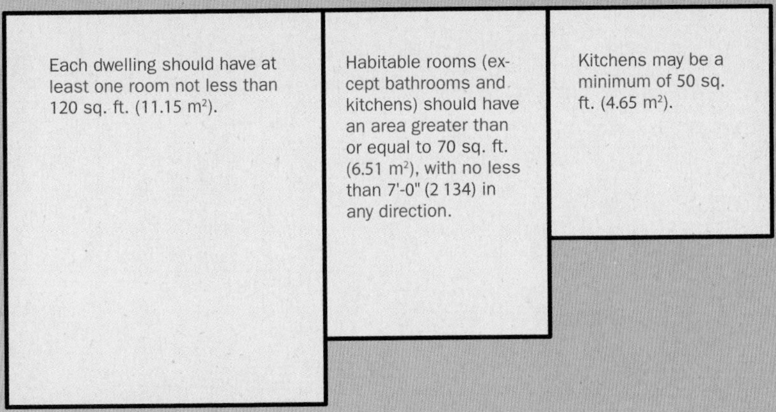
Each dwelling should have at least one room not less than 120 sq. ft. (11.15 m²).
Habitable rooms (except bathrooms and kitchens) should have an area greater than or equal to 70 sq. ft. (6.51 m²), with no less than 7'-0" (2 134) in any direction.
Kitchens may be a minimum of 50 sq. ft. (4.65 m²).

Closets

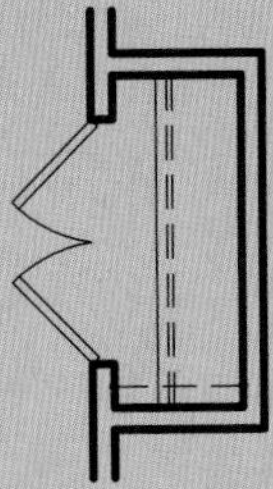

22"–30" (559–762) clear inside depth

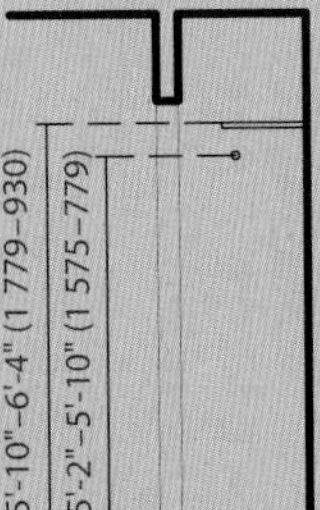
5'-10"–6'-4" (1 779–930)
5'-2"–5'-10" (1 575–779)

48"–72" (1 219–829) of hanging space per person

12" (305) = 6 suits, 12 shirts, 8 dresses, or 6 pairs of pants

Garages

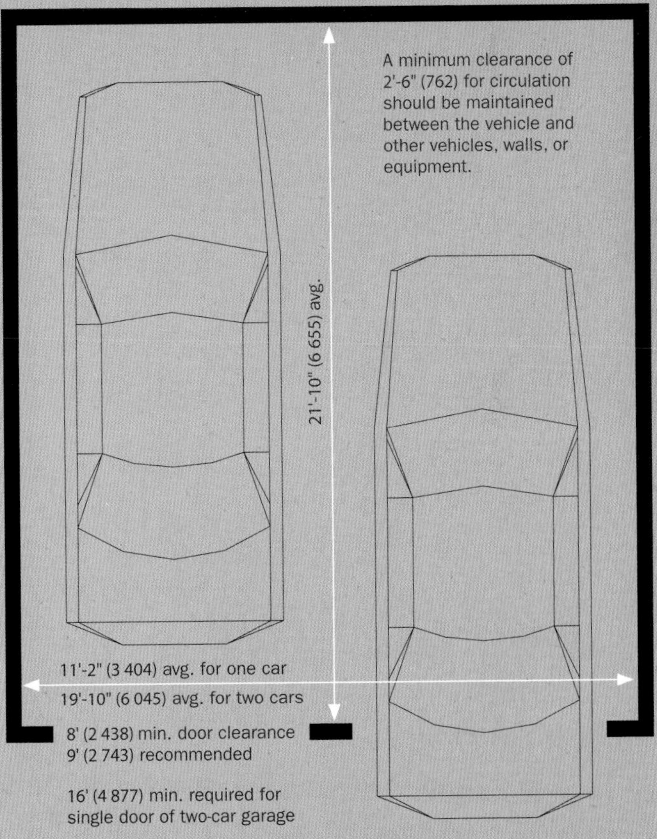
A minimum clearance of 2'-6" (762) for circulation should be maintained between the vehicle and other vehicles, walls, or equipment.
21'-10" (6 655) avg.
11'-2" (3 404) avg. for one car
19'-10" (6 045) avg. for two cars
8' (2 438) min. door clearance
9' (2 743) recommended
16' (4 877) min. required for single door of two-car garage

EATING

Seating Types

Booths

Booth tables may be 2" (51) shorter than bench seats, and with rounded corners to facilitate getting in and out of the booth.

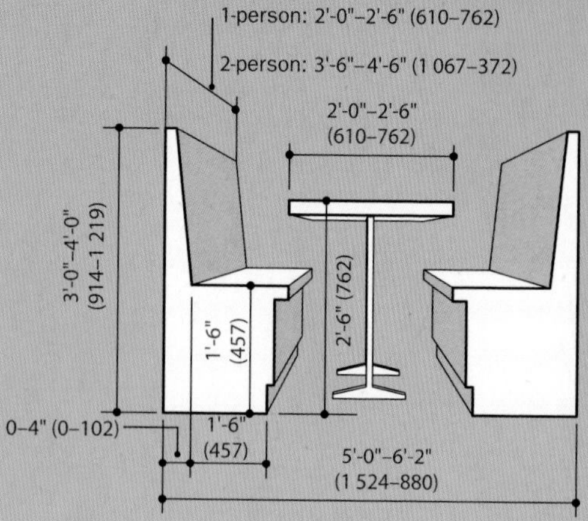
1-person: 2'-0"–2'-6" (610–762)
2-person: 3'-6"–4'-6" (1 067–372)
2'-0"–2'-6"
(610–762)
3'-0"–4'-0"
(914–1 219)
1'-6"
(457)
2'-6" (762)
0–4" (0–102)
1'-6"
(457)
5'-0"–6'-2"
(1 524–880)

Tables

Chair seat dimensions average 1'-2"–1'-6" (356–457).

Tables with widespread bases (shown here) are more practical for sitting down and getting up than four-legged tables.

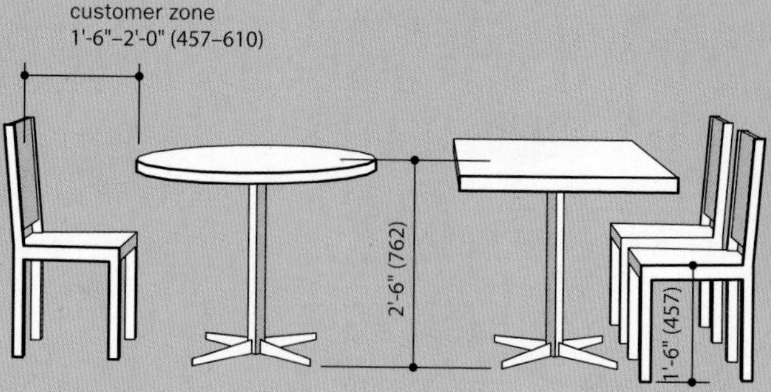
customer zone
1'-6"–2'-0" (457–610)
2'-6" (762)
1'-6" (457)

Bars and Counters

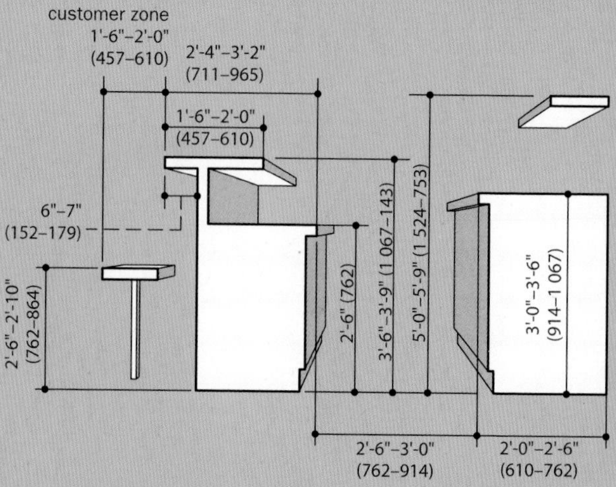
customer zone
1'-6"–2'-0"
(457–610)
2'-4"–3'-2"
(711–965)
1'-6"–2'-0"
(457–610)
6"–7"
(152–179)
2'-6"–2'-10"
(762–864)
2'-6" (762)
3'-6"–3'-9" (1 067–143)
5'-0"–5'-9" (1 524–753)
3'-0"–3'-6"
(914–1 067)
2'-6"–3'-0"
(762–914)
2'-0"–2'-6"
(610–762)

Counter stools should average ten per server.

Seating Clearances

Clear floor area for wheelchairs is 30" × 48" (762 × 1 219), of which 19" (483) may be used for required under-table knee space. At least 5 percent (but not less than 1) of tables must be accessible.

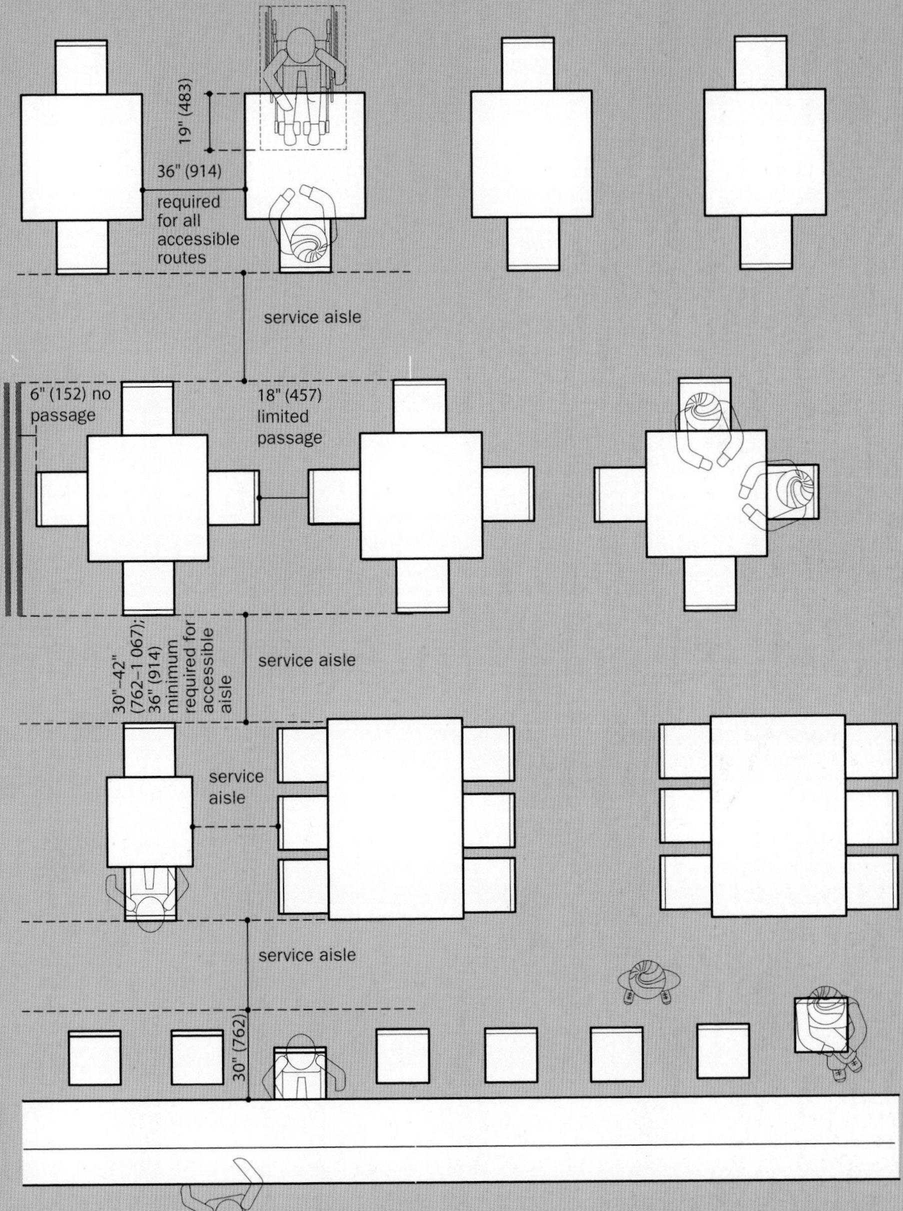

19" (483)
36" (914)
required for all accessible routes
service aisle
6" (152) no passage
18" (457) limited passage
30"–42" (762–1 067); 36" (914) minimum required for accessible aisle
service aisle
service aisle
service aisle
30" (762)

PUBLIC SEATING

Accessible spaces of 36" × 60" (914 × 1 524) should be open, on level ground, and provided as follows:

Total Seating	Wheelchair Spaces
4–25	1
26–50	2
51–300	4
301–500	6
500+	6 (+1 per each additional 100 seats)

Also, 1 percent of all fixed seats (but not less than one) must have removable or folding armrests on the aisle side and must be identified with appropriate signage.

Typical Chair Widths

Chair widths typically run 18"–24" (457–610); the ideal width is 21" (533).

Plumb Line Clearance

The distance between an unoccupied chair in the up position and the back of the chair in front of it. Local codes should be consulted for minimum clearances.

Row Spacing

Row spacing, like tread, runs 32"–40" (813–1 016) and higher.

Closer spacing may cause uncomfortable conditions for the seated person, as well as difficulty for anyone trying to pass in front of a seated person. Conversely, whereas wider spacing of rows provides more comfort while sitting and passing in front of seated persons, too wide a spacing may make the audience feel overly spread out. In addition, the wider spacing may encourage some people to try to squeeze through when exiting, causing a jam that could be dangerous in the event of an emergency.

An ideal spacing that accounts for all of these factors is 36" (914).

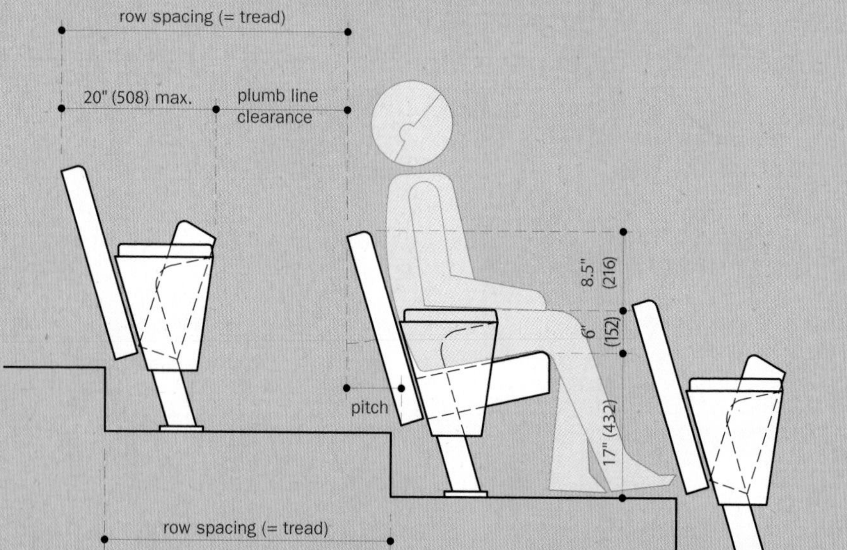
row spacing (= tread)
20" (508) max.
plumb line clearance
8.5" (216)
6" (152)
17" (432)
pitch
row spacing (= tread)

OFFICE WORKSPACES

Flexible Workspaces

Many companies produce flexible office furniture and workspace modules, in a wide variety of styles and finishes. These diagrams are for general layout purposes only and to illustrate a range of possibilities for office privacy, interaction, and space allocation.

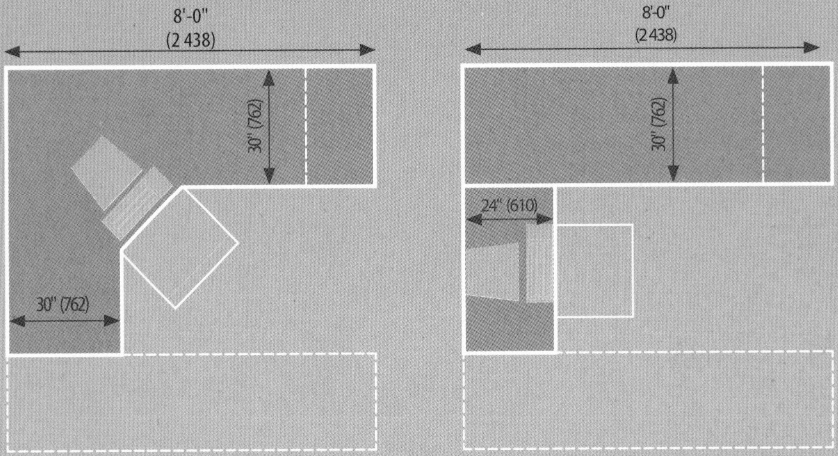
8'-0"
(2 438)
30" (762)
30" (762)
8'-0"
(2 438)
30" (762)
24" (610)

Various arrangements of four 8' × 8' (2 438 × 2 438) workspaces, allowing for a wide range of levels of interaction.

The primary advantage of flexible office furniture is precisely its ability to adjust to changing staff levels, changing personnel type, and even shifts in the nature of work being performed in the space.

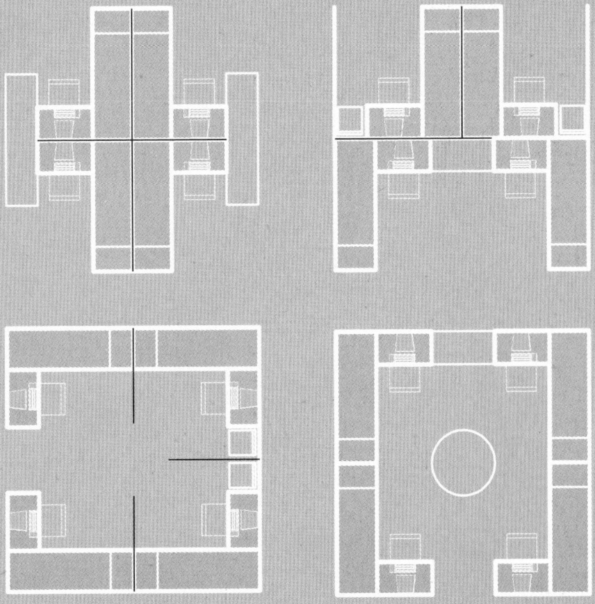

CONTEXT 6.

The art of architecture is not easily quantified or defined. It is certainly more than the sum of the systems and materials that give it shape, though architecture would not exist without the standardized procedures that erect its forms. The preceding chapters have provided the rudimentary tools for making buildings. It is in how architects use these tools to transform limitations into possibilities that allow them to navigate challenging situations and ultimately produce a better built environment.

The breadth of practical information about basic systems and concepts that this book has so far touched on is also a way of describing the world of architecture to all its users. What follows is a broad overview of how these basic systems have become a history of our overlapping cultures.

We live in the built world: whether it is well designed or poorly designed, it is the space and surface of our existence. By inhabiting architecture and moving around it, we have knowledge of it. To enhance our understanding, this book ends with a beginning: an introduction to a range of resources within the enormous, endless scope of architectural information and discussion.

3500 BCE (increments of 250 years) → 3250 BCE 3000 BCE

Chapter 22: Timeline

The history of architecture is a history of civilization. Buildings are artifacts intrinsically linked to the epoch and society of their creation, clearly exposing the varied conditions of how they came to be. To understand a piece of architecture is to gain insight into countless aspects of a place and a moment in time—geography, weather, social hierarchies, religious practices, and industrialization. And because architecture is rarely portable, it is virtually impossible to disengage a building from its origins.

The fluidity of history can make for unwieldy attempts to classify periods succinctly, and architectural styles and movements reflect this difficulty: though some styles may have come into sudden existence as the result of a specific event, most evolve slowly and taper off gradually. The distillation of any history presents obvious limitations; therefore, many dates shown here are approximations, serving the overall purpose of this timeline, which is to illustrate relationships among movements.

Bronze Age (ca. 3200–1050 BCE)

Mesopotamian
(ca. 4500–539 BCE)

Egyptian
(ca. 3500–30 BCE)

BCE (Before Common Era) = BC
CE (Common Era) = AD
b. = before; c. = century; ca. = circa

2750 BCE

2500 BCE

2250 BCE

Imhotep

Stonehenge
(ca. 2900–1400 BCE)
Salisbury Plain, England

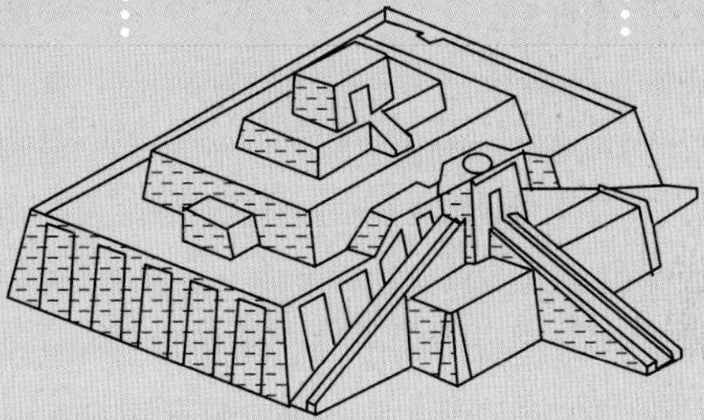

Ziggurat at Ur
(ca. 2100 BCE)
Mesopotamia

Great Sphinx of Giza
(ca. 2500 BCE) Egypt

Mentuhotep Mortuary Temple
(2061–2010 BCE)
Deir el-Bahari, Egypt

Stepped Pyramid of Zoser
(c. 2700 BCE) Egypt
Imhotep

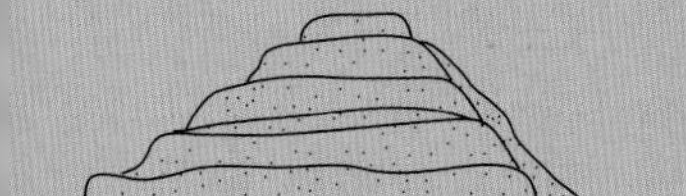

Great Pyramids of Giza
(2570–2500 BCE) Egypt

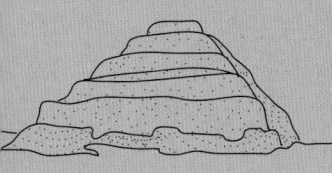

1750 BCE

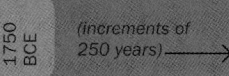

(increments of 250 years) →

1500 BCE

1250 BCE

Amenhotep III
ca. 1411 BCE

Bronze Age (ca. 3200–1050 BCE)

Greek

(ca. 2000–31 BCE)

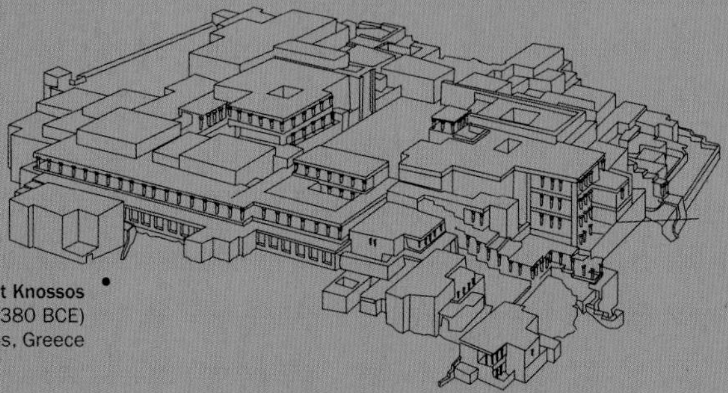

Palace at Knossos
(1700–1380 BCE)
Knossos, Greece

Mesopotamian

(ca. 4500–539 BCE)

Egyptian

(ca. 3500–30 BCE)

Great Temple of Ramses II
(ca. 1285–1225 BCE)
Abu Simbel, Egypt

Hypostyle Hall at Karnak
(ca. 1300 BCE)
Egypt

1000 BCE | 750 BCE | 500 BCE

Homer's
The Iliad and *The Odyssey*
ca. 750 BCE

Plato

Stoa of Attalus
(150 BCE)
Athens, Greece

Parthenon (448–432 BCE)
Athens, Greece

Temple of Paestum
(ca. 530-460 BCE) Paestum, Italy

Temple of Apollo
(310 BCE) Paeonis
and Daphnis, Turkey

Classical Orders

DORIC

IONIC

CORINTHIAN

Temple of Hera
(460 BCE) Paestum, Italy

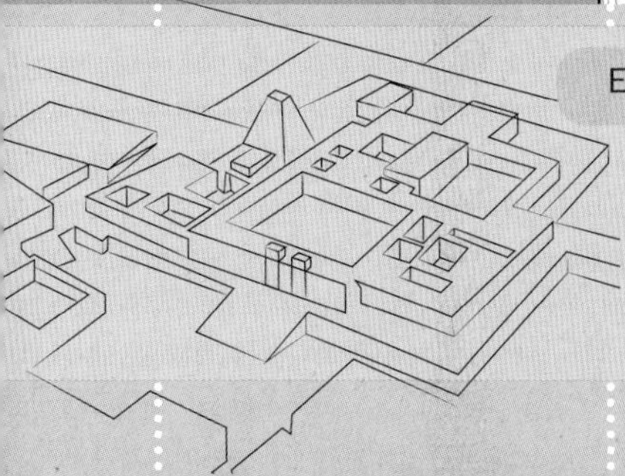

Etruscan (ca. 8th c.-4th c. BCE)

Citadel of Sargon II
(742–706 BCE)
Khorsabad

Roman
(510 BCE–476 CE)

Library at Alexandria
(c. 3rd BCE)
Egypt

0 (increments of 100 years) → 100 200

Augustus emporer: 27 BCE–14 CE

Vitruvius' *De Architetura* c. 15 BCE

Greek
(ca. 2000–31 BCE)

Stoa of Attalus
(150 BCE)
Athens, Greece

Roman
(510 BCE–479 CE)

Pont du Gard Aqueduct
(15 BCE)
Nîmes, France

Pantheon
(118–128 CE)
Rome, Italy

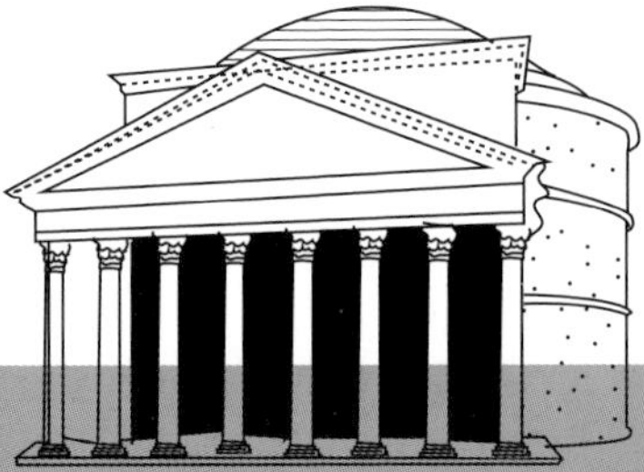

Colosseum (72–80 CE)
Rome, Italy

Baths of Caracalla
(215 CE)
Rome, Italy

Egyptian
(ca. 3500–30 BCE)

300

400

500

MIDDLE AGES

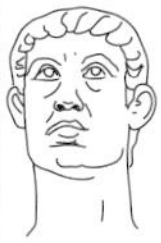

Constantine the Great

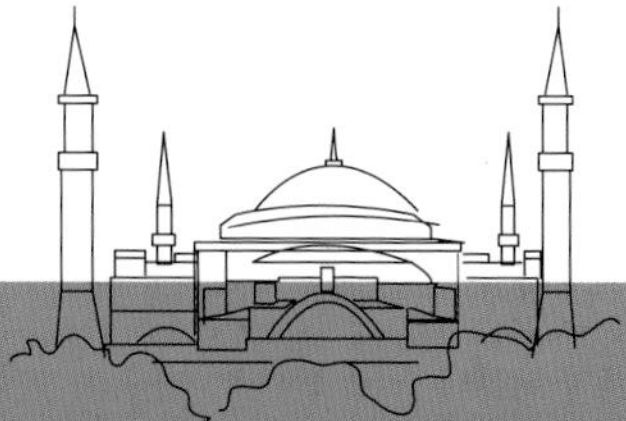

Hagia Sophia (537)
Istanbul
(Constantinople),
Turkey

San Vitale (526)
Ravenna, Italy

Byzantine
(324–12th c.)

Arch of Constantine
(312–15 CE)
Rome, Italy

Romanesque
(500–1200 CE)

S. Apollinaire Nuovo
(ca. 490)
Ravenna, Italy

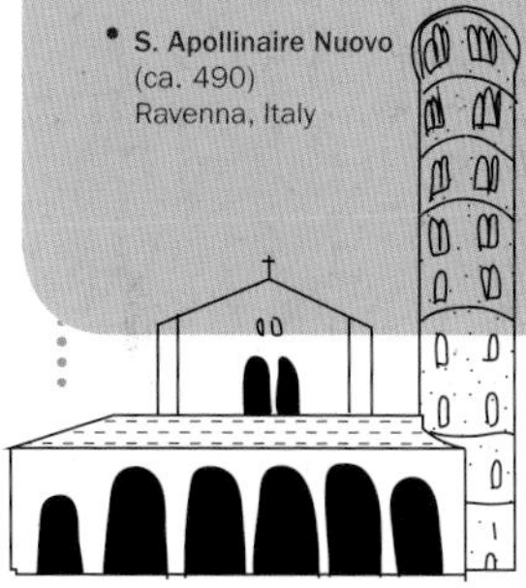

700 (increments of 100 years) → 800 900

MIDDLE AGES (ca. 500–1500 CE)

Byzantine
(324–12th c.)

Basilica of San Marco
(830)
Venice, Italy

Romanesque
(500–1200 CE)

Dome of the Rock
(687–89 CE)
Jerusalem

El Castillo
(850 CE)
Chichen Itza,
Yucatan, Mexico

1000

1100

1200

Angkor Wat
(b. ca. 1120)
Cambodia

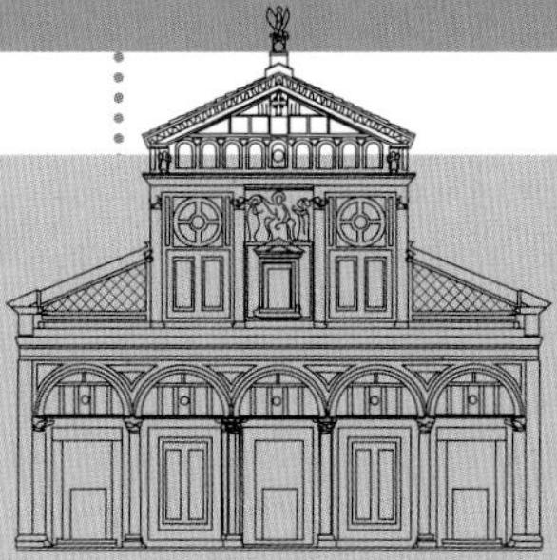

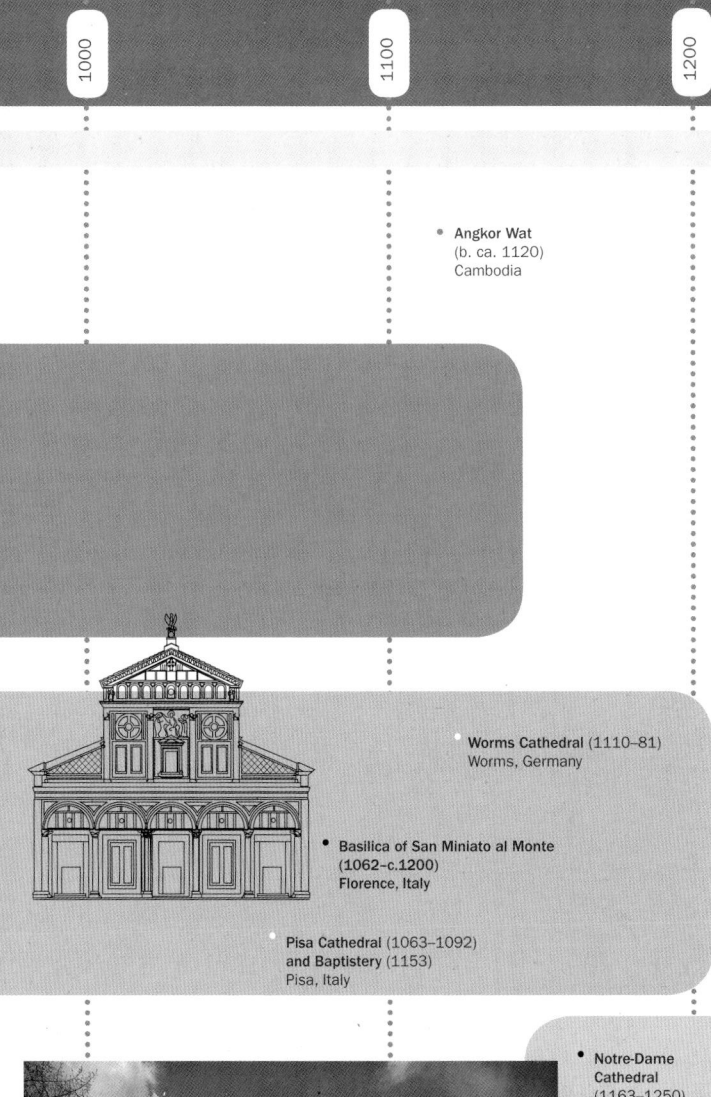

Worms Cathedral (1110–81)
Worms, Germany

Basilica of San Miniato al Monte
(1062–c.1200)
Florence, Italy

Pisa Cathedral (1063–1092)
and Baptistery (1153)
Pisa, Italy

Notre-Dame Cathedral
(1163–1250)
Paris, France

Strasbourg Cathedral
(begun 1277)
Alsace, France

Chartres Cathedral
(1194–1220)
Chartres, France

Gothic
(ca. 1140–1500)

Salisbury Cathedral
(1220–1260)
Salisbury, England

Amiens Cathedral
(1220–1247)
Amiens, France

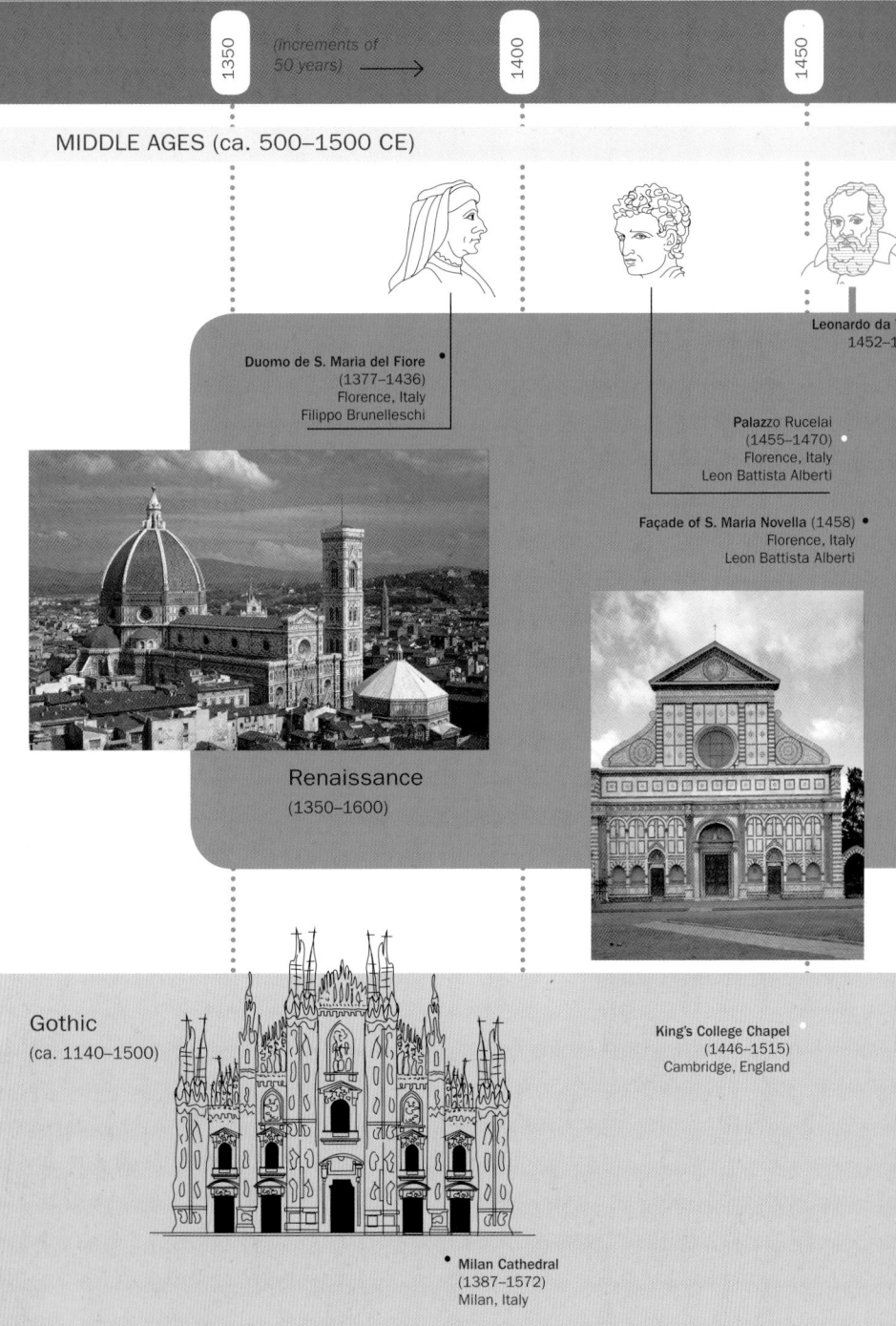

1350 *(increments of 50 years)* → 1400 1450

MIDDLE AGES (ca. 500–1500 CE)

Leonardo da Vi
1452–15

Duomo de S. Maria del Fiore
(1377–1436)
Florence, Italy
Filippo Brunelleschi

Palazzo Rucelai
(1455–1470)
Florence, Italy
Leon Battista Alberti

Façade of S. Maria Novella (1458)
Florence, Italy
Leon Battista Alberti

Renaissance
(1350–1600)

Gothic
(ca. 1140–1500)

King's College Chapel
(1446–1515)
Cambridge, England

Milan Cathedral
(1387–1572)
Milan, Italy

1500

1550

1600

Galileo Galilei
1564–1642

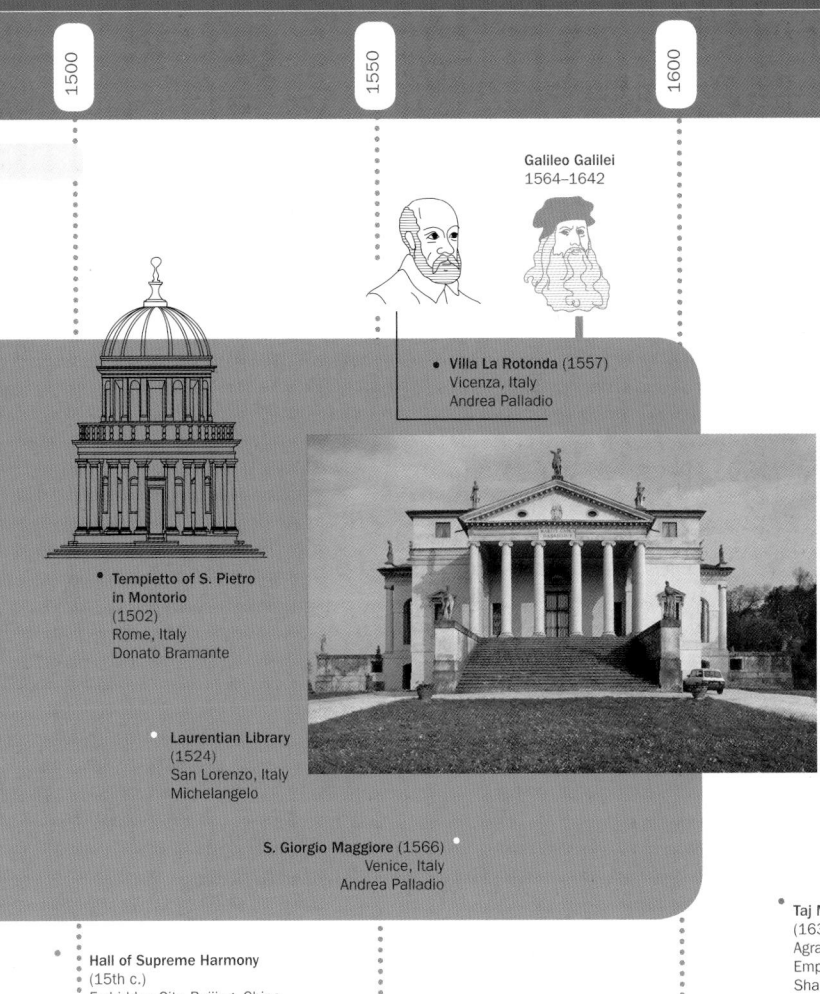

Villa La Rotonda (1557)
Vicenza, Italy
Andrea Palladio

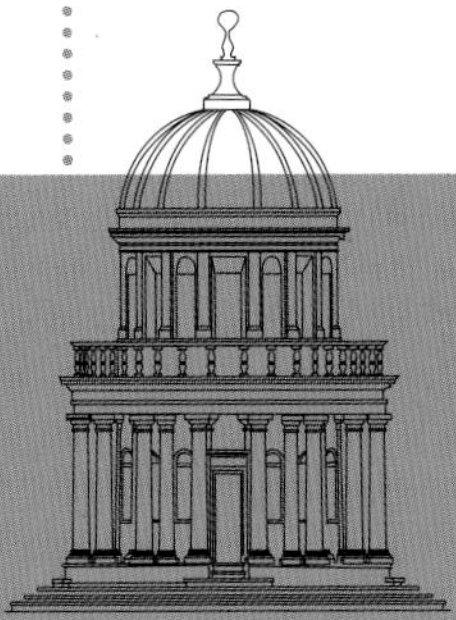

Tempietto of S. Pietro in Montorio
(1502)
Rome, Italy
Donato Bramante

Laurentian Library
(1524)
San Lorenzo, Italy
Michelangelo

S. Giorgio Maggiore (1566)
Venice, Italy
Andrea Palladio

Hall of Supreme Harmony
(15th c.)
Forbidden City, Beijing, China

Taj Mahal
(1630–1653)
Agra, India
Emperor
Shah Jahan

Façade of S. Susanna
(1603)
Rome, Italy
Carlo Maderno

Palais de Justice
(1493–1508)
Rouen, France

Baroque
(1600–1700)

1700 (increments of 20 years) → 1720 1740

S. Carlo alle Quattro Fontane
(b. 1634) Rome, Italy
Francesco Borromini

Rococo
(1700–1780)

Spanish Steps
(1723–1725)
Rome, Italy
Francesco de Sanctis

Baroque
(1600–1700)

Colonnade Piazza of St. Peter's
(1656) Rome, Italy
Gianlorenzo Bernini

Karlskirche (b. 1656)
Vienna, Austria
Johann Fischer van Erlach

Georgian
(1714–1830)

Chiswick House
(1725–1729)
London, England
Lord Burlington

1760

1780

1800

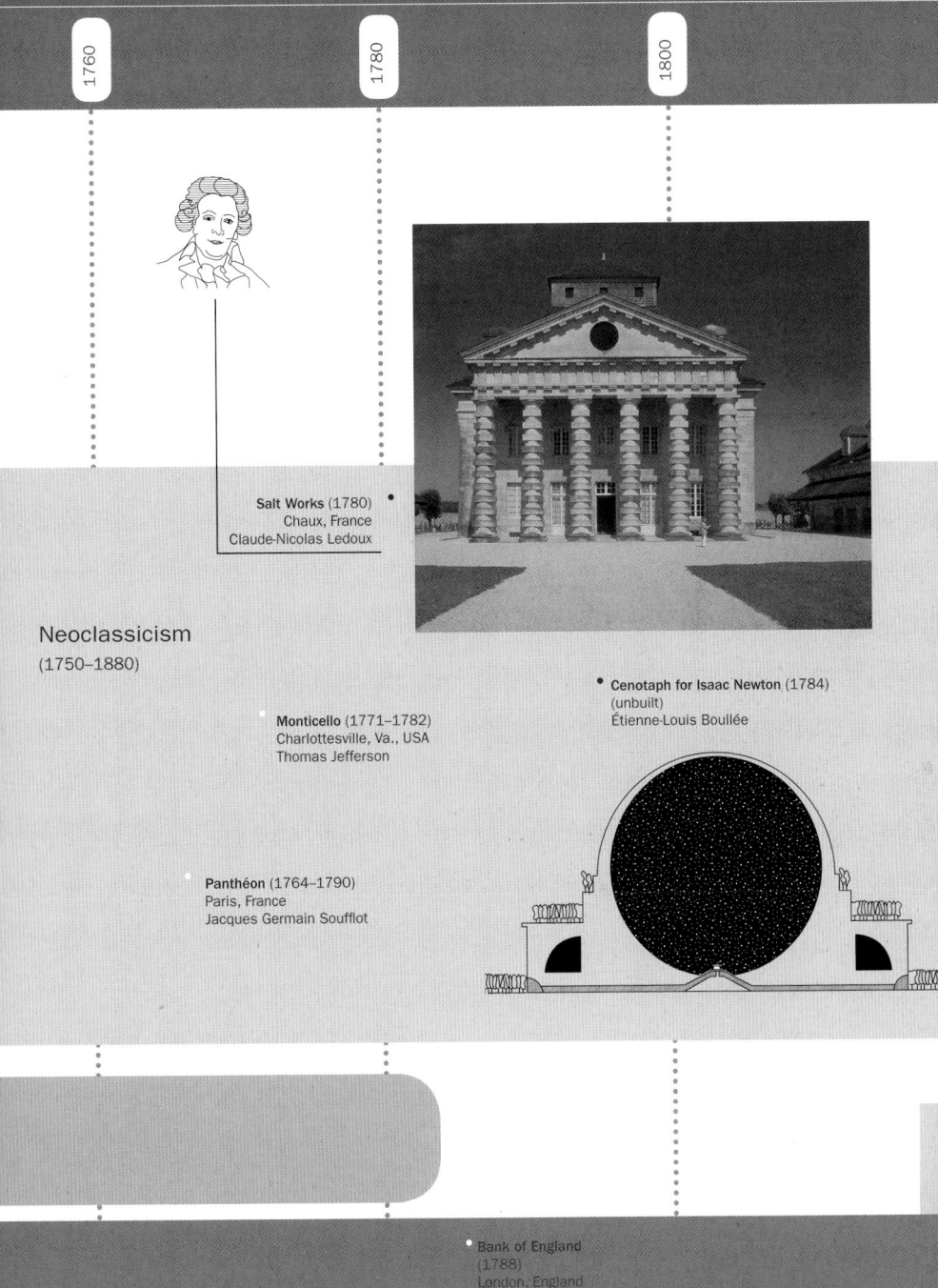

Salt Works (1780)
Chaux, France
Claude-Nicolas Ledoux

Neoclassicism
(1750–1880)

Cenotaph for Isaac Newton (1784)
(unbuilt)
Étienne-Louis Boullée

Monticello (1771–1782)
Charlottesville, Va., USA
Thomas Jefferson

Panthéon (1764–1790)
Paris, France
Jacques Germain Soufflot

Bank of England
(1788)
London, England
John Soane

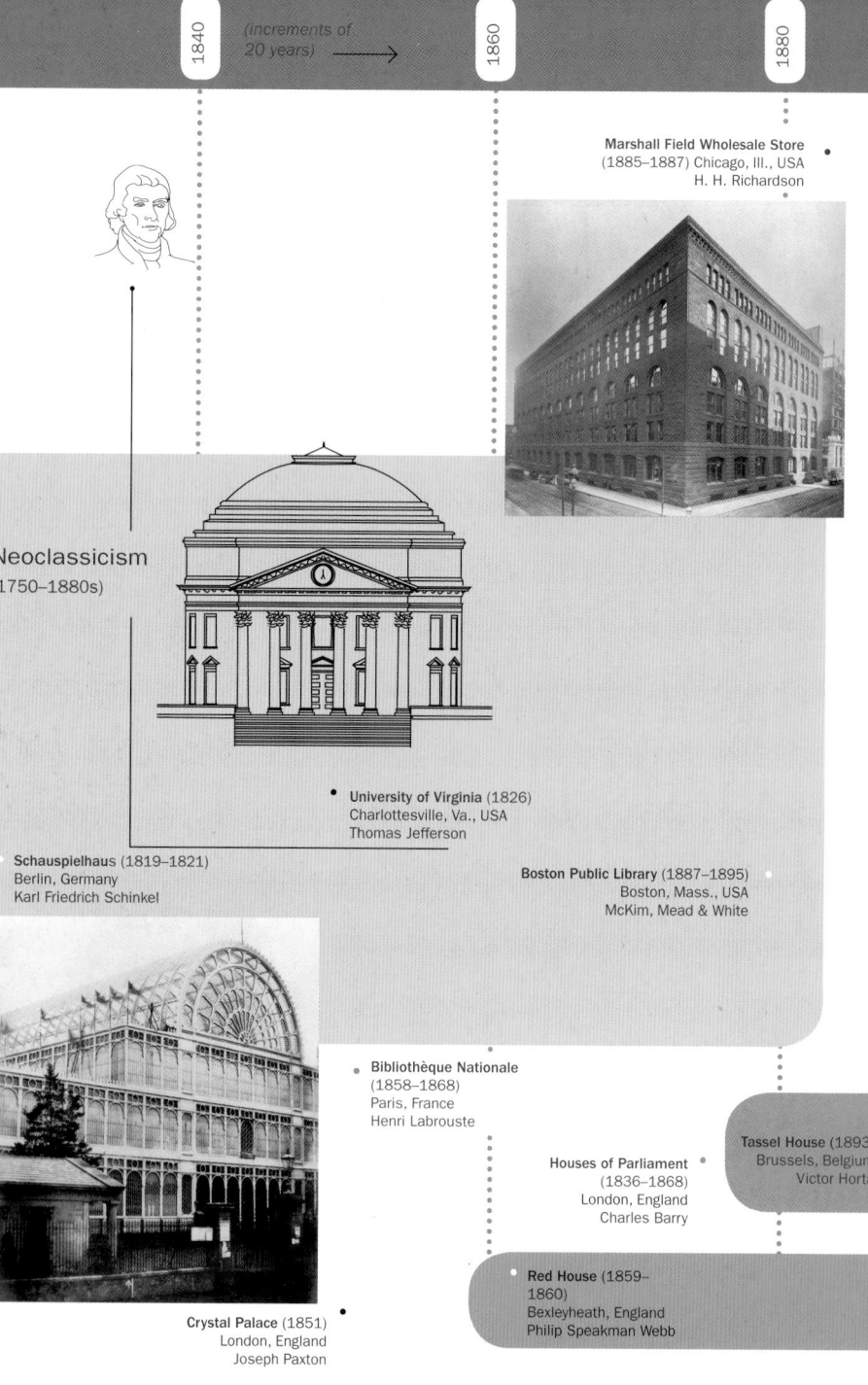

1840 (increments of 20 years) → 1860 1880

Marshall Field Wholesale Store
(1885–1887) Chicago, Ill., USA
H. H. Richardson

Neoclassicism
(1750–1880s)

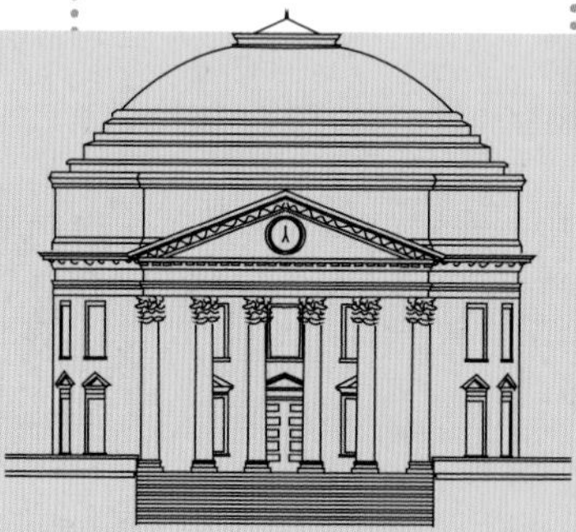

University of Virginia (1826)
Charlottesville, Va., USA
Thomas Jefferson

Schauspielhaus (1819–1821)
Berlin, Germany
Karl Friedrich Schinkel

Boston Public Library (1887–1895)
Boston, Mass., USA
McKim, Mead & White

Bibliothèque Nationale
(1858–1868)
Paris, France
Henri Labrouste

Tassel House (1893)
Brussels, Belgium
Victor Horta

Houses of Parliament
(1836–1868)
London, England
Charles Barry

Red House (1859–1860)
Bexleyheath, England
Philip Speakman Webb

Crystal Palace (1851)
London, England
Joseph Paxton

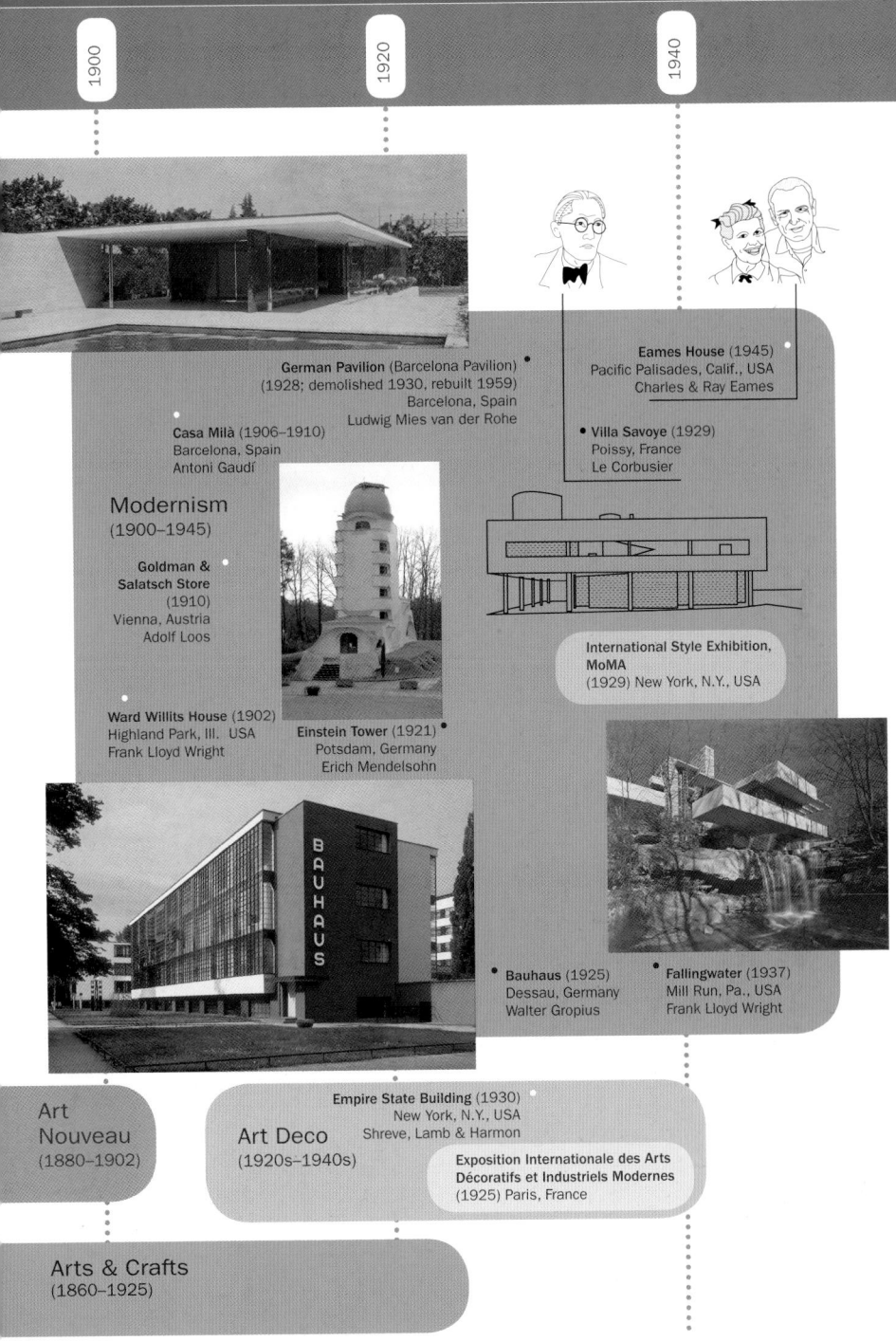

1900 — 1920 — 1940

German Pavilion (Barcelona Pavilion)
(1928; demolished 1930, rebuilt 1959)
Barcelona, Spain
Ludwig Mies van der Rohe

Eames House (1945)
Pacific Palisades, Calif., USA
Charles & Ray Eames

Casa Milà (1906–1910)
Barcelona, Spain
Antoni Gaudí

Villa Savoye (1929)
Poissy, France
Le Corbusier

Modernism
(1900–1945)

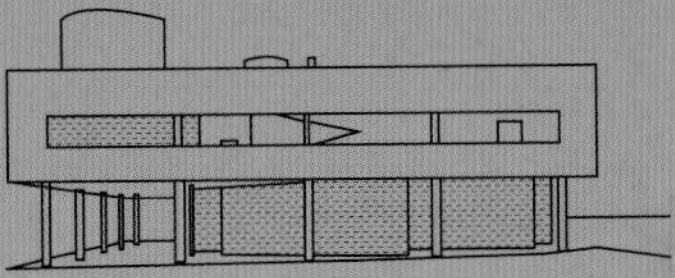

Goldman & Salatsch Store
(1910)
Vienna, Austria
Adolf Loos

International Style Exhibition, MoMA
(1929) New York, N.Y., USA

Ward Willits House (1902)
Highland Park, Ill. USA
Frank Lloyd Wright

Einstein Tower (1921)
Potsdam, Germany
Erich Mendelsohn

BAUHAUS

Bauhaus (1925)
Dessau, Germany
Walter Gropius

Fallingwater (1937)
Mill Run, Pa., USA
Frank Lloyd Wright

Art Nouveau
(1880–1902)

Art Deco
(1920s–1940s)

Empire State Building (1930)
New York, N.Y., USA
Shreve, Lamb & Harmon

Exposition Internationale des Arts Décoratifs et Industriels Modernes
(1925) Paris, France

Arts & Crafts
(1860–1925)

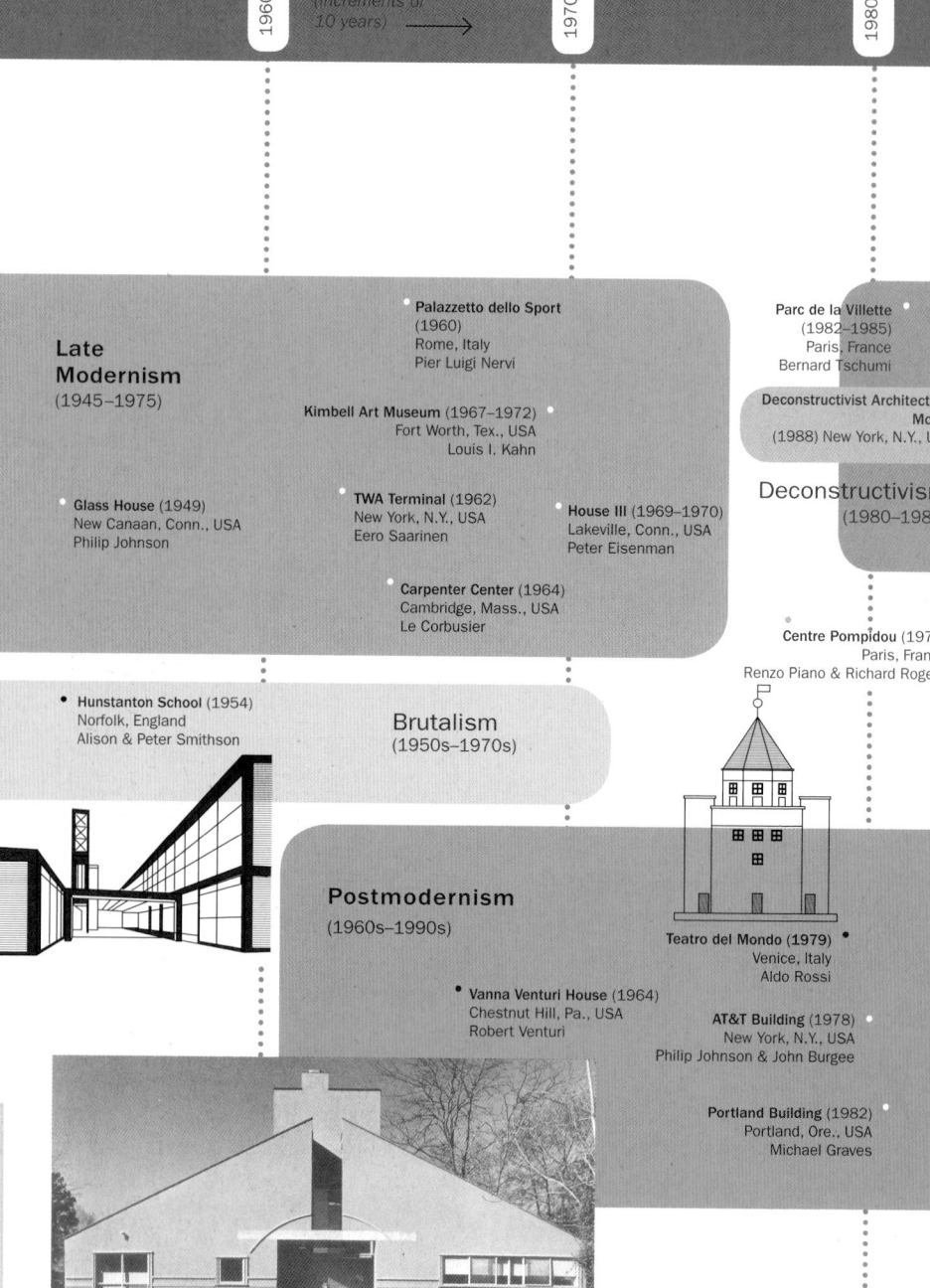

1960 *(increments of 10 years)* → 1970 1980

Late Modernism
(1945–1975)

Glass House (1949)
New Canaan, Conn., USA
Philip Johnson

Palazzetto dello Sport (1960)
Rome, Italy
Pier Luigi Nervi

TWA Terminal (1962)
New York, N.Y., USA
Eero Saarinen

Carpenter Center (1964)
Cambridge, Mass., USA
Le Corbusier

Kimbell Art Museum (1967–1972)
Fort Worth, Tex., USA
Louis I. Kahn

House III (1969–1970)
Lakeville, Conn., USA
Peter Eisenman

Deconstructivism
(1980–1988)

Parc de la Villette
(1982–1985)
Paris, France
Bernard Tschumi

Deconstructivist Architecture, MoMA
(1988) New York, N.Y., USA

Centre Pompidou (1976)
Paris, France
Renzo Piano & Richard Rogers

Brutalism
(1950s–1970s)

Hunstanton School (1954)
Norfolk, England
Alison & Peter Smithson

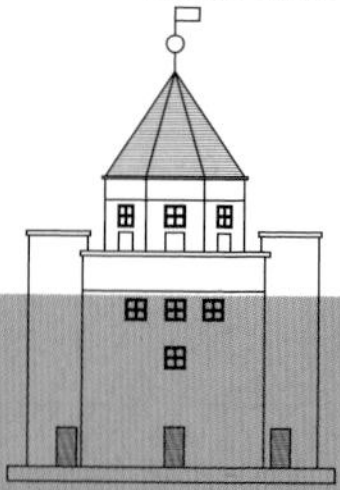

Postmodernism
(1960s–1990s)

Teatro del Mondo (1979)
Venice, Italy
Aldo Rossi

Vanna Venturi House (1964)
Chestnut Hill, Pa., USA
Robert Venturi

AT&T Building (1978)
New York, N.Y., USA
Philip Johnson & John Burgee

Portland Building (1982)
Portland, Ore., USA
Michael Graves

1990

2000

2010

Wexner Center for the Arts (1989)
Columbus, Ohio, USA
Peter Eisenman

Seattle Public Library (2004)
Seattle, Wash., USA
Rem Koolhaas (OMA)

Vitra Fire Station (1990)
Weil am Rhein, Germany
Zaha Hadid

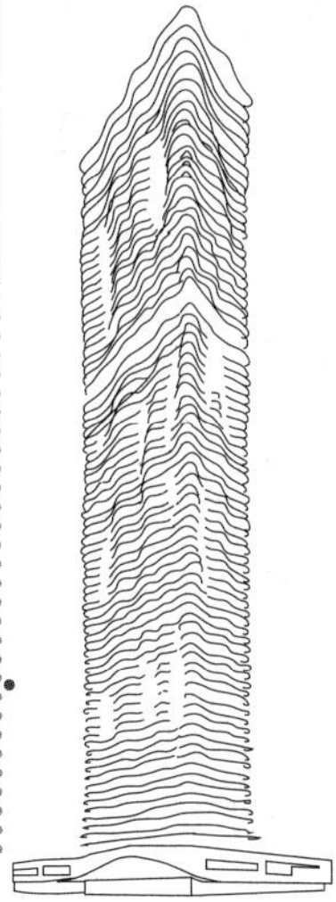

Aqua Tower (2010)
Chicago, Il., USA
Studio Gang

Chapter 23: Architectural Elements and Ideas

ANCIENT EGYPT

For over 3,000 years, ancient Egyptian civilization prospered, producing significant and monumental built forms that not only still stand, but from which contempory building practices were born. Egypt introduced the use of columns and capitals, dressed stones, and pure geometric forms.

Egyptians built with stones such as limestone, granite, and sandstone, as well as bricks (both fired and not) and even wood carpentry assemblages. Compact construction was a primitive form of concrete, and combined clay with chopped straw in a manner that allowed it to be poured into forms. This was, however, inferior in strength and durability to stone.

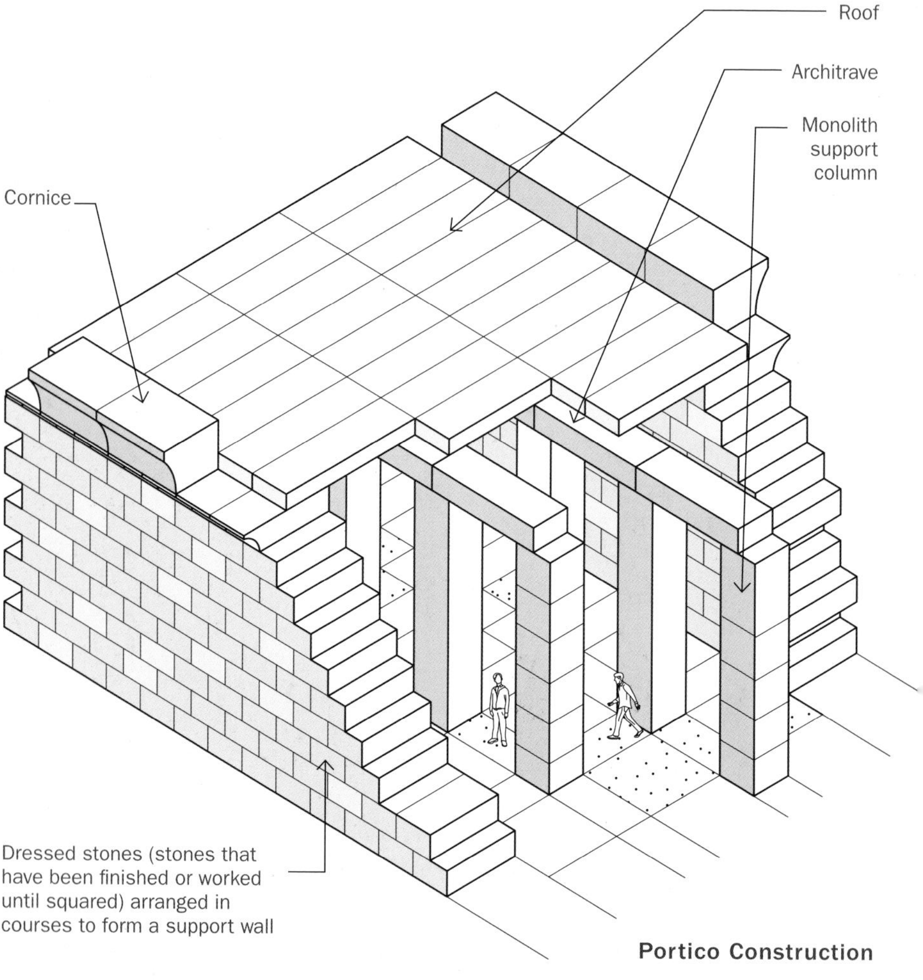
Roof
Architrave
Monolith support column
Cornice
Dressed stones (stones that have been finished or worked until squared) arranged in courses to form a support wall

Portico Construction

COLUMNS

Egyptian column designs were highly varied in height, diameter, ornamentation, spacing, and form. The capitals could become very fanciful in their interpretatios of plants, such as lily, papyrus, lotus flowers, palm, and bundles of reeds.

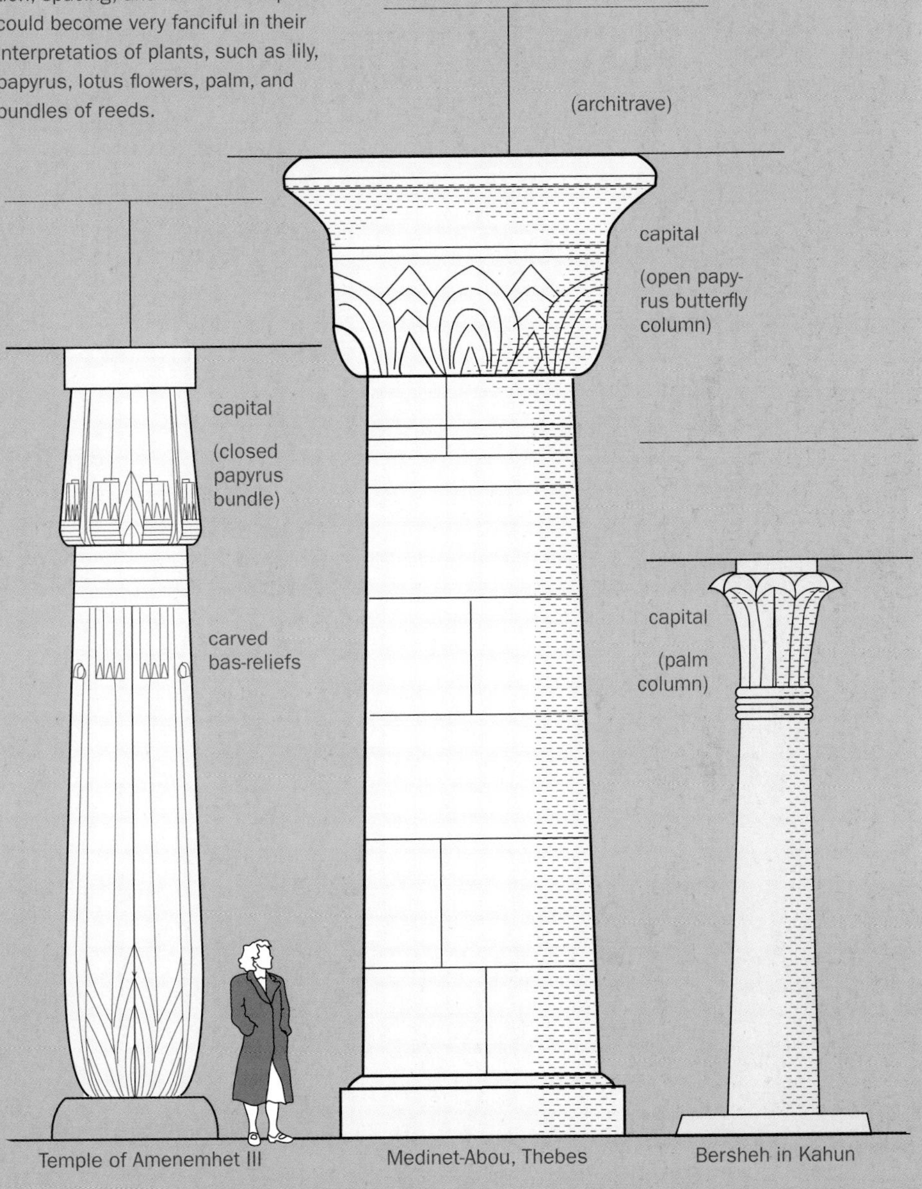
(architrave)
capital
(closed papyrus bundle)
carved bas-reliefs
capital
(open papyrus butterfly column)
capital
(palm column)
Temple of Amenemhet III
Medinet-Abou, Thebes
Bersheh in Kahun

CLASSICAL ORDERS

Elements of the classical orders are distinguished by their unique proportioning system based on the shaft diameter of the columns, from which pedestal, shaft, and entablature heights are derived. Using a common shaft diameter, the five orders are shown here in their proportional relationship to each other.

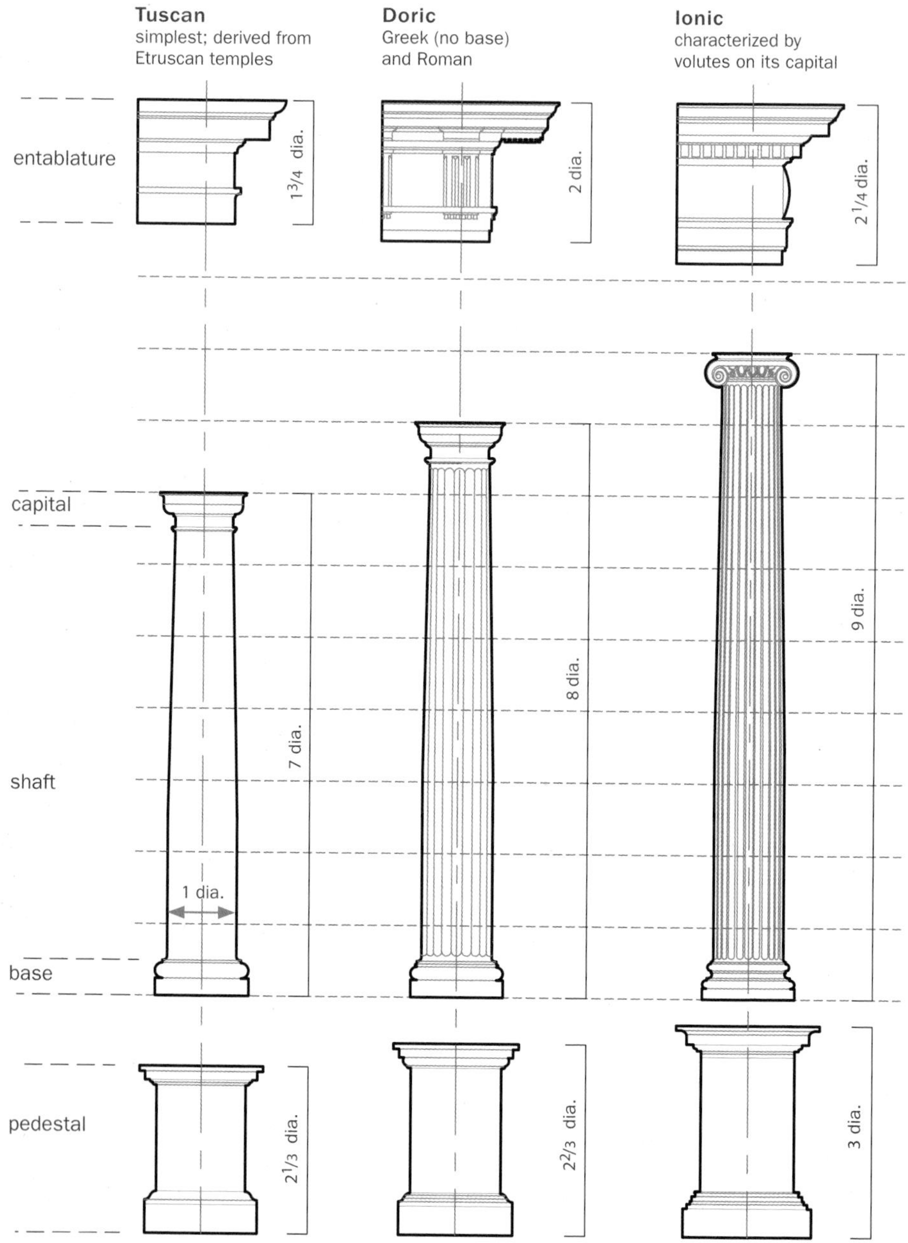
Tuscan
simplest; derived from Etruscan temples
Doric
Greek (no base) and Roman
Ionic
characterized by volutes on its capital
entablature
capital
shaft
base
pedestal
1 3/4 dia.
2 dia.
2 1/4 dia.
7 dia.
8 dia.
9 dia.
1 dia.
2 1/3 dia.
2 2/3 dia.
3 dia.

Corinthian
Greek and Roman, fluted or not; characterized by acanthus leaves on its capital

Composite
Roman combination of Ionic and Corinthian orders

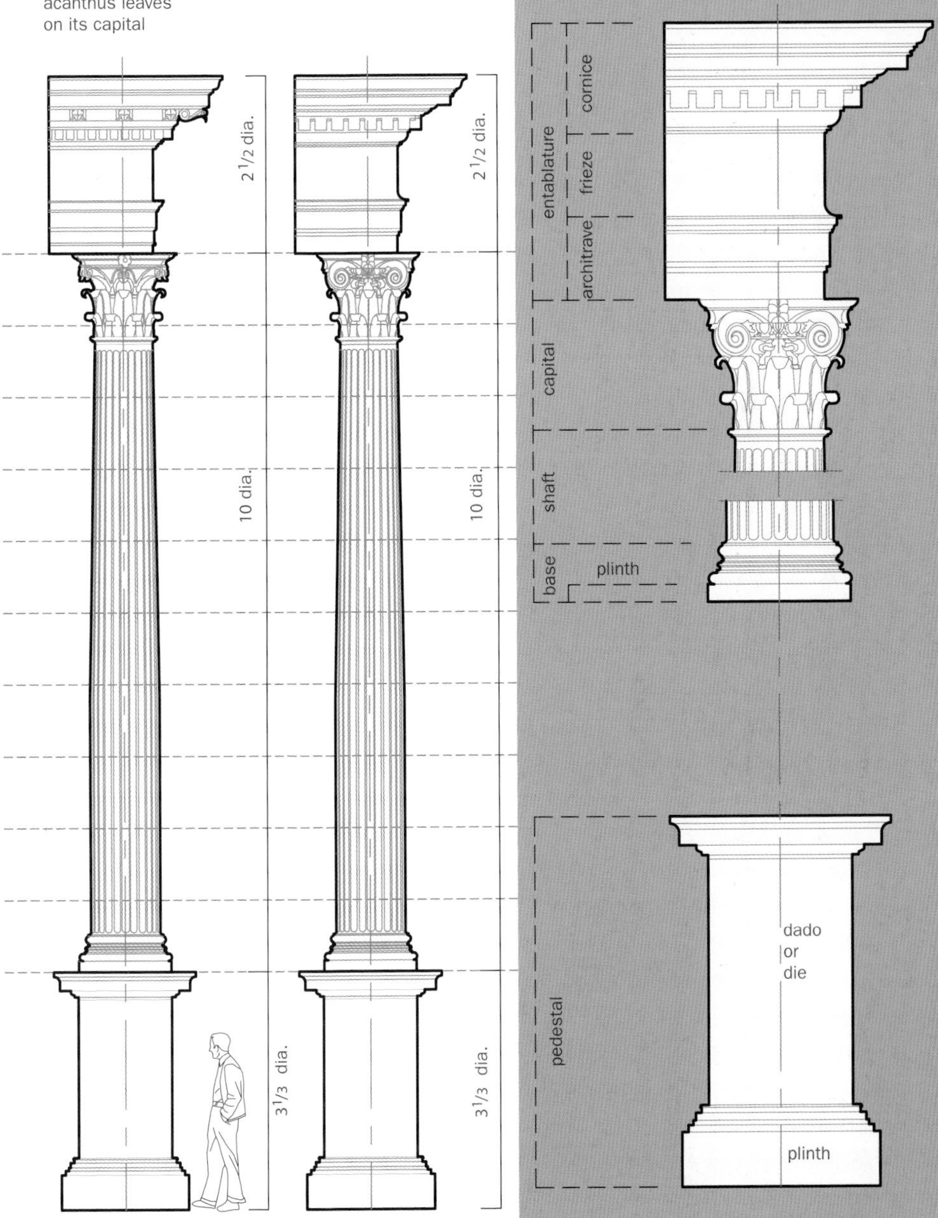
2 1/2 dia.
10 dia.
3 1/3 dia.
2 1/2 dia.
10 dia.
3 1/3 dia.
entablature
cornice
frieze
architrave
capital
shaft
base
plinth
pedestal
dado
or
die
plinth

ANCIENT GREECE

Classical architecture typically refers to the styles of both ancient Greece and Rome, which are based around the fixed columnar proportions and ornamentation of the classical orders. Both Greek and Roman classicism have been the bases of revivals throughout history, and the ideals behind their form and proportion continue to have resonance today.

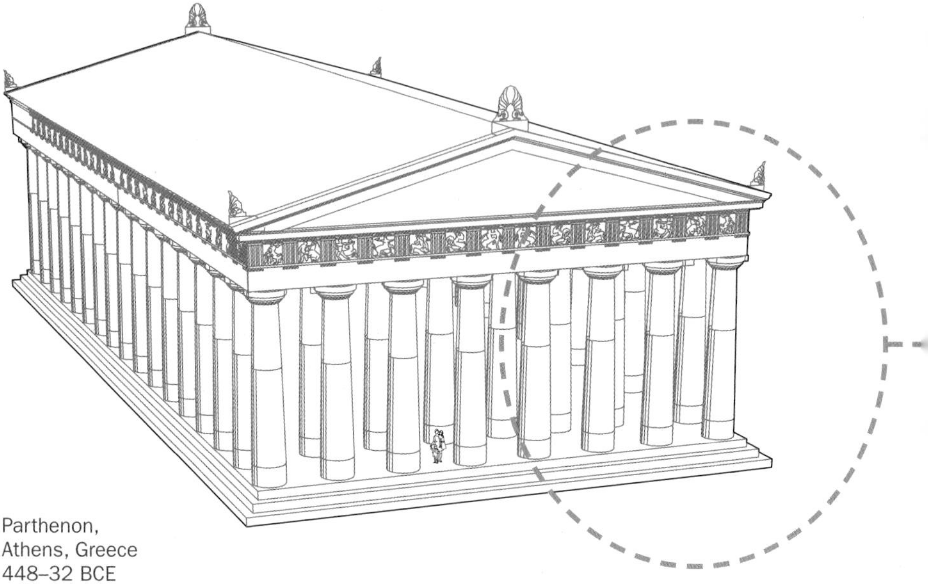

Parthenon,
Athens, Greece
448–32 BCE

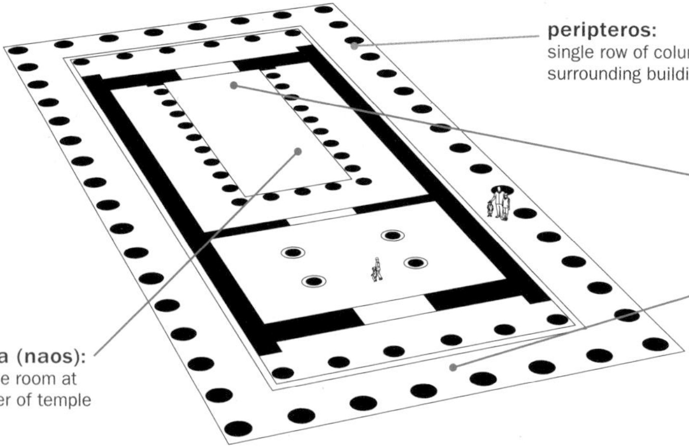
peripteros:
single row of columns surrounding building
pronaos:
vestibule
opisthodomos:
enclosed section at the rear of the temple
cella (naos):
shrine room at center of temple

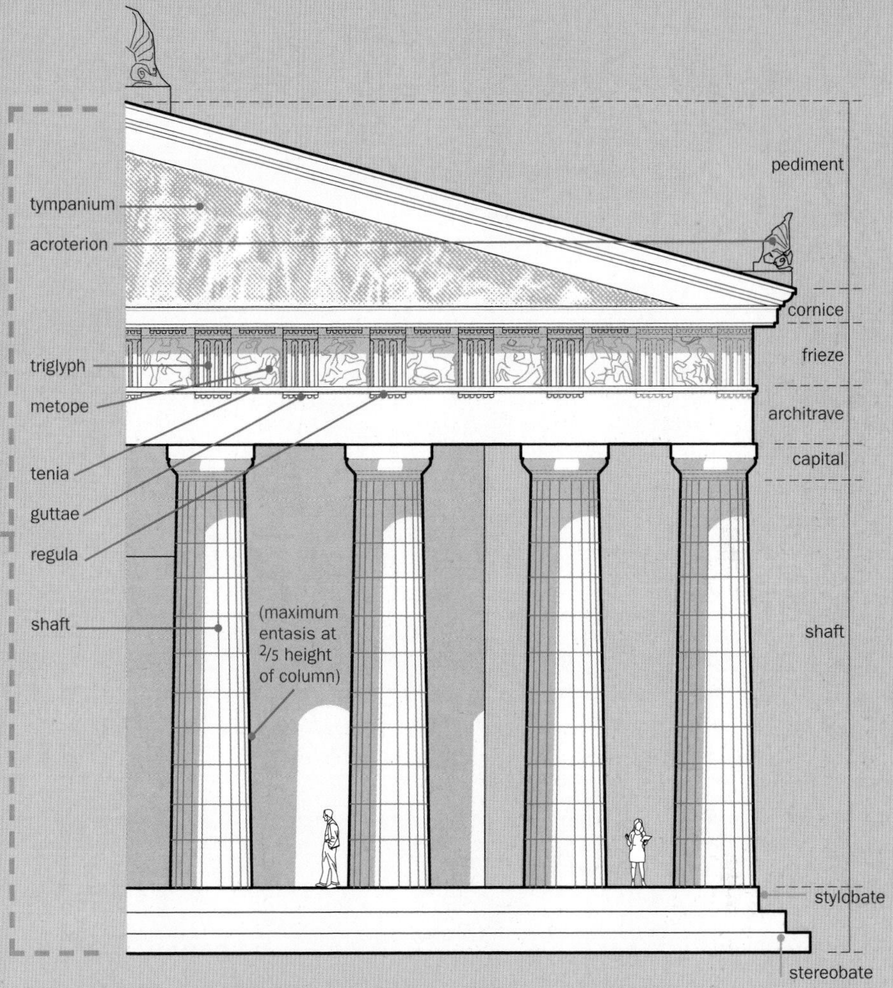
pediment
tympanium
acroterion
cornice
frieze
triglyph
metope
architrave
tenia
capital
guttae
regula
shaft
(maximum
entasis at
2/5 height
of column)
shaft
stylobate
stereobate

Entasis: Slight convex curvature of classical columns, used to counteract the optical illusion of concavity produced by straight lines. Other adjustments, such as reclining the columns slightly away from the vertical and making the end columns larger and closer together, also produce a more pleasing visual effect.

ANCIENT GREECE

A caryatid was a sculpted (from marble) female figure used as a column to support an entablature. Other forms include atlantes or telamones (male caryatids), canephorae (females with baskets on their heads), herms (three-quarter-height figures), and terms (pedestals that taper upward, terminating in a sculptured human or animal).

Ornately carved braids provided extra strength to the maiden's neck, making the figure's head a strong capital.

Erechtheion, Athens (421 BCE)
Porch of the Maidens

ANCIENT ROME

The engineering and architectural accomplishmets of the Roman Empire included the invention of concrete, the arch, the vault, and the dome. These allowed for the creation of large volumes of enclosed space uninterrupted by columns and other supports.

The Pantheon employed a combination of concrete, marble, and brick. The rotunda, housing a soaring hemisphere dome, is fronted by the classical Greek-inspired portico porch.

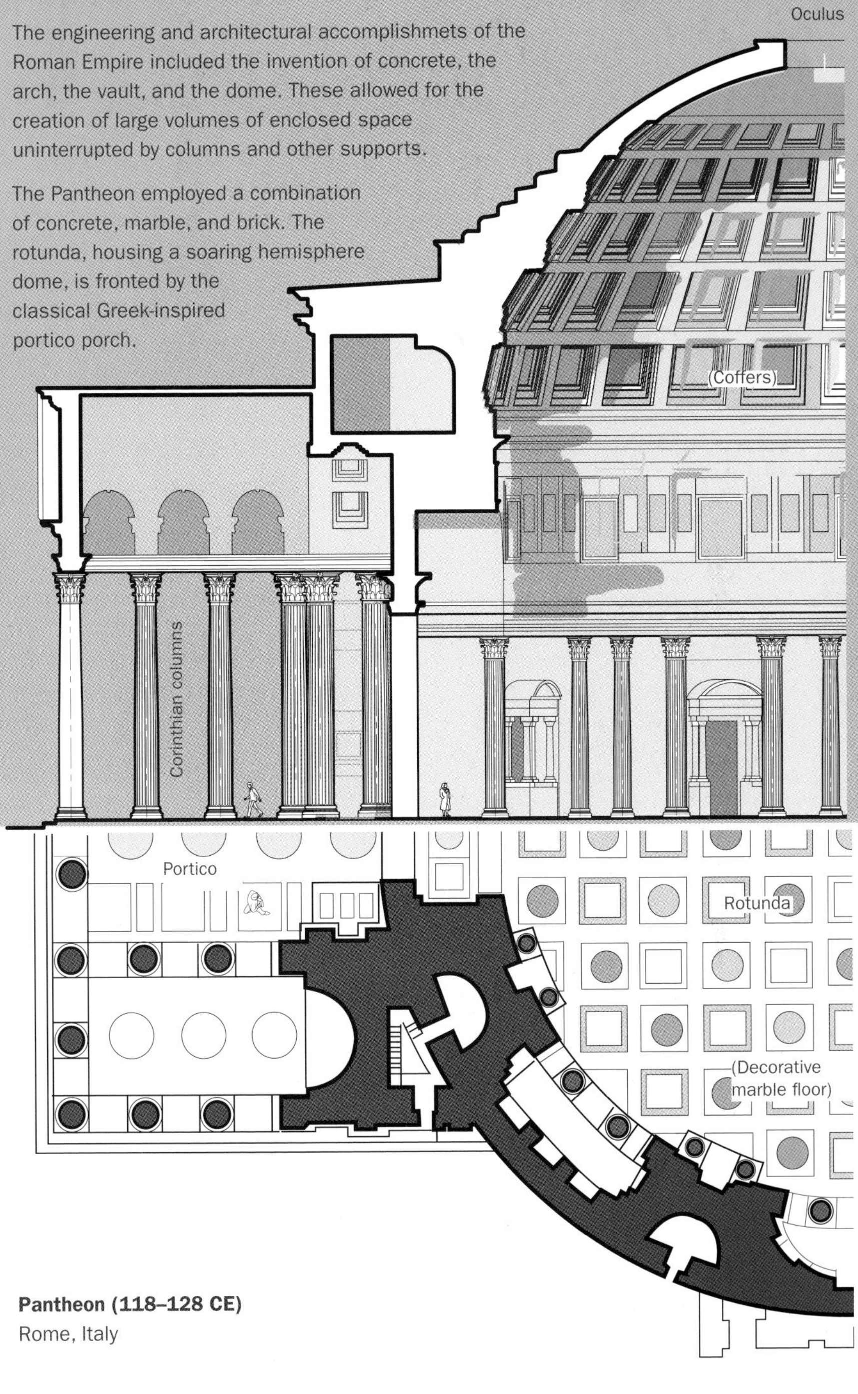
Oculus
(Coffers)
Corinthian columns
Portico
Rotunda
(Decorative marble floor)

Pantheon (118–128 CE)
Rome, Italy

ARCHES

1 | abutment
2 | voussoirs
3 | keystone
4 | intrados (soffit)
5 | extrados
6 | crown
7 | haunch
8 | span
9 | springing line
10 | center

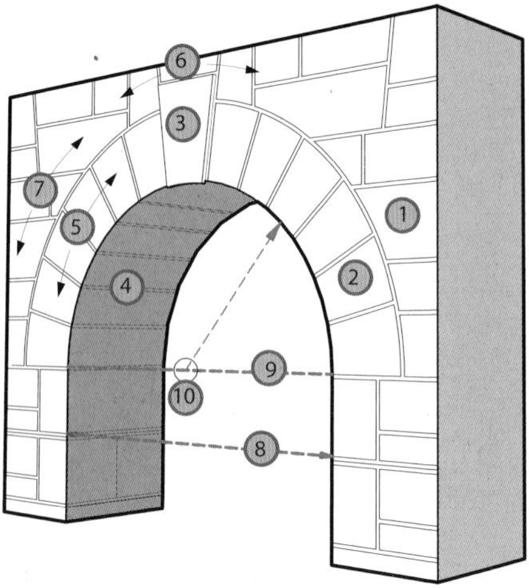
6
3
7
5
1
2
4
9
10
8

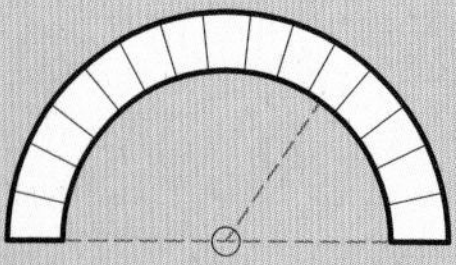
Semicircular

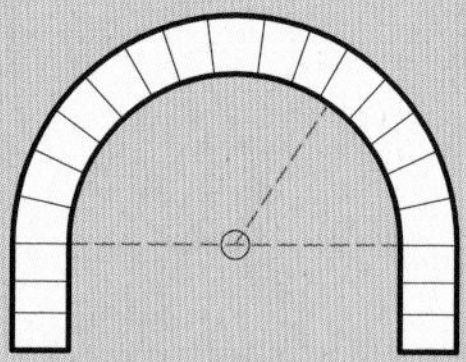
Semicircular Stilted

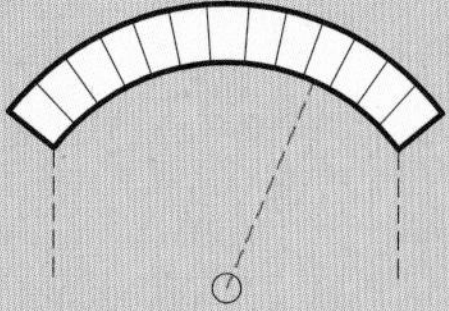
Segmental

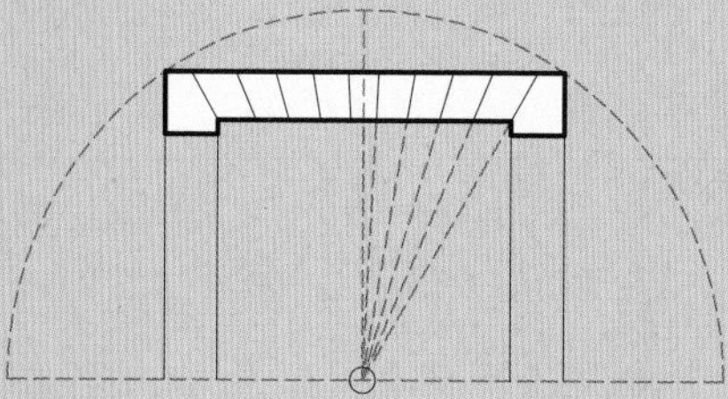
Jack

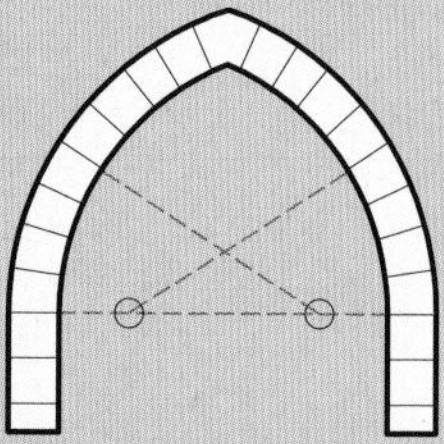
Pointed Saracenic (Gothic)

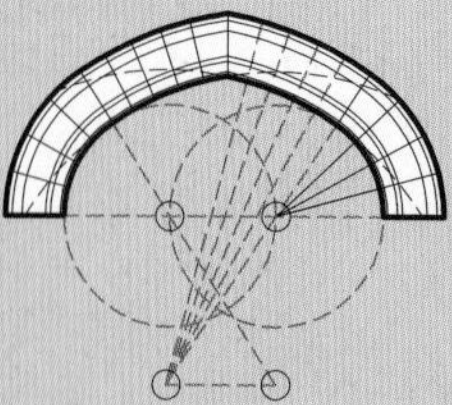
Tudor (Four-Centered)

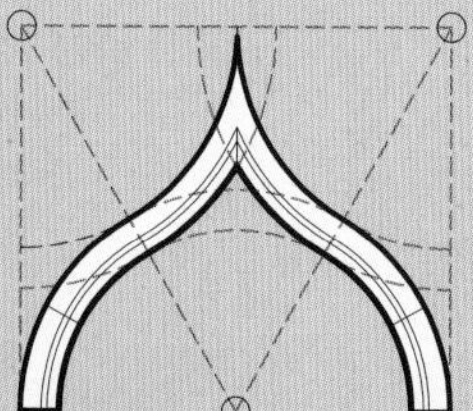
Ogee

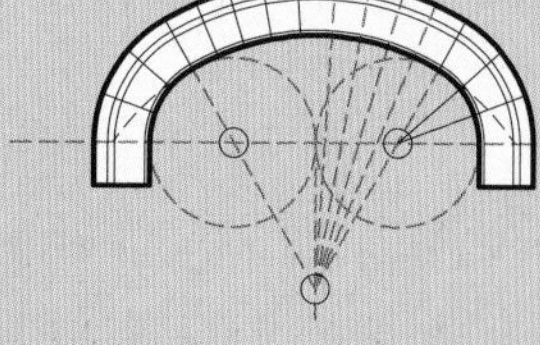
Three-Centered

VAULTS

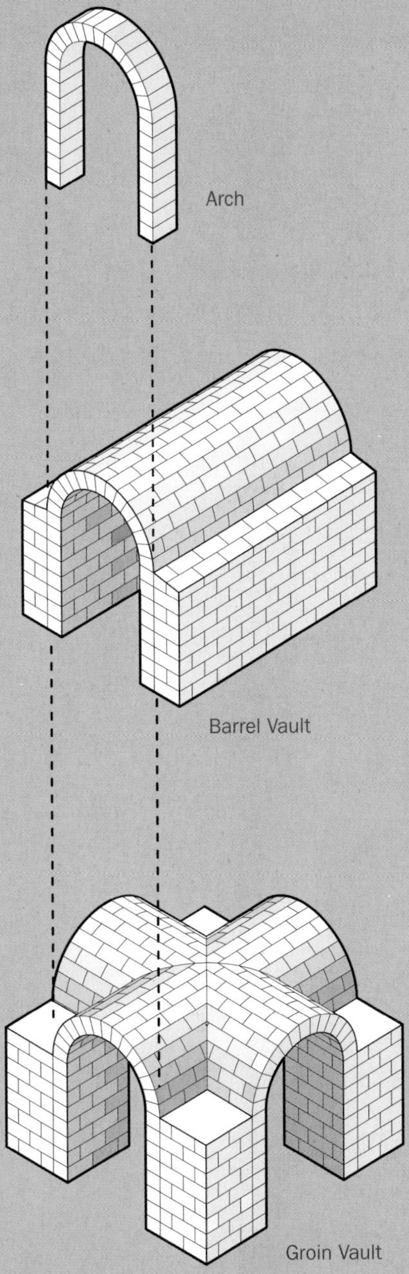
Arch
Barrel Vault
Groin Vault

DOMES

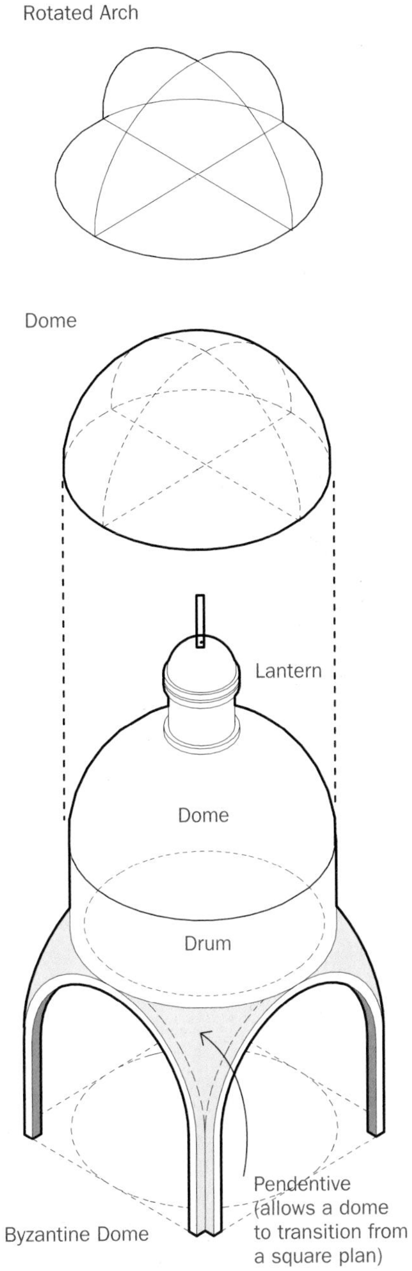
Rotated Arch
Dome
Lantern
Dome
Drum
Byzantine Dome
Pendentive (allows a dome to transition from a square plan)

THE MIDDLE AGES

The Middle Ages in Europe (roughly 500 to 1500 CE) fell between the Roman Empire and the coming enlightenment of the Renaissance. In this period, Byzantine architecture flourished in Constantinople in the east. The domed basilica of the Hagia Sophia (532 CE) was a marvel of engineering that appeared to "float" through the use of pendentives. Ultimately, Byzantine influence extended back to central Europe.

The innovations of the Hagia Sophia reached northern Europe through returning Crusaders, who brought new technologies and insights with them. These enabled the development of the pointed arch, the flying buttress, and the rib vault. All were used in service of new ways to open up tall, light-filled spaces for gathering and worship, in the form of the Gothic cathedral.

BYZANTINE

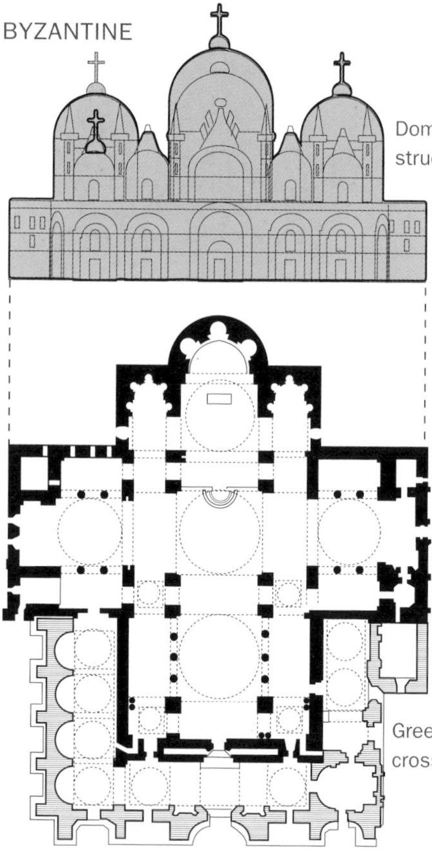
Domed structure
Greek cross plan

Basilica of San Marco (830 CE)
Venice, Italy

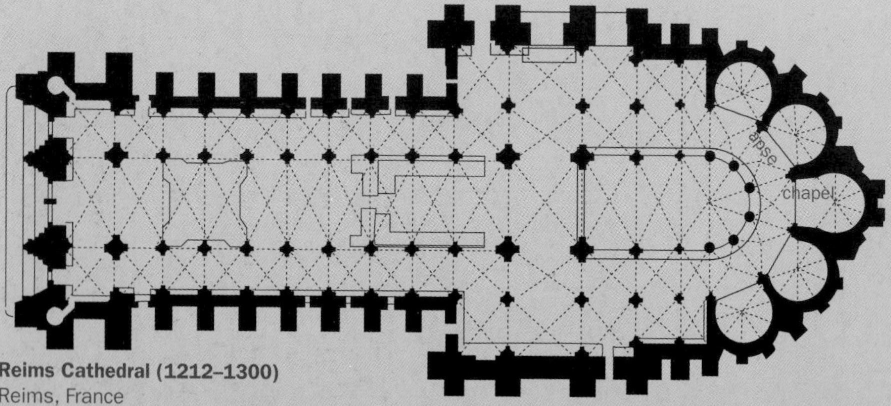
apse
chapel

Reims Cathedral (1212–1300)
Reims, France

GOTHIC

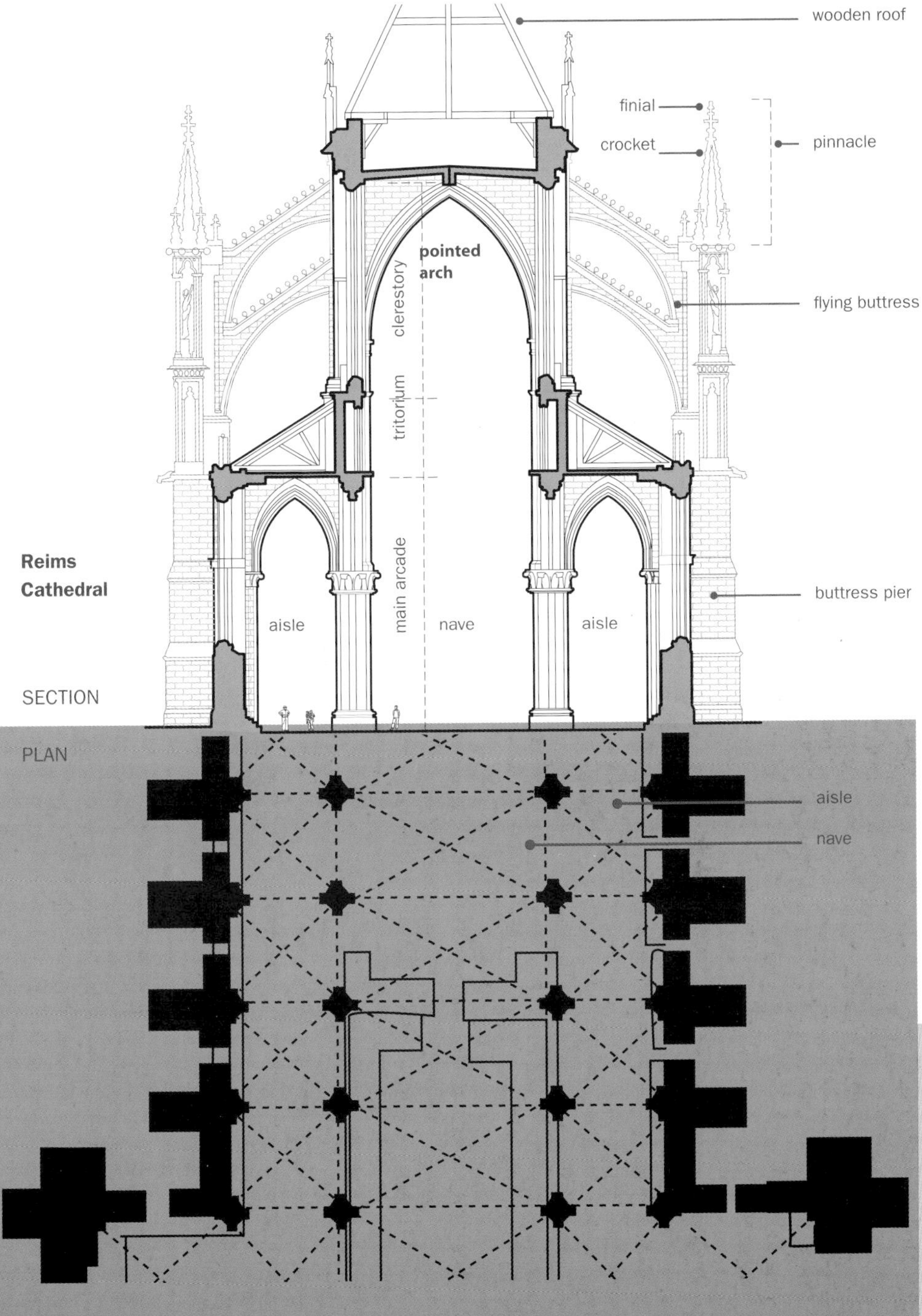

wooden roof
finial
crocket
pinnacle
pointed arch
clerestory
flying buttress
tritorium
main arcade
Reims Cathedral
buttress pier
aisle
nave
aisle
SECTION
PLAN
aisle
nave

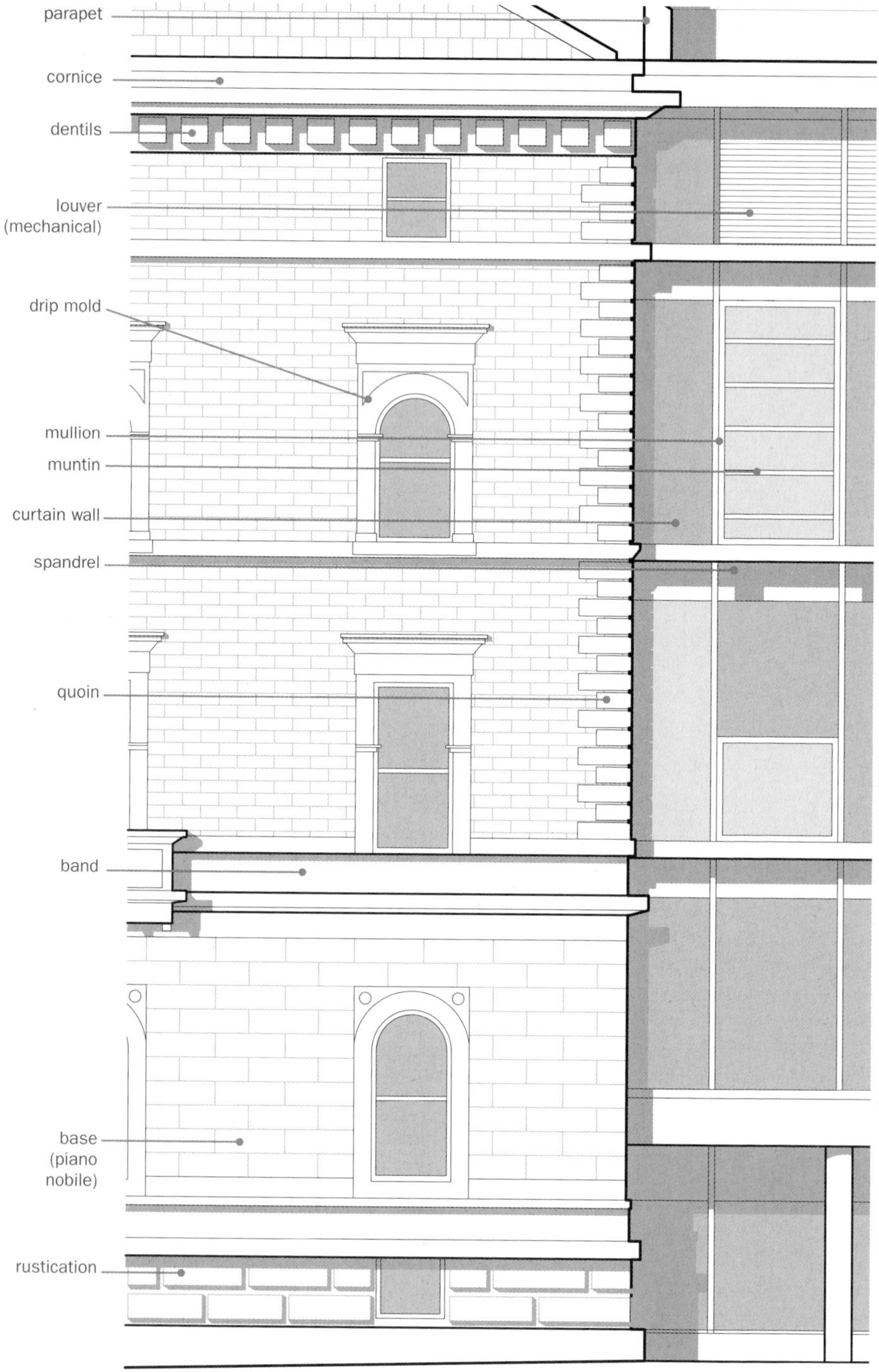
parapet
cornice
dentils
louver (mechanical)
drip mold
mullion
muntin
curtain wall
spandrel
quoin
band
base (piano nobile)
rustication

MODERNISM

Architectural modernism opposed following the forms and styles of the past in favor of embracing contemporary technology and opportunities. Industrialization and innovative methods of using iron, steel, and concrete for structural systems opened up new and flexible ways to design buildings that no longer depended on heavy masonry bearing walls. Swiss architect Le Corbusier (1887–1965) developed the Domino House system (1914), in which he separated building structure from enclosure, freeing up both plan and façade.

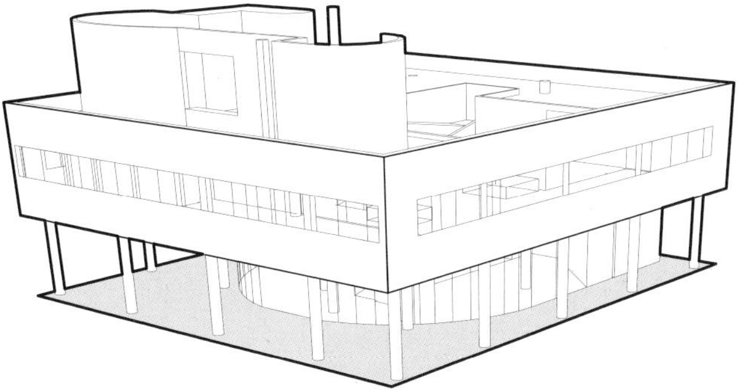

Le Corbusier's five points are supports (pilotis), roof gardens, free plans, horizontal windows, and free design of the façade. His 1929 Villa Savoye (which he dubbed a "machine for living") in Poissy, France, illustrates all five points clearly.

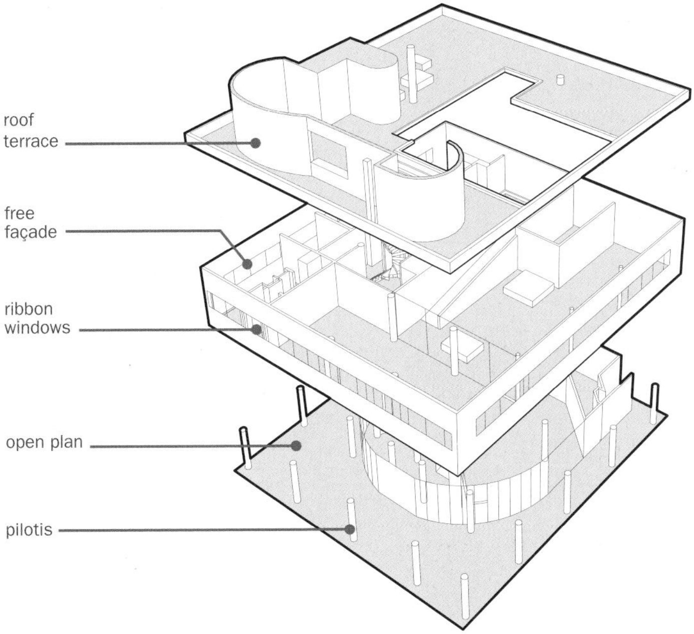
roof terrace
free façade
ribbon windows
open plan
pilotis

CANONICAL ARCHITECTURAL PUBLICATIONS

MARCUS VITRUVIUS POLLIO (c. 80–15 BCE)

De Architectura (in English, *Ten Books on Architecture*)

Vitruvius was an architect, engineer, and writer, who wrote his *Ten Books* around 15 BCE and dedicated them to Emperor Augustus. The books provide explanation and insight into the architecture, engineering, and city planning of classical antiquity, though it was not until the Renaissance that they were rediscovered and ultimately published in 1486. Vitruvius proposed *firmitas*, *utilitas*, and *venustas* as three elements forming the basis for architecture:

firmness (structural stability and integrity)
commodity (efficient and functional spatial arrangement)
delight (pleasing proportion and beauty)

Book 1: *Education of the architect; principals of architecture; city planning*
Book 2: *Materials for building; origin of the dwelling house*
Book 3: *Symmetry and proportion; temples; architectural orders*
Book 4: *Temples; origins of the three orders (continuation of Book 3)*
Book 5: *Civic buildings (Forum, Basilica, Senate); theater design*
Book 6: *Domestic buildings*
Book 7: *Stucco; plasterwork; colors*
Book 8: *Water; aqueducts and cisterns*
Book 9: *Zodiac; planets; astrology*
Book 10: *Machines and instruments*

LEON BATTISTA ALBERTI (1404–1472)

De Re Aedificatoria (*On the Art of Building*)

Written between 1443 and 1452, this became the first printed book on architecture with its publication in 1485 (followed by the publication of Vitruvius's *Ten Books* finally in 1486).

1. *Lineaments*
2. *Materials*
3. *Construction*
4. *Public Works*
5. *Works of Individuals*
6. *Ornament*
7. *Ornament to Sacred Buildings*
8. *Ornament to Public Secular Buildings*
9. *Ornament to Private Buildings*
10. *Restoration of Buildings*

ANDREA PALLADIO (1508–1580)
I quattro libri dell'architettura
(*The Four Books of Architecture*)

A Renaissance architect, Palladio wrote a highly illustrated treatise that included his own designs and the ancient Roman inspirations for his and other work of the Renaissance.

Book 1: Building materials and techniques; the orders of architecture

Book 2: Private houses

Book 3: Streets, bridges, piazzas

Book 4: Reproductions of ancient Roman temple designs

LE CORBUSIER (1887–1965)
Oeuvre Complète
(*Complete Works in Eight Volumes*)

Published regularly throughout the prolific working life (and beyond) of Swiss architect Le Corbusier, the *Oeuvre Complète* comprises over 1700 pages. Contained within is a comprehensive collection of his sketches, drawings, projects both built and unbuilt, texts and manifestos, paintings, and sculptures.

Volume 1: 1910–1929
Volume 2: 1929–1934
Volume 3: 1934–1938
Volume 4: 1938–1946
Volume 5: 1946–1952
Volume 6: 1952–1957
Volume 7: 1957–1965
Volume 8: 1965–1969 (last works)

SEBASTIANO SERLIO (1475–1554)
I sette libri dell'architettura (*Seven Books of Architecture*) also known as: *Tutte l'opere d'architettura et prospetiva* (*All the Works on Architecture and Perspective*)

1. *On Geometry*
2. *On Perspective*
3. *On Antiquities*
4. *On the Five Styles of Buildings*
5. *On Temples*
6. *On Habitations*
7. *On Situations*

The first of Serlio's books was published in 1537; they were highly illustrated and written in Italian in order to appeal to architects and builders of the day—in contrast to Alberti's books, which were written in Latin and did not focus on illustration. Many of Serlio's books were published long after his death.

Chapter 24: Form and Organization

PRIMARY ELEMENTS

The primary elements of form are points, lines, planes, and volumes, each growing from the other. A point is a position in space and the prime generator of form. A line is a point extended; its properties are length, position, and direction. A plane is a line extended; its properties are width and length, shape, surface, orientation, and position. A volume is a plane extended; its properties are length, width, and depth, form and space, surface, orientation, and position.

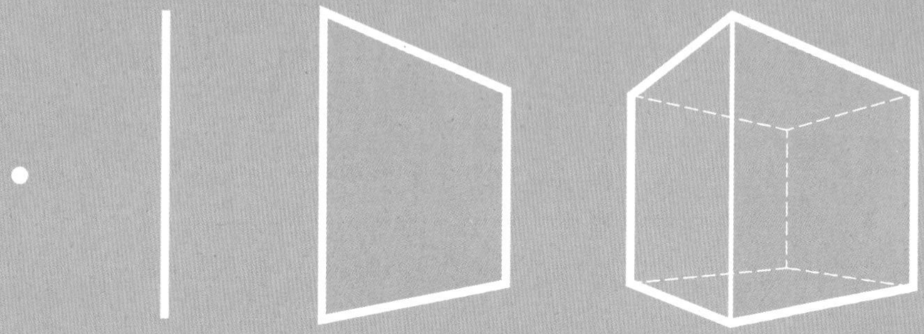

PRIMARY SHAPES

Square

Triangle

Circle

PLATONIC SOLIDS

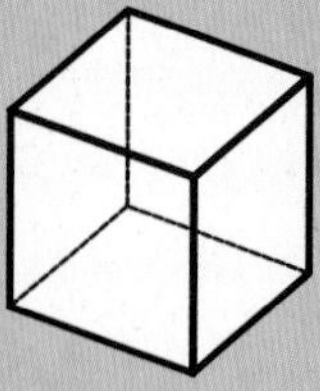

Cube

Pyramid

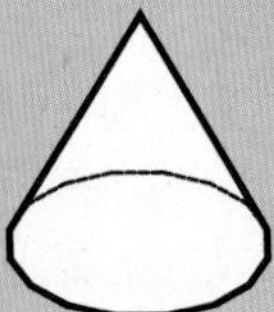

Cone

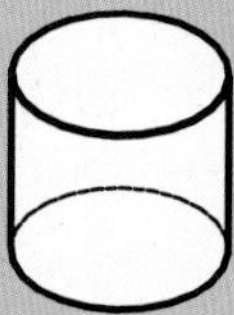

Cylinder

Sphere

POLYHEDRA

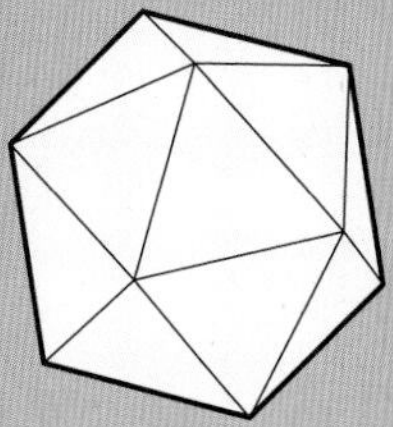

Icosahedron (20-Sided Solid)

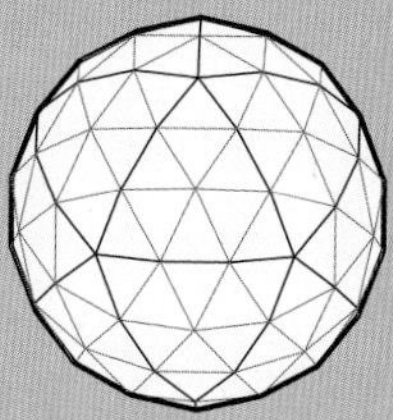

Geodesic Sphere

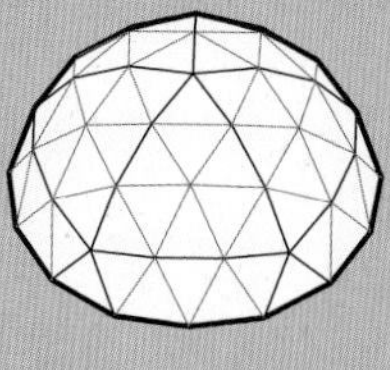

Geodesic Dome

A geometric polyhedron is a three-dimensional solid made up of a collection of polygons, usually joined at the edges.

Geodesic spheres and domes are designed by filling each face of a solid, such as an icosahedron, with a regular pattern of triangles, bulged out so that their vertices are not coplanar but are in the surface of the sphere instead. As a structural concept, the subpattern of triangles form geodesics that distribute stresses across the structure.

BOOLEAN OPERATIONS

Joining together or subtracting of one solid from one or more sets of solids.

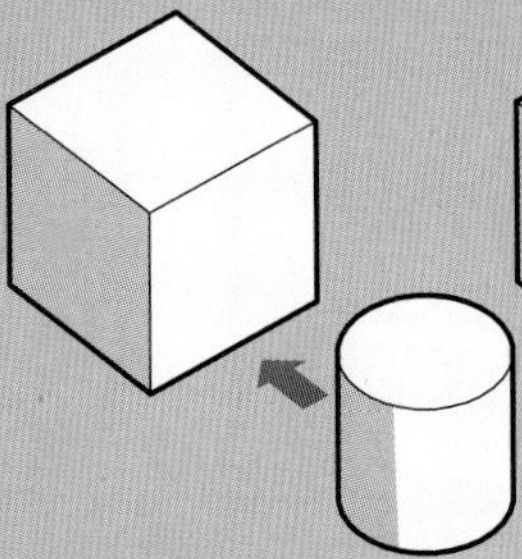

Union

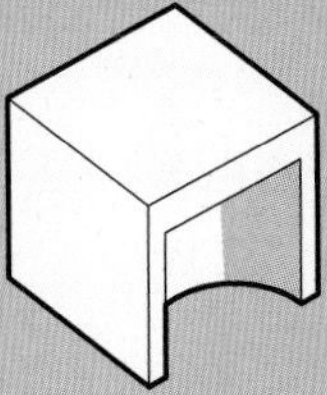

Extraction

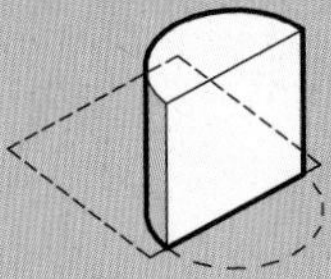

Intersection

RULED SURFACES

A ruled surface, which is the surface generated by connecting line segments between corresponding points, can take many forms.

Hyperboloid of Revolution

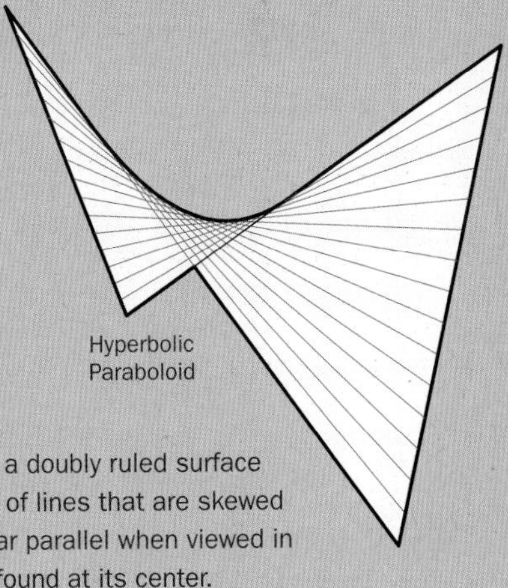

Hyperbolic Paraboloid

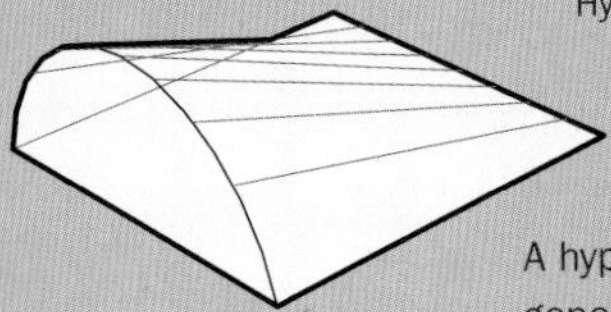

Conoid

A hyperbolic paraboloid is a doubly ruled surface generated by two meshes of lines that are skewed from each other but appear parallel when viewed in plan. The saddle point is found at its center.

THE GOLDEN SECTION

The properties of proportion of the golden section have been employed by architects, artists, mathematicians, and musicians since the ancient Greeks recognized its proportional ordering in the human body. Even today many believe it to contain mystical qualities, whose unique mathematical and geometrical relationships create a harmonic condition that is nature's aesthetically "perfect" balance between symmetry and asymmetry.

Constructing a Golden Rectangle

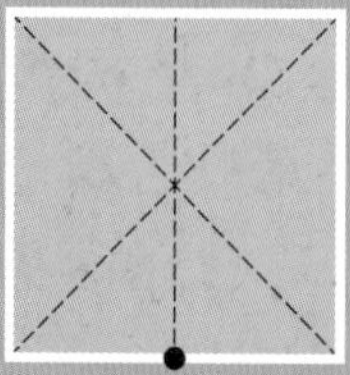

1. Create a square and locate the midpoint of one side.

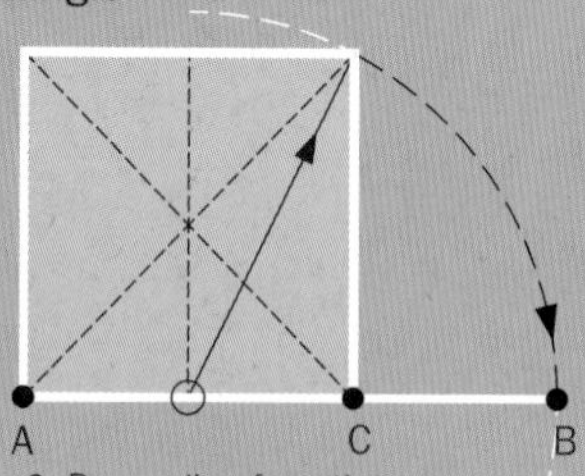
A
C
B

2. Draw a line from the midpoint to a corner that does not share a line with the midpoint.

3. This is the radius of a circle with its center at the midpoint; the point where the circle and the line AC intersect becomes point B.

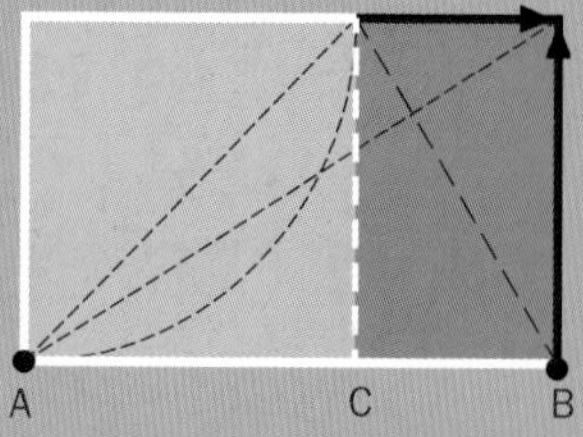
A
C
B

4. Line AB is the long leg of the golden rectangle.

5. A golden rectangle has been added to the original square, and together they also form a larger golden rectangle.

6. The process can be repeated infinitely, creating proportionally larger or smaller series of squares and rectangles.

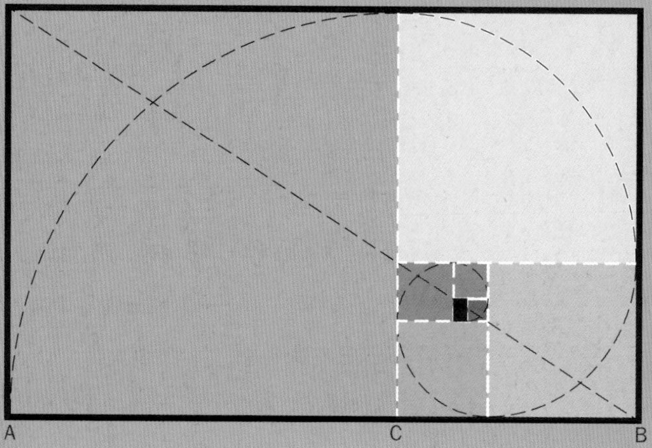
A
C
B

In mathematics, the golden section is the ratio of the two divisions of a line such that the smaller is to the larger as the larger is to the sum of the two. In addition to its many uses in the arts and music, there are practical uses for the mathematical integrity of the golden section in its proportions as related to structure.

Calculating the Golden Mean

AC/CB = AB/AC (a unique characteristic)
If AB = 1, let AC = x

$$x=\frac{\sqrt{5}-1}{2} = 0.61803398\ldots \text{ (infinite).}$$

Therefore: the ratio of AC to AB is approximately 61.8%; the inverse (1/61.8) is 1.61803398 . . .

THE FIBONACCI SEQUENCE

The Fibonacci Sequence is a recursive series of numbers, where each number in the sequence is the sum of the two numbers preceding it. A simple sequence beginning with 0 follows:

0, 1, 1, 2, 3, 5, 8, 13, 21, 34, 55...

Any two adjacent numbers in the sequence may be divided, the lower number by the higher number (for example, 34/55), to achieve a very close approximation of the golden section (in this case, 0.6181818 . . .). The higher the numbers, the more accurate the answer will be (for example: 377/610 = 0.6180327 . . .).

REGULATING LINES

The guiding lines that indicate the proportional and alignment relationships in drawings, such as those depicting the golden rectangle, are known as regulating lines. They are used, for instance, both to determine and to illustrate proportional relationships in a design. Rectangles whose diagonals are either perpendicular or parallel to each other have similar proportions (even if they are not golden rectangles), and the use of such lines is a common proportional ordering tool.

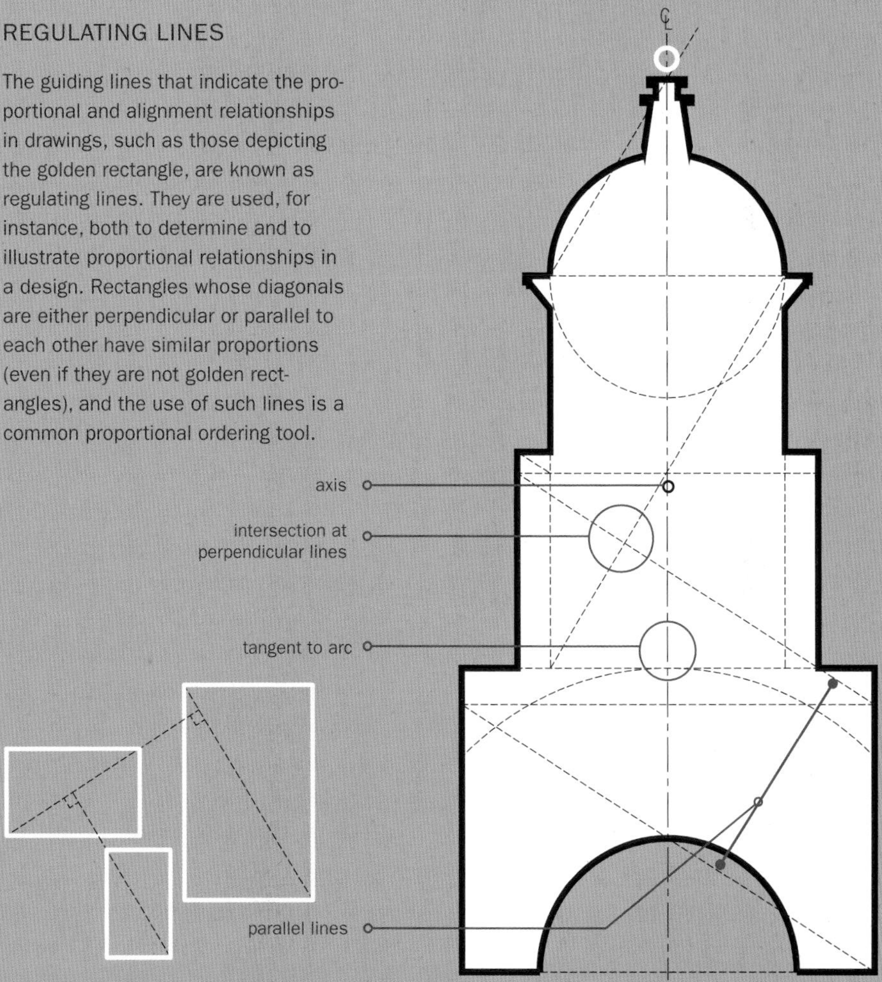

axis
intersection at perpendicular lines
tangent to arc
parallel lines

Chapter 25: Glossary

2 × 4: A standard American lumber size equal to 1½" × 3½" (38 × 89). A roughly equivalent standard SI size would be 40 × 90 or 50 × 100.

AASM: Association of American Steel Manufacturers

AGCA: Associated General Contractors of America

AIA: American Institute of Architects

AISC: American Institute of Steel Construction.

AISI: American Iron and Steel Institute

ANSI: American National Standards Institute

APA: American Plywood Association

ASHRAE: American Society of Heating, Refrigerating, and Air Conditioning Engineers

ASTM: American Society for Testing and Materials

CSI: Construction Specifications Institute

IESNA: Illumination Engineering Society of North America

ICC: International Code Council

ICED: International Council on Environmental Design

ISO: International Organization for Standardization

LEED: Leadership in Energy & Environmental Design

NIBS: National Institute of Building Sciences

NFPA: National Fire Protection Association

RAIC: Royal Architecture Institute of Canada

RIBA: Royal Institute of British Architects

UIA: Union Internationale des Architectes

UL: Underwriters' Laboratory

A

Aalto, Alvar: (1898–1976) Finnish architect and designer; notable buildings include the Municipal Library in Viipuri, Finland, Paimio Sanatorium, and Baker House at MIT.

Access flooring: Removable finish floor panels raised above the floor structure to allow installation of wiring and ductwork below.

Accessible: Capable of being reached by all persons, regardless of levels of disability.

Acoustical ceiling: System of fibrous removable tiles in the ceiling that absorb sound.

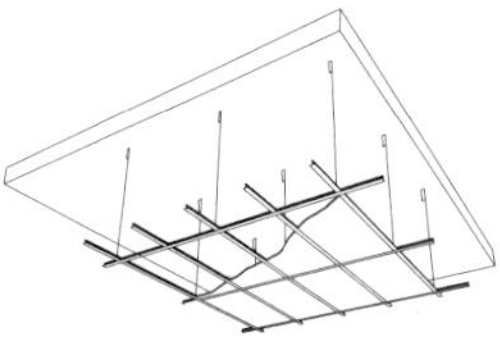

ADA: Americans with Disabilities Act.

Adaptive reuse: Changing a building's function in response to the changing needs of its users.

AFF: Above finish floor.

Aggregate: Particles such as sand, gravel, and stone used in concrete and plaster.

Alberti, Leon Battista: (1404–1472) Italian architect, artist, and Renaissance humanist polymath; notable work includes the facade of the Santa Maria Novella in Florence, Italy, and numerous treatises on art and architecture, with scientific study of perspective.

Alloy: Substance made of two or more metals or a metal and another substance.

Anchor bolt: Concrete-embedded bolt that fastens a building frame to masonry or concrete.

Angle: L-shaped steel or aluminum structural section.

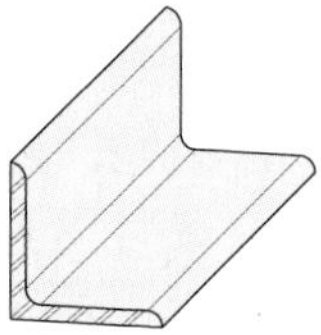

Annealed: Metal cooled under controlled conditions.

Arcade: Series of arches on columns or piers.

Arch: Structural device that supports vertical loads by translating them into axial forces.

Area: Quantity expressing the size of a figure in a plane or surface.

Atelier: Workshop or studio.

Atrium: Open-roofed entrance court of a Roman dwelling; also, a many-storied court in a building, usually skylit.

Axial: Force, load, tension, or compression in a direction parallel to the long axis of a structural member.

B

Ballast: In roofing, a heavy material such as crushed stone installed over a roof membrane to minimize wind uplift; in lighting, a device that provides starting voltage for a fluorescent or high-intensity discharge lamp, then regulates the current during operation.

Balloon frame: Wood-frame construction in which vertical studs run from the sill to the eave instead of resting on intermediate floors.

Baluster: Vertical member used to support a stair railing or a railing in a continuous banister.

Balustrade: Railing system, usually around a balcony, that consists of balusters and a top rail.

Band/banding: Continuous horizontal division on a wall created by different materials, colors, or textures.

Bar: Small rolled steel shape.

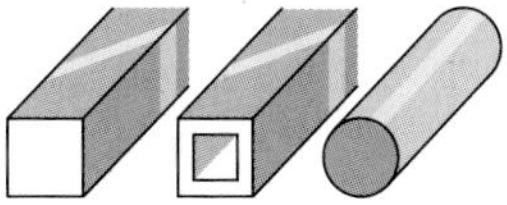

Bar joist: Truss type used for floor and roof support, with steel members on top and bottom and heavy wire or rod web lacing.

Base plate: Steel plate between a column and foundation that distributes the column's load to the foundation.

Bay: Rectangular area of a building defined at its four corners by adjacent columns; projecting portion of a façade.

Beam: Horizontal linear element that spans an opening and is supported at both ends by walls or columns.

Bearing wall: Wall that supports floors or roofs.

Bed joint: Horizontal layer of mortar between units in a masonry wall.

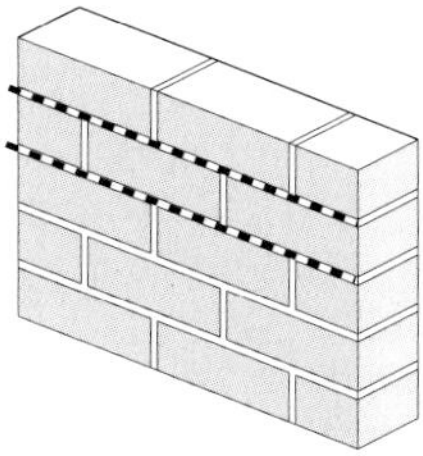

Bending moment: Force acting on a structure, causing it to curve.

Blocking: Pieces of wood placed between joists, studs, or rafters to stabilize the structure or provide a nailing surface for finishes.

Blueprint: Photographic print on specially coated paper; ideal for making precise and undistorted copies of large-scale drawings. Blueprint technology is rapidly being superseded by computer plotters and printers.

Board foot: Unit of measuring lumber volume (nominally: 144 cu. in.).

Bond beam: Top course of a masonry wall, filled with concrete and reinforcing steel, and used to support roof loads.

Bramante, Donato: (1444–1514) Italian Renaissance architect; notable buildings include St. Peter's Basilica and the Tempietto, both in Rome.

Brise-soleil: Shading screen attached to the exterior of a building.

Brunelleschi, Filippo: (1377–1446) Italian Renaissance architect and engineer; notable buildings include the Dome of the Cathedral of Florence and the Basilica of Santo Spirito in Florence.

Building code: Legal restrictions meant to enforce safety and health in the built environment.

Built-up roof: Roof membrane composed of asphalt-saturated felt layers laminated together and bonded with bitumen or pitch.

Buttress: Masonry or concrete reinforcement applied to a wall to resist diagonal forces from an arch or vault.

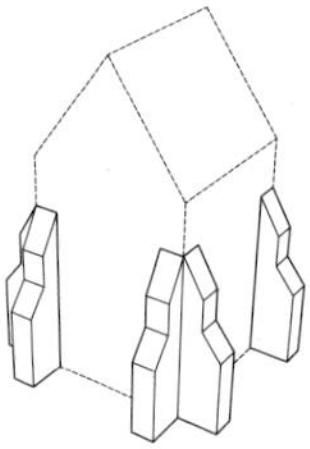

C

CAD: Computer-aided drafting.

Caisson: Long cylindrical foundation element formed by drilling deep into firm clay and pouring concrete into the hole.

Canopy: Projection over doors or windows.

Cantilever: Beam or slab extending beyond its last point of support.

Capital: Uppermost element of a column.

Cavity wall: Masonry wall with a continuous airspace between wythes.

Cement: Dry powder that combines chemically with water and bonds aggregate particles together to form concrete. Also known as portland cement.

Change order: Written document between the owner and contractor of a project authorizing a change in the project.

Chase wall: Cavity wall containing electrical runs or plumbing pipes in its cavity.

Chord: Structural member of a truss.

Clear floor space: Minimum unobstructed floor or ground space required to accommodate a single, stationary wheelchair and occupant.

Clerestory: Windows placed high in a wall, usually above lower roof levels. Also called clearstory.

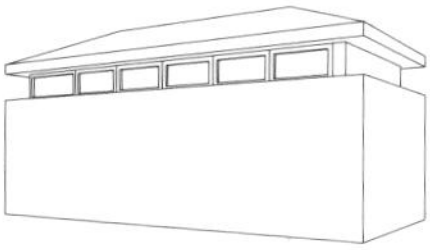

Coefficient of expansion: Fractional change in length, area, or volume or an object per unit change in temperature at a given constant pressure.

Cold rolling: Rolling of metal at room temperature and stretching its crystals to harden the metal.

Colonnade: Linear series of columns carrying an entablature or arches.

Column: Upright structural member.

Concrete: Mix of cement, aggregates, and water that forms a structural material.

Concrete masonry unit (CMU): Solid or hollow block of cured concrete.

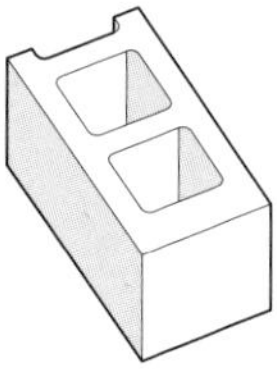

Coping: Protective cap or cover on top of a wall to throw off water.

Corbel: Series of spanning stones or bricks in which each successive course projects over the course below it; also, a projecting masonry or concrete bracket.

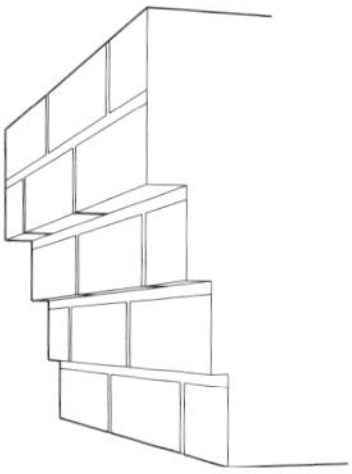

Cornice: Projecting molding at the top of a building; also, the uppermost element of an entablature.

Course: Horizontal layer of one-unit-high masonry units.

Cricket: Component used to divert water away from roof curbs, platforms, chimneys, walls, or other roof forms.

Cripple stud: Short wood framing member in walls interrupted by a header or sill.

Cupola: Domed roof structure rising from a building.

Curtain wall: Non-load-bearing exterior wall system supported on the building's frame.

D

Deck: Horizontal surface spanning across joists or beams.

Deflection: Under an applied load, the amount of bending movement of any part of a structural member perpendicular to that member's axis.

Deliverables: Set of items such as construction documents provided by the architect to the client, and as agreed on in the owner-architect agreement.

Detail: Drawing that provides very specific information about the materials and construction of a component of a project and that is keyed into larger-scale drawings.

Dimensional stability: Ability of a section of wood to resist changes in volume at fluctuating moisture levels.

Dome: Bowl-shaped volume created by rotating an arch about its vertical axis.

Dormer: Protrusion in a sloping roof, usually containing a window.

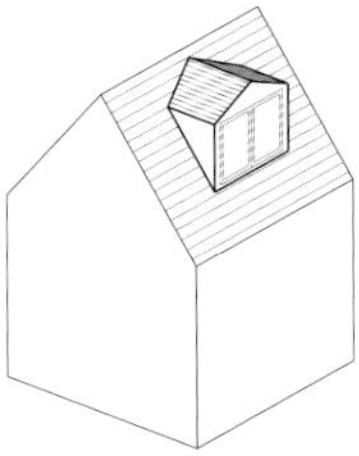

Duct: Hollow conduit for circulating and directing air.

DWG: Computer drawing file.

E

Eave: Edge of a roof plane, usually projecting over the exterior wall.

Egress: Means of exiting safely.

Eisenman, Peter: (1932–) American architect; notable buildings include House VI, Wexner Center for the Arts, and the University of Phoenix Stadium.

Elevation: Architectural drawing of a view of the vertical planes of the building, showing their relationship to each other.

Encroachment: Portion of a building that extends illegally beyond the property owned and onto another property.

Energy efficiency: Reducing energy requirements without reducing the end result.

Engaged column: Non-freestanding column attached to a wall.

Entablature: Uppermost part of a classical order, comprised of architrave, frieze, and cornice and supported on a colonnade.

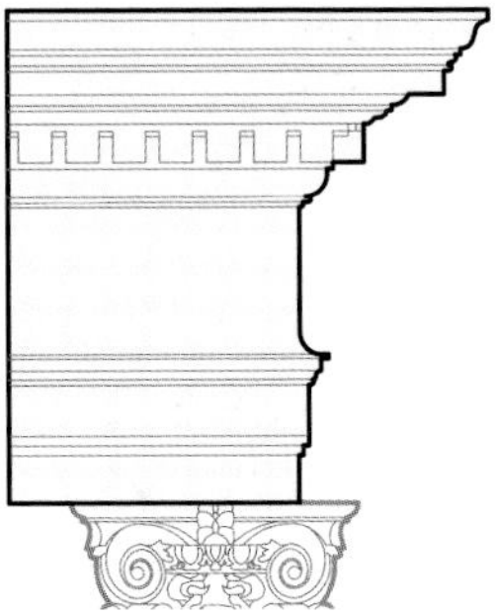

Expansion joint: Surface divider joint allowing for surface expansion.

F

Façade: Face or elevation of a building.

Fascia: Exposed vertical face of an eave.

Fenestration: Windows and window arrangements on a façade.

Finial: Ornament at the top of a spire or roof.

Fire-resistance rating: Determination of the amount of time (in fractions of an hour) that an assembly or material will resist fire.

Flashing: Continuous sheet of thin metal, plastic, or other waterproof material used to divert water and prevent it from passing through a joint into a wall or roof.

Float glass: Common plate glass made by floating the material on a bed of molten metal, producing a smooth, flat surface.

Footing: Widened base of a foundation that spreads a building's loads across the soil.

Foundation: Lowest portion of a building that transfers the building's structural loads into the earth.

G

Galvanic action: Corrosion resulting from an electrical current between two unlike metals.

Girder: Large horizontal beam that supports other beams.

Girt: Horizontal beam that supports wall cladding between columns.

Golden section: Unique proportional ratio of two divisions of a line such that the smaller of the two is to the larger as the larger is to the sum of the two.

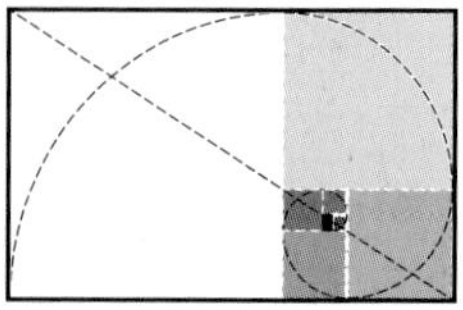

Grab bar: Bar attached parallel to a wall to provide a handgrip for steadying oneself.

Grade: Classification of size or quality; the surface of the ground; the act of moving earth to make the ground level.

Gropius, Walter: (1883–1969) German architect and founder of the Bauhaus. Notable buildings include the Bauhaus School and the Pan Am Building in New York.

Guardrail: Protective railing to prevent falling into stairwells or other openings.

Gusset plate: Flat steel plate to which truss chords are connected at a truss joint.

Gypsum wallboard (GWB): Interior facing board with a gypsum core between paper facing. Also called drywall and plasterboard.

H

Hadid, Zaha: (1950–) Iraqi-British architect; notable buildings include Vitra Fire Station in Weil-am-Rhein, Germany, the London Aquatics Centre for the 2012 Olympics, and the Broad Art Museum in Lansing, Michigan.

Half-timbered: Timber wall with the spaces between filled with masonry.

Handrail: Railing running parallel to the rise of a stairway or ramp, providing a continuous gripping surface.

Hard metric: Conversion of component sizes to fall within a rational metric module, not a strict translation of other units into their exact metric equivalents.

Hardwood: Wood from deciduous trees.

Head joint: Vertical layer of mortar between units in a masonry wall.

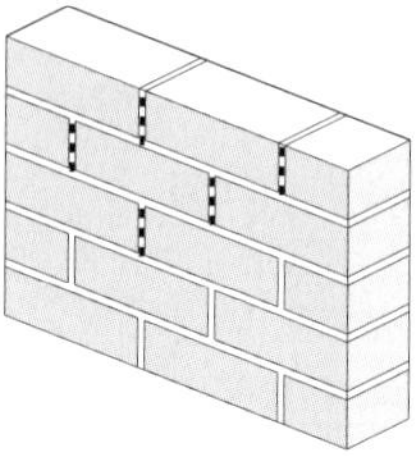

Header: Lintel; in steel, a beam that spans between girders; also, masonry unit laid across two wythes, exposing its end in the face of the wall.

Heavy timber: Structural lumber having a minimum width and thickness of 5" (127).

Hot-rolled steel: Steel formed and shaped by being heated and passed through rollers.

HSLA: High-strength low-alloy grade of steel.

HUD: Housing and Urban Development.

HVAC: Heating, Ventilating, and Air-Conditioning.

I

IBC: International Building Code.

I-beam: Obsolete term for American Standard steel section that is I- or H-shaped.

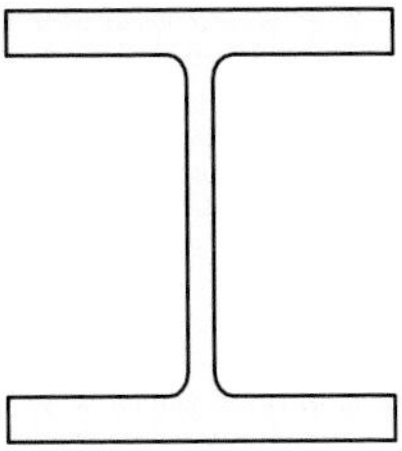

Insulation: Any material that slows or retards the flow or transfer of heat.

J

Jamb: Vertical frame of a window or door.

Johnson, Philip: (1906–2005) American architect; notable work includes the Glass House in New Canaan, Connecticut, the AT&T Building in New York, and the Four Seasons Restaurant in New York.

Joists: Light, closely spaced beams supporting floors or flat roofs.

K

Kahn, Albert: (1869–1942) German-American architect; notable buildings include Hill Auditorium at the University of Michigan, the Packard Automotive Plant in Detroit, and the Detroit Athletic Club.

Kahn, Louis: (1901–1974) American architect; notable buildings include the Philips Exeter Academy Library in New Hampshire; the Salk Institute in La Jolla, California; and the Kimbell Art Museum in Fort Worth, Texas.

Keystone: Central wedge-shaped stone at the top of an arch.

Koolhaas, Rem: (1944–) Dutch architect; notable buildings include the Kunsthal in Rotterdam, the Seattle Central Library, and the CCTV Headquarters in Beijing.

L

Laminate: Material produced through bonding together layers of other materials.

Le Corbusier: (1887–1965) Swiss architect notable for the Villa Savoye (1929), the Unite d'Habitation, and the chapel at Ronchamp.

Ledoux, Claude Nicolas: (1736-1806) French neoclassical architect; notable designs include the Royal Saltworks at Arc-et-Senan, and the Theatre of Besancon.

Lintel: Beam over a door or window that carries the load of the wall above.

Lite: Pane of glass; also "light," though often spelled differently to avoid confusion with visible light.

Loads: Forces acting on a structure. Dead loads are fixed and static elements such as the building's own skin, structure, and equipment; live loads are the changing weight on a building and include people, snow, vehicles, and furniture.

Longitudinal: Lengthwise.

Loos, Adolf: (1870–1933) Austro-Hungarian architect; notable buidlings include the Kärntner Bar in Vienna, the Villa Müller in Prague, and Maison Tzara in Paris.

Louver: Opening with horizontal slats that permit passage of air, but not rain, sunlight, or view.

M

Masonry: Brickwork, blockwork, and stonework; also, the trade of a mason.

Metrication: Act of changing from the use of customary units to metric units.

Mezzanine: Intermediate level between a floor and ceiling that occupies a partial area of the floor space.

Mild steel: Steel with a low carbon content.

Millwork: Interior wood finish components of a building, including cabinetry, windows, doors, moldings, and stairs.

Model: Physical representation (usually at a reduced scale) of a building or building component; in computer drafting and modeling, it is the digital two- or three-dimensional representation of a design.

Molding: Strip of wood, plaster, or other material with an ornamental profile.

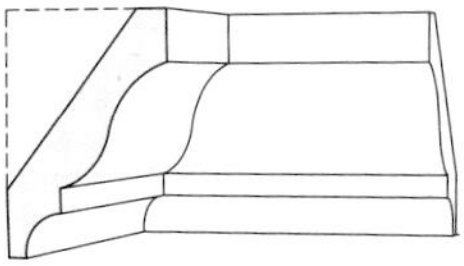

Mortar: Material composed of portland cement, hydrated lime, fine aggregate (sand), and water, used to adhere together and cushion masonry units.

Mullion: Horizontal or vertical bar or divider in the frames of windows, doors, or other openings, and that holds and supports panels, glass, sashes, or sections of a curtain wall.

Muntin: Secondary system of horizontal or vertical divider bars between small lites of glass or panels in a sash.

Mylar: Polyester film that, when coated, can be used as drafting sheets.

N

Niche: Recess in a wall, usually for holding a sculpture.

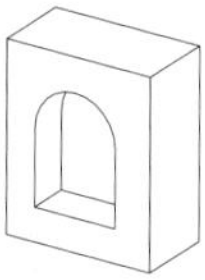

Nominal: Approximate rounded dimensions given to materials for ease of reference.

O

Occupancy: Category of the use of a building for determining specific code requirements.

Ogee: Profile section with a reverse-curve face (that is, concave above and convex below).

Overhang: Projection beyond the face of a wall below.

P

Palladio, Andrea: (1508–1580 Italian architect; notable work includes numerous villas in the Veneto region of Italy, the Teatro Olimpico in Vicenza, and his treatise *The Four Books of Architecture*.

Parametric: Having one or more variables (parameters) that can be altered to achieve different results. In parametric modeling, a database tracks changes to all elements of a design simultaneously.

Parapet: Low wall projecting from the edge of a platform, usually on a roof.

Parti: Central idea governing and organizing a work of architecture.

Partition: Interior non-load-bearing wall.

Passive solar: Technology of heating and cooling a building naturally, through the use of energy-efficient materials and proper site placement.

Pedestal: In classical architecture, a base supporting a column or statue.

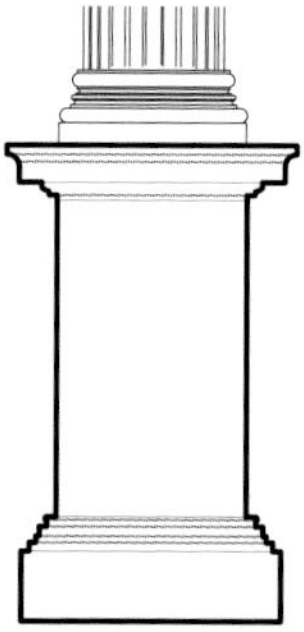

Pediment: Triangular space that forms the gable end of a low-pitched roof, often filled with relief sculpture.

Pendentive: Curved, triangular support that results from transforming a square bay into a dome.

Penthouse: Enclosed space above the level of the main roof used for mechanical equipment; an above-roof apartment.

Peristyle: Colonnaded courtyard.

Pier: Caisson foundation; also, a structural element that supports an arch.

Pilaster: Pier engaged in a wall.

Pillar: Columnar support that is not a classical column.

Pilotis: Columns or pillars that lift a building from the ground.

Pitch: Slope of a roof or other inclined surface, usually expressed as inches of rise per foot of run (X:12, when × is a number between 1 and 12).

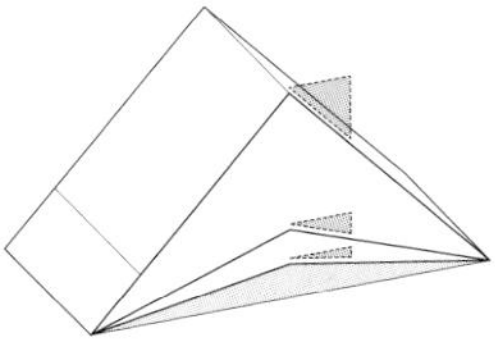

Plan: Architectural drawing of a view of the horizontal planes of the building, showing their relationship to each other, and acting as a horizontal section.

Plenum: Space between a suspended ceiling and the structure above, used for mechanical ductwork, piping, and wiring.

Pointing: Process of applying mortar to the outside surface of a mortar joint after laying the masonry, as a means of finishing the joint or making repairs to an existing joint.

Portico: Entrance porch.

Precast concrete: Concrete that is cast and cured in a location other than its final position.

Prefabricated building: Buildings consisting of components such as walls, floors, and roofs that are built off-site (often in a factory), then shipped to the site for assembly.

Purlin: Beams spanning across the slope of a roof that support the roof decking.

Q

Quoin: Corner stones in a wall made distinct from the surrounding wall by being larger, of a different texture, or having deeper joints to make the stones protrude.

R

Rabbet: Notch in wood for joining pieces or recessed parts in a typical door frame.

Rafter: Roof framing member that runs in the direction of slope.

Reflected ceiling plan: Upside-down plan drawing that documents the ceiling plane.

Retaining wall: Site wall built for resisting lateral displacement of soil, water, or other material.

RFP (Request for Proposal): Official invitation for architects to submit qualifications and proposals to perform a project.

Rib: Fold or bend in a sheet of deck.

Ridge: Horizontal line created at the connection of two sloping roof surfaces.

Rise: Vertical difference in elevation, as in the rise of a stair.

Riser: Vertical face between two treads of a stair; also, vertical run of plumbing, ductwork, or wiring.

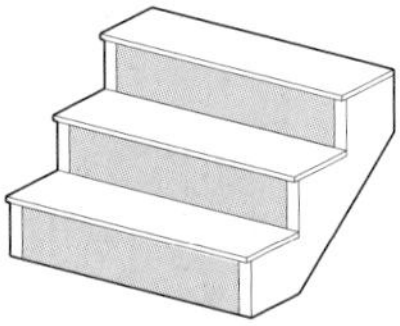

Room cavity ratio: Ratio of room dimensions used to determine how light will interact with the room's surfaces.

Rotunda: Space that is circular in plan and covered by a dome.

Run: Horizontal dimension of a stair, ramp, or other slope.

Rustication: Masonry pattern consisting of large blocks with deep joints.

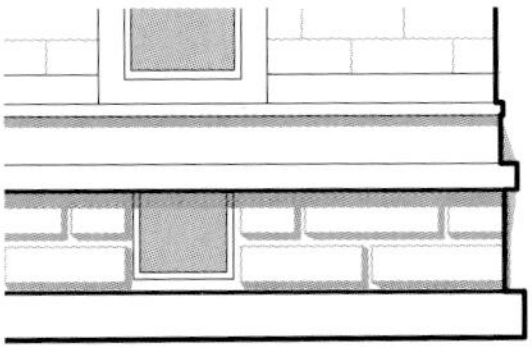

R-value: Measure of the capacity of a material to resist the transfer of heat.

S

Saarinen, Eero: (1910–1961) Finnish-American architect and son of Eliel Saarinen. Notable buildings include the Miller House in Columbus, Indiana; the Gateway Arch in St. Louis; and the TWA Terminal at JFK Airport.

Saarinen, Eliel: (1873–1950) Finnish architect and father of Eero Saarinen. Notable buildings include the Kleinhans Music Hall in Buffalo, New York, and the Cranbrook Educational Community in Bloomfield Hills, Michigan.

Schedule: Chart or table in a set of architectural drawings, including data about materials, finishes, equipment, windows, doors, and signage; also, plan for performing work.

Schinkel, Karl Friedrich: (1781–1841) Prussian architect, city planner and painter; notable buildings include the Altes Museum, the Neues Schauspielhaus, and the Neue Wache, all in Berlin.

Scope of work: Written range of view or action for a specific project.

Section: Architectural drawing of a view of a vertical cut through the building's components, acting as a vertical plan.

Shaft: Trunk of a column between base and capital; also, enclosed vertical clear opening in a building for the passage of elevators, stairs, ductwork, plumbing, or wiring.

Sheetrock: Brand name for gypsum wallboard, often incorrectly used to describe any gypsum board or drywall.

SI: Système International d'Unités (metric system).

Sitecast: Concrete that is poured and cured in its final position; also called cast-in-place or poured-in-place.

Slab on grade: Concrete slab that rests directly on the ground

Soane, Sir John: (1753–1837) English architect; notable buildings include the Bank of England and Sir John Soane's Museum.

Soffit: Finished underside of a lintel, arch, or overhang.

Soft metric: Precise conversion between customary and metric units.

Softwood: Lumber from coniferous (evergreen) trees.

Spall: Splitting off from a surface, in concrete or masonry, as a result of weathering.

Span: Distance between supports.

Spandrel: Exterior panels of a wall between vision areas of windows that conceal structural floors; the triangular space between the curve of an arch and the rectangular outline enclosing it.

Specifications: Written instructions about the materials and means of construction for a building, and included as part of the construction document set.

STC: Sound Transmission Class, a number rating of airborne sound transmission loss as measured in an acoustical laboratory under carefully controlled test conditions.

Stile: Framing member in a door.

Stud: Vertical structural member used in light-frame wall construction and made of dimension wood or metal.

Stringer: In a stair, the sloping wood or steel member that supports the treads.

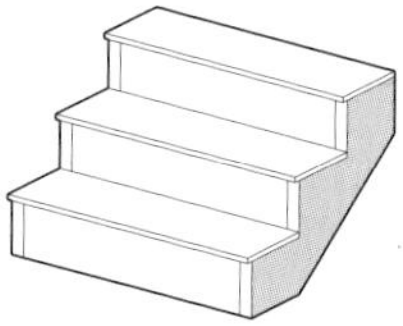

Strut channel: Standardized metal framing system used for light structural support of electrical wiring, mechanical ductwork, and plumbing. Commonly referred to by many of its manufacture trade names, including Unistrut, Flex-Strut and G-Strut

Sustainable design: Environmentally aware design using systems that meet present needs without compromising the needs of future generations.

T

Thermal performance: Ability of a glass unit to perform as a barrier to the transfer of heat.

Transom: Opening above a door or window that may be filled with a glazed or solid operable panel.

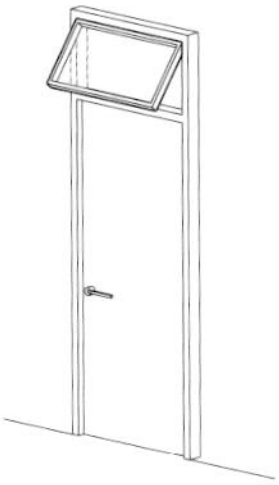

Transverse: Crosswise.

Tread: Horizontal surface between two risers of a stair.

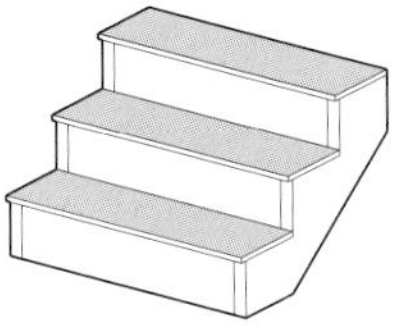

Trompe-l'oeil: Two-dimensional painting or decoration made to look three-dimensional; literally, "trick the eye."

Truss: Structural element made up of a triangular arrangement of members that transforms the nonaxial forces acting on it into a set of axial forces on the truss members.

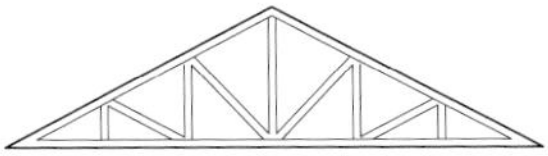

U

Undressed lumber: Lumber that is not planed.

V

Valley: Trough formed at the intersection of two sloping roofs.

Value engineering: Analyzing the materials and processes in a project in an effort to achieve the desired function at the lowest overall cost.

van der Rohe, Ludwig Mies: (1886–1969) German architect; notable buildings include the New National Gallery in Berlin, the Seagram Building in New York (with Philip Johnson), and Crown Hall and other buildings at the Illinois Institute of Technology.

Vault: Arched form.

Veneer: Thin layer, sheet, or facing.

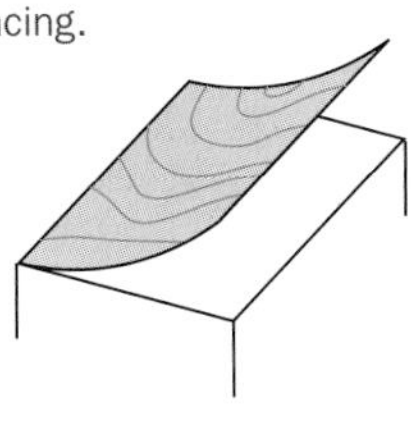

Vernacular: Structures built with indigenous materials, methods, and traditions.

Vitruvius: (c. 80–15 BCE) Roman architect, engineer, and writer; most notable for his treatise *De Architectura* (*On Architecture*).

W

Waler: Horizontal support beam used in concrete formwork.

Winder: L-shaped staircase that used wedge-shaped treads to turn a 90-degree corner.

Wright, Frank Lloyd: (1867–1959) American architect; notable buildings include Fallingwater, the Johnson Wax Building, and the Solomon R. Guggenheim Museum.

Wythe: One-unit-thick vertical layer of masonry.

Z

Ziggurat: Stepped-back pyramid temple.

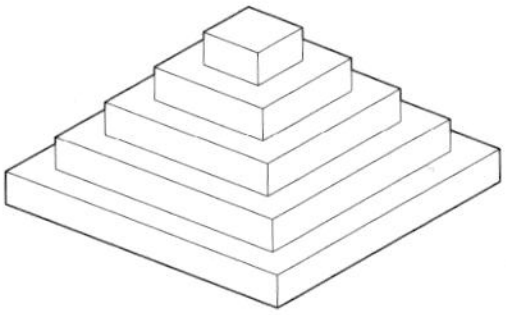

Chapter 26: Resources

The contents of this book offer a quick-reference reflection of numerous sources of information on architectural design and construction—the tip of a formidable iceberg. Any reader wishing to find out more on a specific topic is advised to consult the listing of sources that follow, which is itself an abridged acknowledgment of a wealth of available information. Many of these sources can be found in a well-stocked architecture firm's in-office library, in the libraries of most schools of architecture, and even in some local libraries. Websites have quickly established themselves as excellent resources for (usually) free information on many subjects, and are especially invaluable for exploring the offerings of product manufacturers or trade-related information. It should be noted, however, that Web-based content and addresses are always subject to change.

Architecture and Design Professions

JOURNALS & PERIODICALS

Architecture (monthly, USA); www.architectmagazine.com

Architectural Record (monthly, USA); www.archrecord.construction.com

Architectural Review (monthly, UK); www.architectural-review.com

Arquitectura Viva (bimonthly, Spain); www.arquitecturaviva.com

a+u (Architecture and Urbanism) (monthly, Japan); www.japan-architect.co.jp

Casabella (monthly, Italy)

Detail (bimonthly, Germany); www.detail.de

El Croquis (five times yearly, Spain); www.elcroquis.es

JA (Japan Architect) (quarterly, Japan); www. japanarchitect.co.jp

Lotus International (quarterly, Italy); www.editorialelotus.it

Metropolis Magazine (monthly, USA); www.metropolismag.com

WEBSITES

www.archinect.com

www.archinform.net

www.archdaily.com

www.designboom.com

www.dezeen.com

Primary Sources

Architectural Graphic Standards
Charles George Ramsey, Harold Sleeper, and John Hoke; John Wiley & Sons. 12th edition in 2017; previous editions: 1 (1932); 4 (1951); 5 (1956); 6 (1970); 9 (1994); 10 (2000); 11 (2007)

Neufert Architects' Data, 4th ed.
Blackwell Publishers, 2012

Fundamentals of Building Construction: Materials and Methods, 5th ed.
Edward Allen and Joseph Iano; John Wiley & Sons, 2008

Pocket Ref, 4th ed.
Thomas J. Glover, Sequoia Publishing, 2010

Understanding Buildings: A Multidisciplinary Approach
Esmond Reid; MIT Press, 1994

Building Construction Illustrated, 4th ed.
Francis D. K. Ching and Cassandra Adams; John Wiley & Sons, 2008

The Architect's Studio Companion, 4th ed.
Edward Allen and Joseph Iano; John Wiley & Sons, 2006

Skins for Buildings: The Architect's Materials Sample Book
David Keuning et al.; Gingko Press, 2004

Annual Book of ASTM Standards
American Society for Testing Materials, 2013
Seventy-plus volumes contain more than *12,000* standards available in print, CD-ROM, and online formats.

www.ansi.org (American National Standards Institute)

www.nist.gov (National Institute of Standards and Technology)

01 MATERIALS

01 Wood

Laminated Timber Construction
Christian Müller; Birkhäuser, 2000

Wood Handbook: Wood as an Engineering Material
Forest Products Laboratory, U.S. Department of Agriculture

Timber Construction Manual
Thomas Herzog et al.; Birkhäuser, 2004

Detail Praxis: Timber Construction—Details, Products, Case Studies
Theodor Hughs et al.; Birkhäuser, 2004

AITC Timber Construction Manual, 5th ed.
American Institute of Timber Construction, 2004

AWI Quality Standards, 7th ed., 1999

www.awinet.org (Architectural Wood Institute)

www.lumberlocator.com

02 Masonry and Concrete

Masonry Construction Manual
Günter Pfeifer et al.; Birkhäuser, 2001

Masonry Design and Detailing for Architects and Contractors, 5th ed.
Christine Beall; McGraw-Hill, 2004

Complete Construction: Masonry and Concrete
Christine Beall; McGraw-Hill

Design of Reinforced Masonry Structures
Narendra Taly; McGraw-Hill Professional, 2000

Reinforced Masonry Design
Robert R. Schneider; Prentice-Hall, 1980

Indiana Limestone Handbook, 21st ed.
Indiana Limestone Institute, 2002

www.bia.org (Brick Industry Association)

Concrete Construction Manual
Friedbert Kind-Barkauskas et al.; Birkhäuser, 2002

Construction Manual: Concrete and Formwork
T. W. Love; Craftsman Book Company, 1973

Precast Concrete in Architecture
A. E. J. Morris; Whitney Library of Design, 1978

Concrete Architecture: Design and Construction
Burkhard Fröhlich; Birkhäuser, 2002

www.fhwa.dot.gov (Federal Highway Administration)

www.aci-int.org (American Concrete Institute)

03 Metals

SMACNA Architectural Sheet Metal Manual, 7th ed.
2012

Metal Architecture
Burkhard Fröhlich and Sonja Schulenburg, eds.; Birkhäuser, 2003

Steel and Beyond: New Strategies for Metals in Architecture
Annette LeCuyer; Birkhäuser, 2003

www.corrosion-doctors.org

04 Building Enclosures

Glass Construction Manual
Christian Schittich et al.; Birkhäuser, 1999

Detail Praxis: Translucent Materials—Glass, Plastic, Metals
Frank Kaltenbach, ed.; Birkhäuser, 2004

www.GlassOnWeb.com (glass design guide)

www.glass.org (National Glass Association)

www.nrca.net (National Roofing Contractors Association)

05 Finishes

The Graphic Standards Guide to Architectural Finishes: Using MASTERSPEC to Evaluate, Select, and Specify Materials
Elena S. Garrison; John Wiley & Sons, 2002

Interior Graphic Standards
Maryrose McGowan and Kelsey Kruse; John Wiley & Sons, 2003

Detail Magazine—Architectural Details 2003
Detail Review of Architecture, 2004

Extreme Textiles: Designing for High Performance
Matilda McQuaid; Princeton Architectural Press, 2005

Sweets Catalog
McGraw-Hill Construction, ongoing; www.sweets.com

02 SYSTEMS

06 Structural Systems

LRFD (Load and Resistance Factor Design) Manual of Steel Construction, 3rd ed.
American Institute of Steel Construction, 2001; www.aisc.org

Steel Construction Manual, 14th ed.
American Institute of Steel Construction, 2010

Steel Construction Manual
Helmut Schulitz, Werner Sobek, and Karl J. Habermann; Birkhäuser, 2000

Structural Steel Designer's Handbook
Roger L Brockenbrough and Frederick S. Merritt; McGraw-Hill Professional, 1999

Steel Designers' Manual
Buick Davison and Graham W. Owens, eds.; Steel Construction Institute (UK).

Graphic Guide to Frame Construction: Details for Builders and Designers
Rob Thallon; Taunton Press, 2000

www.awc.org (American Wood Council)

07 Mechanical Systems

Mechanical and Electrical Systems in Construction and Architecture, 4th ed.
Frank Dagostino and Joseph B. Wujek; Prentice Hall, 2004

Mechanical and Electrical Equipment for Buildings, 9th ed.
Ben Stein and John S. Reynolds; John Wiley & Sons, 1999

Mechanical Systems for Architects
Aly S. Dadras; McGraw-Hill, 1995

www.buildingwell.org

www.homerepair.about.com

www.efftec.com

www.saflex.com

Sustainable Architecture White Papers (Earth Pledge Foundation Series on Sustainable Development)
David E. Brown, Mindy Fox, Mary Rickel Pelletier, eds.; Earth Pledge Foundation, 2001

Cradle to Cradle: Remaking the Way We Make Things
William McDonough and Michael Braungart; North Point Press, 2002

www.greenbuildingpages.com

www.buildinggreen.com (Environmental Building News)

www.usgbc.org (U.S. Green Building Council)

www.ashrae.org (American Soc. of Heating, Refrigeration, and Air-Cond. Eng.)

08 Lighting

Lighting Handbook Reference, 9th ed.
Mark S. Rea, ed.; IESNA, 2000

Lighting the Landscape
Roger Narboni; Birkhäuser, 2004

1000 Lights, vol. 2: 1960 to Present
Charlotte and Peter Fiell; Taschen, 2005

www.archlighting.com

www.iesna.org (Illuminating Engineering Society of North America)

www.iald.org (International Association of Lighting Designers)

09 Plumbing

Fire Protection Systems
A. Maurice Jones, Delmar Cengage Learning, 2008

Plumbing Engineering Design Handbook
American Society of Plumbing Engineers, 2004

03 MEASURE AND DRAWING

10 Measurement and Geometry

Measure for Measure
Thomas J. Glover and Richard A. Young; Sequoia Publishing, 2001

Metric Handbook Planning & Design, 2nd ed.
David Adler, ed.; Architectural Press, 1999

www.onlineconversion.com

www.metrication.com

11 Architectural Drawing Types

Design Drawing
Francis D. K. Ching and Steven P. Juroszek; John Wiley & Sons, 1997

Graphics for Architecture
Kevin Forseth with David Vaughan; Van Nostrand Reinhold, 1980

Basic Perspective Drawing: A Visual Approach, 4th ed.
John Montague; John Wiley & Sons, 2004

12 Architectural Documents

The Architect's Handbook of Professional Practice, 13th ed.
Joseph A. Demkin, ed.; American Institute of Architects, 2005

www.uia-architectes.org

www.aia.org

www.iso.org

www.constructionplace.com

www.dcd.com (Design Cost Data)

MasterSpec Master Specification System for Design Professionals and the Building/Construction Industry
ARCOM, ongoing; www.arcomnet.com

Construction Specifications Portable Handbook
Fred A. Stitt; McGraw-Hill Professional, 1999

The Project Resource Manual–CSI Manual of Practice
Construction Specifications Institute and McGraw-Hill Construction, 2004

www.csinet.org (Construction Specifications Institute)

Masterformat 2012
CSI Construction Specifications Institute, 2012

13 Hand Drawing

Architectural Drawing: A Visual Compendium of Types and Methods, 2nd ed.
Rendow Yee; John Wiley & Sons, 2002

Architectural Graphics, 4th ed.
Francis D. K. Ching; John Wiley & Sons, 2002

14 Digital Production

U.S. National CAD Standard, version 3.1
2004; www.nationalcadstandard.org

AutoCAD User's Guide
Autodesk, 2001

AutoCad 2006 Instructor
James A. Leach; McGraw-Hill, 2005

www.nibs.org (National Institute of Building Sciences)

www.pcmag.com

04 CODES AND GUIDELINES

15 Building Codes

2012 International Building Codes
International Code Council, 2012
The complete collection is available in book or CD-ROM format at www.iccsafe.org.

Building Codes Illustrated: A Guide to Understanding the International Building Code, 4th ed.
Francis D. K. Ching and Steven R. Winkel; John Wiley & Sons, 2012

Code Check series
Redwood Kardon, Michael Casey, and Douglas Hansen; The Taunton Press, ongoing. This series is available at www.codecheck.com.

Illustrated 2009: Building Code Handbook
Terry L. Patterson; McGraw-Hill Professional, 2009

16 ADA and Accessibility

ADA Standards for Accessible Design
U.S. Department of Justice - www.ada.gov
1991 and 2010 Standards

ADA and Accessibility: Let's Get Practical, 2nd ed.
Michele S. Ohmes; American Public Works Association, 2003

Guide to ADA & Accessibility Regulations: Complying with Federal Rules and Model Building Code Requirements
Ron Burton, Robert J. Brown, and Lawrence G. Perry; BOMA International, 2003

Pocket Guide to the ADA: Americans with Disabilities Act Accessibility Guidelines for Buildings and Facilities, 2nd ed.
Evan Terry Associates; John Wiley & Sons, 1997

17 Parking

Parking Structures: Planning, Design, Construction, Maintenance & Repair, 3rd ed.
Anthony P. Chrest et al.; Springer, 2001

The Dimensions of Parking
Urban Land Institute and National Parking Association, 2000

The Aesthetics of Parking: An Illustrated Guide
Thomas P. Smith; American Planning Institute, 1988

Parking Spaces
Mark Childs; McGraw-Hill, 1999

www.apai.net (Asphalt Paving Association of Iowa – Design Guide)

www.bts.gov (Bureau of Transportation Services)

18 Stairs

Stairs: Design and Construction
Karl J. Habermann; Birkhäuser, 2003

Staircases
Eva Jiricna; Watson-Guptill Publications, 2001

Stairs: Scale
Silvio San Pietro and Paola Gallo; IPS, 2002

19 Doors

Construction of Buildings: Windows, Doors, Fires, Stairs, Finishes
R. Barry; Blackwell Science, 1992

05 PROPORTION AND FORM

20 The Human Scale

The Measure of Man and Woman: Human Factors in Design, rev. ed.
Alvin R. Tilley; John Wiley & Sons, 2002

Human Scale, vol. 7: Standing and Sitting at Work, vol. 8: Space Planning for the Individual and the Public, and vol. 9: Access for Maintenance, Stairs, Light, and Color
Niels Diffrient, Alvin R. Tilley, and Joan Bardagjy; MIT Press, 1982
Both above-cited books draw on information produced by Henry Dreyfuss Associates, a leading firm in the development of anthropometric data and its relationship to design.

21 Interior Spaces

In Detail : Single Family Housing
Christian Schittich; Birkhäuser, 2000

Dwell Magazine (bimonthly, USA); www.dwellmag.com

www.residentialarchitect.com

www.nkba.org (National Kitchen & Bath Association)

Time-Saver Standards for Interior Design and Space Planning, 2nd ed.
Joseph De Chiara, Julius Panero, and Martin Zelnik; McGraw-Hill Professional, 2001

The Architects' Handbook
Quentin Pickard, ed.; Blackwell Publishing, 2002

In Detail: Interior Spaces: Space, Light, Material
Christian Schittich, ed.; Basel, 2002

06 CONTEXT

22 Timeline

History of Architecture on the Comparative Method: For Students, Craftsmen & Amateurs, 16th ed.
Sir Banister Fletcher; Charles Scribner's, 1958

Modern Architecture: A Critical History, 3rd ed.
Kenneth Frampton; Thames & Hudson, 1992

A World History of Architecture
Marian Moffett et al.; McGraw-Hill Professional, 2003

Source Book of American Architecture: 500 Notable Buildings from the 10th Century to the Present
G. E. Kidder Smith; Princeton Architectural Press, 1996

Architecture: From Prehistory to Postmodernism, 2nd ed.
Marvin Trachtenberg and Isabelle Hyman; Prentice-Hall, 2003

Encyclopedia of 20th-Century Architecture
V. M. Lampugnani, ed.; Thames and Hudson, 1986

Modern Architecture Since 1900
J. R. Curtis, Phaidon Press, 1996

23 Architectural Elements and Ideas

A Visual Dictionary of Architecture
Francis D. K. Ching; John Wiley & Sons, 1996

De architectura (Ten Books on Architecture)
Marcus Vitruvius Pollio, ca. 40 B.C.

The Four Books of Architecture
Andrea Palladio, 1570

The Annotated Arch
Carol Strickland, Ph.D. ; Andrews McMeel Publishing, LLC, 2001

The Egyptian Plant Column
Ludwig Borchardt, 1897

A History of Art in Ancient Egypt
Georges Perrot and Charles Chipiez, 1883

On the Art of Building
Leon Battista Alberti, 1443-1452

Seven Books of Architecture
Sebastiano Serlio, 1537

24 Form and Organization

Architecture: Form, Space and Order, 2nd ed.
Francis D. K. Ching; John Wiley & Sons, 1995

Harmonic Proportion and Form in Nature, Art and Architecture
Samuel Colman; Dover Publications, 2003

25 Glossary

The Penguin Dictionary of Architecture and Landscape Architecture, 5th ed.
John Fleming, Hugh Honour, and Nikolaus Pevsner; Penguin, 2000

Dictionary of Architecture, rev. ed.
Henry H. Saylor; John Wiley & Sons, 1994

Dictionary of Architecture and Construction, 3rd ed.
Cyril M. Harris; McGraw-Hill Professional, 2000

Means Illustrated Construction Dictionary
R. S. Means Company, 2000

Architectural and Building Trades Dictionary
R. E. Putnam and G. E. Carlson; American Technical Society, 1974

Index

PHOTOGRAPHY CREDITS

Pyramid of Giza: Erich Lessing, Art Resource, New York; 236

Stonehenge: Anatoly Pronin, Art Resource, New York; 236

Parthenon: Foto Marburg, Art Resource, New York; 237

Colosseum: Alinari, Art Resource, New York; 237

El Castillo: Vanni, Art Resource, New York; 237

San Vitale: Scala, Art Resource, New York; 238

Notre-Dame: Scala, Art Resource, New York; 238

Duomo, S. Maria del Fiore: Scala, Art Resource, New York; 239

S. Maria Novella: Erich Lessing, Art Resource, New York; 239

Villa La Rotonda: Vanni, Art Resource, New York; 239

S. Carlo alle Quattro Fontane: Scala, Art Resource, New York; 240

Salt Works of Chaux: Vanni, Art Resource, New York; 241

Crystal Palace: Victoria & Albert Museum, Art Resource, New York; 241

Marshall Field Wholesale Store: Chicago Historical Society / Barnes-Crosby; 241

Barcelona Pavilion: Museum of Modern Art / licensed by Scala, Art Resource, New York. © 2006 Artists Rights Society (ARS), New York / VG Bild-Kunst, Bonn; 242

Einstein Tower: Erich Lessing, Art Resource, New York; 242

Bauhaus: Vanni, Art Resource, New York. © 2006 Artists Rights Society (ARS), New York / VG Bild-Kunst, Bonn; 242

Fallingwater: Chicago Historical Society / Bill Hedrich, Hedrich-Blessing; 242

Vanna Venturi House: Rollin R. La France, Venturi, Scott Brown and Associates; 243

Seattle Public Library: LMN Architects / Pragnesh Parikh; 243

Dedication

For Walter, Matthew, and John

Acknowledgments

Special thanks to Anna Buzolits, Adam Balaban, Dan Dwyer, John McMorrough, Rick Smith, and Ron Witte.

Every attempt has been made to cite all sources; if a reference has been omitted, please contact the publisher for correction in subsequent editions.

About the Author

Julia McMorrough is Associate Professor of Practice in Architecture at the Taubman College of Architecture and Urban Planning at the University of Michigan, and partner in studioAPT (Architecture Project Theory). While working professionally in architecture firms in Kansas City, New York, Boston, and Columbus, Ohio, she was the lead designer on a range of projects throughout the country, including libraries, academic buildings, and housing.